Software Best Practice 4

ESSI Practitioners' Reports

Springer
Berlin
Heidelberg
New York
Barcelona
Hong Kong
London
Milan
Paris
Tokyo

Michael Haug   Eric W. Olsen
Lars Bergman (Eds.)

Software Process Improvement: Metrics, Measurement, and Process Modelling

Software Best Practice 4

With 46 Figures and 30 Tables

Springer

Editors:

Michael Haug
Eric W. Olsen
HIGHWARE GmbH
Winzererstraße 46
80797 München, Germany

Michael@Haug.com
ewo@home.com

Lars Bergman
Swedisch Institute for Systems
Development (SISU)
Electrum 212
16440 Kista, Sweden

lars@sisu.se

ISBN 3-540-41787-7 Springer-Verlag Berlin Heidelberg New York

Library of Congress Cataloging-in-Publication Data
Software best practice.
    p. cm.
    Includes bibliographical references and index.
    1. Software quality approaches : testing, verification, and validation / M. Haug,
E. W. Olsen, L. Consolini, eds. -- 2. Managing the change : software configuration and
change management / M. Haug ... [et al.], eds. -- 3. Software management approaches :
project management, estimation, and life cycle support / M. Haug ... [et al.], eds. --
4. Software process improvement : metrics, measurement, and process modelling /
M. Haug, E. W. Olsen, L. Bergman, eds.
    ISBN 3540417842 (v. 1) -- ISBN 3540417850 (v. 2) -- ISBN 3540417869 (v. 3) --
ISBN 3540417877 (v. 4)
    1. Software engineering. I. Haug, Michael, 1951-

QA76.758 .S6445 2001
005.1--dc21   2001041181

Springer-Verlag Berlin Heidelberg New York,
a member of BertelsmannSpringer Science + Business Media GmbH

http://www.springer.de

© Springer-Verlag Berlin Heidelberg 2001
Printed in Germany

Cover design: design & production GmbH, Heidelberg
Typesetting: Camera-ready by editors
Printed on acid-free paper   SPIN: 10832695   45/3142 GF – 543210

Foreword

C. Amting
Directorate General Information Society, European Commission, Brussels

Under the 4th Framework of European Research, the European Systems and Software Initiative (ESSI) was part of the ESPRIT Programme. This initiative funded more than 470 projects in the area of software and system process improvements. The majority of these projects were process improvement experiments carrying out and taking up new development processes, methods and technology within the software development process of a company. In addition, nodes (centres of expertise), European networks (organisations managing local activities), training and dissemination actions complemented the process improvement experiments.

ESSI aimed at improving the software development capabilities of European enterprises. It focused on best practice and helped European companies to develop world class skills and associated technologies to build the increasingly complex and varied systems needed to compete in the marketplace.

The dissemination activities were designed to build a forum, at European level, to exchange information and knowledge gained within process improvement experiments. Their major objective was to spread the message and the results of experiments to a wider audience, through a variety of different channels.

The European Experience Exchange (EUREX) project has been one of these dissemination activities within the European Systems and Software Initiative. EUREX has collected the results of practitioner reports from numerous workshops in Europe and presents, in this series of books, the results of Best Practice achievements in European Companies over the last few years.

EUREX assessed, classified and categorised the outcome of process improvement experiments. The theme based books will present the results of the particular problem areas. These reports are designed to help other companies facing software process improvement problems.

The results of the various projects collected in these books should encourage many companies facing similar problems to start some improvements on their own. Within the Information Society Technology (IST) programme under the 5th Framework of European Research, new take up and best practices activities will be launched in various Key Actions to encourage the companies in improving their business areas.

Preface

M. Haug
HIGHWARE, Munich

In 1993, I was invited by Rainer Zimmermann and David Talbot to participate in the industrial consultation group for the then-new ESSI initiative. Coming from a Software Engineering background and having been responsible for industrial software production for more than 20 years, I was fascinated by the idea of tackling the ubiquitous software quality problem in a fresh new way, in helping not only a particular organisation to improve their software process, but to create the framework for an exchange of the experience gained among those organisations and beyond, to spread this experience throughout the European Software Industry.

While serving as an evaluator and reviewer to the Commission within the ESSI initiative, I had the opportunity to have a more or less superficial look at more than 100 Process Improvement Experiments (PIEs) at workshops, conferences and reviews. Consequently, the desire to collect and consolidate information about and experience from *all* of the more than 300 PIEs in a more organised way became immanent. In short, the idea for EUREX was born.

EUREX is an ESSI dissemination project. The budget limitations applicable to such projects did not allow us to conduct reviews or interviews of all of the more than 300 projects. Therefore, a distributed and staged approach was taken: a set of regional workshops became the platform to collect the information. The results of these 18 workshops held in Europe over a period of two years, together with contributions from representative PIEs and with expert articles rounding out the experience reports, is now in your hands: a series of books focussing on the central problem domains of Software Process Improvement.

Each of the books concentrates on a technical problem domain within the software engineering process, e.g. software testing, verification and quality management in Vol. 1. All of the books have a common structure:

Part I SPI, ESSI, EUREX describes the context of the European Software and Systems Initiative and the EUREX project. While Part I is similar in all books, the problem domains are differentiated for the reader. It consists of the chapters:

    1 Software Process Improvement

    2 The EUREX project

    3 The EUREX taxonomy.

In Part II we present the collected findings and experiences of the process improvement experiments that dealt with issues related to the problem domain addressed by the book. Part II consists of the chapters:

4 Perspectives

5 Resources for Practitioners

6 Experience Reports

7 Lessons from the EUREX Workshops

8 Significant Results

Part III offers summary information for all the experiments that fall into the problem domain. These summaries, collected from publicly available sources, provide the reader with a wealth of information about each of the large number of projects undertaken. Part III includes the chapters:

9 Table of PIEs

10 Summaries of Process Improvement Experiment Reports

A book editor managed each of the books, compiling the contributions and writing the connecting chapters and paragraphs. Much of the material originates in papers written by the PIE organisations for presentation at EUREX workshops or for public documentation like the Final Reports. Whenever an author could be identified, we attribute the contributions to him or her. If it was not possible to identify a specific author, the source of the information is provided. If a chapter is without explicit reference to an author or a source, the book editor wrote it.

Many people contributed to EUREX[P1], more than I can express my appreciation to in such a short notice. Representative for all of them, my special thanks go to the following teams: David Talbot and Rainer Zimmermann (CEC) who made the ESSI initiative happen; Mechthild Rohen, Brian Holmes, Corinna Amting and Knud Lonsted, our Project Officers within the CEC, who accompanied the project patiently and gave valuable advice; Luisa Consolini and Elisabetta Papini, the Italian EUREX team, Manu de Uriarte, Jon Gómez and Iñaki Gómez, the Spanish EUREX team, Gilles Vallet and Olivier Bécart, the French EUREX team, Lars Bergman and Terttu Orci, the Nordic EUREX team and Wilhelm Braunschober, Bernhard Kölmel and Jörn Eisenbiegler, the German EUREX team; Eric W. Olsen has patiently reviewed numerous versions of all contributions; Carola, Sebastian and Julian have spent several hundred hours on shaping the various contributions into a consistent presentation. Last but certainly not least, Ingeborg Mayer and Hans Wössner continuously supported our efforts with their professional publishing know-how; Gabriele Fischer and Ulrike Drechsler patiently reviewed the many versions of the typoscripts.

The biggest reward for all of us will be, if you – the reader – find something in these pages useful to you and your organisation, or, even better, if we motivate you to implement Software Process Improvement within your organisation.

Table of Contents

List of Contributors

R. Barbati
Dataspazio S.p.A., Rome

José D. Carrillo Verdún
AEMES, Madrid

Kevin Daily
Improve QPI Ltd.

S. Farina
Intecs Sistemi, Pisa

Alfonso Fuggetta
CEFRIEL, Italy

Michael Haug
HIGHWARE

T. R. Judge,
Parallax Solutions Ltd, Coventry

Jens-Otto Larsen
The Norwegian Technical University, Trondheim

Luigi Lavazza,
CEFRIEL, Italy

Markku Oivo
Schlumberger SMR, France

Eric W. Olsen
HIGHWARE

Duncan Brown
Rolls-Royce plc, Derby

Stefano Cinti,
Digital Equipment SPA, Italy

Gerd Eickelpasch
KoDa GmbH, Würzburg

Norman Fenton
City University, London

Christiane Gresse,
UKL/STTI-KL, Germany

Barbara Hoisl,
UKL/STTI-KL, Germany

John S. Keenan
Systems and Software Engineering Centre, Defence Evaluation and Research Agency

Frank van Latum,
Schlumberger RPS, Netherlands

Sandro Morasca
CEFRIEL, Italy

Giandomenico Oldano,
Digital Equipment SPA, Italy

Elena Orazi
Digital Equipment SPA, Italy

Terttu Orci
SISU, Stockholm University

Anthony Powell
Rolls-Royce University Technology Centre/University of York

Erik Rodenbach, Schlumberger
RPS, Netherlands

Günther Ruhe
UKL/STTI-KL, Germany

Rini van Solingen
Schlumberger RPS, Netherlands

A. Williams
Parallax Solutions Ltd, Coventry

P. Panarono
Intecs Sistemi, Pisa

Helge M. Roald
Sysdeco GIS AS, Kongsberg

Dieter Rombach
UKL/STTI-KL, Germany

G. Sabbatici
Alenia, Rome

Otto Vinter

Helmut Woda
Robert Bosch GmbH, Germany

Part I

SPI, ESSI, EUREX

1 Software Process Improvement
A European View

1.1 Introduction[1]

Enterprises in all developed sectors of the economy – not just the IT sector – are increasingly dependent on quality software-based IT systems. Such systems support management, production, and service functions in diverse organisations. Furthermore, the products and services now offered by the non-IT sectors, e.g., the automotive industry or the consumer electronics industry, increasingly contain a component of sophisticated software. For example, televisions require in excess of half a Megabyte of software code to provide the wide variety of functions we have come to expect from a domestic appliance. Similarly, the planning and execution of a cutting pattern in the garment industry is accomplished under software control, as are many safety-critical functions in the control of, e.g., aeroplanes, elevators, trains, and electricity generating plants. Today, approximately 70% of all software developed in Europe is developed in the non-IT sectors of the economy. This makes software a technological topic of considerable significance. As the information age develops, software will become even more pervasive and transparent. Consequently, the ability to produce software efficiently, effectively, and with consistently high quality will become increasingly important for all industries across Europe if they are to maintain and enhance their competitiveness.

1.2 Objectives – Scope of the Initiative

The goal of the European Systems and Software Initiative (ESSI) was to promote improvements in the software development process in industry, through the take-up of well-founded and established – but insufficiently deployed – methods and

---

[1] All material presented in Chapter 1 was taken from publicly available information issued by the European Commission in the course of the European Systems and Software Initiative (ESSI). It was compiled by the main editor to provide an overview of this programme.

technologies, so as to achieve greater efficiency, higher quality, and greater economy. In short, the adoption of Software Best Practice.

The aim of the initiative was to ensure that European software developers in both user and vendor organisations continue to have the world class skills, the associated technology, and the improved practices necessary to build the increasingly complex and varied systems demanded by the market place. The full impact of the initiative for Europe will be achieved through a multiplier effect, with the dissemination of results across national borders and across industrial sectors.

1.3   Strategy

To achieve the above objectives, actions have been supported to:

- Raise awareness of the importance of the software development process to the competitiveness of all European industry.
- Demonstrate what can be done to improve software development practices through experimentation.
- Create communities of interest in Europe working to a common goal of improving software development practices.
- Raise the skill levels of software development professionals in Europe.

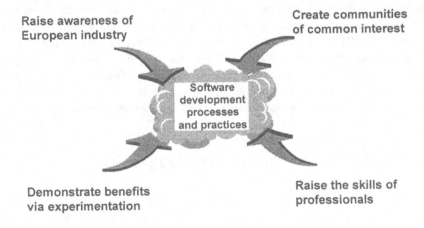

Fig. 1.1 A focused strategy for achieving Best Practice

1.4   Target Audience
(Who can participate, Who will benefit)

Any organisation in any sector of the economy, which regards generation of software to be part of its operation, may benefit from the adoption of Software Best Practice. Such a user organisation is often not necessarily classified as being in the software industry, but may well be an engineering or commercial organisation in which the generation of software has emerged as a significant component of its operation. Indeed as the majority of software is produced by organisations in the non-IT sector and by small and medium sized enterprises (SMEs), it is these two groups who are likely to benefit the most from this initiative.

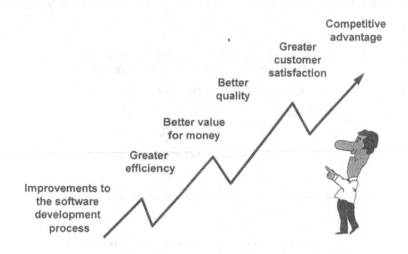

Fig. 1.2 The benefits of Software Best Practice

In addition to the user organisations participating directly in the initiative, software vendors and service providers also stand to benefit, as demand for their methodologies, tools and services is stimulated and valuable feedback is given on the strengths and weaknesses of their offerings.

1.5   Dimensions of Software Best Practice

Software Best Practice activities focus on the continuous and stepwise improvement of software development processes and practices. Software process improvement should not be seen as a goal in itself but must be clearly linked to the business goals of an organisation. Software process improvement starts with addressing the organisational issues. Experiences in the past have shown that before any investments are made in true technology upgrades (through products like tools and infrastructure computer support) some critical process issues need to be addressed and solved. They concern how software is actually developed: the methodology and methods, and, especially, the organisation of the process of development and maintenance of software.

Organisational issues are more important than methods and improving methods is, in turn, more important than introducing the techniques and tools to support them.

Finding the right organisational framework, the right process model, the right methodology, the right supporting methods and techniques and the right mix of skills for a development team is a difficult matter and a long-term goal of any process improvement activity. Nevertheless, it is a fundamental requirement for the establishment of a well-defined and controlled software development process.

1. Business: *market, customers, competition, ...*
& People issues: *skills, culture, teamwork, ...*

Business & People　⬇　driven

2. Process

⬇

3. Technical approach: *methods, procedures, ...*

⬇

4. Technical support: *tools, computers, ...*

Fig. 1.3 Anatomy of a successful SPI programme

Software development is a people process and due consideration should be given to all the players involved. Process improvement and implementation concerns people and needs to take into account all people related aspects (human factors). These are orthogonal to the technology and methodology driven approaches and are crucial to the success of adopting best practice.

Successful management of change includes staff motivation, skilling and promotion of the positive contributions that staff can make.

The people aspects cover all the different groups which have an input to the software development process including Management, and Software Engineers.

In order to ensure an appropriate environment for the successful adherence to a total quality approach it is imperative that Senior Management are fully aware of all the issues. Their commitment and involvement are crucial to the successful implementation of the improvement process and it might be necessary to raise their awareness regarding this issue.

It is important to identify clear milestones that will enable the software developer to measure progress along the road of software improvement. Certification through schemes such as ISO 9000, while not an end in itself, can play a valuable role in marking and recognising this progress.

1.6 European Dimension

The objectives of Software Best Practice can be accomplished by understanding and applying the state-of-the-art in software engineering, in a wide range of industries and other sectors of the economy, taking into account moving targets and changing cultures in this rapidly evolving area. The full impact for Europe will then be achieved by a multiplier effect, with the dissemination of results across national borders and across industrial sectors.

The definition of best practice at the European level has three main advantages. Firstly, there is the matter of scale. Operating on a European-wide basis offers the possibility to harness the full range of software development experience that has been built up across the full spectrum of industry sectors in addition to offering exposure to the widest selection of specialist method and tool vendors. In the second place, it maximises the possibility to reduce duplication of effort. Finally, it offers the best possibility to reduce the present fragmentation of approaches and, at the same time, to provide a more coherent and homogeneous market for well-founded methods and tools.

Moreover, as we move towards the Information Society, we need to develop and build the technologies necessary to create the Information Infrastructure (such as is envisaged in the Commission White Paper on "Growth, Competitiveness and Employment"); a dynamic infrastructure of underlying technologies and services to facilitate fast and efficient access to information, according to continually changing requirements. Within this context, software is seen as a major enabling technology and the way in which we develop software is becoming a key factor for industrial competitiveness and prosperity.

All of the above factors can be enhanced through the creation and use of standards, including de-facto standards for "best practice" and, indeed, standards are vital in the long term. However, the proposed actions should not, at this stage of evolving standards, be restricted to one particular standard. Furthermore, the actions cannot wait for a full and accepted set to be established before being able to implement improvement. Nevertheless, a close look at the ISO-SPICE initiative and active contribution to it is suggested.

1.7   Types of Projects

The European Commission issued three Calls for Proposals for Software Best Practice in the Fourth Framework Programme in the years 1993, 1995 and 1996. The first call was referred to as the "ESSI Pilot Phase". The aim was to test the perceived relevance of the programme to its intended audience and the effectiveness of the implementation mechanisms. Before the second call in 1995 a major review and redirection took place. Following the revision of the ESPRIT Work programme in 1997, a further call was issued of which the results are not been reviewed in this book. The four calls varied slightly in their focus. In the following, all types of projects supported by the ESSI initiative will be presented.

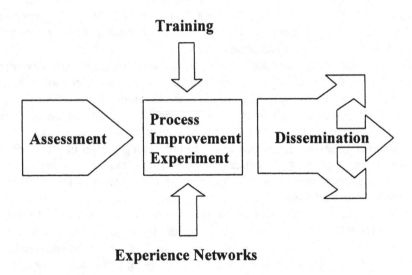

Fig. 1.4 Lines of complementary action

1.7.1   Stand Alone Assessments[2]

The main objective of the Stand Alone Assessments action was to raise the awareness of user organisations to the possibilities for improvement in their software development process, as well as give the momentum for initiating the improve-

---

[2]   Stand Alone Assessments have been called only in the year 1995.

ment process. Assessments were targeted particularly at organisations at the lower levels of software development maturity.

It was expected that assessments will stimulate the pursuit of quality through continuous improvement of the software development process.

An underlying methodology was needed to carry out an assessment. This methodology had to recognise that software development is governed by the processes which an organisation uses to capitalise upon the potential talent of its employees (people) in order to produce competitive, top quality, software systems and services (products).

Most assessment methods are based on questionnaires and personnel interviews. An assessment resulted in the identification of an organisation's strengths and weaknesses, provides a comparison with the rest of the industry, and was accompanied by a series of recommendations on how to address the weak aspects of the software development process, from a technological and organisational point of view.

No single standard methodology was advocated; however, the adopted approach had to be a recognised assessment methodology, such as BOOTSTRAP, TickIT, etc.

The following types of assessment have been envisaged:

Self-assessments, which were conducted if the organisation had the required resource capacity to allow it to absorb the load of conducting the assessment. In this case, it was expected that an internal assessment team was set up, trained in the selected methodology, and that it carried out the assessment according to an agreed schedule. This type of assessment may have conducted with the support of the methodology provider or under the guidance of external assessors.

Assessments carried out by external assessors. The organisation was expected to select an external assessor who conducted the assessment. Again, an internal assessment team was expected to be set up to collaborate with the assessors.

Both types of assessment had to cater for measuring the organisation's existing situation, positioning the organisation relatively to the rest of the industry in terms of software development process and allowing the organisation to plan and prioritise for future improvements.

1.7.2 Process Improvement Experiments (PIEs)[3]

PIEs are aimed at demonstrating software process improvement. These followed a generic model and demonstrated the effectiveness of software process improve-

---

[3] Process Improvement Experiments have been called in the years 1995, 1996 and 1997. As the project type "Application Experiment" can be considered the predecessor of PIEs, it is legitimate to say that PIEs have been subject to all ESSI calls and have formed not only the bulk of projects but also the "heart" of the initiative.

ment experiments on an underlying baseline project that is tackling a real development need for the proposing organisation.

Process Improvement Experiments (PIEs) formed the bulk of the Software Best Practice initiative. Their aim was to demonstrate the benefits of software process improvement through user experimentation. The results had to be disseminated both internally within the user organisations to improve software production and externally to the wider community to stimulate adoption of process improvement at a European level.

The emphasis was on continuous improvement through small, stepped actions. During a PIE, a user organisation undertook a controlled, limited experiment in process improvement, based on an underlying baseline project. The baseline project was a typical software project undertaken by the user organisation as part of its normal business and the results of the experiment should therefore be replicable.

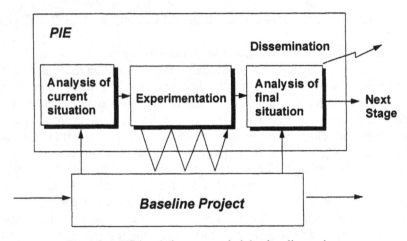

Fig. 1.5 A PIE in relation to an underlying baseline project

The introduction of a Configuration Management System, improvements to the design documentation system, the use of a Computer Aided Design (CAD) tool, the application of Object Oriented Programming techniques, the development of a library for software re-use and the introduction of metrics, are some examples of possible improvement steps for Software Best Practice and the focus of a PIE.

It was expected that a PIE was carried out as part of a larger movement within the user organisation towards process improvement. Participants were expected to have considered their strengths and weaknesses, and to have at least an idea of the general actions required. They also needed to demonstrate that they were aware of quality issues and were considering the people aspects of their actions.

Dissemination of the results of the experiment, from a software engineering and business point of view, to the wider community, was an essential aspect of a PIE and was undertaken with the support of the Software Best Practice Dissemination Actions.

1.7.3 Application Experiments[4]

These experiments were targeted at building up a comprehensive set of examples to show that the adoption of improved software development practices were both possible and had clear industrial benefits. The experiments involved the introduction of state-of-the-art software engineering (e.g. management practices, methodologies, tools) into real production environments that address specific applications, and then evaluating the resulting impact.

Within the context of this book (and the project EUREX) these Application Experiments have been treated like PIEs, i.e. their specific results have been included.

1.7.4 Dissemination Actions[5, 6]

Dissemination Actions aimed at raising awareness and promoting the adoption of software best practice by Industry at large. Actions provided software producing organisations with information concerning the practical introduction of software best practice, how it can contribute to meeting business needs and how those organisations can benefit: particularly, by showing the real life business benefits – and costs – in a way which could be of interest to companies intending to address related problems.

The Dissemination Actions widely disseminated Software Best Practice information by making it available and packaging it in a form suitable for "focused target audiences":

- The experience gained by the participants in PIEs (Process Improvement Experiments): experiences and lessons learned which could be of interest to industry at large.
- Software Best Practice material and experiences available world-wide. For example, valuable and generally useful software engineering material which is representative of a class of processes, methodologies, assessment methods, tools, etc. Relevant world-wide experiences.

---

[4] Application Experiments have only been called in 1993. See also the footnote to Process Improvement Experiments.
[5] Dissemination Actions have been called in 1993, 1995 and 1996.
[6] The ESSI project EUREX which resulted in this book was such a Dissemination Action.

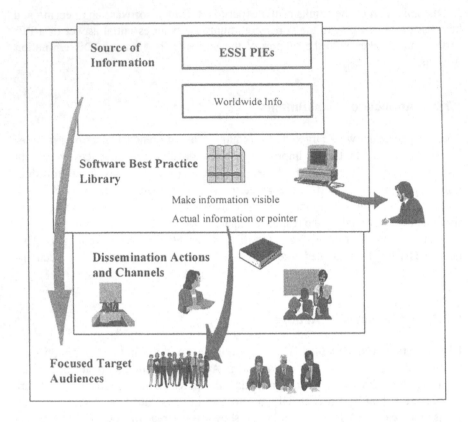

Fig. 1.6 ESSI Dissemination Framework

1.7.5   Experience/User Networks[7]

There was opportunity for networks of users, with a common interest, to pursue a specific problem affecting the development or use of software. Experience/User Networks mobilised groups of users at a European level and provided them with the critical mass necessary to influence their suppliers and the future of the software industry through the formulation of clear requirements. A network had to be trans-national with users from more than one Member or Associated State.

By participating in an Experience/User Network, a user organisation helped to ensure that a particular problem – with which it is closely involved – is addressed and that it is able to influence the choice of proposed solution.

Software suppliers (methodologies, tools, services, etc.) and the software industry as a whole took benefit from Experience/User Networks by receiving valuable

---

[7] Experience/User Networks have only been called in 1995.

feedback on the strengths and weaknesses of their current offerings, together with information on what is additionally required in the marketplace.

1.7.6 Training Actions[8]

Training actions have been broad in scope and covered training, skilling and education for all groups of people involved – directly or indirectly – in the development of software. In particular, training actions aimed at:

- increasing the awareness of senior managers as to the benefits of software process improvement and software quality
- providing software development professionals with the necessary skills to develop software using best practice

Emphasis had been placed on actions which served as a catalyst for further training and education through, for example, the training of trainers. In addition, the application of current material – where available and appropriate – in a new or wider context was preferred to the recreation of existing material.

1.7.7 ESSI PIE Nodes (ESPINODEs)[9]

The primary objective of an ESPINODE was to provide support and assistance, on a regional basis, to a set of PIEs in order to stimulate, support, and co-ordinate activities. ESPINODEs acted closely with local industry and were particularly aimed at helping to facilitate exchange of practical information and experience between PIEs, to provide project assistance, technical and administrative support, and to exploit synergies.

On a regional level, an ESPINODE provided a useful interface between the PIEs themselves, and between the PIEs and local industry. This included improving and facilitating access to information on ESSI/PIE results, and raising interest and awareness of local companies (notably SMEs) to the technical and business benefits resulting from software process improvement conducted in the PIEs.

At the European level, an ESPINODE exchanged information and experience with other ESPINODEs, in order to benefit from the transfer of technology, skills and know-how; from economies of scale and from synergies in general – thus creating a European network of PIE communities.

---

[8] Training Actions have been called in 1993 and 1996. Whereas the projects resulting from the call in 1996 were organised as separate projects building the ESSI Training Cluster ESSItrain, the result of the call in 1993 was one major project ESPITI which is described in chapter 2.3.2.

[9] ESSI PIE Nodes have only been called in 1997.

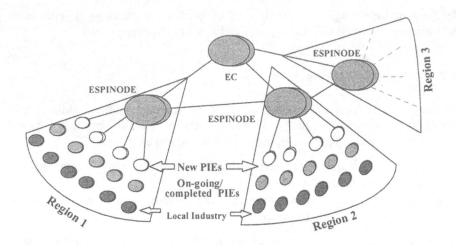

Fig. 1.7 ESPINODE collaboration model

1.7.8   Software Best Practice Networks (ESBNETs)[10]

The objective of an ESBNET was to implement small scale software best practice related activities on a regional basis, but within the context of a European network. A network in this context was simply a group of organisations, based in different countries, operating together to implement an ESBNET project, according to an established plan of action, using appropriate methods, technologies and other appropriate support. By operating on a regional level, it was expected that the specific needs of a targeted audience will be better addressed. The regional level was complemented by actions at European level, to exploit synergies and bring cross-fertilisation between participants and their target audiences. A network had a well defined focus, rather than being just a framework for conducting a set of unrelated, regional software best practice activities.

The two ESSI tasks newly introduced in the Call for Proposals in 1997 – ESPINODEs and ESBNETs – aimed to continue and build upon the achievements of the initiative so far, but on a more regional basis. ESPINODEs aim with first priority to provide additional support to PIEs, whilst ESBNETs aim to integrate small-scale software best practice actions of different type implemented on a regional basis – with an emphasis on the non-PIE community.

By operating on a regional level, it was expected that ESPINODEs and ESBNETs will be able to tailor their actions to the local culture, delivering the message and operating in the most appropriate way for the region. Further, it was expected that such regional actions will be able to penetrate much more into the very corners of Europe, reaching a target audience which is much broader and

---

[10] Software Best Practice Networks have only been called in 1997.

probably less experienced in dealing with European initiatives. Such an approach should be of particular interest to SMEs and other organisations not in the traditional IT sector, for which it is perhaps difficult to deal directly with an organisation based in a different country, due to – for example – a lack of resources, cultural and language reasons.

Regional Support within European Networks

• **Disseminate the results beyond those directly involved in ESSI**

• **Ensure that projects act as a 'catalyst' for further action**

• **Increase the participation in ESSI**

• **Reach organisations never involved before**

Fig. 1.8 ESPINODEs and ESBNETs

2 The EUREX Project

M. Haug, E.W. Olsen
HIGHWARE, Munich

The European Experience Exchange project (EUREX) was conceived, proposed, and carried out as an ESSI Dissemination Action (see Chapter 1). The overall objective of EUREX was to evaluate the experiences of several hundred ESSI Process Improvement Experiments (PIEs) and to make this experience accessible to a broad European audience in a convenient form. In particular, the goal was to collect and make available to interested practitioners information about Software Best Practice and its introduction in specific problem domains.

In the following sections, we briefly review the history of the EUREX project.

2.1 Target Audience and Motivation

Over 70% of the organisations that participated in events organised during the course of the ESPITI project (see section 1.3.2 below) were Small or Medium Enterprises (SMEs), and many of which had substantially fewer than 250 employees. This response rate demonstrated a significant interest on the part of SMEs in finding out more about Software Process Improvement (SPI). Therefore, the primary target audience for EUREX was those European SMEs, and small teams in the non-IT organisations, engaged in the activity of developing software. Within these organisations, the focus was on management and technical personnel in a position to make decisions to undertake process improvement activities.

The ESPITI User Survey presents a clear picture of the needs and requirements of SMEs concerning software process improvement. For example, 25% of those who responded requested participation in working groups for experience exchange. However, SMEs are faced with many difficulties when it comes to trying to implement improvement programmes.

For example, SMEs are generally less aware than larger companies of the benefits of business-driven software process improvement. It is perceived as being an expensive task and the standard examples that are quoted in an attempt to convince them otherwise are invariably drawn from larger U.S. organisations and therefore bear little relevance for European SMEs. ESSIgram No 11 also reported that "peer review of experiment work in progress and results would be helpful."

Thus, SMEs need to see success among their peers, using moderate resources, before they are prepared to change their views and consider embarking upon SPI actions.

For those SMEs that are aware of the benefits of SPI, there are frequently other inhibitors that prevent anything useful being accomplished. Many SMEs realise that they should implement software process improvement actions but do not know how to do this. They do not have the necessary skills and knowledge to do it themselves and in many cases they do not have the financial resources to engage external experts to help them. Consequently, SPI actions get deferred or cancelled because other business priorities assume greater importance. Even those SMEs that do successfully initiate SPI programmes can find that these activities are not seen through to their natural completion stage because of operational or financial constraints.

Many of the concerns about the relevance of SPI for SMEs were addressed by EUREX in a series of workshops in which speakers from similarly characterised companies spoke about their experiences with SPI. The workshops were in integral part of the EUREX process and provided much of the data presented in this volume.

The Commission funded EUREX in large measure because the evaluation of approximately 300 PIEs was too costly for an independent endeavour. Even if some resource-rich organisation had undertaken this task, it is likely that the results would not have been disseminated, but would rather have been used to further competitive advantage. Commission support has insured that the results are widely and publicly distributed.

Many ESSI dissemination actions have been organised as conferences or workshops. PIE Users register in order to discharge their obligations to the Commission; however, the selection and qualification of contributions is often less than rigorous. In addition, many public conferences have added PIE presentation tracks with little organisation of their content. Small audiences are a consequence of the competition of that track with others in the conference. The common thread in these experiences is that organisation of the actions had been lacking or passive.

EUREX turned this model on its end. PIE Users were approached proactively to involve them in the process. In addition, the information exchange process was actively managed. The EUREX workshops were organised around several distinct problem domains and workshop attendees were supported with expert assistance to evaluate their situations and provide commentary on solutions from a broadly experienced perspective. (See chapter 3 for a detailed discussion of the domain selection process.) Participants were invited through press publications, the local chambers of commerce, the Regional Organisations of EUREX and through co-operation with other dissemination actions.

This approach provided a richer experience for attendees. Since the workshops were domain-oriented, the participants heard different approaches to the same issues and were presented with alternative experiences and solutions. This was a more informative experience than simply hearing a talk about experiences in a vacuum, with no background and no possibility for comparison or evaluation. The opportunity to exchange views with one's peers and to hear advice from respected experts provides substantial benefit not found using a passive approach to dissemination.

Our approach also offered a better experience for European Industry as a whole. Since we have categorised and evaluated approximately 300 different improvement experiments, we present a broad practical view of the selected problem domains. This is distinctly different from purely academic approaches that offer little practical experience. EUREX is an opportunity to derive additional benefit from the PIEs, beyond that of obligatory presentations. We hope to lend an authoritative voice to the overall discussion of Software Process Improvement.

2.2 Objectives and Approach

As mentioned above, the objective of EUREX was to assess, classify, categorise, and exploit the experience of the ESSI PIE Prime Users and Associated Partners (collectively referred to here simply as Users or PIE Users) and then to make this experience accessible. In particular, we sought to provide a broad European audience with data about Software Best Practice and its introduction in selected problem domains.

The approach is broken down into two phases. The first phase required the classification and collection of data and the second phase involves the analysis, distribution and dissemination of the resulting information. The phases were implemented in three steps:

1. Classify and categorise the base of PIE Users and the Problem Domains addressed by them. All of the available material from over 300 PIEs was assessed, the categorisation was designed such that over 90% of the material under consideration fell into one of the selected Problem Domains (see chapter 3).
2. Plan and conduct a series of Regional Workshops in order to collect information from PIE projects as well as for disseminating the PIE's experiences at a regional level. 18 workshops in 8 European countries were undertaken. (Refer to chapter 7 for the best of the workshop material.)
3. Publish the first four of the Software Best Practice Reports and Executive Reports to detail the experiences. In addition, a Web-site provides access to the background material used by EUREX.

Steps 1 and 2 fall within phase one and steps 2 and 3 are within phase two. Notice that, because multiple benefits are derived from the same activity, the two phases overlapped somewhat. This approach is intended to convey to the largest possible audience the experiences of the Commission's Process Improvement Experiment program.

The EUREX Software Best Practice Reports (of which this volume is one) and Executive Reports are directed at two distinct audiences. The first is the technically oriented IT manager or developer interested in the full reports and technology background. The second is senior management, for whom the Executive Reports a summary of benefits and risks of real cases are appropriate.

2.3   Partners

The EUREX project was carried out by the following partners:

- HIGHWARE GmbH, Germany (Coordinator)
- Editions HIGHWARE sarl, France
- GEMINI Soc. Cons. A, Italy
- SOCINTEC, Spain
- SISU, Sweden
- MARI Northern Ireland Ltd., United Kingdom.

The fact that MARI has left the consortium (as they did with other projects as well) caused some disruption and delay for the project. The partners were able to compensate largely, e.g. the number of workshops held and the countries covered. Even the book about the domain assigned to MARI, Object Orientation, was prepared with the help of FZI Forschungszentrum Informatik, Karlsruhe, Germany.

2.4   Related Dissemination and Training Actions

Other ESSI Dissemination Actions that have also generated significant results that may be of interest to the reader. These actions include SISSI and ESPITI, both described briefly below.

2.4.1   Software Improvement Case Studies Initiative (SISSI)

European companies must face the challenge of translating software engineering into a competitive advantage in the market place, by taking full advantage of the existing experiences and results. The process of overcoming existing barriers is not an easy one, particularly if individual companies must face them on their own. It is a major issue to put at the disposal of companies a set of written case studies providing a practical view of software process improvement (SPI) impact and best practices. Successful experiences can demonstrate that existing barriers can be dismantled. This learning process, which takes time and requires continuity in the long term, is being fostered by the SISSI project.

2.4.1.1 Overview

The target audience for the SISSI case studies is senior executives, i.e. decision-makers, in software producing organisations through Europe. This includes both software vendors and companies developing software for in-house use. The material has been selected in such a way that it is relevant for both small and large organisations.

SISSI produced a set of 33 case studies, of about 4 pages each, and distributed 50 case studies overall, together with cases from previous projects. Cases are not exclusively technical; rather, they have a clear business orientation and are focused on action. Cases are a selected compendium of finished Process Improvement Experiments (PIEs) funded by the ESSI program of the EC. They are classified according to parameters and keywords so tailored and selective extractions can be made by potential users or readers. The main selection criteria are the business sector, the software process affected by the improvement project and its business goals.

The dissemination mechanisms of SISSI were the following: a selective telephone-led campaign addressed to 500 appropriate organisations together with follow up actions; an extensive mailing campaign targeting 5000 additional organisations which have selected the relevant cases from an introductory document; joint action with the European Network of SPI Nodes –ESPINODEs– to distribute the SISSI material and provide continuity to the SISSI project; WWW pages with the full contents of the case studies; synergic actions with other Dissemination Actions of the ESSI initiative, like EUREX, SPIRE, RAPID; co-operation with other agents like European publications, SPI institutions, or graduate studies acting as secondary distribution channels.

SISSI developed an SPI Marketing Plan to systematically identify and access this target market in any European country and distributed its contents through the European Network of SPI Nodes both for a secondary distribution of SISSI Case Studies, and for a suitable rendering of the ESPINODEs services. The plan was implemented for the dissemination of the SISSI Case Studies in several European countries, proving its validity.

2.4.1.2 Objectives

The main goals of the approach taken in the SISSI project have been as follows:

- The material produced has been formed by a wide variety of practical real cases selected by the consultants of the consortium, and documented in a friendly and didactic way to capture interest between companies.
- The cases have clearly emphasised the key aspects of the improvement projects in terms of competitive advantage and tangible benefits (cost, time to market, quality).

- Most of the cases have been successful cases, but also not successful ones have been sought in order to analyse causes of failure, i.e. inadequate analysis of the plan before starting the project.
- The project has not been specially focused on particular techniques or application areas, but it has been a selected compendium of the current and finished Process Improvement Experiments –PIEs–. They have been classified according to different parameters and keywords so tailored and selective extractions can be made by potential users or readers. The main selection criteria have been: business sector (finance, electronics, manufacturing, software houses, engineering, etc.), the software process, the business goals and some technological aspects of the experiment.
- The Dissemination action should open new markets promoting the SPI benefits in companies not already contacted by traditional ESSI actions.
- The SISSI Marketing Plan should provide the methodology and the information not only to disseminate the SISSI material, but has to be generic enough to direct the marketing of other ESSI services and SPI activities in general.

The SISSI material should be used in the future by organisations and other dissemination actions and best practices networks as a reference material to guide lines of software improvement and practical approaches to face them. In particular, SISSI has to provide continuity of the action beyond the project itself supporting the marketing of SPI in any other ESSI action.

2.4.2   ESPITI

The European Software Process Improvement Training Initiative (ESPITI) was officially launched on 22 November 1994 in Belfast, Northern Ireland. The final event was held in Berlin, Germany in Spring 1996. The Initiative aimed to maximise the benefits gained from European activities in the improvement and subsequent ISO 9000 certification of the software development process through training. A sum of 8.5 million ECU was allocated to the Initiative for a period of 18 months, to support actions intended to:

- Identify the true needs of European industry for training in software process improvement (SPI).
- Increase the level of awareness of the benefits of software process improvement and ISO 9001.
- Provide training for trainers, managers and software engineers.
- Support the development of networks between organisations at regional and European levels to share knowledge and experience and form links of mutual benefit.
- Liase with similar initiatives world-wide and transfer their experiences to Europe.

2.4.2.1   Organisational Structure

The Initiative was implemented through a network of 14 Regional Organisations addressing the local needs of 17 EU and EFTA countries. Regional Organisations (ROs) have been existing commercial organisations that were contracted to carry out a specific range of activities in support of the ESPITI goals. The ROs were divided into 2 sets, each set supported by a Partner. The two Partner organisations, Forschungszentrum Karlsruhe GmbH from Germany and MARI (Northern Ireland) Ltd from the United Kingdom, have been co-ordinating and supporting co-operation at European level through the provision of services to the ROs. These services included provision of:

- Preparation of a user survey in all countries involved to determine the local SPI needs.
- An electronic communication network for exchanging SPI information of mutual interest.
- Guidelines on event organisation, e.g. seminars, training courses and working groups.
- Awareness material for project launches, software process improvement and ISO 9001.
- Assistance in evaluating performance at project and event levels.
- Guidance in programme planning and control.
- Assistance in PR activities.
- Assistance in experience exchange and co-operation between the ROs.

The European Software Institute ESI was also involved in ESPITI, providing the Partners with valuable assistance, including the merging of the European user survey results, liaison with other initiatives and contributions to RO meetings.

2.4.2.2   The ESPITI Approach

The ESPITI project adopted a multi-pronged strategy for improving the competitiveness of the European software industry.

- Survey of European needs was carried out to ascertain the needs and the best approach to adopt to satisfy these needs within each region.
- Seminars for raising awareness of the benefits and approaches to quality management and process improvement.
- Training courses for improving know-how in initiating, assessing, planning and implementing quality management and process improvement programmes.
- Workshops, which aim to teach participants about a subject and direct them in implementing the subject in their Organisations.
- Working groups for enabling dissemination of experience in a subject, and to allow participants to discuss and learn about those experiences.
- Case studies for demonstrating the successes and difficulties in software process improvement.

- Liaisons with similar, related initiatives world-wide to understand their approaches and successes and to transfer the lessons learned there to Europe.
- Public relations activities to promote the aims and objectives of ESPITI and to ensure participation in ESPITI events.
- Evaluation of the ESPITI project to assess the effectiveness of the initiative, and to determine how the initiative could progress from there.

2.4.2.3   The Partners and Regional Organisations

The Partners

- MARI (Northern Ireland) Ltd, United Kingdom
- Forschungszentrum Karlsruhe GmbH, Germany

The Regional Organisations

- Austrian Research Centre, Austria
- Flemish Quality Management Centre, Belgium
- Delta Software Engineering, Denmark
- CCC Software Professionals Oy, Finland
- AFNOR, France
- Forschungszentrum Karlsruhe GmbH, Germany
- INTRASOFT SA, Greece
- University of Iceland, Iceland
- Centre for Software Engineering, Ireland
- ETNOTEAM, Italy
- Centre de Recherche Public Henri Tudor, Luxembourg
- SERC, The Netherlands
- Norsk Regnesentral, Norway
- Instituto Portugues da Qualidade, Portugal
- Sip Consultoría y formación, Spain
- SISU, Sweden
- MARI (Northern Ireland) Ltd., United Kingdom

3   The EUREX Taxonomy

M. Haug, E.W. Olsen
HIGHWARE, Munich

One of the most significant tasks performed during the EUREX project was the creation of the taxonomy needed to drive the Regional Workshops and, ultimately, the content of these Software Best Practice Reports. In this chapter, we examine in detail the process that led to the EUREX taxonomy and discuss how the taxonomy led to the selection of PIEs for the specific subject domain.

3.1   Analysis and Assessment of PIEs

Over 300 Process Improvement Experiments (PIEs) funded by the Commission in the calls of 1993, 1995 and 1996 were analysed using an iterative approach as described below. The technical domain of each of the PIEs was assessed by EUREX and each PIE was attributed to certain technological areas.

Early discussions proved what others (including the Commission) had already experienced in the attempt to classify PIEs: there is no canonical, "right" classification. The type, scope and detail of a classification depends almost entirely on the intended use for the classification. The EUREX taxonomy was required to serve the EUREX project. In particular, it was used to drive the selection of suitable subject areas for the books and, consequently, the selection of regional workshop topics to insure that good coverage would be achieved both by the number of PIEs and by the partners in their respective regions.

3.2   Classification into Problem Domains

A set of more than 150 attributes was refined in several iterations to arrive at a coarse grain classification into technological problem domains. These domains were defined such that the vast majority of PIEs fall into at least one of these domains. There were seven steps used in the process of discovering the domains, as described in the following paragraphs.

In part because of the distributed nature of the work and in part because of the necessity for several iterations, the classification required 6 calendar months to complete.

3.2.1   First Regional Classification

Each partner examined the PIEs conducted within its region and assigned attributes from the list given above that described the work done within the PIE (more than one attribute per PIE was allowed). The regions were assigned as shown in Table 3.1.

Table 3.1 Regional responsibilities of consortium partners

Partner	Region
SISU	Denmark, Finland, Norway, Sweden
MARI	United Kingdom, Ireland
GEMINI	Italy
SOCINTEC	Spain, Portugal, Greece
HIGHWARE Germany	Germany, Austria, The Netherlands, Israel and all other regions not explicitly assigned
HIGHWARE France	Benelux, France

3.2.2   Result of First Regional Classification

HIGHWARE Germany (the consortium co-ordinator) began with a classification of the German PIEs according to the above procedure. This first attempt was distributed among the partners as a working example.

Using the example, each partner constructed a spreadsheet with a first local classification and returned this to HIGHWARE Germany.

3.2.3   Consolidation and Iteration

HIGHWARE Germany prepared a consolidated spreadsheet using the partners' input, and developed from that a first classification and clustering proposal. This was sent to the other partners for review and cross-checking.

3.2.4   Update of Regional Classification

All partners reviewed their classification, in particular the assignment of attributes to PIEs. Corrections were made as necessary.

3.2.5 Mapping of Attributes.

HIGHWARE Germany mapped all key words used by the partners into a new set of attributes, normalising the names of attributes. No attribute was deleted, but the overall number of different attributes decreased from 164 to 127. These attributes were further mapped into classes and subclasses that differentiate members of classes. This second mapping lead to a set of 24 classes each containing 0 to 13 subclasses. The resulting classes are shown in table 3.2.

Table 3.2 Attributes of the Classification

Assessment	Case Tools	Change Management
Configuration Management	Decision Support	Documentation
Estimation	Formal Methods	Life Cycle: Analysis & Design
Life Cycle: Dynamic System Modelling	Life Cycle: Installation & Maintenance	Life Cycle: Requirements & Specification
Life Cycle: Product Management.	Metrics	Modelling & Simulation
Object Orientation	Process Model: Definition	Process Model: Distributed
Process Model: Iterative	Process Model: Support	Project Management
Prototyping	Quality Management	Reengineering
Reuse & Components	Reverse Engineering	Target Environment
Testing, Verification & Validation	User Interface	

3.2.6 Review of Classification and Mapping into Subject Domains

The classification achieved by the above mentioned process was reviewed by the partners and accepted with minor adjustments. It is important to note that up to this point, the classification was independent of the structure of the planned publications. It simply described the technical work done by PIEs in the consolidated view of the project partners.

In the next step this view was discussed and grouped into subject domains suitable for publications planned by the consortium.

3.2.7 Subject Domains Chosen

Out of the original 24 classes, 7 were discarded from the further consideration, either because the number of PIEs in the class was not significant or because the domain was already addressed by other ESSI Dissemination Actions (e.g. formal methods, reengineering, and so on). The 17 final classes were grouped into the subject domains shown in table 3.3 such that each of the resulting 5 domains forms a suitable working title for one of the EUREX books.

Table 3.3 Final Allocation of Domains

Partner	Domain
SISU	Metrics, Measurement and Process Modelling
MARI	Object Orientation, Reuse and Components
GEMINI	Testing, Verification, Validation, Quality Management
SOCINTEC	Configuration & Change Management, Requirements Engineering
HIGHWARE France	Project Management, Estimation, Life Cycle Support

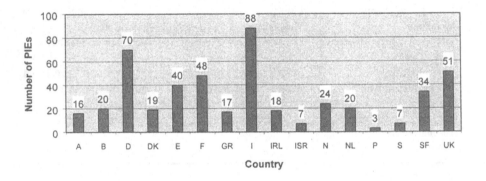

Fig. 3.1 All PIEs by Country

The breakdown of all (unclassified) PIEs on a per-country basis is shown in Fig. 3.1. The distribution of PIEs is somewhat related to population, but there are notable exceptions (e.g. Italy and France).

The classification breakdown of PIEs Europe-wide is worth examining. Referring to Fig. 3.2, notice first that the classification has resulted in a relatively even distribution of projects, only the Project Management classification dips noticeably below the average. The number of PIEs without any classification was held below 10% of the total. (Further discussion of the "No Classification" category appears below.)

3.2.8   Unclassified PIEs

There we 33 PIEs that were not classified by EUREX. There were generally two reasons for lack of classification.

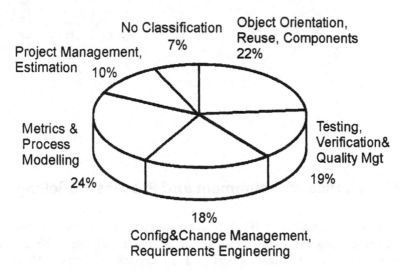

Fig. 3.2 Classification of PIEs Europe-wide

1. Neither the EUREX reviewer alone nor the consortium as a whole was able to reach a conclusion for classification based on the PIE description as published.
2. The PIE addressed a very specific subject that did not correspond to a class defined by EUREX and/or the PIE was dealt with by other known ESSI projects, e.g. formal methods. The consortium tried to avoid too much overlap with other projects.

When one of these rules was applied, the corresponding PIE was given no classification and was not considered further by the EUREX analysis. Fig. 3.3 shows the breakdown of unclassified PIEs by country.

As can be seen in Fig. 3.3, there were 33 PIEs that remained unclassified once the EUREX analysis was complete.

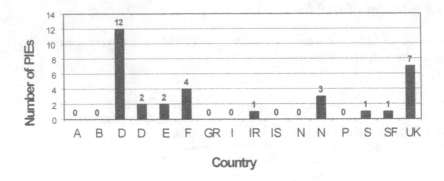

Fig. 3.3 Unclassified PIEs.

3.3 Metrics, Measurement and Process Modelling

Part II presents the results of EUREX project with respect to the Metrics, Measurement & Process Modelling classification. The attributes associated with this classification were Metrics, Measurement and all aspects of Process Modelling. Within this classification there were a total of 116 PIEs that were assigned one or more of these attributes. The distribution of these PIEs throughout Europe is shown in figure 3.4.

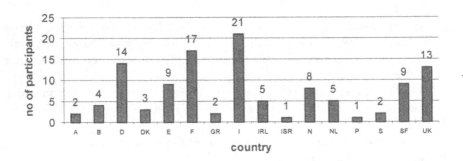

Fig. 3.4 Metrics, Measurement and Process Modelling PIEs by Country

Part II

Metrics, Measurement and Process Modelling

4 Perspectives

Lars Bergman
SISU, Kista

Three perspectives on Software Process Improvement through Metrics are given in this chapter. The views of Norman Fenton and José D. Carrillo Verdun were presented at EUREX Metrics Workshops in the UK and Spain respectively. Terttu Orci was an active member of the Nordic EUREX team and made a study of Metrics Quality in relevant Process Improvement Experiments.

Norman Fenton offers a witty state of the art overview of the academic and industrial fields. He treats the use of metrics as a means of assessing Software Methods provides an analysis of the problems concerning faults metrics. Mr. Fenton's presentation is thought provoking reading for anyone using or planning to use fault metrics in their measurement programme.

José D. Carrillo Verdun, takes the management point of view in his presentation, which gives a normative management consultancy perspective on the why's and how's of deploying metrics in a software development organisation. For those considering or planning the deployment of measurement programmes, this presentation should work nicely as a checklist and as a base for internal discussions about adapting the process to the organisational environment.

Terttu Orci studied 13 PIEs (most of which were involved in EUREX Metrics Workshops) to determine the quality of the metrics used. Following an introduction to basic metrics, which is a worthwhile brush-up, she analyses the choice and application of metrics in the selected PIEs. The conclusion is that there remains ample room for improvement in the measurement practice in those organisations. The findings should provide valuable and practical advice for organisations in their measurement work.

4.1   Metrics for Software Process Improvement

Norman Fenton
City University, London

Norman Fenton is Professor of Computing Science at the Centre for Software Reliability, City University, London and also Managing Director of Agena Ltd, a company specialising in risk management for critical computer systems. He is a Chartered Engineer who previously held academic posts at University College Dublin, Oxford University and South Bank University where he was Director of the Centre for Systems and Software Engineering. He has been project manager and principal researcher in many major collaborative projects. His recent and current projects cover the areas of: software metrics; safety critical systems assessment; Bayesian nets for systems' assessment; software reliability tools. Professor Fenton has written several books on software metrics and related subjects.

Abstract

One of the reasons for the massive increase in interest in software metrics has been the perception that metrics are needed for process improvement. In fact the only successful uses of metrics arise from very well-defined and specific objectives. A vague requirement of process improvement is not sufficient. It is not surprising therefore that the practical take-up of anything other than the crudest techniques has been extremely poor. I will offer my own explanation for this situation, citing what I feel have been the successes and failures of software metrics. I will look especially at the role of metrics for methods/process evaluation and highlight the problems associated with defects-based metrics and how these can be overcome. The talk provides some guidelines on defining simple metrics programmes to meet specific objectives.

4.1.1   Metrics for Software Process Improvement

Major issues:

- Need for clearly defined objectives
- Chasm between academic research and industrial use of software metrics
- Poorly defined/motivated role of metrics for "process improvement"
- Measurement to evaluate software process methods has been poor
- Software metrics are poor predictors of the things we are really interested in
- Fundamental problems with the way we currently monitor and predict software defects

Different reasons for software measurement:

- To assess software products
- To assess software methods
- To help improve software processes
- Need to start with a specific objective before defining your "metrics programme"

There is no single motivation for using software metrics. For this reason, there is no such thing as a generic software metrics "programme" or a generic set of software metrics. The most (and possibly only) successful metrics programmes are those which started out with a very specific and focused objective.

Although these high level goals are not terribly well-defined they encompass most sensible software measurement activities.

Assessing software products: here we treat software as an artefact (we include documentation as part of this). We are interested in measuring/predicting attributes such as reliability, maintainability, internal complexity etc.

Assessing software methods: here we are interested in using measurement for experimentation purposes. We want to know which competing software engineering methods are most cost-effective. The only effective way of doing this is via measurement-based case studies.

Improving software processes: this is where the bulk of software measurement activities lie. Examples include measurement for cost/effort estimation, measurement for quality control etc.

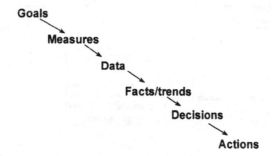

Fig. 4.1 From Goals to Actions

Unless the end result of a measurement programme is a potential set of actions, the programme is doomed to failure. Thus measurement results must lead to decisions which can be actioned. For example, if your goal is to assess the effectiveness of a new design tool being used by several members of staff, then the measurement results may lead you to the decision that the tool is overpriced and does not improve the quality of designs. In that case you need to take the decision not to continue with the tool. If such action was always out of your control then the measurement programme in this case was a waste of time.

The Metrics Plan
For each technical goal this contains information about

- *why* metrics can address the goal
- *what* metrics will be collected, how they will be defined, and how they will be analysed
- *who* will do the collecting, who will do the analysing, and who will see the results
- *how* it will be done – what tools, techniques and practices will be used to support metrics collection and analysis
- *when* in the process and how often the metrics will be collected and analysed
- *where* the data will be stored

Any measurement programme should have a documented plan containing the above information.

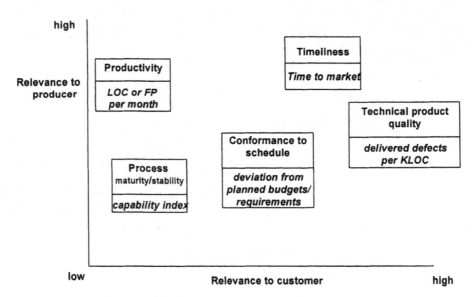

Fig. 4.2 Software metrics from different software quality perspectives

Different views on software quality have different relevance to customers and developers. The graph shows some different views and where they fit on the axes.

Along with each view of quality we have indicated (below the lines) a popular way of measuring this view of quality.

Note that a process oriented view of quality such as process maturity/stability provides the least direct evidence of quality.

4.1.2 Software Metrics: Successes and Failures

4.1.2.1 A Brief History of Software Metrics

- First book (Gilb 1976) but LOC-based measures since 1960's
  - "productivity"=LOC/effort
  - "quality"=defects/LOC
  - "effort"=f(LOC)
- LOC used as surrogate notion of size, complexity
- Drawbacks led to new metrics:
  - Halstead, McCabe, Function Points
- Drawbacks in these led to further metrics:
  - Design level metrics, metrics for different language paradigms

Meta-level Activities

- Setting up a metrics program
  - notably Grady and Caswell
- Goal-oriented metrics
  - Basili et al's GQM
- Use of metrics in empirical software engineering
- Theoretical underpinnings

Good news about metrics:
- Phenomenal success judged by academic/research output
- Significant increase in industrial metrics activity
  - most IT companies have some kind of metrics program
  - massive increase in last 10 years

There are 1600 papers, 40 text books, dedicated conferences. Software metrics are accepted as core software engineering topic. Many companies with "metrics programs" may not regarded them explicitly as such.

Bad news about metrics:
- No match in content between the increased level of metrics activity in academia and industry
- Much academic metrics research is inherently irrelevant to industrial needs
- Much industrial metrics activity is poorly motivated
  - grudge purchase

- CMM/assessment the major trigger
- Much industrial metrics activity is poorly executed

Much of the increased metrics activity in industry is based almost entirely on metrics that were around in the early 1970s.

Much academic work has focused on metrics which can only ever be applied/computed for small programs, whereas all the reasonable objectives for applying metrics are relevant primarily for large systems. Irrelevance in scope also applies to the many academic models which rely on parameters which could never be measured in practice.

Whereas the pressing industrial need is for metrics that are relevant for process improvement, much academic work has concentrated on detailed code metrics. In many cases these aim to measure properties that are of little practical interest.

All too often the decision by a company to put in place some kind of a metrics program is inevitably a "grudge purchase"; it is something done when things are bad or to satisfy some external assessment body. For example, in the US the single biggest trigger for industrial metrics activity has been the CMM; evidence of use of metrics is intrinsic for achieving higher levels of CMM. Just as there is little empirical evidence about the effectiveness of specific software development methods so there is equally little known about the effectiveness of software metrics. Convincing success stories describing the long-term payback of metrics are almost non-existent. What we do know is that metrics will always be an overhead on your current software projects (we found typically it would be 4-8%) .

We have come across numerous examples of industrial practice which ignores well known guidelines of best practice data-collection and analysis and applies metrics in ways that were known to be invalid twenty years ago. For example, it is still common for companies to collect defect data which does not distinguish between defects discovered in operation and defects discovered during development.

Metrics successes ?

- The enduring LOC metric
- Metrics relating to defect counts
- McCabe's cyclomatic number
- Function Points

... but only in their level of use.

This is if we judge success by reasonably widespread industrial use. The problem is that, used in isolation, these kind of metrics are worse than useless.

4.1.2.2 The Problem with Measuring "Problems"

The following are used interchangeably:

- Defects
- Faults
- Failures

- Anomalies
- Bugs
- Crashes

One of the major weaknesses of software metrics work (and indeed much empirical software engineering) has been the failure to distinguish between different classes of "problems" during measurement and data-collection. For example, "defects" irrespective of whether they are discovered before or after release are often lumped together. Next we investigate the ramifications of doing this.

Fig. 4.3 Human errors, faults, and failures

- Human Error: Designer's mistake
- Fault: Encoding of an error into a software document/product
- Failure: Deviation of the software system from specified or expected behaviour

A *fault* occurs when a human error results in a mistake in some software product. That is, the fault is the encoding of the human error. For example, a developer might misunderstand a user interface requirement, and therefore create a design that includes the misunderstanding. The design fault can also result in incorrect code, as well as incorrect instructions in the user manual. Thus, a single error can result in one or more faults, and a fault can reside in any of the products of development.

On the other hand, a *failure* is the departure of a system from its required behaviour. Failures can be discovered both before and after system delivery, as they can occur in testing as well as in operation. It is important to note that we are comparing actual system behaviour with required behaviour, rather than with specified behaviour, because faults in the requirements documents can result in failures, too.

In some sense, you can think of faults and failures as inside and outside views of the system. Faults represent problems that the developer sees, while failures are problems that the user sees. Not every fault corresponds to a failure, since the conditions under which a fault results in system failure may never be met.

Actual example:

Human error: Failure to distinguish signed and absolute value numbers in an algorithm resulted in:

Fault: "X:=Y" is coded instead of "X:= ABS(Y)" which in turn led to Failure: Nuclear reactor shut down because it was determined wrongly that a meltdown was likely.

The "Defect Density" Measure: an Important Health Warning
- Defects = {faults} $\cup$ {failures}
  - but sometimes defects = {faults} or defects = {failures}
- System defect density $= \dfrac{\text{number of defects found}}{\text{system size}}$
  - where size is usually measured as thousands of lines of code (KLOC)
- Defect density is used as a de-facto measure of software quality.
  - Adams' data shows this is very dangerous

Faults vs. Failures
There is much inconsistency in the terminology for software "problems". Many people refer to defects as the union of faults and failures, but this is not universal.

However, the biggest problem is the assumption that somehow faults and failures are "equally bad" and that defects are therefore in some sense homogeneous.

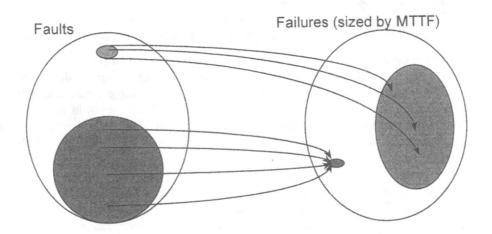

35% of all faults only lead to very rare failures (MTTF>5000 years)

Fig. 4.4 Relationship between faults and failures (Adams 1984)

In real systems most faults are "benign" in the sense that they lead only to very rare failures. Conversely a small proportion of faults account for most common failures.

Below MTTF = Mean Time To Failure

Adams looked at the failure data for these products. If a product was running on n installation each for y years when a particular failure is first observed at one of the installations then the Time to Failure is n × y years.

What the chart shows is that 35% of all failures are "very rare" failures, i.e. those with MTTF of > 5000 years. In practical terms such failures are almost certainly only observed at one installation out of the many thousands which use the software. Conversely, a very small proportion of all failures (< 2%) are the "common" failures, i.e. those with MTTF of < 50 years. The Adams' data highlights the danger of associating a measure of fault density with software quality (especially if quality is synonymous with reliability which is defined as the probability of failure-free operation in a given time period under given operational conditions).

See [Adams 84] for more details.

The relationship between fault and failures:

- Most faults are benign
- For most faults: removal will not lead to greatly improved reliability
- Large reliability improvements only come when we eliminate the small proportion of faults which lead to the more frequent failures
- Does not mean we should stop looking for faults, but warns us to be careful about equating fault counts with reliability

This does not mean that fault removal does not lead to improved reliability. It is possible (if we are unlucky enough with our test selection) to remove 98% of all faults in a system without achieving any real reliability improvement. In practice, without any prior knowledge about the faults we would hope that our testing does discover a reasonable proportion of the 2% of the important faults.

4.1.2.3   Implications for Metrics Data-Collection

Identifying the "smallest component":

- Unit
- Module
- Subsystem
- System

Incidents need to be traceable to identifiable components.

Therefore generic data, which has to be applicable to failure, fault or change is needed:

- *Location*: Where is it?
- *Timing*: When did it occur?

- *Mode*: What was observed?
- *Effect*: Which consequences resulted?
- *Mechanism*: How did it arise?
- *Cause*: Why did it occur?
- *Severity*: How much was the user affected?
- *Cost*: How much did it cost the developer?

The data required on failures is mainly:

- *Location*: Installation where failure observed
- *Timing*: Some measure of amount of software execution (e.g. CPU time) and real time
- *Mode*: e.g. type of error message
- *Effect*: e.g. classify as: "operating system crash", "services degraded", "loss of data", "wrong output", "no output" etc.
- *Mechanism*: Chain of events, e.g. keyboard commands
- *Cause*: Refer to fault
- *Severity*: e.g. classify as "critical", "major", "minor"
- *Cost*: cost to fix plus lost future business

The data required on faults is mainly:

- *Location*: e.g. module or document identifier
- *Timing*: Normally classified by life-cycle phase
- *Mode*: Normally either category (missing/wrong/extra) or type of fault (logic, data-flow etc)
- *Effect*: mode of failure when activated
- *Mechanism*: How was fault created, detected, corrected
- *Cause*: Type of human error that lead to fault
- *Severity*: severity of worse possible resulting failure
- *Cost*: Time/effort to locate and correct

Classifications:

- Choose orthogonal "entity" classification schemes
- Appropriate schemes will be context dependent but consult, e.g. IEEE P1044/D5 "Standard Classification for Software Anomalies"
- The following classification scheme for fault type is non-orthogonal:
  - critical
  - data
  - logic
  - documentation
  - misc other

4.1.3   Using Metrics to Evaluate Software Process Methods

The ESSI principle of using metrics:

- Need to assess quantitatively the impact of software technologies
- Implies careful experimentation and measurement
- Not always carried out

What we Need to Measure:
- The extent to which method has been used
- The cost of using the method
- The extent to which the method produces "good" products
  - identify key success criteria
  - problems with simplistic "quality" measures

If you omit any of these three dimensions then you cannot really evaluate the effectiveness of the method.

The Uncertainty of Software Engineering Methods
- Software engineering is dominated by revolutionary methods that are supposed to solve the software crisis
- Most methods focus on fault avoidance
- Proponents of methods claim theirs is best
- Adopting a new method can require a massive overhead with uncertain benefits
- Potential users have to rely on what the experts say

Empirical Evidence About Software Engineering Methods
- Limited support for n-version programming
- No public evidence to support claims made for formal methods or OOD
- Conflicting evidence on CASE
- No conclusive evidence even to support structured programming
- Inspection techniques are cost-effective (but ill-defined)

We know almost nothing about which (if any) software engineering methods really work.

Use of Measurement in Evaluating Methods
- Measurement is the only truly convincing means of establishing the efficacy of a method/tool/technique
- Quantitative claims must be supported by empirical evidence

We cannot rely on anecdotal evidence. There is simply too much at stake.

Table 4.1 A Study in Relative Efficiency of Testing Methods[11]

Testing Type	Defects found per hour
Regular use	0.21
Black bow	0.282
White Box	0.322
Reading/Inspections	1.057

The Evidence for Structured Programming

"The precepts of structured programming are compelling, yet the empirical evidence is equivocal"[12]

It is hard to know which claims we can believe.

OO Case Studies

- Similar C and C++ systems
  - each approx 50KLOC
- Higher quality in C version?
  - 2.4 faults/KLOC in C, 2.9 faults/KLOC in C++
- Higher maintainability in C version
  - Avg. defect correction time in C++ is 2.6 times as long as C.[13]
- Value of inheritance?
  - Study of 133KLOC C++ system showed components involved in inheritance has 6 times more defects.[14]

SMARTIE Formal Methods Study

CDIS Air Traffic Control System

Best quantitative evidence yet to support FM:

- Mixture of formally (VDM, CCS) and informally developed modules.
- The techniques used resulted in extraordinarily high levels of reliability (0.81 failures per KLOC).
- Little difference in total number of pre-delivery faults for formal and informal methods (though unit testing revealed fewer errors in modules developed using formal techniques), but clear difference in the post-delivery failures.

Praxis built an air traffic control information system for the UK Civil Aviation Authority in the early 1990s using a variety of formal methods. The Central Con-

---

[11] See [Grady92].
[12] See [Vessey84].
[13] See [Hatton98].
[14] See [Cartwright97].

trol Function Display Information System (CDIS) provides controllers at the London Air Traffic Control Centre with key information, allowing them to manipulate the approach sequence of aircraft for the one of the busiest airspaces in the world. Praxis had used formal methods before, but not to the extent used in CDIS. Several different formal methods were involved in the development. The functional requirements were developed using three techniques:

- an entity-relationship analysis to describe the real-world objects, their properties and interrelationships (such as arrivals, departures, workstations, plasma display screens)
- a real-time extension of Yourdon's structured analysis to define the processing requirements
- a formal specification language, to define the data and operations.

Praxis expressed the requirements for critical system elements using VDM. The team approached the system specification from three points of view: an abstract definition of the required functionality; a concrete user interface definition; a concurrency specification.

The abstract specification was written in a formal language called VVSL, similar to VDM. The user interface definitions, derived from a prototyping exercise, were expressed as pictures, text and state-transition diagrams. The concurrency specification was a mixture of data flow diagrams and formal notation using Robin Milner's CCS. The overall CDIS design was described in a design overview, containing the overall system architecture and design rationale. Then, each of the four major parts of the system had its own design document. The application code was designed by writing VDM-like specifications of the application modules, created as refinements of the core specification. The user interface code was designed informally, using pseudocode for each window class. The processes needed to achieve concurrency and invoke the application code were defined as finite state machines (FSMs).The local area network software was designed formally, using a mixture of VDM and a formal method called CCS. Because this area was particularly difficult, some formal proofs were done to find faults in the design.

As a problem was identified, a fault report number was assigned, as well as a category to describe the likely source of the problem: specification, design or code. A brief description of the problem was written on the fault report form, plus suggestions about which code modules, specification documents or design components might be the source. Following contractual obligations, a severity designation was assigned at the same time, with severity categories defined by the Civil Aviation Authority according to the following criteria:

- Category 1: Operational system critical
- Category 2: System inadequate
- Category 3: System unsatisfactory

When the problem was fixed, the responsible party would list on the form all documents and modules actually changed; sometimes the severity designation was changed, too, to indicate the true nature of the problem. Indeed, the designation could be changed to 0, meaning that the perceived problem either was not a problem at all or had been reported previously.

CDIS FAULT REPORT		S.P0204.6.10.3016
ORIGINATOR:	Joe Bloggs	
BRIEF TITLE:	Exception 1 in dps_c.c line 620 raised by NAS	

FULL DESCRIPTION   Started NAS endurance and allowed it to run for a few minutes. Disabled the active NAS link (emulator switched to standby link), then re-enabled the disabled link and CDIS exceptioned as above. (I think the re-enabling is a red herring.)   (during database load)

ASSIGNED FOR EVALUATION TO: DATE:

CATEGORISATION: 0 ①2 3 Design Spec Docn
SEND COPIES FOR INFORMATION TO:
EVALUATOR: DATE: 8/7/92

CONFIGURATION ID	ASSIGNED TO	PART
dpo_s.c		

COMMENTS: dpo_s.c appears to try to use an invalid CID, instead of rejecting the message. AWJ

ITEMS CHANGED

CONFIGURATION ID	IMPLEMENTOR/DATE	REVIEWER/DATE	BUILD/ISSUE NUM	INTEGRATOR/DATE
dpo_s.c v.10	AWJ 8/7/92	MAR 8/7/92	6.120	RA 8-7-92

COMMENTS:

CLOSED

FAULT CONTROLLER: DATE: 9/7/92

Fig. 4.5 CDIS fault report form

There were 910 fault reports designated "0" by the developers. We restricted ourselves only to those faults rated non-zero and thereby to those documents and code modules that were actually the source of problems. Moreover, the data was separated so that faults arising from code could be analysed separately from faults arising from specification or design problems. (Pre-delivery changes affecting test code were not usually counted in the fault reports, but some were recorded accidentally.) However, since the Civil Aviation Authority's severity categories and related contractual obligations considered faults that affected documentation and configuration management, we counted as faults not only the changes made to delivered code but also changes affecting configuration management files and documents.

A look at the post-delivery failures and their relationship to formal methods provides a very different picture of the effects of formal design methods. The 147 non-zero problems reported during the analysis period led to 549 changes to modules or documents; of these, 21 changes were to formal-derived documents and 37 to informally-derived ones. Of the 185 changes to delivered code, 6 were to FSM-designed modules, 9 to VDM/CCS, 44 to VDM, and 126 to informally-designed modules, as shown in this table. The remaining changes were to informally-designed or -specified user documents, test documents or test modules. In other words, far fewer changes were required to formally-designed parts of the delivered system than to informally-designed parts.

Table 4.2 Changes to delivered code as a result of post-delivery problems

Design Type	Number of Changes	Number of Lines of Code Having This Design Type	Number of Changes Normalised by KLOC	Number of Modules Having This Design Type	Number of Changes Normalised by Number of Modules
FSM	6	19064	.31	67	.09
VDM	44	61061	.72	352	.13
VDM/CCS	9	22201	.41	82	.11
Formal	59	102326	.58	501	.12
Informal	126	78278	1.61	469	.27

Results of SQE's extensive survey were summarised as:

"Best projects do not necessarily have state of the art methodologies or extensive automation and tooling. They do rely on basic principles such as strong team work, project communication, and project controls. Good organisation appears to be far more of a critical success factor than technology or methodology."[15]

4.1.4   A Case Study[16]

Motivation for complexity metrics:

- In large systems a small number of modules account for most "defects"
- Metrics can help identify these defect-prone modules
- Complexity metrics assumed to be better predictors than simple size metrics like LOC
- Hence metrics can help save testing effort, and identify reliability and maintenance "hotspots"

  ... hence metrics for defect prediction

---

[15] See [Hetzel93].
[16] See [Fenton99a].

- Much metrics work has focused on "quality prediction" as measured by defect density
- Much of this work is poor
  - methodological and theoretical flaws
  - model mis-specification
  - use of inappropriate data
  - regression based approaches inappropriate
  - size and structure alone clearly insufficient
- Many problems attributable directly to flaws in use of "defect density"

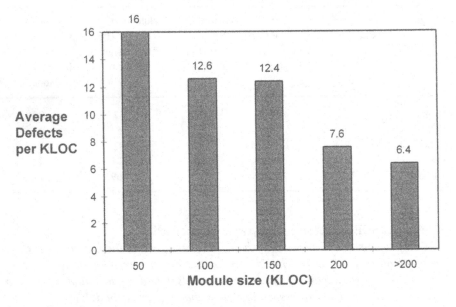

Fig. 4.6 Defect density case study: Basili and Pericone

Basili and Perricone[17] looked at a number of factors influencing the fault and failure proneness of modules. One of their most notable results was that larger modules tended to have a lower fault density than smaller ones. This result was also observed by other authors in subsequent studies. Possible explanations on these results are provided later.

Typical metrics validation study:
- Define a metric that can be extracted from the code (archetypal example: McCabe's cyclomatic complexity)
- Metric is "valid" if it correlates with "unreliability"

---

[17] See [Basili84].

- modules with higher "complexity" values will have higher incidence of failures in operation
- a valid metric will therefore be a good predictor of reliability "hot spots" that require special attention
- Testing fault data used as surrogate for operational failure data
  - fault density is surrogate measure of module's "unreliability"

The basic assumption in using (testing) fault density as a surrogate "unreliability" is that modules which are especially fault prone in testing are assumed to be the "rogue" modules. In fact we will show that this assumption is fundamentally flawed.

Table 4.3 Basic case study data

Release	Number of faults			
	Function test	System test	Site test	Operation
n (sample size 140 modules)	916	682	19	52
n+1 (sample size 246 modules)	2292	1008	238	108

- Major switching system software
- Modules randomly selected from those that were new or modified in each release
- Module is typically 2,000 LOC
- Only distinct faults that were fixed are counted
- Numerous metrics for each module

The data presented here is based on two major consecutive releases of a large legacy project developing telecommunication switching systems. We refer to the earlier of the releases as *release n*, and the later release as *release n+1*. For this study 140 and 246 modules respectively from release *n* and *n+1* were selected randomly for analysis from the set of modules that were either new or had been modified. The modules ranged in size from approximately 1000 to 6000 LOC. Both releases were approximately the same total system size.

Hypotheses relating to Pareto principle of faults distribution:

- 1a: A small number of modules contain most of the faults discovered during testing.
- 1b: If a small number of modules contain most of the faults discovered during pre-release testing then this is simply because those modules constitute most of the code size.
- 2a: A small number of modules contain most of the operational faults.
- 2b: If a small number of modules contain most of the operational faults then this is simply because those modules constitute most of the code size.

1a: For release *n*, 20% of the modules were responsible for nearly 60% of the faults found in testing. An almost identical result was obtained for release *n+1*. This is also almost identical to the result in earlier work where the faults from both testing and operation were considered [Ohlsson96]. This, together with other results such as [Munson92], provides very strong support for hypothesis 1a), and even suggests a specific Pareto distribution in the area of 20-60. This 20-60 finding is not as strong as the one observed by [Compton90] (they found that 12% of the modules, referred to as packages, accounted for 75% of all the faults during system integration and test), but is nevertheless important.

Since we found strong support for hypothesis 1a, it makes sense to test hypothesis 1b. It is popularly believed that hypothesis 1a is easily explained away by the fact that the small proportion of modules causing all the faults actually constitute most of the system size. For example, [Compton90] found that the 12% of modules accounting for 75% of the faults accounted for 63% of the LOC. In our study we found no evidence to support hypotheses 1b. For release *n*, the 20% of the modules which account for 60% of the faults (discussed in hypothesis 1a) actually make up just 30% of the system size. The result for release *n+1* was almost identical.

2a: We discovered not just support for a Pareto distribution, but a much more exaggerated one than for hypothesis 1a. For release *n*, 10% of the modules were responsible for 100% of the failures found. The result for release *n+1* is not so remarkable but is nevertheless still quite striking: 10% of the modules were responsible for 80% of the failures.

2b: we found strong evidence in favour of a converse hypothesis: most operational faults are caused by faults in a small proportion of the code.

For release n, 100% of operational faults contained in modules that make up just 12% of entire system size. For release n+1, 80% of operational faults contained in modules that make up 10% of the entire system size.

Hypothesis 3: Higher incidence of faults pre-release implies higher incidence of faults post-release ?

- At the module level
- This hypothesis underlies the wide acceptance of the fault-density measure
- No evidence for this hypothesis – in fact evidence of a counter-hypothesis

The rationale behind this hypothesis is that the relatively small proportion of modules in a system that account for most of the faults are likely to be fault-prone both pre- and post release. Such modules are somehow intrinsically complex, or generally poorly built. "If you want to find where the faults lie, look where you found them in the past" is a very common and popular maxim. For example, [Compton90] have found as much as six times greater post delivery defect density when analysing modules with faults discovered prior to delivery.

In many respects the results in our study relating to this hypothesis are the most remarkable of all. Not only is there no evidence to support the hypothesis, but again there is strong evidence to support a converse hypothesis. In both release *n* and release *n+1* almost all of the faults discovered in pre-release testing appear in modules which subsequently reveal almost no operation faults. Specifically, we found:

In release *n*, 93% of faults in pre-release testing occur in modules which have NO subsequent operational faults (of which there were 75 in total). Thus 100% of the 75 failures in operation occur in modules which account for just 7% of the faults discovered in pre-release testing.

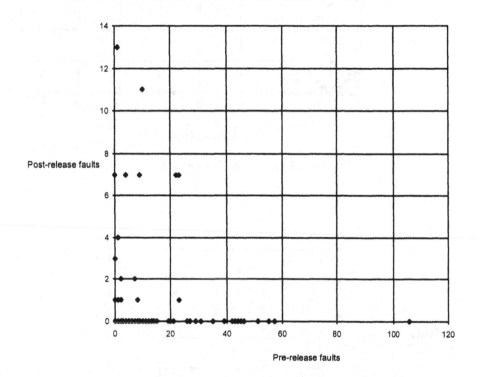

Fig. 4.7 Hypothesis 3: Release n

In release *n+1* we observed a much greater number of operational faults, but a similar phenomenon to that of release *n*. Some 77% of pre-release faults occur in modules which have NO post-release faults. Thus 100% of the 366 failures in operation occur in modules which account for just 23% of the faults discovered in function and system test.

These remarkable results are also exciting because they are closely related to the Adams' phenomenon. The results have major ramifications for one of the most commonly used software measures, *fault density*. Specifically it appears that modules with high fault density pre-release are likely to have low fault-density post-release, and vice versa.

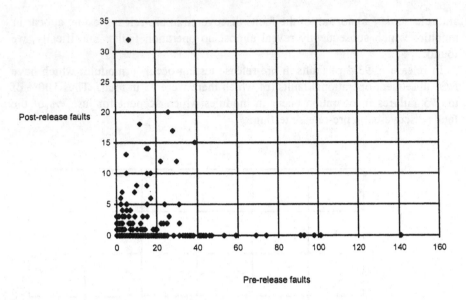

Fig. 4.8 Hypothesis 3: Release n+1

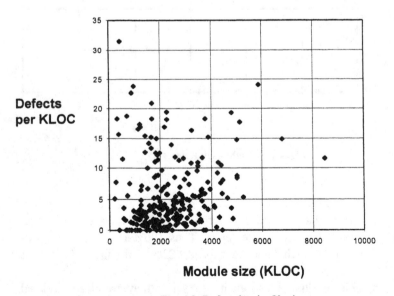

Fig. 4.9 Defect density Vs size

The approach to grouping data as done in [Basili84] is highly misleading. What
Basili and Perricone failed to show was a simple plot of fault density against mod-

ule size, as we have done in here for release $n+1$. Even though the grouped data for this release appeared to support the Basili and Perricone findings, this graph shows only a very high variation for the small modules and no evidence that module size has a significant impact on fault-density. Clearly other explanatory factors, such as design, inspection and testing effort per module, will be more important.

Complexity metrics vs. simple size metrics:

- Are complexity metrics better predictors of fault and failure-prone modules than simple size metrics : Not really, but they are available earlier.
- Results of hypothesis 3 are devastating for metrics validation.
- A "valid" metric is implicitly a very bad predictor of what it is supposed to be predicting.
- However
  - complexity metrics can help to identify modules likely to be fault-prone pre-release at a very early stage (metrics like SigFF are available long before LOC),
  - complexity metrics may be good indicators of maintainability.

"Complexity metrics" is the misleading term used to describe a class of measures that can be extracted directly from source code (or some structural model of it, like a flow graph representation). Occasionally (and more beneficially) complexity metrics can be extracted before code is produced, such as when the detailed designs are represented in a graphical language like SDL (as was the case for the system in this study). The archetypal complexity metric is McCabe's cyclomatic number CC, but there have in fact been many dozens that have been published. Of special interest in this study was the metric *SigFF* – the count of the number of new and modified signals.

Size is a reasonable predictor of number of faults (although not of fault density). An implicit assumption is that complexity metrics are better than simple size measures in this respect (for if not there is little motivation to use them).

When the cyclomatic complexity and the pre- and post-release faults were graphed we found the most "complex" modules appear to be more fault-prone in pre-release, but appear to have nearly no faults in post-release. The most fault-prone modules in post-release appear to be the less "complex" modules. This could be explained by how test effort is distributed over the modules: modules that appear to be complex are treated with extra care than simpler ones. Analysing in retrospect the earlier graphs for size versus faults reveal a similar pattern. To explore the relations further the scatter plots were also graphed with normalised data. The result showed even more clearly that the most-fault prone modules in pre-release have nearly no post-release faults.

The results do not paint a very glowing report of the usefulness of complexity metrics, but it can be argued that "being a good predictor of fault density" is not an appropriate validation criteria for complexity metrics. Nevertheless there are some positive aspects. The combined metric *CC*SigFF* is shown to be a reasonable predictor of fault-prone modules. Also, measures like *SigFF* are, unlike LOC, available at a very early stage in the software development. The fact that it correlates so closely with the final LOC, *and* is a good predictor of total number of faults, is a major benefit.

Conclusions:

- Increased industrial metrics activity not influenced by academic research
- A "Metrics Programme" should be based on a specific well-defined objective
- Need to distinguish between different types of "defects" and collect data accordingly
- Fundamental problems with defect density measure and complexity metrics
- Hence limitations in metrics-based process assessment

With respect to the defect density measure and complexity metrics, we showed:

- Pareto principles confirmed, but normal explanations are wrong
- "Complexity metrics" not significantly better than simple size measures
- Modules which are especially fault-prone pre-release are not especially fault-prone post-release
- No causal link between size and defect density
- Interpreting metrics in isolation
- Currently using Bayesian Belief Nets to address these problems.

Bibliography

[Adams84]
> Adams E., *Optimising preventive service of software products*, IBM Research Journal, 28(1), 2-14, 1984.

[Basili84]
> Basili V.R. and Perricone B.T., *Software Errors and Complexity: An Empirical Investigation*, Communications of the ACM 27(1), pp. 42-52, 1984.

[Cartwright97]
> Cartwright M. and Shepperd M., *An empirical investigation of an object-oriented software system*, Tech Report TR 96/01, Dept Computing, Bournemouth University, 1997.

[Fenton99a]
> Fenton N.E. and Neil M., *A Critique of Software Defect Prediction Models*, IEEE Transactions on Software Engineering, to appear, 1999.

[Fenton99b]
> Fenton N.E. and Ohlsson N., *Quantitative Analysis of Faults and Failures in a Complex Software System*, IEEE Transactions on Software Engineering, to appear, 1999.

[Fenton96]
> Fenton N.E. and Pfleeger S.L., *Software Metrics: A Rigorous and Practical Approach (2nd Edition)*, International Thomson Computer Press, 1996.

[Grady92]
  Grady R. B., *Practical Software metrics for Project Management and Process Improvement*, Prentice Hall, 1992
[Hatton98]
  Hatton L., *Does OO sync with how we think?*, IEEE Software. 15(3), 1998, 46-54.
[Hetzel93]
  Hetzel B., *Making Software Measurement Work*, QED, 1993.
[Ohlsson96]
  Ohlsson N. and Alberg H., *Predicting error-prone software modules in telephone switches*, IEEE Transactions on Software Engineering, 22(12), 886-894, 1996.
[Vessey84]
  Vessey I. and Webber R., *Research on structured programming: an empiricists evaluation*, IEEE Transactions on Software Engineering, 10, July 1984, 397-407.

4.2   Software Metrics as a Support in Business Management

José D. Carrillo Verdún
AEMES, Madrid

The expert in the area José D. Carrillo, Caja Madrid, and Secretary of AEMES (Spanish Metric Software Association) gave the following presentation on the EUREX Metrics workshop in Spain.

"The main difference between a well developed science such as Physics and other less developed ones such as Psychology or Sociology, is the level with which things are measured."   Fred S. Robert (1979)

4.2.1   Introduction

Measurement techniques have a long tradition in any scientific field. As early as the end of the last century, the physicist, Lord Kelvin defined the importance of measurement in the Sciences by stating:

"When spoken words can be measured and expressed in numbers, we begin to know something about them, but when this is not possible, the knowledge is insufficient and unsatisfactory. One can be at the beginning of this knowledge but there has been little progress when considering it as a Science."

These measurements produce a quantitative description of the key processes and the obtained products which provide to their knowledge as well as to the quality of the results. This knowledge permits the selection of the best techniques and tools, as well as the optimisation of the product and process quality and the use of resources.

Since Engineering is the application of the Sciences to the real world based on measurements, Software Engineering requires the construction of a solid theoretical base founded on data such as this for its maturity.

For more than 25 years, researchers on software measurements have been divided into two fields: those that say that software can be measured and those that say that it cannot be analysed with measurements. In any case, both sides are worried by the quality of software and the need to quantify it. As a result of this worry, more than one thousand software measures have been proposed and more than 5000 documents have been published on this subject, with a significant increase in the last few years.

The extent of the costs involved in the development and maintenance of software as well as the importance it has acquired in all aspects of life, have increasingly accelerated the need to provide this engineering field with a scientific foundation which supports the programming standards and helps take decisions based on quantitative data.

So much so that in 1980 Curtis stated: "Strict scientific procedures should be applied to the study and development of software systems, if programming is to be transferred into an engineering field. The nucleus of these procedures contains the development of measurements, techniques and the determination of cause-effect relationships".

With these objectives in mind, software measurements should respond the following questions:

- Is it possible to predict errors in a system using measurements from the design stage?
- Is it possible to extract quantitative aspects from the design of the software that facilitate the system's maintenance level?
- Are there key and quantifiable aspects in the code of a programme that could facilitate the prediction of the level of difficulty of the tests and the number of residual errors in a programme or module after having completed a determined number of tests?
  Is it possible to extract quantifiable aspects from software design that would help the prediction of the amount of effort required to make the designed software?
- Do quantifiable aspects exist that can be obtained from the code of a subroutine and which may help to predict the amount of effort required to test this subroutine?
- Are there aspects that allow the prediction of the size of the project from the specification stage?
- What qualities should the software metrics have to determine the quality of the design?
- Which are the software measurements that form the basis of the quality attributes in the ISO 9001 quantitatively?

Answering these questions has been the task for researchers since 1974 when Wolverton first tried to formally measure the productivity of a programmer using code lines.

Anyone who wants to use or is using software metrics should ask himself this question: What benefits do these metrics provide in practice? (ed ital)

Possibly it was Grady in 1992 that best expressed the relevance of metrics.

Software metrics are used to measure specific attributes of a software product, a development process or the resources used.

The following can be obtained from these measurements:

- A base for assessment.
- To follow the progress of the project.
- To determine the complexity of a product.
- To help understand when a certain level of quality has been reached.

- To analyse defects.
- To evaluate the practice that allows the maturity to advance in the software development processes.

In conclusion, software metrics allow better decision making.

Today, nobody doubts that metrics constitute an important method of reaching higher software quality.

Dieter Rombach says "we should not ask if we should measure, the question is how".

In the past, metrics research has Centred on the definition, choice and collection of data. As part of the effort used to examine the scientific basis of Software Engineering, *the attention is now Centred on the analysis of the information obtained.*

The developers continue using what is available and easy to use, without taking into account if it is applicable. This in part is the responsibility of the researchers that have not described the limitations of the techniques put into practice.

Finally, *technology transfer is a global problem*. It is not reasonable to hope that developers become experts in statistics, probabilities, measurement theories or in code complexity calculations or parameter modelling.

In its place, *it is necessary to motivate researchers into providing techniques and tools that the developers can easily understand and apply.*

In the same way, *the objectives of the measurements should be based on the objectives of the clients and developers.*

If they request early measurements in the development cycle, efforts should be Centred on the measurement of design requirement analysis aspects.

If they request measurements to assess commercial software, product metrics that support the purchase decisions should be provided.

If they insist on higher levels of reliability, functionality, usability, reusability and maintenance, the researchers should work closely with the developers for them to understand the processes and resources that contribute to obtaining better results.

Researchers will have to work closer to the developers if the software to be produced is better in theory and in practice.

4.2.2 Importance of Metrics for Companies

There has been a growing interest during the last few years in the introduction of software measurement programmes in companies.

The reason for this must be found in the importance that software has acquired in all types of business activity, giving way to important increases in development costs which require the application of strict selection criteria in the investments to be carried out.

This fact, together with the large amounts of investment in Information Technologies are not automatically reflected in a large investment return for companies, as shown in Paul Strassman's study amongst others, and therefore require a change in their management. These investments are even more doubtful when they have been determined by technical management and not by the business.

This change of perspective in the management has four main components:

- A change from the technological to the business vision.
- A change in the support of the administrative corporate to the business services.
- A change in the vision of the development of the information applications and technologies to that of Information Systems Architecture and departmental infrastructure.
- A change in the vision of Information Technology services to reach leadership in the business.

It is necessary for the implementation of these changes that the management and control of technology be based on quantitative data as occurs with the remaining business resources.

As Peter Drücker states: "the fewer controls necessary, the more efficient they will be" and defines five numbers that should be used to manage any activity sector:

- A measurement of the quantity to be produced. In the case of function point and code line software.
- A time limit to complete the project.
- A measurement of the production cost.
- A measurement of the quality of the resulting product.
- A measurement the activity's productivity.

The measurement of these five quantities is well known in the case of the manufacturing or construction industry. They are the basis of any kind of management activity and therefore also in the software industry. They are the basis for planning for all types of project and this plan is the basis of the key management activities:

- To provide the cost in order to calculate the price to give to the client or user.
- To establish a delivery date.
- To provide people with the appropriate experience and knowledge, as well as the tools when the plan needs them.
- To provide a reference base through which the management can follow the process and incorporate corrective actions.

4.2.3 To Make the Management of Directors Measurable

These management concepts are not specifically software and can be found in other contexts within management.

On the other hand, there is an increasing problem today that affects computer technicians in many companies; people are losing confidence in them in spite of their experience.

As Barbara J. Bashein and M. Lyme state in a study published recently in Sloan Management Review, the reasons for this lack of confidence, although due to their behaviour towards their clients on the whole, are also based on the lack of visibility in their work and the repeated unfulfillment of delivery times and costs, as well as in the quality of the delivered products.

These circumstances are leading to the need for quantitative measurements on the processes, products and resources used and to redrive the management of the Information Technologies in the direction required today by companies.

Behind this change there are really two problems to which companies must respond:

- To improve the quality of the software produced.
- To obtain a set of measurements that allows a better visibility of the value that technology supplies the business and to improve the credibility of its management.

Software quality improvement requires that the quality of processes be improved first, which at the same time brings about the need for having the measurements at one's disposal in order to learn the level of progress reached. If these basic measurements do not exist the second problem cannot be resolved.

4.2.3.1   How to Improve the Quality of Software

A recent study carried out by Capers Jones covering over 700 software projects carried out by 600 organisations all over the world, summarizes the experiences from these companies in the improvement of their software development processes using the CMM model.

As well as providing information on costs using ACB techniques and of the time spent passing from one level to the next, the study establishes a new scale of the management processes that should be developed in the company to reach excellence in software. If this is being achieved, how can it be measured?

To improve software, the process used to create it should be improved first. A combination of metrics and costs based on the activity can help measure exactly what is happening.

These measurements can also demonstrate that process improvement generates benefits in terms of quality, time, effort, costs, user satisfaction and other quantifiable factors.

Significant improvements in software processes do not occur by following an aleatory process.

When analysing the models used by companies that have experienced the most progress, it is observed in all cases that the following has existed: an assessment of the software process, a series of measurements that constitute a reference base and finally a benchmarking activity.

This Model Identifies Six Stages:

Stage 0: Assessment of the software process, reference base and benchmarking activity.

Stage 1: Centred on technology management.

Stage 2: Centred on software and methodology processes.

Stage 3: Centred on new tools.

Stage 4: Centred on infrastructure and specialisation.

Stage 5: Centred on reusability.

Stage 6: Centred on market leadership.

Each company is different and its improvement strategies should be defined according to its culture and requirements.

The sequence in which the six stages should be carried out is based on practical considerations.

For example, any development manager that should justify costs for any large investment should first assess all the process flows, which correspond to the last stages.

Moreover, unless excellence has been achieved in project management, it is very unlikely that the final stages be reached.

Stage 0: Assessment of the Software Process, Reference Base and Benchmarking Activity

This stage is out of range because neither an assessment nor a benchmarking activity can produce tangible improvements by themselves. Some companies ignore this important fact and think that they will achieve the expected improvement with the results they have obtained.

Nevertheless, the improvement strategy begins with a formal assessment process and the establishment of a reference metrics base of the productivity and the present quality levels.

The assessment is a diagnosis used to find all the strengths and weaknesses associated with software.

The reference base provides a base of measurements on productivity, time, costs and quality, as well as on user satisfaction. This enables the company to pass judgment on the progress of the improvement.

Benchmarking is a formal comparison with other organisations of the software development methods and of the results obtained.

Stage 1: Centred on Technology Management

Project management is the weakest stage in software development, and therefore the first stage should concentrate on introducing management to technologies such as planning, estimation, tracking, risk analysis, measurements and value analysis.

It is important to start with the management as they should be the ones that calculate the investment return that will come later. They should collect the information to demonstrate the progress which therefore may very dangerous if the management is not properly trained in their roles.

Stage 2: Centred on Software and Methodology Processes
This stage is Centred on reaching a solid base of requirements, design, development and quality control. As tools support processes, the processes should be selected before large investments are carried out.

Some of the processes implemented include JAD, formal design methods, inspections and change management procedures.

Stage 3: Centred on New Tools
Once the previous objectives have been reached different advanced tools should be acquired.

It is also the moment to explore more complex technologies with pronounced training curves such as client/server and object orientation.

A premature jump to client/server projects or a quick analysis and design oriented towards objects, results in problems due to the lack of training of the developers.

Stage 4: Centred on Infrastructures and Specialization
This stage deals with the organisation and specialization problems. It begins by establishing specialized teams in testing, maintenance, integration and configuration management.

The creation of a quality assurance function and the existence of continuous training policies are also very important.

Stage 5: Centred on Reusability
Reusability is the best investment return in any technology, but it is not a game that can be played by amateurs. If quality control is not carried out strictly, what will be reused is rubbish and costs will increase.

Efficient reusability includes a minimum of six reusable elements: requirements, design and specifications, strong code, user documentation, testing plans and test cases.

Stage 6: Centred on Leadership in Industry
The organisations that reach the sixth stage are usually leaders in their respective industries. They are often in a position to buy out their competitors or of supplying services to other companies.

Leadership in industry is something that many companies desire but which is achieved by very few.

The attributes of leader companies can be identified as follows:

- Use of powerful tools to manage projects.
- Use of powerful development tools.
- Tools to assure quality and testing.
- Efficient software development processes.

To be successful, each company must create an individualised plan and a budget for its improvement strategy. Usually, the plan and budget should be carried out after stage 0 and during stage 1.

Cost elements include training, equipment, software licenses and improvements in office conditions.

Process improvements take various years and the maximum benefit is not obtained until stage 5 has been reached and the reusability plans have been implemented.

A frequently asked question is why reusability is not started in the first stage if it is what creates the largest investment return. The reason is that reusability depends mainly on the quality of software, the use of techniques such as formal inspection and correct development processes.

In many cases the function points show that, in spite of their problems, they are the most effective metrics available to measure activities that are not related to coding such as requirements, design, user documentation, and management.

4.2.3.2 Achieving a Set of Metrics for Management

This requires the implementation of a measurement programme based on basic metrics which leads to the derivatives requested by the business.

What is important in the first stage of the programme's implementation is its validity and the precision of the continuous procedure of data collection that permits continuous process improvement and the refining of the quality of the collected data.

The information should be collected with the sole aim of satisfying specific information requirements. These requirements should be joined to the business objectives that the organisation pursues.

It can be concluded from these ideas that measurements can therefore by carried out in two levels:

- Strategic level
- Tactical level

The application on a strategic level is centred on the use of metrics for the continuous improvement of the development process and to measure the impact of the possible changes that may arise when improving this process. On this level, subjects related with the plans of the organisation, market competition, the orientation and goals of the company are all considered. The measurements used on this level would pursue the following objectives.

4.2.4   To Obtain Information for the Management

It is necessary to be aware of this information at precise moments as well as during the whole process in order to see the tendencies. Two objectives are always sought when a process is being managed: to maximise output and to minimise costs. In order to achieve this it is necessary to have information at one's disposal to supervise and predict the values of the information with reference to:

1. Productivity
In terms of software development productivity would be: function points divided by the development effort. This definition is centred on the performance of the Software Engineering process.

Two important aspects should be mentioned briefly:

In reality the most important things are not the absolute values of productivity but the tendency obtained throughout time. A continuous improvement should be expected.

Productivity will never be measured on a personal level as this can generate a lack of motivation in staff.

2. Quality
Quality is one of the key factors if a good competitive level is to be achieved. Although it is a difficult term to define, it implies:

* conformity with requirements
* user satisfaction
* reliability, maintenance and other attributes

Quality should be measured and predicted with anticipation but to do this is complicated because quality has a subjective nature. What we can really consider when talking about quality are the different attributes or factors that characterise it. When determining the attributes or factors that characterise software quality we can use different classification outlines such as Grady or Pressman's FURPS model.

The main indicators of quality in software are the defects. To guarantee quality in software one must:

* predict the appearance of defects: a set of techniques and methods should be applied to reduce complexity as well as the tendency in committing errors, and
* eliminate the defects that already exist: this aspect should be measured tangibly and with high precision. Reports on the defects for each of the elimination activities should be collected as soon as possible and as many times as possible.
* Compare the process to those followed in other companies.

The measurements taken for this comparison require that the organisation make an effort to compare the benefits with the costs. When making these comparisons one must consider the definitions of the measurements that are used and their consistency.

Carry out an experimental validation to verify which are the most appropriate practices to which the organisation can opt.

The choice can be made from those activities that are carried out within Software Engineering and that have been measured and tested in practical environments. For example: inspections, graphic representations, structured design, verification and validation methods.

4.2.5 Tactical or Project Level

The application on a tactical or project level is centred on the use of metrics for project management and for product design The measurements on this level deal with specific projects and with the factors that affect them directly. These metrics help in the following tasks:

Estimation of the Size, Duration and Cost of the Project

The correct estimation of the software project is difficult to obtain because it depends on lots of variables. Even so it is the base for other project activities and therefore the results obtained should be as reliable as possible. The whole problem should thus be broken down into smaller sub-functions. The size of each one will be estimated individually by using Function Points (FP). The estimated productivity figures will then be applied to these values to obtain the effort estimations. By joining the estimations of each sub-function, the total project estimation can be obtained.

Control of the Project

This task should take into account three activities: initial project planning, its management and the supervision of progress as the development advances.

1. Initial Planning

This first control activity is carried out to correctly define the product. To begin with it is necessary to identify the scope and objectives that the project aims at without specifying how they will be reached. From this information the appropriate effort and cost estimations will be carried out. It is now the moment to take into consideration other planning activities: the analysis and management of the risks related to the project, as well as the temporary planning of each of the activities that should be developed. The result of this initial stage will be a project plan that will guide its subsequent management.

2. Management

The objective of this activity is to carry out the project efficiently. The result of the development process is not only the code; during this process (specification, design, coding and testing) there are products that we could call work products: they follow a standard presentation and are supported by tools that carry out controls and obtain data that facilitate progress tracking.

3. Supervision of the Progress

The company's aim is to deliver the product within the budgets and time limits established. In order to verify if this objective is achieved or not, the progress against the foreseen plans must be supervised. It will be necessary to reunite the members of the team to discuss the state of the project, to assess the results of the revisions carried out in the different stages of the development project and to check if the established milestones have been reached in the dates planned. To help this activity, the work products mentioned previously can also be used.

4.2.6   Metrics Applied to the Design of the Software Product

It includes a set of techniques based on the measurements applied to design with the aim of assessing its complexity. This is interesting because frequently designs that present high levels of complexity are also unreliable and difficult to maintain. These characteristics usually define a low quality product. If we take Goodman's definition we could say that complexity is the level of complication of a system or of its components.

The measurements applied to design can be classified into two groups:
- Inter-measured: these refer to the complexity of the connection between modules, and
- Intra-measured: these refer to the existing complexity inside each module.

Two sets of metrics applied to software design are frequently used: McCabe metrics and metrics on information flow.

As can be appreciated, there are many application fields. When implementing Software Metrics, we must decide which areas are the most appropriate to our needs. To achieve this it is necessary to identify and satisfy the most important requirements for the organisation. It is neither good nor advisable to try to cover all the areas at once.

The application of methodologies such as audience analysis or GQM permit obtaining the metrics necessary to respond to the business objectives.

4.2.7   Implementation of a Metrics Programme

Weighing the advantages and disadvantages, a Software Metrics Programme is of great use for any organisation. If one decides to take this opportunity, how should the programme implementation be put forward ?

By acting appropriately and following a method, it will be possible to gain the company's acceptance. The staff will change their way of working without fearing the negative results provoked by the implementation of the new programme.

The implementation of a Software Metrics Programme implies an important change in the way of working and thinking in people. Success will only be reached if the implementation is dealt with as if it were a project, with its corresponding plans, budgets, resource assignments, progress controls, revisions and above all with management commitment.

This project, like any other, will follow a life cycle. The measurement process to be implemented will have to be adaptable and manageable.

Any life cycle model requires:

- A previous stage of adaptation to the company's specific environment.
- It will be sufficiently flexible as to change according to its needs.
- It has to be planned and the activities planned will be communicated to all the staff.

The measurement process will be directed, carried out and controlled according to the established plan.

The problem posed today is not the deficiencies in the technology of the software measurement process, but the cultural resistance that exists in the people working with the software.

This resistance is due to the fear that the measurements will be used against them. It is of vital importance to promote that the objective of the measurement is to provide useful information that permits a better estimation, management and control of the projects.

The challenge is found in destroying this fear by demonstrating that the results obtained are necessary for the company to maintain its competitive edge.

The strategy that should be followed is to apply a method in which this programme undergoes a similar treatment to that followed by any other project.

For this, it is necessary to develop a general life cycle model. The activities that should be carried out during this cycle can be increased or reduced according to the needs of each organisation in particular. These needs define the magnitude and scope of the programme. It has already been stated that Software Metrics should be taken on little by little, fixing objectives, which once reached will give way to the establishment of new goals.

- Start: the person to start this process and the motives that trigger this initiative off are identified.
- Requirements Definition: what is wanted, which needs should be covered and what problems are to be solved? The client's ideas will be taken into account as it is he who will define the scope of the initiative. The use of methods such as Audience Analysis and techniques such as GQM are fundamental.
- Design of components: the programme will include various requirements that have been defined in the previous specification stage. The components that will

satisfy each of these requirements have to be designed. For example, a component must be designed to achieve appropriate estimation of size, duration and cost of a programme. It is now that we must start to think about metrics, about the people that will help to achieve the measurements and about the complete infrastructure that surrounds this activity.

Construction of components: the design obtained in the previous stage takes shape in this phase and should be carried out mechanically.

- Implementation of the Software Metrics (to improve the process): the programme must be put into practice and to achieve this, the people affected by its implementation must be convinced. It is necessary that these people be sure that the development process will improve with this programme.

When this last stage has finished the people involved should have the desire to start the process again. The company will learn from this experience and will widen its metrics programme by repeating the cycle to cover new needs that were left uncovered.

Why is it Important to Invest in a Software Metrics Programme?

The application of metrics is focused on surpassing the continuous crisis symptoms in Software:

- the budgets and planning foreseen are surpassed (unrealistic expectations);
- there are important problems in reliability and quality;
- the cost of quality is very high;
- there are not sufficient resources.

4.2.8   Benefits

The measurement process that is applied to control and improve software projects produce benefits that are difficult to quantify, usually more than the costs that carrying out this process implies.

A good metrics programme demands that a wide study of the software development process be carried out. More exact knowledge of this process will be obtained as a result of this study. It is now possible to elaborate a diagnosis in which all the problems that need solving are identified.

The implementation of the metrics programme produces rigor in the measurements. A precise reference base on which we can support ourselves will be created little by little. This reference base can be used to determine what the progress achieved by the company is as time passes.

As stated above, as well as measuring the process, it can also measure the product. Product quality can be improved from the information obtained. If both the process and product are improved the company will be more competitive and its clients will be feel more satisfied. Metrics orient the development process towards the search for company strategic objectives.

Measurement activities and tools help the company to reach a higher level in Software Engineering techniques, which in turn improves the level of professionalism. Management and engineers are more able to carry out their work: to better plan, manage and supervise projects.

Adopting the programme will help to acquire a common terminology which is very necessary when measuring and interpreting the information generated by the metrics programme. In other words, the terminology offers consistency in its measurements.

Lastly, we can highlight that with metrics it is possible to assess which are the methods, techniques and tools that will appear in the future and that will be most appropriate (and beneficial) to improve the software development process. The information obtained will also serve to support new proposals.

4.2.9 Difficulties

The implementation of the metrics programme faces a series of important problems:

The first obstacle are people. The team that is in charge of implementing the Software Metrics Programme should convince them that data collection and its later analysis produces improvements and that their personal capacity will not be measured. This last idea is vital if the programme is to be successful.

Another problem is to integrate metrics within the organisation in such a way that the programme can easily adapt to the new circumstances when their business objectives or the conditions of their environment change.

An important obstacle is related to the cost of the metrics programme, especially the cost of starting up the programme. As costs are difficult to identify, it is much easier to understand the costs of not implementing a programme as this position signifies an important loss of competitivity.

In any case there are more advantages than disadvantages. To be able to completely take advantage of these benefits it is necessary that the measurement be applied systematically and this is where the need arises for the company to use a method to reach them.

"The bridges built by the Romans in ancient history were very inefficiently structured. For modern standards they used too many stones and as a consequence worked too hard in their construction. Over the years we have learned to build bridges more efficiently, using less material and less work to carry out the same task"   Tom Clancy

References

[Zuse95]
Zuse, Horst. *History of software measurement*, 1995.

[Oman96]
Oman P. and Pfleeger, S.L. *Applying software metrics*, IEEE Computer Society Press, Los Alamitos, 1996.

[Fenton96]
Fenton N. and Pfleeger S.L., *Software Metrics: A rigorous and practical approach*, International Thomson Press, London, 1996.

[Grady96]
Grady R.B. and Caswell D.L., *Practical software metrics for project management and process improvement*, Prentice Hall, 1996.

[Drücker73]
Drücker P.F., *Management: Task, Responsibilities, Practices*, Harper & Row, New York, 1973.

[Pfleeger97]
Pfleeger S. L., Jeffery R. , Curtis B., Kitchenham B., *Status report on software measurement*, IEEE Software, March/April 1997.

[Jones97]
Jones C., *Polishing the software process*, Software Development, pg. 47-54, December 1997.

4.3   Software Metrics Applications in a European Perspective

Terttu Orci
SISU, Stockholm University, Stockholm

4.3.1   Introduction

Software metrics has been quite an intensive research area for more than two decades, yet its practical applications have been rather limited. The 70's being the era for software size metrics, introduced lines of code, and Albrecht's Function Points [Albrecht97], to measure the size and functionality of a software product. The size measurement, useful in its own right, serves also as a component in measuring productivity, and as an estimated parameter to estimation models [Boehm81], [Putnam79], which were mainly introduced in the 80's. In the 90's, the main focus is on software processes, and to improve the software processes is commonly agreed to be the solution for software companies fighting against delivery delays, cost overriding, and quality flaws in the end product. As measurement is inherent in the concept of improvement, in the stream of software process improvements currently undertaken, the number of practical applications of software metrics can be expected to increase.

A software process improvement may be undertaken with different intentions: to get certified according to a standard, e.g. ISO9001 [Oskarsson95], to follow the maturity ladder of the Capability Maturity Model (CMM) [Paulk95], or to solve a specific problem, e.g. the lack of configuration control.

Some of the large software companies in USA have published their long term process improvement programs including introduction of metrics, e.g. [Grady92], [SEI96]. We are not aware of any corresponding publications from large European companies concerning organisation wide improvement or metrics programs. Yet, in software process improvement area, several activities are in place today, the most widely known and influential being the ESSI programme (European Software and Systems Initiative) supported by CEC.

SISU – the Swedish Institute of Systems Development, is responsible for the Nordic PIEs (Sweden, Denmark, Norway, and Finland) as well as for the subject domain Software Metrics. At the time of writing, two workshops have been organised by SISU. In the context of those workshops, ten PIEs have presented and/or made their final reports available. In addition to that, the final reports from three PIEs presented at a metrics workshop given by Socintec's (ES) have been made available to us. Those 13 PIEs are the basis for the study presented in this paper.

4.3.2   Software Metrics

Software metrics, presented in various textbooks, e.g. [Fenton96], [Fenton95], [Kan95], [Shepperd95] and conferences, has a long tradition in theory, while considerably shorter in terms of industrial applications. Software metrics relies on the underlying theory, called representational measurement theory, posing some requirements on a correct definition, validation, and use of software metrics. From practical point of view, there are several further questions of importance, e.g. how to identify the right metrics to use, how to introduce a metrics programme, and how to keep it alive. In the following, these aspects will be discussed in more detail.

4.3.2.1   *Measurement – What is It?*

Software measurement is an activity assigning a number or a symbol to an entity in order to characterise a property of the entity according to given rules. The informal definition, even though giving an idea, must be more precisely defined. The message of the definition is that there should be an entity, a property, a measurement mapping and rules for the mapping. The measurement mapping and the rules is usually called metric. An example of an entity is code. An attribute characterising the code is size, and one possible metric for measuring size of code is the number of lines of code (LOC).

Initially, there must be an intuitive understanding of the property of the entity of interest, otherwise there is no way to define an adequate metric. For example, for the entity person, we can intuitively understand the property length, which can be measured in inches or centimetres. If observing two persons, we usually get an understanding who is taller, i.e. whose length would get a larger value if measured. The intuitive understanding can be represented in an empirical relation system, a pair consisting of the set of entities, and a set of relations, e.g. "taller than". For the measurement, there must be a corresponding numerical relation system, a pair, with symbols representing the entities and numerical relations corresponding to the empirical relations. For the relation "taller than", an adequate numerical relation would be >. There is also a so called representation condition requiring that a measurement mapping must map the entities into numbers and empirical relations into numerical relations in such a way that the empirical relations preserve and are preserved by the numerical relations. In practice, this means that if we have an intuitive understanding that A is taller than B, then also the measurement mapping M must give that M(A) > M(B). The other way around, if M(A) > M(B), then it must be that A is intuitively understood be taller than B.

In the above example, the representation condition is easy to understand and accept. The difficulties arise as soon as we are talking about metrics which have been defined although there does not exist such an intuitive understanding of the property. Good candidates in this class are complexity of code and quality of a product. The complexity is often measured by McCabe's cyclomatic number, while the most used quality metrics are related to the defects: the number of defects/KLOC, or the number of defects discovered by the customer. None of those metrics paint the whole picture, mainly because there does not exist that intuitive understanding in the first place. Both metrics give only a partial view of the property of interest.

The measurement mapping, the empirical and numerical relations are usually called the scale of the measurement. There are five different scales:

- nominal scale
- ordinal scale
- interval scale
- ratio scale, and
- absolute scale

A measurement on a nominal scale is a classification of the entities into a set of disjoint classes without any ordering between the classes, i.e. the classes form a partition. An example of measurement on a nominal scale is a categorisation of defects, if no ordering of the defects is of interest. The ordinal scale extends the nominal by adding an order for the classes. An example of the ordinal scale is categorising defects with respect to severity. The interval scale adds the concept of distance, and poses the requirement that the distance between any two consecutive classes is to be equal. Celsius and Fahrenheit for measuring temperature are on interval scale. Ratio scale is the interval scale extended with zero-element, i.e. it includes the total absence of the property in case, e.g. size of code measured by LOC, which in principle could be zero. An absolute scale measurement is counting the occurrences of entities, e.g. hours spent on a particular task.

It is important to establish the scale of the measurement in that different scales allow different manipulations with the measurement data. On the nominal scale, only the frequency and mode are relevant. On ordinal scale we can calculate the median of the values. On interval scale also the arithmetic mean is meaningful to calculate, while on ratio scale, also geometric mean makes sense. On absolute scale, we can do all the calculations by numbers.

If a measure has components from different scales, the scale with the weakest manipulation possibilities determines the scale of the composite measure. For example, productivity calculated by dividing the size of the output by effort needed to produce that output is on ratio scale because size is on ratio scale, although effort is on absolute scale.

Attributes can be classified as internal and external attributes. Measuring internal attributes of an entity, no other entities or attributes are involved. An example of an internal attribute is size. Measuring an external attribute of an entity, other entities or attributes may be needed for measurement. An example of an external attribute of the entity code is maintainability. To measure maintainability, it is not enough to study the code, but the code in the process of error detection and correction must be studied. The external attributes are the challenging ones when it comes to define and validate metrics. If there is no adequate metric for an external attribute, e.g. maintainability, it may be possible to predict from an internal attribute. This is what we always do when buying a car: we cannot measure the external attributes like how well the car behaves under certain circumstances, but use internal attributes like tire dimension, brake system, or whatever, as a predictor.

4.3.2.2   What is the Thing Being Measured?

There are three main classes of entities of interest for measurement in software engineering, namely product, process, and resource. Product is an output from a process, e.g. code, a document, a script. A process is one or several activities. Resource is an input to a process, e.g. staff, tool, method.

Sometimes, we need to measure attributes for a global entity, namely the entire organisation, e.g. average delivery delays in all the projects undertaken during a certain period of time, or the maturity of the organisation in software development on a CMM scale.

Why is the Triangle – the Entity, Attribute, and Metric – Needed?

Unless there is a clear statement of the entity, attribute, and a metric, it does not make much sense to talk about measurement. For example, the statement "the size is 20 measured in LOC" does not make sense unless we know the entity in question. Unless the attribute is defined, we do not know what property of the entity is supposed to be characterised by the metric. For example "The code has FOG number 50" does not make any sense unless we know what attribute we are measuring by the FOG number. Unless the metric is defined, we do not know even the scale of the measurement, nor can we get an understanding of the relative value of the measurement. For example, the statement "The code size is 70000" does not make sense unless we know if size has been measured in LOC or bytes, or something else.

What Types of Use are There for the Measurement Data?

The measurement data has two principal types of use: assessment, i.e. to understand the state of the affairs, and prediction, i.e. to make a statement about the future state of the affairs. Possible uses of measurement data in prediction are as input to a prediction model, to calibrate a prediction model, or to serve as the basis for defining a prediction model. An example of an assessment is measuring complexity of code by McCabe's cyclomatic number. An example of use of McCabe's cyclomatic number is as input to a prediction model to predicting the attribute maintainability of the code. There are studies showing that McCabe's metric is not a valid predictor of maintainability, nor is it an acceptable complexity metric [Fenton96]. Yet it is often used in both senses.

4.3.2.3   Validating Metrics and Prediction Systems?

The software metrics literature offers a large number of metrics, yet there are severe limitations in terms of adequate metrics missing, e.g. metrics for complexity and quality of different kind of products, size and structure of products other than code, to take a few examples. If there does not exist a metric adequate to the purpose, an organisation can always define its own metrics. When defining metrics, empirical data is needed to validate the metric in case. The validation is intended to assure that the representation condition is fulfilled, i.e. that the empirical relations are preserved and preserve the numerical relations. First of all, there must exist consensus, an intuitive understanding of the attribute. The basic idea of the metrics validation is that it should measure the attribute it is intended to measure. A good example of an attribute, the metric of which is often said to fail in this respect, is the IQ test. It is claimed that the test does not measure the attribute intelligence, but something else, for example logical ability. Logical ability, although possibly being a component of intelligence, is not the lone carrier of intelligence. The problem with the metric for intelligence is that there is no commonly agreed definition of intelligence in the first place.

The validation requirement applies also to prediction systems. A prediction system is valid if it correctly predicts what it is intended to predict. In validation of a prediction system, the empirical data must cover the predictive capability of the prediction system, i.e. to give a measure how much the estimates differ from the actuals. Metrics for this purpose are MRE (Mean Relative Error) and PRED (Prediction accuracy).

4.3.2.4   How to Identify Right Metrics?

It is stressed by most authors that the identification of metrics should be goal oriented, i.e. unless you know the purpose of the measurement, you should not start a metrics programme. The most well-known methods for identifying the right metrics from the goals are the Goal-Questions-Metrics method (GQM) [Basili88] and Application of Metrics in Industry (AMI) [AMI93]. Although the methods are not difficult as such, the difficulty lies in inventing the right questions and metrics, which is not trivial at all. Knowledge and training in software metrics as well as familiarity with the application domain are needed.

4.3.2.5   What is Good Data?

The measurement data collected should fulfil certain quality criteria to be useful in an analysis. We do not attempt to give an exhaustive list of quality criteria, rather to present some requirements which are commonly accepted as necessary requirements on measurement data, namely

- correctness
- consistency

- time precision
- right granularity

The correctness requirement means that the data should be collected according to the rules of metrics definition. For example, if measuring the code size by LOC, and the rules state that reused code should be excluded, correct data would not include reused lines of code. Needless to say, this requirement implies that there should be precise definitions in the first place. The consistency criteria means that different people measuring a product for some purpose should use the same version of the product, i.e. the product to be measured should be under configuration control. The time precision means that if a process is measured, there should be distinct start and end of the process, otherwise the process measurement is meaningless. The right granularity means that the granularity should be determined with respect to the goals of the measurement. If the granularity is too fine for the purpose, unnecessary effort must be put into data collection, while in the opposite case, the usefulness of the data might be reduced.

4.3.2.6   How to Introduce a Metrics Programme and to Keep it Alive?

It is often argued that only simple metrics should be used, whatever is meant by simple metrics, and that metrics should be automatically collected, otherwise the programme will fail in the long run. The first question to ask is how long the program should run? Has the programme been introduced with the purpose of assessing the state of the affairs, to solve a particular problem, or has the measurement programme been included in a continuous process improvement programme, intended to run long term. There are a number of guidelines and good advice for introducing a metrics programme and to keep it alive [Fenton96], [SEI96], e.g.

- get and keep a commitment from the top management
- measure anything, but individuals
- give feedback to those who collect the measurement data
- metrics should be automatically collected if possible
- do not measure unless there is a clear purpose with it

The guidelines do not, of course, guarantee a success of a metrics programme, but the lack of the requirements may easily lead to a failure. Of particular importance is the commitment from the top management. Without that support, the programme has not much chance to survive.

4.3.3   The Study

In this study, 13 PIEs have been analysed. The basis for the structure of the analysis has been the theoretical aspects and the questions of practical interest presented in the previous section. In particular, we analyse the PIEs with respect to the following questions:

- Is the measurement well-defined?
- Have the metrics and prediction systems been validated?
- What is the distribution of the entity types product, process, and resource?
- Has expert support been needed in metrics definition?
- How have the right metrics been identified?
- What are the lessons learned and problems encountered?

4.3.3.1   Is the Measurement Well-Defined?

With this question we try to understand the metrics maturity of the PIEs, which can be said to represent the European software community. There are several requirements on being well-defined. For example, if LOC is used to measure the size of code, the model of the entity should be precisely defined, e.g. will comments be included or not. In this study, we only ask whether or not each of entity, attribute, and metric have been defined in the context of a metric presented. If a concept is not explicitly stated, but obvious from the context, it is regarded as defined.

In the 13 PIEs analysed, 51 different metrics were presented in total. Only nine of the metrics definitions (18%) included the entity, attribute and metric, while in the remaining cases, one or two of the concepts were not explicitly stated, nor clear from the context.

In 27 of the metrics (53%), the entity was not defined. For example, the metric "number of errors discovered within three months after release" might be intended to measure a process, e.g. development or testing. Alternatively, it might be intended to give an indication of the error density of the products delivered to a customer. To take another example, the metric "percentage of the problems solved at the first level", is stated to measure the attribute quality, but it is not clear which entity it refers to. In principle, it could be a product or a process.

In 28 of the 51 metrics (55%), the attribute was not defined, in some of them with the entity defined, in some without. An example of a missing attribute with defined entity is the metrics "the number of nodes in the design tree" characterizing the entity design document. The attribute intended might be the size of the design document. This metric could also be used to predict some attribute for another entity, e.g. maintainability of the code. Another example of a missing attribute with a defined entity is "the number of software problem reports" for a product. This attribute is often used to assess the quality of a product. In that case, the number of software problem reports should rather be related to the size of the product, instead of giving it as an absolute number. An example of both entity and attribute missing is the metric "the number of software errors per function point". It might been used to assess the attribute "error density" of a product, or it could be a metric for assessing the quality of the development process.

In five of the 51 metrics presented (10%), the metric was not defined. An example of a missing metric with other concepts in place is "risk" assessment for a process. An example of both metric and entity missing, is the attribute "productivity", usually a resource metric, but without explicit definition, we do not know what kind of resource is intended, neither how it is measured.

In 20 of the 51 metrics presented (39%), neither the entity nor the attribute were defined. Examples of such metrics are "percent of cost per function point", "the number of claims", "the number of problems registered", "the number of test cases", and "the number of unnecessary modifications related to the total number of modifications".

4.3.3.2   Have the Metrics and Prediction Systems been Validated?

Unless the metrics and prediction systems have been validated, the value of the measurement data is not of much interest. Even worse, it may be misleading in that the measurement data can be interpreted in several ways.

Only two of the 13 PIEs (4%) have presented experiments for validation, both validating prediction systems. Two of the PIEs have used an invalid metric, McCabe cyclomatic number to measure the complexity of the code. With a closer look, it seems that the real use of McCabe metric has in those PIEs been to predict the maintainability of the code, the higher the McCabe number, the more efforts can be expected to be needed in maintenance. However, McCabe metric is neither a valid predictor of maintainability [Fenton96].

4.3.3.3   What is the Distribution of the Entity Types Product, Process, and Resource?

The PIEs are supposed to measure the improvement obtained because of the process improvement experiment. It could be expected that process measurement would be the main entity type in the measurements. However, of the 24 metrics with entity defined at all, the distribution of the entity types is as follows: eight process metrics (33%), 13 product metrics (55%), one resource metric (4%), and two global metrics (8%) measuring the organisation maturity. It seems that product metrics are to a large extent used to measure some external attribute of a process, e.g. the product quality measured by the number of problems can be used to measure the quality of the software process, or some of its activities.

4.3.3.4   Has Expert Support been Needed in Metrics Definition?

A need of expert support in defining metrics would imply some lack knowledge and training in software metrics in the organisations.

Of the 13 PIEs studied, seven of them (54%) state explicitly having used expert support to define the metrics. This number could be higher in reality, as there is no reason for the PIEs to present this fact unless the metrics expert was a partner in the project.

4.3.3.5   How have the Right Metrics been Identified?

With this question we intend to capture the methodologies used to identify right metrics.

The methods for identifying the right metrics have been Goal-Question-Metric (GQM) in one case (8%), and AMI (Application of Metrics in Industry) in one case (8%). As 46% of the PIEs had expert support in metrics definition, the explicit method of identifying the metrics might not be known to the PIE, and therefore not mentioned.

4.3.3.6   What are the Lessons Learned and Problems Encountered?

The reason for this question is to investigate whether the lessons learned and problems encountered confirm or conflict the common knowledge of introducing metrics programs. A further reason is to use the problem statements to support the discussion and conclusions of the study. We state all the problem and experience types explicitly and once. Most of them are shared by several PIEs.

- Data was not consistently collected
- The purpose of measurement was not clear
- Reliability and accuracy of the measurement data is important
- There was resistance by people to collect metrics data
- Collection of data must be integrated in working processes
- Metrics program was too ambitious
- It was difficult to measure
- Metrics must be defined and validated
- Relationships between metrics must be defined
- There must be templates for metrics data collection
- Collection of data was a big effort
- It was useful to get the metrics
- Use simple metrics

None of the statements is new, nor in conflict with the common knowledge in the area. It is worth to observe that the PIEs stress the requirements on correctness, reliability, accuracy, consistency, definition, and validation, especially as the metrics presented in large extent lack these properties. The need for templates for data collection can also be interpreted as supporting the need of precise definition of data. The statement of ideally using simple metrics may be interpreted as the defined metrics have been difficult to understand, the metrics data collection has been difficult, or the analysis part has been difficult. Similarly, the difficulty in measuring may be based on difficulty of understanding because of lacking precise definitions. It is well-known that resistance for metrics data collection and filling in the forms is common, and that it may be, to some extent, be reduced by giving feedback of the measurement results.

4.3.3.7   Conclusions

We have analysed 13 PIEs with the focus on how the improvement has been measured in the process improvement experiments undertaken. The basis for the analysis consists of a number of aspects, originating from both theory and practice.

The aspect which we believe is of most importance, is the definition and validation of the metrics used. Although this issue has its origin in theory, it is not only an academic issue to be discussed between software metrics researchers, but it is an essential issue for the practical applications. Without a well-defined and validated metrics and prediction systems, measurement has no value to the organisation. Even worse, the measurement data may be misleading as without precise definitions, all interpretations become possible. Without precise and validated metrics, comparing measurement data from different organisations does not make sense either.

From this point of view, the PIEs under study appear considerably weak. Naturally there is always bias in this kind of studies, and so may be even here: the reality might in some cases been better than it seems from the final report. Still, it seems correct to draw the conclusion that there is major potential for improvement in the software metrics maturity and understanding the importance of the underlying theory. The conclusion is also supported by the lessons learned, presented in the previous section: Without a precise metrics definitions it is not surprising at all that it has been difficult to measure, and that the reliability, accuracy, correctness, consistency, definition, and validation aspects have been included in the lessons learned. Another supporting fact is that more than half of the PIE organisations needed expert support in metrics definition. Yet, the attributes measured were, with a few exceptions, internal attributes, the metrics of which are easier to define and validate than metrics for external attributes.

To obtain an improvement in the software metrics maturity on a European level, software engineering research with the focus on empirical studies, especially in defining and validating metrics, is needed. The empirical data needed for the research should ideally originate from the industry. A co-operation between research and industry is needed to getting started in a larger scale towards a software metrics maturity improvement. To ensure a continuous improvement in metrics maturity, software metrics should be included in the software engineering curricula, to train the top management and engineers of tomorrow.

4.3.3.8   References

[Albrecht97]
  Albrecht, A.J., Measuring Application Development, in Proceedings of IBM
  Applications Development Joint SHARE/GUIDE Symposium, Monterey, CA,
  pp. 83-92, 1979.

[AMI93]
AMI – Application of Metrics in Industry, ESPRIT metrics technology transfer project 1991-1993.

[Basili88]
Basili, V.R., Rombach, H.D., The TAME project: Towards improvement-oriented software environments, in IEEE Transactions on Software Engineering 14(6), pp.758-773, 1988.

[Boehm81]
Boehm, B.W., Software Engineering Economics, Prentice Hall, 1981.

[EUREX]
EUREX – European Experience Exchange, Project Number 24478, ESSI Dissemination Action, Annex I, Project Programme.

[Fenton96]
Fenton, N.E., Pfleeger, S.L., Software Metrics – A Rigorous & Practical Approach, International Thomsom Publishing Inc., 1996.

[Fenton95]
Fenton, N. Whitty, R., Iizuka, Y., Software Quality – Assurance and Measurement. A Worldwide Perspective. International Thomson Computer Press, 1995.

[Gillies97]
Gillies, A.C., Software Quality – Theory and Management, 2nd ed, International Thomson Computer Press, 1997.

[Grady92]
Grady, R.B., Practical Software Metrics for Project Management and Process Improvement. Prentice Hall, 1992.

[Kan95]
Kan, S.H., Metrics and Models in Software Quality Engineering. Addison-Wesley, 1995.

[Oskarsson95]
Oskarsson, Ö., Glass, R.L., ISO 9000 i programutveckling – att konstruera kvalitetsprodukter, Studentlitteratur, 1995.

[Paulk95]
Paulk, M.C. et al, The Capability Maturity Model – Guidelines for Improving the Software Process, Addison-Wesley, 1995.

[Putnam79]
Putnam, L.H., Fitzsimmons, A., Estimating software costs, in Datamation, Deptember, October and November 1979, pp. 312-315.

[SEI96]
SEI, Managing Software Development with Metrics, Course material, 1996.

[Shepperd95]
Shepperd, M. Foundations of Software Measurement. Prentice Hall, 1995.

5 Resources for Practitioners

Lars Bergman
SISU, Kista

The following is a consolidation of the many resources used by the various PIE teams studied.

5.1 Books

[ami92]
The ami consortium, *ami, a quantitative approach to software management,* South Bank University, London, 1992

[Basili94a]
Victor R. Basili, Gianluca Caldiera and H. Dieter Rombach, *Goal Question Metric Paradigm,* Encyclopaedia of Software Engineering, Volume 1, Pages 528-532, John Wiley & Sons, 1994

[Basili94b]
Victor R. Basili, Gianluigi Caldiera, and H. Dieter Rombach, *Measurement,* Encyclopaedia of Software Engineering, volume 1, pages 646- 661, John Wiley & Sons, 1994

[Basili92]
Victor R. Basili, *Software modelling and measurement: The Goal/Question/Metric paradigm.,* Technical Report CS-TR-2956, Department of Computer Science, University of Maryland, College Park, MD 20742, 1992

[Basili94]
Basili, Victor R., Caldiera, Gianluigi, Rombach, Dieter H, *The Experience Factory,* in: Encyclopaedia of Software Engineering, 2 Volume Set, John Wiley & Sons, Inc, 1994

[Beizer90]
B. Beizer, *Software Testing Techniques,* USA, 1990

[Boehm95]
Boehm, B. et. al , *Cost Models for Future Software Life Cycle Processes : CO-COMO 2.0,* Annals of Software Engineering, Special Volume on Software Process and Product Measurement., 1995

[Boehm 81]
  Boehm, B.W., *Software Engineering Economics*, Prentice Hall, 1981
[Booch94]
  Booch, G., *Object Oriented Analysis with Applications 2nd Edition*, Benjamin/Cummings Publishing Co. Inc, Redwood City, CA, 1994
[Booch97]
  Booch G., Jacobsen I., Rumbaugh J., *UML Reference Version 1.0*, Rational Corp, 1997
[Cagan96]
  M. Cagan, *Various articles on the Continuus Software Corporation WWW pages*, Not published, 1996
[Jones91]
  Jones, Capers, *Applied Software Measurement*, McGraw-Hill, 1991
[Capers96]
  Capers Jones, *Applied Software Measurement-Assuring Productivity and Quality*, McGraw-Hill, USA, 1996
[Capers97]
  Capers Jones, *Polishing the software process*, Software Development, Pages. 47-54, 1997
[Jones97]
  Jones, Capers, *The Impact of Project Management Tools on Software Failures and Successes*, Article, Software Productivity Research Inc, 1997
[Crosby80]
  Crosby, Philip B, *Quality is free – The Art of making quality certain*, Mentor (Penguin Books), USA, 1980
[Drücker73]
  P.F. Drücker, *Management: Task, Responsibilities, Practices*, Harper & Row, N.Y., 1973
[Dumke94]
  Dumke, Reiner, Zuse, Horst (Ed.):, *Theorie und Praxis der Softwaremessung*, Deutscher Universitäts Verlag, Germany, 1994
[Fenton96]
  Fenton NE and Pfleeger SL, *Software Metrics: A Rigorous and Practical Approach (2nd Edition)*, International Thomson Computer Press, 1996
[Fenton95]
  Fenton, N. Whitty, R., Iizuka, Y., *Software Quality – Assurance and Measurement. A Worldwide Perspective*, International Thomson Computer Press, 1995
[Firesmith93]
  Firesmith D, *Object Oriented Requirements Analysis and Logical Design, A Software Engineering Approach*, John Wiley, 1993
[Frost95]
  Stuart Frost, *The SELECT Perspective*, ISBN 1-899340-01-7, SELECT Software Tools Ltd, 1995

[Frost95]
  Frost S., *The SELECT Perspective, Developing Enterprise Systems using Object Technology,* SELECT Software Tools Inc, 1995
[Gillies97]
  Gillies, A.C., *Software Quality – Theory and Management, 2nd ed.,* International Thomson Computer Press, 1997
[Goldberg89]
  Adele Goldberg, David Bobson, *Smalltalk-80 The Language,* ISBN 0-201-13688-0, Addison Wesley, 1989
[Goldberg95]
  Adele Goldberg, Kenneth S. Rub, *Succeeding with Objects,* ISBN 0-201-62878-3, Addison Wesley, 1995
[Grady92]
  Grady, R.B., *Practical Software Metrics for Project Management and Process Improvement,* Prentice Hall, 1992
[Grady96]
  R.B. Grady, D.L. Caswell, *Practical software metrics for project management and process improvement,* Prentice Hall, 1996
[Graham94]
  Graham I, *Migrating to Object Technology,* Addison-Wesley, 1994
[Gresse95]
  Christiane Gresse, Barbara Hoisl and Jürgen Wüst, *A Process Model for GQM-Based Measurement,* Software Technology Transfer Initiative, Technical Report STTI-95-04-E October, University of Kaiserslautern, Department of Computer Science, Germany, 1995
[Hartkopf]
  S. Hartkopf, *Analysis in GQM-Based Measurement: Feedback Sessions with Rough Sets,* Diplomarbeit, Universität Kaiserslautern
[Henderson-Sellers96]
  Henderson-Sellers, B., *Object Oriented Metrics – Measures of Complexity,* Prentice Hall, Upper Saddle River, NJ., 1996
[Hoisl94]
  Barbara Hoisl, *A process model for planning GQM-based measurement,* Technical Report STTI-94-06-E Software Technology Transfer Initiative, April, University of Kaiserslautern Department of Computer Science, Germany, 1994
[Watts89]
  Watts S. Humphrey, *Managing the SoftWare Process,* ISBN 0-201-18095-2, Addison Wesley, 1989
[Hunter97]
  R. Hunter, M. Light, *Methodology and Productivity Study: The Data,* ADM: SPA-480-1505 June, GartnerGroup Continuous Services, 1997
[IFPUG94]
  IFPUG, *Function Point Counting Practices Manual Release 4.0,* IFPUG, Westerville, OH, 1994

[Jacobson92]
    Jacobson, I., et al, *Object-Oriented Software Engineering: A Use Case Driven Approach*, Addison-Wesley, Reading, MA, 1992
[Kaikkonen 98]
    Kaikkonen T., Oivo M., Puputti J. and Vierimaa M., *Practical Process Improvement Meets DSP Software Development.*, Software Quality Management: Quality Improvement Issues, April, pp. 15-25, Springer-Verlag, 1998
[Kan95]
    Kan, S.H., *Metrics and Models in Software Quality Engineering*, Addison-Wesley, 1995
[Even-André95]
    Even-André Karlsson, *Software Reuse A Holistic Approach*, ISBN 0-471-95819-0, John Wiley & Sons, 1995
[Kitchenham96]
    Barbara A. Kitchenham, *A procedure for analysing unbalanced datasets*, Dept of Computer Science Technical Report TR10, ISSN 1353-7776, 1996
[van Latum a]
    Frank van Latum, Markku Oivo, Barbara Hoisl and Günther Ruhe, *No Improvement without Feedback: Experiences from goal-oriented measurement at Schlumberger*, (to be submitted)
[van Latum b]
    Frank van Latum, Markku Oivo, Barbara Hoisl, Dieter Rombach and Günther Ruhe, *Shifting towards goal-oriented measurement: Experience of Schlumberger*, (in preparation)
[Lorenz93]
    Lorenz, M., *Object-Oriented Software Development: A Practical Guide*, p. 227, Prentice Hall, Englewood, NJ, 1993
[Manca96]
    S. Manca, M. R. Pagone, *Personalizzazione CCC per SIA*, Document code: SIA/GNR/0100T/5-SSI-CFG-01, SIA, 1996
[Marven94]
    Marven C. and Ewers G., *A simple approach to Digital Signal Processing*, Texas Instruments, 1994
[Marick95]
    B. Marick, *The Craft of Software Testing*, Prentice Hall, 1995
[Melton96]
    Melton, Austin, *Software Measurement*, International Thomson Computer Press, UK, 1996
[Minkiewicz98]
    Arlene F. Minkiewicz, *Cost Estimation Using Predictive Object Points*, The Tenth Annual Software Technology Conference, Knowledge Sharing – Global Information Networks conference proceedings, Salt Lake City, Utah, 1998
[NASA94]
    National Aeronautics and Space Administration, *Software measurement guide-*

book, Technical Report SEL-84-101, July, NASA Goddard Space Flight Center, Greenbelt, MD 20771, 1994

[Oliver97]
Oliver D.W., Kelliber T.P., Keegan Jr. J.G, *Engineering Complex Systems with Models and Objects,* Computing, McGraw-Hill, 1997

[Oman96]
P. Oman, S.L.Pfleeger, *Applying software metrics",* IEEE Computer Society Press, Los Alamitos, California, 1996

[Oskarsson 95]
Oskarsson, Ö., Glass, R.L., *ISO9000 i programutveckling – att konstruera kvalitetsprodukter,* Studentlitteratur, 1995

[Paulk93]
Paulk M.C., Curtis B., Chrissis and Weber C.V., *Capability Maturity Model for Software, Version 1.1,* Technical Report CMU/SEI-93-TR-025, Software Engineering Institute, USA, 1993

[Paulk95]
Mark C. Paulk, Charles V.Weber, Bill Curtis, Mary B.Chrissis, *The Capability Maturity Model Guidelines for Improving the Software Process ,* ISBN 0-201-54664-7, Addison Wesley, 1995

[Pawlak91]
Z. Pawlak, *Rough Sets: Theoretical Aspects of Reasoning about Data,* Kluwer, 1991

[Pfaff85]
G.E.Pfaff, *User Interface Management Systems,* Springer, 1985

[Pulford96]
K. Pulford, A. Kuntzmann-Combelles, S. Shirlaw, *A quantitative approach to Software Management – The ami Handbook,* ISBN 0-201-87746-5, Addison-Wesley Publishing Company, 1996

[Reenskaug 96]
Trygve Reenskaug, *Working With Objects ,* ISBN 0-13-452930-8 , Manning Publication Co, 1996

[Rigg95]
W. Rigg, C. Burrows, P. Ingram, *Ovum Evaluates: Configuration Management Tools,* Ovum Ltd, 1995

[Rombach91a]
H. Dieter Rombach, *Practical Benefits of goal-oriented measurement, Software Reliability and Metrics*, Elsevier Applied Science, London, 1991

[Rumbaugh91]
J. Rumbaugh, M. Blaha, W. Premerlani, F. Eddy, W. Lorensen, *Object-Oriented Modelling and Design ,* ISBN 0-13-630054-5, Prentice-Hall International, 1991

[Curran98]
Joc Sanders Eugene Curran, *Software Quality – A Framework for Success in software Development and Support,* AQUIS'98 Proceedings – 4th International

Conference on Achieving Quality In Software, ISBN : 0-201-63198-9 , Addison Wesley, 1998

[SEI95]
Software Engineering Institute, *The Capability Maturity Model: guidelines for improving the software process*, Addison Wesley, 1995

[Shepperd 95]
Shepperd, M., *Foundations of Software Measurement*, Prentice Hall, 1995

[Solingen95]
R. van Solingen, *Goal-oriented software measurement in practice: Introducing software measurement in Schlumberger Retail Petroleum Systems*, Master Thesis Report, Schlumberger, 1995

[Sommerville 96]
Sommerville I., *Software Engineering Fifth Edition*, Addison-Wesley, 1996

[Susmaga96]
R. Susmaga and R. Slowinsky, *Rough Processing of Fuzzy Information Tables (ProFIT).*, Institute of Computing Science. Poznan University of Technology, Poznan, 1996

[Ward85]
Ward P.T. and Mellor S.J., *Structured Development of Real-Time Systems*, Yourdon Press, USA, 1985

[Zuse95]
Horst Zuse, *History of software measurement*, 1995

5.2   ESSI PIE Projects

Documentation from the ESSI PIE projects is one of the important sources of information for this book. Generally, the following types of documents are available for each PIE:

- Snapshot, a short presentation based on the project proposal written before the project is undertaken;
- Final report, including executive summary, which is written after the project is completed and before being put on the web; and
- SISSI presentation, which is a condensed summary of the project made after the final report.

The material above is published on the European Commission funded web at http://www.esi.es/ESSI/. This site also includes search facilities and is very useful for anyone looking for documented software improvement experiences.

5.3 Articles in Journals

[Adams84]

Adams E, *Optimising preventive service of software products*, IBM Research Journal, 28(1), 2-14, 1984

[Albrecht83]

Albrecht, A & Gaffney, J, *Software Function, Source Lines of Code, and Development Effort Prediction: A Software Science Validation*, IEEE Transactions on Software Engineering, Vol. SE-9, No. 6 November, pp. 639-648, 1983

[Banker92]

Banker, R.D, et. al., *An Empirical Test of Object-based Output Measurement Metrics in a Computer Aided Software Engineering (CASE) Environment*, Journal of Management Information Systems, Vol. 8, No. 3, Winter., pp. 127-150, 1992

[Banker94]

Banker, R. D. et. al., *IEEE, Automating Output Size and Reuse Metrics in a Repository-Based Computer Aided Software Engineering (CASE) Environment*, Transactions on Software Engineering, Vol. 20, No. 3, March., pp. 169-186, 1994

[Basili84a]

Victor R. Basili and David M. Weiss, *A methodology for collecting valid software engineering data*, IEEE Transactions on Software Engineering, SE-10(6), pp. 728-738 November, 1984

[Basili86]

Victor R. Basili, Richard W. Selby, and David H. Hutchens, *Experimentation in software engineering*, IEEE Transactions on Software Engineering, SE-12(7) July, pp. 733- 743, 1986

[Basili84b]

Basili V.R. and Perricone B.T., *Software Errors and Complexity: An Empirical Investigation*, Communications of the ACM, 27(1), pp. 42-52, 1984

[Basili98]

V. R. Basili, and H.D.Rombach, *The TAME project. Towards improvement-orientated software environments*, IEEE Transactions on Software Engineering., 14(6), pp 758-773, 1988

[Brown95]

D. Brown, B. Waldman, M. Light, *The Value of Applications Development Benchmarking*, ADM: R-930-126, September, GartnerGroup RAS Services, 1995

[Chidamber94]

Chidamber, S. R. & Kemerer C. F, *A Metrics Suite for Object Oriented Design*, IEEE Transactions on Software Engineering, Vol. 20, No. 6, June, pp. 476-493, 1994

[Chillarege92]

R. Chillarege, I. S. Bhandari, J. K. Chaar, M. J. Halliday, D. S. Moebus, B. K.

Ray, and M-Y. Wong, s, *Orthogonal Defect Classification – A Concept for In-Process Measurement*, IEEE Transactions on Software Engineering, 18(11), pp. 943 – 956., 1992

[Churcher95]
Churcher, N.I. & Shepperd M. J., *Comments on A Metric Suite for Object Oriented Design*, IEEE Transactions on Software Engineering, Vol. 21, No. 3, March, pp. 263-264, 1995

[Fenton99a]
Fenton N.E. and Neil M., *A Critique of Software Defect Prediction Models*, IEEE Transactions on Software Engineering, to appear, 1999

[Fenton99b]
Fenton N.E. and Ohlsson N., *Quantitative Analysis of Faults and Failures in a Complex Software System*, IEEE Transactions on Software Engineering, 1999

[Fuggetta96]
Alfonso Fuggetta, Luigi Lavazza, Sandro Morasca, Stefano Cinti, Giandomenico Oldano and Elena Orazi., *Applying GQM in an industrial software factory*, submitted to the IEEE Transactions on Software Engineering)., 1996

[Grigoletti96]
Marco Grigoletti and Cristiano Gusmeroli, *Software metrics, il paradigma GQM* (in Italian), Informatica Oggi, January, 1996

[Jenson91]
Jenson, R. L. & Bartley, J. W., *Parametric Estimation of Programming Effort: An Object-Oriented Model*, Journal of Systems and Software, Vol. 15, pp. 107-114, 1991

[Joos94]
Joos, R., *Software Reuse at Motorola*, IEEE Software, September, pp. 42-47, 1994

[Karjalainen96]
Karjalainen J., Mäkäräinen M., Komi-Sirviö S. and Seppänen V, *Practical process improvement for embedded real-time software*, Quality Engineering, Vol. 8, no 4, pp. 565-573, 1996

[Kitchenham95]
B. A. Kitchenham, S. L. Pfleeger, and N.E. Fenton, *Towards a framework for software measurement validation*, IEEE Transaction on Software Engineering, 21(12), December, Keele University, 1995

[Lam97]
Lam, W., *Achieving Requirements Reuse: A Domain-Specific Approach from Avionics*, Journal of Systems and Software, 1997

[Laranjeira90]
Laranjeira, L., *Software Size Estimation of Object-Oriented Systems*, IEEE Transactions on Software Engineering, Vol. 16, No. 5, May, pp. 510 – 522, 1990

[Lim94]
Lim, W. C. , Effects of Reuse on Quality, Productivity and Economics, IEEE Software, September, pp. 23-31, 1994
[McCabe76]
McCabe T.J., *A complexity measure*, IEEE Transactions on Software Engineering, Vol. No. 4, April, 1976
[Minkiewicz 97]
Minkiewicz, A.F., *Objective Measures*, Software Development, June 1997, pp. 43-47, 1997
[O'Connor 94]
O'Connor, C. and Mansour, J. Turner-Harris, G. Campbell, *Reuse in Command and Control Systems*, IEEE Software, September, pp. 70-79, 1994
[Ohlsson96]
Ohlsson N and Alberg H, *Predicting error-prone software modules in telephone switches*, IEEE Transactions on Software Engineering, 22(12), pp. 886-894, 1996
[Pawlak82]
Z. Pawlak, *Rough Sets*, International Journal of Computer and Information Sciences, 11(5), pp. 341-356, 1982
[Pfleeger97]
S. L. Pfleeger, Roos Jeffery , Bill Curtis, Barbara Kitchenham, *Status report on software measurement*, IEEE Software, Marzo/Abril, 1997
[Pittman93]
Pittman, M., *Lessons Learned in Managing Object-Oriented Development*, IEEE Software, January, 1993
[Putnam97]
Putnam, L.H., Fitzsimmons, A., *Estimating software costs*, Datamation, pp. 312-315, 1979
[Vaishnavi96]
Vijay K. Vaishnavi, Rajendra K. Bandi, *Measuring Reuse*, Object Magazine, April, pp. 53-57, 1996
[Weyuker88]
Weyuker, E., *Evaluating software complexity measures*, IEEE Transactions on Software Engineering, Vol. 14, No. 9, September, 1988

5.4   Conference Papers

[ISERN95]
The ISERN Group, International Software Engineering Research Network, *Annual Meeting,* October, University of Maryland, 1995
[Albrecht97]
Albrecht, A.J., *Measuring Application Development,* Proceedings of IBM Ap-

plications Development Joint Share/Guide Symposium, pp. 83-92, Monterey, CA, 1979

[Barbati98]
R. Barbati, *4th International Conference on Achieving Quality In Software,* pp.301-307, Venice, Italy, 1998

[Bröckers96]
Bröckers, Alfred, Differding, Christiane, Threin, Günter, *The Role of Software Process Modelling in Planning Industrial Measurement Programs,* in: Proceedings of the 3rd International Metrics Symposium, IEEE, Berlin, 1996

[Falck97]
Falck, W., Gaupås, M., Kautz, K., Oppøyen, A. and Vidvei, T, *Implementing Configuration Management in Very Small Enterprises,* European Conference on Software Process Improvement, Barcelona, 1997

[Cugola97]
G. Cugola, A. Fuggetta, P. Fusaro, C. Gresse, L. Lavazza, S. Manca, M. R. Pagone, G. Ruhe, and R. Soro, *An Experience in applying GQM to the evaluation of the impact of Configuration Management,* Fourth International Symposium on Software Metrics (Metrics '97), Albuquerque, New Mexico, 1997

[Gresse96]
Christiane Gresse, Barbara Hoisl, H. Dieter Rombach and Günther Ruhe, *Kosten-Nutzen- Analyse von GQM-basiertem Messen und Bewerten: Eine replizierte Fallstudie (in German,* Conference on Empirical Research in Business Informatics, March, Linz, 1996

[Hill94]
Hill, J. Harper, K. Rimmer, R. McDermid, J. A. Whittle, B. R. and Yates, M., *Reuse of Engine Controller Technology,* presented the Avionics Conference "Systems Integration is the Sky the Limit?", Heathrow, 1994

[Kaikkonen98]
Kaikkonen T. and Vierimaa M., *Practical Process Improvement for DSP Software Development,* The Proceedings of the Embedded Systems Conference Europe, September, pp. 9-23, Miller Freeman, 1998

[Powell98]
Powell, A.L. Mander, K. C. and Brown, D.S., *Strategies for Lifecycle Concurrency and Iteration – A System Dynamics Approach,* Process Modelling and Simulation 98 (ProSim'98, 22-24 June, Silver Falls, Oregon, 1998

[Myers97]
Myers, C. *A Framework for Technology Adoption,* Software Engineering Symposium, June, Software Engineering Institute, Pittsburgh, PA, 1997

[Quaquarelli 96]
B. Quaquarelli, D. Mazzeranghi, L. Consolini, *Improving software quality through a verification process: first findings of the PROVE project,* Proceedings of SPI'96, 1996

[Quaquarelli 97]

B. Quaquarelli, L. Consolini, *Quality Improvement through Verification Process,* Proceedings QWE'97, 1997

[Ruhe96]

G. Ruhe, *Rough Set based Data Analysis in Goal Oriented Software Measurement,* Third Symposium on Software Metrics, p.10-19, IEEE Computer Society Press, Berlin, 1996

[Salvatore97]

C. Salvatore, R. Barbati, *Process Improvement through metrics and standards,* Proc. of CQS '97 Conference on Exploiting Excellence in European Information and Communication Industry, pp.177-179, Roma, Italy, 1997

[Shan 90]

Yen-Ping Shan, *Mode: A UIMS for Smalltalk,* ECOOP/OOPSLA '90 Proceedings, p258-268, 1990

[van Solingen95]

R. van Solingen, F. van Latum, M. Oivo, E. Berghout, *Application of software measurement at Schlumberger RPS: Towards enhancing GQM,* Proceedings of the sixth European Software Cost Modelling Conference (ESCOM), May, 1995

[Weiss96]

Weiss, D., *Family-Oriented Abstraction Specification and Translation: the FAST process,* Proceedings of the 11th Annual Conference on Computer Assurance, pp. 14-22, IEEE Press, New Jersey, Gaithersburg, Maryland, 1996

[Whitmire96]

Whitmire, Scott, *3D Function Points: Applications for Object-Oriented Software,* ASM '96 Conference Proceedings, San Diego, CA, 1996

[Vierimaa 98]

Vierimaa M., Kaikkonen T., Oivo M. and Moberg M., *Experiences of practical process improvement,* Embedded Systems Programming Europe, November, Volume 2, No 13, pp. 10-20, 1998

5.5 References to Standards

AMI ESPRIT

A quantitative approach to Software Management, The AMI Handbook, ISO/IEC TR 15504, 1995

ISO/IEC

Guide to software product evaluation – The evaluator's guide, ISO/IEC CD 14598-5, International Standard Organisation, 1993

IEEE Software Engineering

Standards collection, ISBN 1-55937-080-7, 1991

IEEE
  Standard for Software Test Documentation, ANSI/IEEE 829, IEEE Computer
  Society, 1983
IEEE
  Standard Glossary of Software Engineering Terminology (Std 610.12-1990).,
  Institute of Electrical and Electronics Engineers, Inc, USA, 1991
ISO/IEC
  Information Technology – Software Life Cycle Process, ISO/IEC 12207, Inter-
  national Standard Organisation, 1995
ISO/IEC
  Information technology – Software product evaluation – Part 6: Evaluation
  Modules, ISO/IEC CD 14598-6, International Standard Organisation, 1995
ISO/IEC
  Information technology – Software product evaluation – Quality characteristics
  and guidelines for their use, ISO/IEC International Standard 9126, International
  Standard Organisation, 1991
IDEF0
  Integration Definition for Function Modelling, IDEF0, Federal Information
  Processing Standards Publications, December, 1993
ISO/IEC
  TR 15504 (SPICE) – Software Process Assessment Standard, Vers. 3.02 Nov,
  1997
ISO/IEC
  Software Process Assessment – Part 1 Concept and Introductory Guide,
  ISO/IEC JTC1/SC7 N1405: WD, July 10th, 1995
ISO/IEC
  Software Process Assessment – Part 7 Guide for process improvement,]
  ISO/IEC JTC1/SC7 N1411: WD, July 10th, 1995
SPICE
  ISO/IEC JTC1/SC7 N1592, International Standard Organisation, 1996
SPICE
  Software Process Assessment Standard, 1998
SUP.2
  Perform configuration management Part 2: A model for process management,
  ISO/IEC/SPICE – Software Process Management, 1995

5.6   Organisations

A number of organisations are valuable resources for metrics research, events, and
publications. Many of these organisations have good on-line events calendars as
well.

5.6.1   ESSI of the European Community

This gives a listing of relevant EU items. Those connected to ESSI are the prime interest here:
- CORDIS
  (http://www.cordis.lu/)
- Directorate-General for Information Society
  (http://www.europa.eu.int/comm/dgs/information_society/index_en.htm)
- DG XIII –Telecommunications, Information Market and Exploitation of Research (http://europa.eu.int/comm/dgs/energy_transport/index_en.html)
- Europe Direct
  (http://europa.eu.int/citizens/index_es.html)
- European Commission
  (http://www.europa.eu.int/)
- European IT Prize
  (http://www.it-prize.org/)
- ESI
  (http://www.esi.es/)
- ESPITI
  (http://www.sea.uni-linz.ac.at/espiti/espiti_eng/general.html)
- ESPRIT
  (http://www.cordis.lu/esprit/home.html)
- ESSI
  (http://www.cordis.lu/esprit/src/stessi.htm)
- ESSITrain
  (http://www.affari.com/essi_training/)
- ESSI-SCOPE
  (http://www.cse.dcu.ie/essiscope)
- Fifth Framework Programme
  (http://www.cordis.lu/fp5/home.html)
- Telematics Applications Programme (DG XIIIC/E)
- Software Technologies
  (http://www.cordis.lu/esprit/src/sthome.htm)
- Year 2000 and Euro: IT challenges of the century
  (http://europa.eu.int/information_society/index_en.htm)

5.6.2   ESI

European Software Institute (URL: http://www.esi.es/) has now established itself as one of the world's major centres for software process improvement.

Our strength lies in our close partnership with industry. ESI's business-driven approach focuses on issues that result in a genuine commercial impact, such as reduction of costs and improving productivity.

Our sponsoring and corporate member companies play a key role in setting this policy. Between us, we have developed an exciting and forward-looking programme of activities and services that is helping both individual businesses and the software-related industry as a whole. We hope that, when you have read this brochure, you too will be interested in joining this successful and growing partnership.

Our Mission
To support our members and European industry to improve competitiveness by promoting and disseminating best practice in software.

Our Style
European Software Institute (ESI) is one of the world's leading independent authorities on software process improvement. Established in 1993 and with its headquarters in Spain, ESI is a non-profit making organisation driven by the demands of European industry. It is supported by the European Commission, the Basque Government and through company membership. Our team of 60 people is drawn from all over the world and from a wide variety of disciplines. Our technical staff are not only experts in their field but also experienced in working with business to ensure the practical dissemination and implementation of technology.

At this site you will find vast information on:
- Technologies
- Products & Services
- Models & Tools
- Info Services
- Repositories

And a very comprehensive listing of upcoming events like conferences and seminars:
http://www.esi.es/WorldwideEvents/Search/bydate.html

5.6.3   SEI

The Software Engineering Institute (SEI) (http://www.sei.cmu.edu/sei-home.html) is a federally funded research and development centre sponsored by the U.S. Department of Defence through the Office of the Under Secretary of Defence for Acquisition, Technology, and Logistics [OUSD (AT&L)]. The SEI contract was competitively awarded to Carnegie Mellon University in December 1984. The SEI staff has extensive technical and managerial experience from government, industry, and academia.

The U.S. Department of Defence established the Software Engineering Institute to advance the practice of software engineering because quality software that is produced on schedule and within budget is a critical component of U.S. defence systems.

The SEI mission is to provide leadership in advancing the state of the practice of software engineering to improve the quality of systems that depend on software.

The SEI accomplishes this mission by promoting the evolution of software engineering from an ad hoc, labour-intensive activity to a discipline that is well managed and supported by technology

The SEI carries out its mission through two principal areas of work:

- Software Engineering Management Practices (/managing/managing.html) This work focuses on the ability of organisations to predict and control quality, schedule, cost, cycle time, and productivity when acquiring, building, or enhancing software systems.
- Software Engineering Technical Practices (/engineering/engineering.html) This work focuses on the ability of software engineers to analyse, predict, and control selected properties of software systems. Work in this area involves the key *choices and trade-offs that must be made when acquiring, building, or enhancing* software systems.

Within these broad areas of work, the SEI has defined specific initiatives that address pervasive and significant issues impeding the ability of organisations to acquire, build, and evolve software-intensive systems predictably on time, within expected cost, and with expected functionality.

5.6.4 BCS

As the only chartered professional Institution for the field of information systems engineering, the British Computer Society (http://www.bcs.org.uk) exists to provide service and support to the IS community, including individual practitioners, employers of IS staff and the general public.

Formed in 1957, the Society now operates under a Royal Charter granted in 1984 which requires it, amongst other things, to:

".... promote the study and practice of Computing and to advance knowledge therein for the benefit of the public"

The BCS is also an Engineering Institution, fully licensed by the Engineering Council to nominate Chartered and Incorporated Engineers and to accredit university courses and training schemes

Computerised information systems have developed rapidly since they made their first appearance in the 1950's. That growth has been particularly rapid in recent years and computers are now involved in almost every aspect of human activity. The quality of information systems is a major factor determining the prosperity, even the survival of business organisations, the strength of national economies and, in an ever increasing number of situations, the physical safety of the general public. It is clear that this dependency on the computer will continue to increase for the foreseeable future and, as we move towards the 21st century, it is essential that the work of designing, building and maintaining information systems should be in the hands of qualified, competent professionals working to clearly defined, appropriate standards.

5.6.5   Université du Québec à Montréal

The Mission of the Software Engineering Management Research Laboratory (http://www.lrgl. uqam.ca/mission.html) is to develop, for our software engineering industry, the analytical models and measurements instruments to enable them to improve their decision-making processes in order to meet their business objectives.

In order to achieve its mission, this Laboratory has set for itself a numbers of AIMS :
- To collaborate with the software engineering industry to develop new knowledge to better manage software.
- To collaborate with the software engineering industry in the technological transfer of this knowledge, adapting it to the various industrial contexts.
- To train senior, qualified personnel for the software engineering industry, capable of introducing these new management technologies successfully in the software divisions.
- To develop in Montreal a world centre of expertise in research and development in this specialised domain of software engineering.
- To contribute actively to the development of international standards for the establishment of databases of performance measures for benchmarking purposes, in both software development and maintenance.

5.6.6   FESMA

The Federation of European Software Measurement Associations (http://www.fesma.org). This non-profit making organisation was founded in Amsterdam in 1996 to co-ordinate and supports the activities of the various Software Metrics Associations in Europe. The main objective of these organisations is to promote the use of software metrics, in the broadest sense, to enable best practice in the development and delivery of software products. At the moment software metrics associations from 9 European countries: Austria, Belgium, Denmark, Finland, France, Germany, Great Britain, Spain and the Netherlands are participating in FESMA. Canada and Japan are associated members. The number of members is starting to grow, as the application of software metrics becomes common practice throughout Europe.

5.6.7 IFPUG

The International Function Point Users' Group (IFPUG) is a membership governed, non-profit organisation committed to increasing the effectiveness of its members' information technology environments through the application of function point analysis (FPA) and other software measurement techniques. IFPUG endorses FPA as its standard methodology for software sizing. In support of this, IFPUG maintains the Function Point Counting Practices Manual, the recognised industry standard for FPA.

IFPUG (http://www.ifpug.org/) also provides a forum for networking and information exchange that promotes and encourages the use of software product and process metrics. IFPUG members benefit from a variety of services.

5.6.8 SPIN

The Software Process Improvement Network (http://www.sei.cmu.edu/ collaborating/spins) is comprised of individuals who want to improve software engineering practice. The individuals are organised into regional groups called "SPINs" that meet and share their experiences initiating and sustaining software process improvement programs. They meet annually at the Software Engineering Process Group (SEPG) Conference, which is co-sponsored by the SEI and a regional SPIN.

5.7 Conferences

The following conferences have a long-established metrics focus.

10th International Workshop on Software Measurement
Berlin, Germany
October 4-6, 2000
http://ivs.cs.uni-magdeburg.de/sw-eng/us/IWSM2000/

COCOMO/SCM 15
15th International Forum on COCOMO and Software Cost Estimation
October 24-27, 2000
http://sunset.usc.edu/Activities/oct24-27-00/index.html

FESMA 99
Hamburg, Germany
October 4-7, 1999
http://www.fesma.org/index.html

ESCOM-SCOPE 99
Maximising Quality and Managing Risk
Optimising software Development and Maintenance
Herstmonceux Castle, England
April 27-29, 1999
http://dialspace.dial.pipex.com/town/drive/gcd54/index.shtml

QWE 2000
4th International Software Quality Week
Europe &International Internet Quality Week Europe
Conference Theme: Initiatives for the Future
20-24 November 2000
Brussels, BELGIUM
http://www.soft.com/QualWeek/QWE2K/index.html

6 Experience Reports

Lars Bergman
SISU, Kista

6.1 Selected PIE Reports

Seven PIEs were selected for presentation in this chapter. They were chosen for the range of interesting and important aspects of Metrics for Improvements in Software Organisations.

CEMP is an early PIE that is of interest to the reader from two points of view. Since three companies were involved it was possible to make comparisons and evaluations based on similarities and differences between outcomes in the three companies. The PIE was an experiment on experiments. In addition, considerable effort was put into materialising methods for the practical application of GQM, which makes the reference documentation a goldmine for organisations introducing GQM.

In the **METPRO** PIE, a strategy for establishing a metrics programme covering the company software processes without getting stuck with the existing processes is developed. The goal is twofold. On the one hand, the METPRO participants wanted to establish a "health check" that runs continuously. On the other hand, they wanted to be able to define priorities for various process improvement efforts. This PIE provides valuable ideas to organisations starting or restarting metrics programmes.

OO represents a well-known paradigm shift in software development methods. Among other things, it introduces metrics and estimation issues. These issues are considered in the **MOOD** project. In particular, both metrics and estimation in an OO environment are discussed and Function Points are presented as part of the method.

The **MBM** PIE demonstrates the integration of the metrics of the software organisation with that of the company as a whole. Also, the "Dashboard" metaphor is akin to the Corporate Scorecard concept that is now generally accepted in management circles. This encourages a broad, holistic view of metrics in the context of the organisation.

The **CMEX** PIE deals with improved Configuration Management. It was selected for its generally useful ideas on the improvement process and specifically for having a well thought out and meticulously worked through accompanying metrics process. Also it raises the issue of the "truth" of metrics in software process improvement. It points out the fact that there are almost always several change variables active in the improvement environment and thus it is difficult if not impossible to ascribe the good results to a particular variable. The appendices found at the VASIE web site give an additional and thorough picture of how to apply metrics to a PIE.

Reuse is the primary target of the **PRIME** project. This should be of a wide and general interest since improved reuse in many software producing organisations is viewed as a key to maintaining competitiveness. The PIE deals with the objective of improving reuse by following a stepwise strategy for introduction and by establishing metrics to track of reuse and the resulting improvements in this area.

In **MMM** – metrics, measurement and management – a small software company presents an ambitious introduction of metrics well integrated with its business, technology and personnel. GQM and Function Points are both used. This is a practical example that should be of interest to smaller software organisations on the track to metrics.

6.2   Project 10358 – CEMP[18]
Customised Establishment of Measurement Programs

Helmut Woda
Robert Bosch GmbH, Germany

Erik Rodenbach, Frank van Latum, Rini van Solingen
Schlumberger RPS, Netherlands

Stefano Cinti, Giandomenico Oldano, Elena Orazi
Digital Equipment SPA, Italy

Christiane Gresse, Barbara Hoisl, Dieter Rombach, Günther Ruhe
UKL/STTI-KL, Germany

Markku Oivo
Schlumberger SMR, France

Alfonso Fuggetta, Luigi Lavazza, Sandro Morasca
CEFRIEL, Italy

6.2.1   Structure of the Document

In 6.2.2 an executive summary of the project "Customised Establishment of Measurement Programs" (CEMP) is given. 6.2.3 provides background information on the CEMP project concerning the objectives, involved companies etc. The structure of the main part of the document is related to the specific experimental design of the CEMP project, where in addition to the studies on the three experimental sites a comparative analysis was performed to increase validity of the results. According to this structure, in 6.2.4 "Customised Establishment of Measurement Programs at the Experimental Sites" a documentation of the pilot projects at the experimental sites is given w. r. t.

- the introduction and performance of measurement programs related to the quality aspects of reliability/reusability and
- cost/benefit analysis w. r. t. the introduction of Goal/Question/Metric (GQM) based measurement programs.

---

[18] Final Report of the project CEMP. The project lasted from January 1994 until October 1995

This chapter contains information on the work performed at each company, results and their interpretation summarising all pilot projects. More detailed information on the individual experimental sites are contained in the appendices. In 6.2.5 the comparative analysis across the replicated pilot projects at the experimental sites is documented w. r. t.

- the comparison and analysis of the cost/benefit data of the experimental sites and
- the derivation of guidelines and heuristics for GQM-based measurement programs.

Commonalties and differences of all results and experiences are related to specific application domains and project characteristics. This better enables transfer and application of the overall CEMP project results in other environments and organisations. In 6.2.6 key lessons w. r. t. the introduction of GQM-based measurement programs are given, both from a technical and a business point of view. Conclusions and future actions are described in 6.2.7. All documents related to the CEMP-project are also referenced in 6.2.7. In addition it contains the contact points of all contractors and sub-contractors for getting further information on the project. A glossary of essential terms (used in the context of the measurement programs and the specific application domains) is added to the Final Report in 6.2.8. In 6.2.9 references to secondary literature are included. In the appendices the measurement programs at each experimental site are described in more detail. This includes information on the company-specific starting scenario, work performed and the results of the measurement programs for each company. In Appendix D: "GQM Process Description and Guidelines" a brief summary of the guidelines and heuristics for the GQM method is given, based on [Gresse95].

6.2.2   Executive Summary

The Goal/Question/Metric (GQM) approach to measurement of software processes and products has been used successfully in selected industrial environments. This report summarises results and lessons learned from its application in three European companies: Robert Bosch, Digital, and Schlumberger.

Project Goals

Main objectives of the CEMP ("Customised Establishment of Measurement Programs") project were (i) to introduce and perform measurement programs based on GQM related to quality aspects of reliability and reusability in all three companies, (ii) to compare and analyse their results and experiences, and (iii) to derive replicable cost/benefit data as well as guidelines and heuristics for wide-spread establishment of GQM-based measurement programs in European industries.

Work Done

To increase validity of results, the project was organised as a synchronised and co-ordinated parallel case study. All application experiments performed the following main steps:

- Characterisation of the application environment.
- Definition of GQM-plans for reliability and reusability.
- Planning of measurement programs.
- Realisation of measurement programs.
- Company-specific analysis and interpretation of collected data.
- Packaging of results.

Additionally, comparison of results across companies were done to analyse commonalties and differences. Dissemination of experiences gained in the project was organised. All information on the CEMP project is also available on the WWW-server.

Results Achieved Including their Significance

Measurement programs for reliability and reusability were successfully introduced and realised in all three companies. Additional pilot measurement was included during the 22 months of CEMP project. After careful analysis of measurement results an improved understanding of software development with an increased awareness of strengths and weaknesses of products and processes was achieved. Based on established baselines for all topics under considerations, suggestions for improvement with high impact on quality of software development were derived.

As an additional deliverable, tool support for performing goal-oriented measurement was developed by Digital.

Across the replicated pilot projects at the experimental sites a comparative analysis was done w. r. t. the introduction of GQM-based measurement programs. Commonalties and differences of all results and experiences were related to specific application domains and project characteristics to better enable transfer and application of the overall CEMP project results in other environments and organisations.

From the CEMP experiment it was shown that total effort for introducing GQM based measurement is about one person year. Project team effort devoted to GQM was proven to be less than 3% of total project effort. Taking into account achieved benefits, effort was considered to be an efficient investment even for the first measurement project. Reuse of experiences and results in the second pilot projects resulted in improved cost-benefit ratio. From a methodological point of view, CEMP-project experiences in performing goal-oriented measurement were summarised in a detailed process model which is accompanied by guidelines and heuristics for its implementation. This considerably facilitates the application of the approach by other organisations.

Next Proposed Actions

All three companies achieved a higher maturity in software measurement. They will introduce GQM for an increasing number of projects or even for all software projects as in the case of Schlumberger RPS. Results and experiences of CEMP-project initiated improvement programs for participating companies and will enable other companies to learn when starting with goal-oriented measurement.

6.2.3   Background Information

Almost any business today involves the development or use of software. Software is either the main aspect of the business, the value added to the product or it is on the critical path to project success. It is generally accepted that the quality of the software business is of essential importance for the competitiveness of an organisation. However, the state-of-the-practice is that software engineering processes frequently are of insufficient quality, productivity, and predictability.

To improve this situation we need to understand the specific nature of software and software processes. The problem with software is that its development is influenced by a large spectrum of factors such as human, process, problem, product and resource factors. To get deeper insight into this development process we need formal models and an organisation for reuse of all the knowledge which is gained through explicit modelling and measurement.

6.2.3.1   Objectives of the CEMP-Project

The objective of the CEMP project was to evaluate the Goal/Question/Metric (GQM) approach to goal-oriented measurement in order to ease its transfer into industrial software engineering practice.

The GQM-approach is a very flexible measurement approach by which all kinds of artefacts, e.g. products, processes, resources can be evaluated and dynamic when compared to other measurement approaches. The approach is well-recognised in the scientific software engineering community and has been successfully used in industrial environments such as NASA-SEL. An overview on GQM providing detailed references is given in [Basili94b].

However, the widespread transfer of GQM-based measurement into software engineering practice is made difficult by the lack of empirical data regarding the cost/benefit ratio of the approach and by the lack of precise implementation descriptions including guidelines on how to customise a measurement program to fit the specific needs of an organisation.

The introduction of GQM-based measurement in three representative European companies aimed to:

- Assessment and quantitatively proven improvement of important quality aspects in software development process at the three organisations, mainly w. r. t. reliability and reusability.

- Support for customised establishment of GQM-based measurement programs in other European organisations by comparing cost and benefits of one performed measurement cycle. and the addition of guidelines and heuristics for tailoring the approach to the fundamental methodology.
- Comparative analysis of all the results and experiences to increase their validity and to relate them to specific contexts.

6.2.3.2   Involved Companies and their Roles

The structure of the CEMP-consortium included three industrial partners performing the experiment. In the beginning of the CEMP project the application project of Schlumberger was placed at the site Schlumberger EM. An additional measurement program was established at another division (Schlumberger RPS) in the course of the CEMP project with no additional cost. Because of administrative reasons within the company, the application project at Schlumberger EM was changed and the establishment of the measurement program was stopped, while the experiment was continued at Schlumberger RPS.

At the experimental sites application experiments were conducted within real-life projects. The measurement programs were set up by coaching people coming from either academic institutions or a company research organisation. The role of the GQM consultants is essential for the implementation of the GQM technology. They build the required GQM models, define the detailed measurement procedures, and support the analysis and interpretation of collected data.

All training, the overall experiment design, and supervision, as well as generalisation and packaging of results of the overall experiment were done by the Software Technology Transfer Initiative Kaiserslautern at the University of Kaiserslautern (UKL/STTI-KL). UKL/STTI-KL and CEFRIEL were responsible for dissemination of the generalised results outside the partners.

6.2.3.3   Starting Scenario

The GQM approach to measurement was the object of study within the CEMP experiment. The technological background of this approach is the Quality Improvement Paradigm (QIP), an enhancement of the Total Quality Management customised to the specific needs of software development. An introduction to QIP and detailed references are found in [Basili94a]. GQM was first introduced in [Basili84]; a recent overview providing detailed references is [Basili94b]. For a general introduction to software measurement issues, see [Basili94c]; for practical guidelines on how to establish measurement programs see [NASA94]. The current literature on the GQM approach focused on the description of the GQM paradigm and GQM plans. The process of actually developing and using the GQM plans was not described in detail. Guidance for any part of the GQM process was missing. Furthermore no replicable data about the cost and benefits with respect to GQM-based measurement was available.

The different starting scenarios at the experimental sites are described for each company in detail in the appendices A.1 Robert Bosch , B.1 Digital Italy and C.1 Schlumberger . In the beginning of the CEMP project an initial characterisation of the organisations took place as a part of the GQM process. A broad spectrum of characteristics of the industrial companies has been identified.

At the experimental sites measurement activities have already taken place before the CEMP project started. But these were isolated measurements not oriented to improvement goals. The data collected were incomplete and inconsistent. The measurement data were causing a "data cemetery" instead of a new information source for identification of improvement opportunities, because the data were not analysed and interpreted. The GQM method was not used before the CEMP project at any of the experimental sites.

6.2.3.4 *Workplan*

At three experimental sites GQM-based measurement programs were introduced at some pilot projects w. r. t. reliability and reusability of software process/products. To increase validity of results, the three related case studies were performed in parallel, called a replicated case study.

Based on a common methodology, parallelism of experiments, common object of investigation, and careful description of experimental environments, the analysis of commonalties and differences when comparing three experimental sites was done. Generalisations are related to different environments thus offering experience for reuse of results within participating companies and on a broader basis. In addition the introduction and establishment of the GQM technology was evaluated across the companies.

6.2.3.5 *Expected Outcomes*

The expected results of the CEMP experiment were:

- establishment of company-specific GQM-based measurement programs
- better understanding of the software process regarding reliability and reusability, and the essential influence factors on these quality aspects.
- cost/benefits data regarding the introduction of GQM-based measurement programs.
- guidelines and heuristics for establishing GQM-based measurement programs.
- decision support for improvement of software processes.

The results of the CEMP project were furthermore intended to facilitate the introduction of goal-oriented measurement based on GQM also within other environment and organisations. To that end, cost/benefit models should have been established and heuristics for effective implementation of GQM should have been formulated as results of the CEMP project across the organisations.

6.2.4 Customised Establishment of Measurement Programs

The introduction of GQM-based measurement programs at the three representative European companies is focused in this chapter. The measurement programs aimed to assess and improve certain aspects of their software development processes w. r. t. reliability and reusability and to obtain the cost/benefit ratio for the establishment of GQM-based measurement programs.

6.2.4.1 Work Performed

More detailed information about the work performed at each experimental sites is given in the appendices A.2 Robert Bosch, B.2 Digital Italy, and C.2 Schlumberger.

Organisation

Within the CEMP project GQM-based measurement programs w. r. t. to reliability and reusability were introduced in two pilot projects at each experimental site. The project teams of the pilot projects were involved in all steps of the measurement program. At all experimental sites the measurement program was planned and guided by a separate GQM team. In parallel a cost/benefit analysis w. r. t. the introduction of GQM-based measurement was performed.

The comparative analysis of the company-specific results and the integration of the individual feedback was done by UKL/STTI-KL.

Technical Environment

At the experimental sites changes to the technical environment were made w. r. t. the handling of the GQM plan/measurement, plan/measurement database, the data collection procedures and analysis and interpretation of measurement data.

In order to facilitate the job of GQM consultants CEFRIEL developed a software tool supporting the application of the GQM methodology in a project. The tool delivers support for the definition and maintenance of GQM plans including abstraction sheets, data collection, analysis and interpretation. It was developed during the CEMP project and applied at the experimental sites, which also provided feedback. For a detailed description of the tool see B.2.2 Digital Italy. A prototype of the tool is now public available. Other companies, e.g. the Societá Interbancaria per l'Automazione in Italy are also using the tool now to support their GQM-based measurement programs.

Some already existing tools for data collection at Schlumberger RPS did not provide sufficient support for their GQM-based measurement program. To complement the data collection, additional paper forms to record several metrics were designed. Also the existing tools were adjusted to the requirements of the measurement program.

For the data analysis in the feedback sessions, presentation material based on the GQM plan and the collected data has to be prepared. This process is now also partly supported by tools at the experimental sites.

Training

The GQM teams and project teams were both trained for applying the GQM methodology in the experiment, implying both external and internal training. The GQM teams were trained by experts from UKL/STTI-KL on theoretical backgrounds and practical application of the GQM methodology. During the experiment the GQM teams were continuously coached by UKL/STTI-KL during all steps of the experiment. The project teams attended a GQM introduction training by UKL/STTI-KL, and had further training and coaching from the GQM team.

Role of the Consultants

For training companies in the effective use of GQM, training seminars were performed by UKL/ STTI-KL at all three experimental sites at the beginning of the project. Methodological support and supervision was given by UKL/STTI-KL during all phases of the measurement program and at all experimental sites. In more details, this covers:

- Pre-study.
- Identification of GQM goals.
- Production of GQM plans.
- Production of measurement plans.
- Collection and validation of the data.
- Analysis and interpretation of the data.
- Packaging.

For the definition of GQM plans, support in performing interviews with project team members was given. These interviews were guided by abstraction sheets enabling a better communication between involved people. The refinement of the GQM plans based on the results of the interviews was supported and supervised by UKL/STTI-KL. Especially for company-specific analysis and interpretation of collected data, a regular participation at feedback sessions was done by UKL/ STTI-KL.

Phases of the Experiment

GQM-based measurement programs w. r. t. reliability and reusability

In this section, the activities related to the set up and execution of the measurement programs are described according to the GQM-process description of [Hoisl94], [Gresse95]. All process steps have been performed for each pilot project at each experimental site. A more detailed description of the work performed at the individual sites is given in the appendices.

Pre-study – Objective of the pre-study process is the collection of information which is relevant for the introduction of a GQM-based measurement program. First the given inputs, preconditions and constraints were identified. The organisation was characterised using a predefined questionnaire and the organisational improvement goals were stated. Possible application projects were identified and one project for the introduction of GQM-based measurement was selected at each experimental site. The project goals of the selected project were identified and initiated. Beside these process steps the participants of the GQM-based measurement program were trained to understand the underlying GQM technology.

Identification of GQM goals – Based on the description of the environment, the informal organisational improvement goals and the project goals were refined into GQM goals. The different goals were formulated according to the templates for GQM goals, ranked in a priority list and the ones actually used in the measurement program were selected.

The GQM goals focused in the measurement programs of the CEMP project were:

- *Goal Reliability:* Analyse the software product/process for the purpose of understanding with respect to reliability from the viewpoint(s) of the software development team in the following context: experimental site XYZ.
- *Goal Reuse:* Analyse the software product/process for the purpose of understanding with respect to reuse from the viewpoint(s) of the software development team in the following context: experimental site XYZ.

These GQM goals were further refined at the experimental sites to their specific interests.

Production of GQM plan

According to the identified GQM goals, a GQM plan was developed for each goal at each experimental site. The process was refined into first finding out implicit knowledge of people with respect to the measurement goal by interviewing people representing the viewpoint of the respective GQM goal and documenting the results in an abstraction sheet. Abstraction sheets are a means for knowledge acquisition and also to give a high-level overview on the GQM plan. Then the information resulting from the interviews was merged, a GQM plan using the obtained information was refined by deriving metrics via questions. Existing conflicts, inconsistencies and missing items were clarified by interviewing the people again and the GQM plan was reviewed to find out whether it is complete and correct. These process steps were performed iteratively because it was not possible to complete the GQM plan solely with the information obtained from one interview session. Parts of the company-specific GQM plans are included in the appendices.

Production of Measurement Plan

The main issue to be addressed when producing the measurement plan is the appropriate integration of measurement into the process performed in the software project. Therefore all GQM plans of one measurement program were considered and one measurement plan was developed in accordance to the given project plan of the pilot project. The following sub processes have been performed: definition of the data collection procedures (including design and implementation) and checking whether the prescribed data collection procedures are consistent with the project plan.

Collection and Validation of the Data
During the execution of the measurement plan the measurement data were collected by the defined procedures. Additionally, collected data were validated and subsequently stored in the measurement data base. Both existing measurement tools and new collection sheets were used. An example for a questionnaire used at Digital is given in the appendix B.2.5. The results were stored in a predefined database and presented using spreadsheet tools.

Analysis and Interpretation of the Data
The analysis and interpretation of the collected data was done during feedback sessions within the pilot projects at the experimental sites. The results of this part of the GQM process are described in 6.2.5.2 Results and Analysis.

Packaging the Experiences
The results and experiences gained by the measurement program with respect to the analysed process/product as well as to the measurement program itself were translated into models, considering also environment variables. There is still not much understanding on the way in which this packaging must be done. Some activities have been performed in Schlumberger RPS, for creating possibilities for future reuse of the measurement results.

Those activities were inclusion of metrics in the software development process model, infra-structural support for packaging of GQM products and measurement results and internal dissemination.

At the Bosch site there was no explicit experience factory in place at the beginning of the CEMP project. During the CEMP application experiment it became evident that for the support team structure to be successful on the long run a separate organisation is required and the concept of the experience factory [Basili94a] was introduced in Bosch.

During the CEMP project GQM-based measurement programs were introduced in a second pilot project at all experimental sites according to the steps described above.

Cost/Benefit Analysis
One of the main objective of the CEMP-project was the analysis of the cost/benefit ratio of introducing GQM-based measurement, including the determination of essential influence factors. Therefore the cost/benefit analysis was per-

formed for each pilot project at each experimental site and in addition the individual results were compared across the projects and organisations. For more detailed information see [CEMP95b], [CEMP95c].

This cost/benefit analysis was done by GQM-based measurement according to the following goal:

- Analyse the introduction of GQM measurement technology
- for the purpose of better understanding
- with respect to cost/benefit ratio
- from the viewpoint(s) of the quality organisation and project team
- in the following context: experimental sites of the CEMP project

For ease of usage this goal was broken down into two separate goals, one for measuring the cost of introducing GQM-based measurement and one for determining the benefits.

To describe the goal on a quantitative level, first interviews have been performed to acquire the implicit existing understanding on cost at the experimental sites. This interviews were performed with representatives of the viewpoints of the GQM goals in each pilot project at the experimental sites. The interviews were moderated by GQM experts from UKL/STTI-KL. Based on the information gathered during these interviews five company-specific GQM plans for the three different company environments were developed and summarised across the different viewpoints and organisations.

In this context cost was understood as cost for personnel working hours (effort):

To analyse the cost of the introduction of a GQM-based measurement program the cost was measured in number of additional hours spent due to introduction of GQM-based measurement program in the context of the CEMP project.

In order to represent the project manager's high-level view on effort data the total effort for introducing the GQM-based measurement programs and the effort distribution due to set up vs. performance of the measurement programs was evaluated. The effort for performing the measurement program (data collection and analysis/interpretation) was measured per month of execution of the measurement program.

The quality assurance managers of all sites were interested in a more detailed breakdown of effort data. Therefore the effort per phase according to a detailed phase model and the effort per role (GQM team 1 vs. project team 2) was investigated. The phase model covers the phases of the GQM process [Gresse95] and also support activities (e.g. process modelling, tool development, dissemination activities).

Based on the obtained cost model the data collection forms were derived by UKL/STTI-KL. The effort data were reported by the partners for all pilot projects according to the effort reporting sheet [CEMP95b] from January 1994 until May 1995. The data collection was supervised by UKL/STTI-KL. During the consortium meetings the cost data was analysed and interpreted.

Similarities and differences of the measurement data between the projects and organisations were carefully evaluated under consideration of the environments. An overview on the results is given in "Cost of Introducing GQM-Based Measurement". More detailed information is contained in [CEMP95b].

The second goal of the cost/benefit analysis was related to the benefits of GQM-based measurement programs. The company-specific GQM plans were developed based on the information gained by interviews with the project manager and the quality assurance manager, representatives of the viewpoint stated in the goal, at each site and project. The interviews were moderated by GQM experts from UKL/STTI-KL. Five company-specific GQM plans for the three different company environments resulted from these interviews. The GQM plans include the quality aspects of benefits as well as variation factors that are supposed to influence the quality models related to the benefits at the different experimental sites.

These company-specific GQM plans for evaluating the benefits of GQM-based measurement were analysed and a "generalised GQM plan" was developed by UKL/STTI-KL based on the individual plans in order to include all mentioned aspects on benefits at the different environments. For both the quality aspects and the variation factors the following procedure was performed: all quality aspects/variation factors mentioned in the company-specific GQM plans were merged together and regrouped according to common issues addressed. Several major concepts could be identified that were used for defining quality models for achieved benefits:

Quality model 1: benefits due to availability of data
- data to support systematic improvement cycle: baseline provided, suggestions for improvement identified, realistic scale for improvement goals provided
- data to support planning and proposals: better planning based on data, data to support requests/proposals to higher management
- data to support learning/understanding: better monitoring of the software process, comparison between projects, strengths and weaknesses of products/processes /personnel, cost of bad quality, falsification/confirmation of assumptions
- data to support quality assurance tasks: avoidance of faults improved, external audits prepared

Quality model 2: benefits due to (improved) explicit models
- explicit representation of knowledge, transfer of measurement experience/results, improvement of explicit process model, checklists for reviews

Quality model 3: benefits due to team involvement
- willingness to supply data, customer satisfaction w. r. t. measurement, increased awareness of quality issues, usage of knowledge of personnel, discussion of relationship between high-level and project goals

Quality model 4: improved measurement capability

- retrospective analysis of existing data, better focus of data collection efforts, higher usefulness of available data, higher number of data points available

The following influencing factors have been evaluated w. r. t. their impact on the quality models stated above:

Process Conformance

- state of technologies required for the application of the GQM approach: availability of a detailed product and process model for the GQM method
- allocated resources: resource allocation to the measurement program, availability of a supporting GQM team, proper planning of measured software project
- feedback: feedback structure/feedback mechanisms used, performance of feedback session
- training and understanding of the GQM approach
- characteristics of the application of the GQM-approach: scope of measurement program, effectiveness of multiple measurement programs
- degree of involvement of all relevant roles
- motivation of all relevant roles
- Domain conformance
- characteristics of the software process: completeness, complexity, stability, consistency
- stability of environment: personnel, high-level goals, structure of organisation
- culture/attitude: team (measurement/disclosure of information, open discussion, orientation towards improvement, process orientation), higher management
- internal policies: flexibility w. r. t. SW process,
- availability of historical data
- project team structure

The data according to the GQM plan was collected after the performance of the measurement programs w. r. t. reliability and reusability for each pilot project at the experimental sites. The company-specific data was appended to the GQM plan after the collection of data by UKL/STTI-KL.

The results were analysed and discussed during a meeting with project managers and quality assurance managers.

Internal Dissemination

At the experimental sites the results of the measurement programs were distributed over the organisations.

At Bosch the results of CEMP were disseminated through presentation to software development teams, quality circles and presentation of experience by the experience factory to other departments and divisions of Bosch and their quality organisations.

- At Schlumberger RPS the following communication media were used to disseminate the results of the measurement programs:
- Quality signs in the building to inform the personnel.
- Month End Letter with relevant progress information was distributed every month to all managers in the organisation.
- Project Evaluation Reports were sent to top management every one to two months, describing the progress, results and future actions of the measurement program.
- WWW-server for the presentation of the software measurement programs, the measurement results, and the conclusions and further activities.
- Personal contacts to distribute the measurement results over the organisation is by giving presentations, and by talking to other Schlumberger employees.

At Digital Italy the results of CEMP experiment were presented to the project leaders and development managers of all the projects currently under development. The team that conducted the CEMP experiment has now joined the Digital European Expertise Centre for Technical CASE: in the context of this department, the team members will provide consultancy on the GQM methodology to other Digital software development sites and to key Digital customers.

Within the CEMP consortium experiences were exchanged regularly during project meetings.

6.2.4.2   Results and Analysis

In the CEMP project GQM-based measurement was introduced at three different European companies. The aim of the measurement programs was the investigation of reliability and reusability of the software development process and its related products. More detailed information about the results and analysis at each experimental sites is given in the appendices

A.3 Robert Bosch, B.3 Digital Italy and C.3 Schlumberger.

At all three experimental sites a better understanding of process/products aspects of the software development was achieved by the measurement programs and improvements were initiated (R1-R4).

R1 A better understanding on the effectiveness of testing techniques was achieved by reliability measurement. There upon, improvement steps could be initiated at all experimental sites.

At Schlumberger RPS it was shown that a recently introduced test method had a significant contribution to the defects found (see Fig 6.1), which was not even regarded as an important part of the regular testing process by the project team before the measurement program started. A further analysis showed that a high percentage of these failures found by the Novice User Test were fatal ones. Based on the results of the measurements, the team members decided to change their process and include Novice User Test as a regular part of their testing process.

Investigating failure detection effectiveness through the development process phases, Digital discovered that the field test at customer sites was accounting for only 3% of the total product failures detected by the project team during the development and qualification phases. Moreover only medium priority problems were reported by the customer test sites. Therefore a verification done at the customer sites pointed out that the products were tested very superficially because of the lack of a clear testing program agreed between Digital and the selected customers. Figure 6.2 shows a pie chart of the percentage of total failures detected during development (Phase 2), internal field test (Phase 3 IFT) and external field test (Phase 3 EFT). According to the above results, the field test policy was revised performing an accurate selection of customer sites, defining the test program and monitoring the site during the testing period.

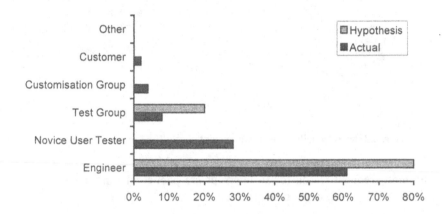

Fig. 6.1 Detection of failures before release at Schlumberger RPS classified by the different groups of people that can detect failures

At the Bosch site the effectiveness of the test at the measurement stand was investigated. It was found out, that 50% of the failures have been seen only after system integration, one third of these could not have been detected during the test at the measurement stand. 40% of all functions have been rated to be complex and therefore difficult to test. This was explained by the fact, that the test at the measurement stand has not enough capability of defect detection as needed. Therefore additional measures are required to filter defects. A very efficient method for defect detection are systematic reviews, which will be part of the software development process of the project.

R2 A baseline for effort spent in the software development process was created by the measurement programs. Context factors influencing the amount of effort were identified. Resulting form this investigation improvement areas for the reduction of effort have become obvious.

At the Bosch site interrupts during the process execution were investigated. Analysing context data collected for the goal reliability it could be seen that interrupts during software development are a frequent source of disturbance during process execution.

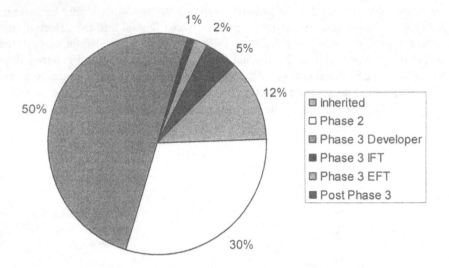

Fig. 6.2 Detected failures vs. Development phases (first project at Digital)

The most frequent reason for an interrupt are phone calls that have to be forwarded or result in messages to be recorded.

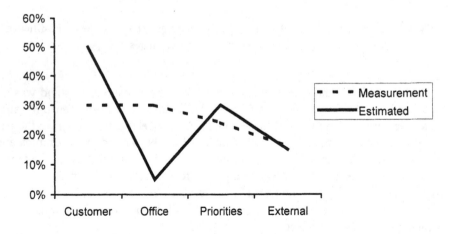

Fig. 6.3 Interrupts (Robert Bosch GmbH)

Therefore a sufficient number of telephone sets (one per person) will be installed immediately.

Concerning the first project at Digital the time between two product base levels has been identified as a bottleneck for failure fix verification, causing unnecessary delays in the product development. Therefore the base level build process was reviewed and management take the decision of purchasing a product configuration management tool allowing to improve the product build frequency.

A result at the Schlumberger site was that faults introduced in the requirement phase cost three times the average time to repair, while faults introduced during detailed design and implementation require 0.6 of the average time to repair. Better formulation of requirements and early customer involvement appears to be valuable with respect of repair costs.

R3 Concepts concerning the reliability of the software process and its related products have been better understood. Characteristics of the concepts and their influence on reliability could be identified.

At the Bosch site the reason for starting a process run is that for 80% of all cases measured the individual functionality was not considered satisfactory when executed in road tests. Changes of the specification are required by the customer even shortly before final delivery. Data showed that the specification has been seen to be complete in most cases, 75% of the specifications have been identified to be evident and clear and only in an insignificantly low number of cases the specification has been seen to be the origin of an error causing failures. The situation was improved by the possibility of simulation of the specification to enable the customer to realise whether the functions required are reasonable.

The distribution of faults found over time per severity category was investigated at the Schlumberger site. The analysis showed that the percentage of fatal faults is stabilising around 25% while the expected number of fatal faults was 10%. The initial assumption at Schlumberger that large and complex modules are error prone is strongly supported by the data. The occurrence of faults depends on a combination of complexity, size and time spent on testing/reviews. This combination is now used in predicting reliability.

In order to achieve some of the GQM goals, Digital had to collect data concerning the tracing of faults to the affected source files. Performing this activity, they understood that the problem tracking tools used by both projects were not to provide a valid support to record this kind of information. In fact, to collect the above data, the developers had to be interviewed in many cases. Therefore the problem tracking tool interfaces were extended to provide the necessary support for entering the above information. A side effect of this modification was an improvement in the efficiency of detection of new faults.

R4 Investigation of dependency between module criticality and reuse.

Schlumberger investigated the dependency between criticality and reuse. A result regarding reusability at the Schlumberger site was that fault density in a module developed from scratch doubles the fault density of new code in a significantly changed module, which on its turn doubles the fault density of new code in a slightly changed module. Due to the selection of fully reused modules, its fault density equals zero. Figure 6.4 shows the number of faults in dependence of different degrees of reuse.

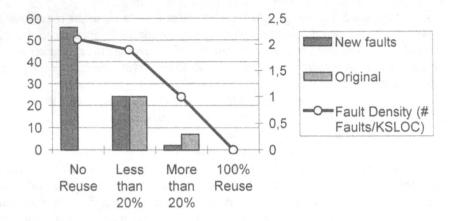

Fig. 6.4 Fault densities of modules categorized by the amount of reuse at Schlumberger RPS

6.2.5   Comparative Analysis Across the Organisations

In this chapter the comparative analysis across the replicated pilot projects at the experimental sites is documented w. r. t. the derivation of guidelines and heuristics for GQM-based measurement programs and the comparison and analysis of the cost/benefit data of the introduction of GQM-based measurement programs in the pilot projects. The comparative analysis of the replicated studies enables the transfer and application of the CEMP project results in other environments and organisations.

6.2.5.1   Work Performed

Derivation of Guidelines and Heuristics for GQM-Based Measurement Programs

The methodological experience with respect to GQM-based measurement was summarised by UKL/STTI-KL in a more detailed and advanced description of the GQM process. At the regular consortium meetings, exchange of experiences with respect to the measurement programs according to the company-related quality goals were organised and the implementation of the GQM measurement method at the different experimental sites was presented by all partners.

Based on the feedback from the practical experiences of the application partners a process model for the GQM-based measurement was formulated, including guidelines and heuristics [Gresse95] for the customised application. This process model was reviewed by all application partners.

Comparison and Analysis of the Cost/Benefit Data of the Experimental Sites

For the cost/benefit analysis w. r. t. the introduction of GQM-based measurement programs at the experimental sites a general framework was developed based on the individual analyses of the application partners (see also "Phases of the Experiment"). Interviews with both quality and project managers of all three companies were performed by UKL/STTI-KL members to realise comparison and analysis across companies. The definition of the general GQM plan/measurement plan was done by UKL/STTI-KL. The data collection was supervised and the analysis of the measurement data was prepared by UKL/STTI-KL. At regular meetings, exchange of experiences with respect to the cost/benefit analyses took place within the CEMP consortium. Based on a careful characterisation of organisational and project environment, differences and commonalties between companies were investigated and possible explanations were given. The results of the comparative analysis are documented in [CEMP95b], [CEMP95c].

6.2.5.2   Results and Analysis

Technical Results w. r. t. the GQM Technology

The GQM-based measurement was successfully introduced at the experimental sites. Based on the experiences of the application partners the method was further refined and the individual process steps were explained in detail and supplemented by guidelines. The process model is described in detail in [Gresse95]. A brief summary of the guidelines and heuristics is given in

"Appendix D: GQM Process Description and Guidelines".

In this chapter the most important results w. r. t. the GQM technology made at the experimental sites during the CEMP project are summarised below:

GQM1 Refinement of the GQM Process Description

Figure 6.5 presents an overview on the steps of the refined GQM method and its relationship to the QIP, which is described in detail in [Gresse95].

GQM2 Preconditions for a Successful Establishment of GQM-Based Measurement

- GQM process has to be customised to the organisation.
- Organisational orientation towards improvement.
- Motivation of the participants in the measurement program.
- Appropriate form of communication and information, e.g. open discussions must be possible.

- Sufficient degree of resource allocation to the measurement program, i.e. supporting
- GQM experts should be available.
- Positive attitude of higher management towards proposals of the project personnel.
- Flexibility of the organisational culture as a basis for the realisation of changes.
- Actual introduction of changes based on suggestions for improvement is mandatory for

GQM3 Guidelines for the Definition of the GQM Goals

Questions concerning the project characteristics, environment identification, project and improvement goal identification and measurement goal selection have been described [Solingen95].

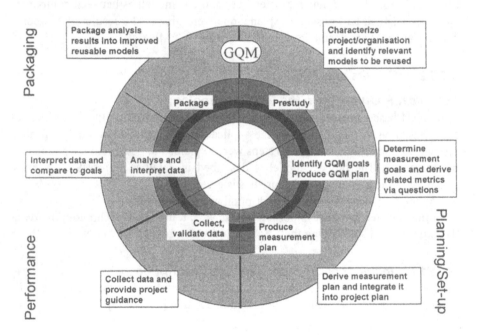

Fig. 6.5 Overview on the GQM method

GQM4 Structured Interviews/Abstraction Sheets are a Means of Knowledge Acquisition

The implicit available knowledge about the analysed process/product has to be made explicit by interviewing the people in the viewpoint of the GQM goal. These interviews, structured by so called "abstraction sheets" were used as a means of knowledge acquisition in defining the GQM plan. Abstraction sheets have been a very useful tool throughout the project, because they also increase the readability of the GQM plans.

GQM5 Hypotheses are a Means of Reflecting the Current State

Hypothesis for each question of the GQM plan are stated, reflecting the current state of concepts or relationships between quality aspects and context variables assumed by the people in the viewpoint of the GQM goals. By the project it was proven that it initiates and supports participation of project team members by discussion and interpretation of deviations between the hypothesis and measurement results.

GQM6 Interpretation of the Data is Supported by GQM

In contrast to earlier measurement at the experimental sites GQM supports the derivation of metrics oriented to the goal of the measurement program and the interpretation of the collected data. The GQM-based measurement programs also allowed a post-mortem analysis of collected data during earlier measurement programs that could not have been evaluated before.

GQM7 Feedback Sessions are the Key Mechanism for Analysis

Feedback sessions as a part of the GQM process were identified as key mechanism of analysis, resulting in acceptance of and motivation for data collection and validity of measurement results. The real value comes from conclusions drawn by the developers themselves with the help and based upon collected data. All the feedback sessions lead to either to modified or new measurement analysis and also to several changes in the GQM plan. This is a constant iterative learning process where the analysis and interpretation of the measurement data lead to better understanding of the underlying models and consequently better understanding lead to new questions or even new goals.

GQM8 Measurement Program Performed as an Iterative Process

Iteration is needed in producing GQM plans and measurement plans. GQM goals, GQM plans and the measurement plan are updated in the course of the measurement program as reaction to changes of the environment or the viewpoint of interest.

*GQM9 Tool Support for the Organisation of Artefacts Related to the
GQM-Based Measurement Program is not Mandatory, but Reduces
the Required Effort*

Business

One of the main objectives of the CEMP-project was the analysis of the
cost/benefit ratio of introducing GQM-based measurement across different organisations. This analysis is based on the cost/benefit data w. r. t. the establishment of
the measurement programs in the pilot projects at the individual experimental
sites.

Cost of Introducing GQM-Based Measurement

In this section the most important results of the analysis on effort w. r. t. the
GQM-based measurement generalised from the parallel analysis at the companies
are reported. All values are averages of the results of the different sites and projects, where support activities are excluded:

*C1 The Total Effort Needed for Introducing GQM Based Measurement
is about 1 Person Year.*

*C2 The Total Effort Needed for Introducing GQM of about 1 Person
Year Comes to 1/3 from the Project Team and to 2/3 from the GQM
Team.*

*C3 The Relation of the Effort of the Set-up and Execution Phase for
the First Projects is about 2/3 (Set-up Phase) to 1/3 (Execution
Phase).*

- The total effort of set-up and execution phase is about 1 person year. A relatively wide range from about 4 – 11 PM w. r. t. the set-up effort between the
  separate projects is explained by the following variation factors:
- degree of involvement of the project team members in activities of the GQM
  process (to be trained in establishing and performing a GQM-based measurement program)
- characteristics of the project team such as size and contribution
- scope of the measurement program
- experience of GQM consultants w. r. t. the GQM technology and the application domain of the project

C4 The Total Effort of Set-up and Execution Phase is about 6 PM in the Second Projects Compared to 11 PM in the First Projects.

The main reason for the decrease are the availability of tool support for the GQM technology at the experimental sites in the second projects.

The comparison of the effort spent in the second projects to the first ones has to be seen carefully in the CEMP project. The second projects at the experimental sites cannot be seen as follow-up projects, because some of the preconditions, such as experience with the GQM technology, which would be expected to be improved in the second projects, did not change compared to the first project. Reasons are different project teams in the second projects etc.

C5 The Project Overhead due to GQM-Based Measurement (Project Team only) For the First Projects was Less than 3% at All Experimental Sites.

The productivity of the project personnel increased at the Digital site, because the developers were very happy to see that the collected data was the direct cause of improvements to their development environment.

C6 The Total Effort for GQM-Based Measurement (for the Set-up and Execution Phase, Including Project Team and the GQM Experts) in Percentage of the Total Project Effort is about 17%.

The range is very wide between only 3% and 41% of the total project effort, depending on the initial situation, the scope of the measurement program and the degree of further activities related to the GQM-based measurement, e.g. tool development.

C7 In the CEMP Project, the Total Effort for GQM-Based Measurement per Month of Execution is Almost the Same in the First and Second Projects with about 0.4 PM.

This is important, because the total effort spent on the measurement program depends on the duration of the execution phase (data collection period).

Results on Achieved Benefits

As an overall result of the goal-oriented measurement programs, all experimental sites viewed GQM as very beneficial. At all sites additional measurement programs for goals beyond the aims of the CEMP project were introduced.

Most important benefits gained by the GQM based measurement are:

B1 Better Understanding of the Products/Processes Related to the Software Process at all Experimental Sites was Achieved.

E.g. the effort for failure/fault fixing is more visible, properties of high-risk modules were identified.

B2 All Experimental Sites could Derive Quantitative Baselines for all Stated Questions/Topics of Interest.
For more information see A.3.1 Robert Bosch, B.3.1 Digital Italy and C.3.1 Schlumberger.

B3 Increased Awareness of Strengths and Weaknesses to the Products or the Processes (w. r. t. to the Respective Quality foci) could be Identified.
E.g. certain testing techniques turned out to be significantly more or less effective than expected. Hypotheses, reflecting the common implicit understanding of the process/product, could be confirmed or rejected based on quantitative data, and explanations for the correctness or falseness of the assumptions could be stated, e.g. the assumed distribution of faults was refuted.

B4 Suggestions for Improvement with Medium/High Impact on the SW Development Process could be Formulated.
For more information see R1-R3 in chapter "6.2.4.2 Results and Analysis".

B5 The Measurement Programs Further Provide Quantitative Support for Project Planning, Sound Proposals/Requests to Higher Management, Tasks of Quality Assurance People.
For more information see R1-R3 in chapter "6.2.4.2 Results and Analysis".

B6 Improved SW Measurement Know-how of the Project People
Improved measurement capabilities and a better understanding on the application of goal-oriented measurement could be identified. This was used to customise the measurement program in the second projects, resulting in decreased efforts.

B7 More Detailed Information about the Application of the GQM Method and Tool Support are Available.
A detailed description of the GQM process was formulated including guidelines and heuristics for the application of GQM-based measurement, see [Gresse95] or "Appendix D: GQM Process Description and Guidelines". A detailed analysis of the cost/benefit ratio was performed [CEMP95b], [CEMP95c]. At the experimental sites also tools for the handling of GQM related products, collecting data and preparing the data analysis were developed.

Since the introduction of a measurement technology alone does not directly lead to cost savings, the benefits to be derived from the establishment of a measurement program were of a qualitative nature and no large-scale process changes for improvement could be measured.

For a complete overview on the achieved benefits in the CEMP project see [CEMP95c].

6.2.6   Key Lessons

6.2.6.1   Technological Point of View

- KLT1 GQM has been proven a powerful measurement approach for systematic improvement within the software domain.
- KLT2 From the application of GQM, a better understanding, assessment and control of processes was initiated. By means of a GQM based measurement program the software development process becomes a practical asset for the day to day development in an industrial environment.
- KLT3 Formalising the GQM process in CEMP is a major improvement over the previous use of GQM methodology.
- KLT4 Models of software development processes/products are required for the implementation of a measurement program.
- KLT5 Definition of measurement goal must be adopted in accordance to organisation objectives and software project description.
- KLT6 Tool support for the organisation of artefacts related to the GQM-based measurement program is not necessary, but reduces the effort.
- KLT7 Integration of the GQM-based measurement into the existing measurement practice is important to gain acceptance and reduce effort.
- KLT8 Feedback sessions are the key mechanism for analysis and interpretation of the data.
- KLT9 Close interaction between the project team and the GQM team is essential to make measurement practices succeed.

6.2.6.2   Business Point of View

From a business point of view GQM-based measurement is regarded as very promising for support for decision making.

KLB1 Effort Spent on GQM-based Measurement

The required additional effort of one person-year for the introduction of GQM-based measurement program is seen as acceptable by the industrial partners compared to the achieved benefits (see also C1-C7 in chapter "Cost of Introducing GQM-Based Measurement"). Especially, because the effort needed for the introduction of GQM-based measurement will decrease in the following measurement programs, as in the second projects at the experimental sites in the CEMP project, because of the experiences with GQM and the availability of tool support and possibility to reuse parts of products related to the GQM process.

KLB2 Human Aspects

One of the key elements for the success of the measurement program is the involvement and motivation of the participants in the projects. The project personnel should be involved from the very beginning and contribute significantly to the design and analysis of the measurement program.

KLB3 Decision Making/Planning

The results of the measurement programs were formulated in terms of guidelines and rules of thumbs. They constitute a well-founded basis for decisions and planning of software development processes and identification of problem and potential improvement areas.

GQM-based measurement also supplies concrete information to substantiate requests and proposals based on collected and analysed measurement data.

KLB4 Context Factors Influencing the Cost and Benefits of a GQM-Based Measurement Program

- initial state of the organisation
  - Are the software process and the related products already modelled?
  - Is a separate quality assurance team available?
  - Are historical data w. r. t. the software process available?
- management support
  - Is the measurement program supported by management?
- organisational culture
  - Is the organisation oriented towards improvement?
  - Is flexibility (e.g. process changes) possible?
  - Does the organisation focus the quality of the products?
- maturity of the GQM method
  - Is a detailed product and process model for the GQM method available?
  - Is tool-support for performing GQM-based measurement available?
- performance of GQM process
  - What is the scope and duration of the measurement program?
  - Can experience from earlier measurement programs be reused?
  - What is the degree of the involvement of project team members in technical activities of the GQM process?
  - Is the communication, information and training for each involved person appropriate?
  - Are sufficient resources allocated to the measurement program, i.e. are a supporting GQM experts available?
- experience with the GQM technology of all roles involved
  - Do all people involved in the measurement program have already experiences with GQM or measurement?
- application project characteristics
  - What are the characteristics of the software process w. r. t. complexity, stability and consistency and software process performance?
  - What are the characteristics of the project team w. r. t. the size and distribution and the experiences of the project team related to the software process?

For a more detailed explanation see [CEMP95b], [CEMP95c].

6.2.6.3   *Strengths and Weakness of the Experiment*

S1 The introduction of GQM-based measurement was highly supported by the environment at the experimental sites.

S2 The structure of the consortium including three experimental sites allowed replicated case studies on the introduction of GQM-based measurement. Therefore a higher significance of the results was achieved, the identification of context factors influencing the application due to different company characteristics was possible and the GQM method was described in detail.

S3 The synchronicity of the performance of the experiments intensifies the statement in S2. The gained knowledge was further enriched by the exchange of experiences, which were discussed openly within the consortium.

S4 The CEMP project is further characterised by a *two-level structure*:

- Experimental sites: qualified to assess and improve certain aspects of their software development process regarding the measurement goals of the CEMP project reliability and reusability.
- Perspective of the European Community: availability of empirical information to European industries regarding cost/benefit ratio of the approach [CEMP95b], [CEMP95c] and precise implementation descriptions including guidelines on how to customise a measurement program to fit the specific needs of an organisation [Gresse95].

S5 The CEMP project was guided and *supervised by one* partner, UKL/STTI-KL, who also provided the technology for the experiment. The organisation also combined the results and experiences of the three experimental sites and to obtain information about the cost/benefit ratio and the GQM method, which is applicable on a broader context.

S6 The frame of the project created the possibility to establish measurement programs at the experimental sites and achieve results at all sites within 22 months.

The following *weaknesses* have been identified:

W1 The presence of a tool for the application of the GQM methodology, that stores GQM plans and analysis procedures allows GQM executors to reuse very easily parts of the GQM plan, already developed for previous projects, and makes it very ease to define and implement the data analysis. The major drawback of the GQM experiment implementation for the first time at one experimental site was related to the effort required to set up the first GQM plan and prepare the measurement environment and tools. In the second target project the benefits of this strategy already were clear.

In contrast to this it was regarded an advantage of the GQM method at another experimental site, that all activities can also be done only on paper.

W2 In the beginning of the CEMP project detailed guidelines for the planning of the GQM-based measurement program and the data collection were available, but guidelines for the analysis of data and packaging were missing, because of the lack of practical experiences with these activities.

W3 The duration of the CEMP project of only 22 months was rather short. Consequently the measurement programs resulted to a better understanding of the analysed products and processes and based on this knowledge first improvement actions took place, but no complete improvement cycle could be performed in this time frame.

6.2.7   Conclusions and Future Actions

6.2.7.1   Conclusions

Con1 GQM-based Measurement Programs were Successfully Introduced at all Three Experimental Sites.

The application of GQM based measurement has been very successful at the experimental sites. The GQM approach has turned out to be suitable for establishing an effective measurement program focusing the attention on the real causes for problems of the development process. As a result of the measurement programs at all experimental sites the GQM based measurement program has significantly increased the understanding of software reliability and quality of the development process as well as the quality of the software product itself. A better understanding of reliability and its causes and effects can be now anticipated. As shown in chapter 3 considerable benefits from applying this technology have been identified. The results of the GQM-based measurement allowed to identify strengths and weaknesses of both the product and process and, therefore, opportunities for improvement based on a quantitative and objective analysis at all industrial partners. As mentioned before some relevant improvement actions have been already started.

Con2 The Participating Companies will Continue and Expand the Measurement Programs.

GQM-based measurement was shown as a very useful foundation for systematic quality improvement. The required additional effort was considered acceptable by all industrial partners, when compared to the achieved benefits.

The CEMP project supported successfully the technology transfer of the GQM method into the participating companies. The technology has been customised to the specific needs of the organisations and people at the experimental sites have been trained as GQM experts and gained experiences with the performance of the measurement programs. All experimental sites will continue and expand their measurement programs.

To improve the practices of the companies, a permanent experience exchange and further technology transfer on a more mature level than in the CEMP project has been requested by the experimental sites.

Con3 The Results and Experiences of the Project can be Applied to Introduce GQM-based Measurement at Other Companies and Organisations and are Publicly Available.

In the CEMP project the company-specific experiences with the GQM-based measurement programs have been summarised and compared. The GQM method has been described in detail based on the experiences of the participating companies [Gresse95] and a cost/benefit analysis regarding the results at all three sites is available now [CEMP95b], [CEMP95c].

Con4 More Experiments/Replicated Case Studies as Funded by ESSI are Necessary to Systematically Establish Experience Bases Enabling Best Practice Experience Exchange Within/Between Companies.

Technology transfer was enabled in the CEMP project. The consortium structure allowed the guidance and supervision of the experiment by UKL/STTI-KL, the comparison of the company-specific results and a lively experience exchange between all partners.

6.2.7.2   Future Actions

The CEMP consortium will continue collaboration for technology transfer and experience exchange. This will be realised in the future through workshops to exchange current experiences of the partners in measurement programs and further need for new technologies by the experimental sites. The specific future actions of the participating organisations are described below.

Future Actions at Robert Bosch GmbH. Continuation/Expansion of the Existing Measurement Projects

For Kompakt the measurement program is expanded to insure project results in terms of timeliness, cost and quality of the delivered product. The expansion concerns development of goals and introducing a focus that will include more than "for the purpose of understanding". For 1996 explicit quantitative improvement goals will be defined. The concept of the experience factory will be used to support the Kompakt project. Starting from verification and tailoring of this concept by practical application in the Kompakt project the experience factory will support software development in all departments. The experience factory will develop concepts for packaging and the development of an experience database for the storage of experience for reuse independently of existing projects. Another instance of the experience factory in another division will be installed beginning of

1996. The mission will be to introduce GQM based measurement and improvement programs.

Planned Dissemination Events
The CEMP experience will be presented to the new experience factory team.

Future Actions at Digital Equipment SPA. Continuation/Expansion of the Existing Measurement Projects
The introduction of GQM in the two target projects gave very good results, hence the measurement activity is going to continue on new releases of the two products. GQM will be used to evaluate the benefits achieved modifying the development process according to the results of the CEMP experiment. New GQM goals will be established to evaluate the effectiveness of the revised field test strategy and of the new product configuration/build environment. GQM plans stored in the database of the GQM support tool will be re-used to define similar parts of the new plans. In parallel with this new GQM analysis, all plans and measurements defined during the CEMP experiment are reviewed and packaged to set-up a first experimental experience factory.

Follow-up Projects
The team that conducted the CEMP experiment at Digital has joined the European Expertise Centre for Technical CASE. This department was created by Digital to provide consultancy and system integration support in the area of technical CASE to Digital key customers and Digital internal software development teams. Within this structure, the members of the Digital CEMP team will provide training and consultancy on the GQM methodology to key customers and to internal software projects.

Planned Dissemination Events
In addition to the dissemination of the GQM knowledge within Digital, the Digital CEMP Team has participated to a dissemination event organised by CEFRIEL. This event was a one day presentation of the GQM methodology and of the results achieved by Digital with the support of CEFRIEL using the methodology, in the framework of the CEMP project. The participants were about 30 people of the major IT and Telecommunication companies operating in Italy. The GQM methodology will be part of the service portfolio of the Digital Expertise Centre for Technical CASE, and it will be advertised to customers and other Digital organisations.

Future Actions at Schlumberger RPS, Continuation/Expansion of the Existing Measurement Projects

Data collection and data analysis is going to continue in both measurement projects. The introduction of GQM was successful, the results are beneficial, so the measurement projects will continue. The Omega 2010 project is currently expanded with a goal on understanding testing, and the DEMP project will soon release it's first design document which will result in data collection during review and inspection.

Because of the valuable experiences with GQM measurement as a supporting mechanism, and because of the need to deliver high quality products, RPS will expand the application of GQM to all projects in Schlumberger RPS. A new project will be selected in which the reliability goal of CEMP (probably) will be replicated. The Omega 2010 measurement products like GQM plan, measurement information system and feedback session presentation material will be applied and reused in this project by which effort reduction is expected.

The current measurement projects are an input product for future measurement projects, resulting in for example reuse of GQM plans, but also the experience in applying GQM will be used in new projects. Therefore all results of the existing measurement projects must be packaged. GQM already emphasises the packaging of results. Not just measurement results, but also results of applying GQM itself.

Follow-up Projects

At Schlumberger currently new projects are planned in which measurement play an important role. Recently Schlumberger RPS started a two year research project which intends to visualise the impact of process improvement activities on reliability characteristics of products. Also a new project will be introduced that is going to measure the effectiveness of inspection techniques in the different phases of the development process. A major part of that project will be a measurement program, to visualise the performance of the inspections, and to create the possibility for drawing empirical relations.

Planned Dissemination Events

Because Schlumberger RPS believes that the results achieved in the CEMP project by introducing goal-oriented software measurement with GQM, are also valuable for the rest of the organisation, those results will be distributed by internal presentations and reports, and (probably) by the Schlumberger WWW-site. A 3-day quality courses for all Schlumberger RPS software engineers will take place in 1996. Issues about improvement, measurement and GQM will be an important part of this course and the CEMP results will be used as examples.

6.2.7.3   CEMP Documentation and Contact Point

The Final Report is supplemented by the following documents:

*   "A Process Model for GQM-Based Measurement" [Gresse95]
    Detailed description of the complete GQM process including guidelines and
    definitions of all required products. A brief summary is given in Appendix D:
    "GQM Process Description and Guidelines".
*   "Cost of Introducing GQM-Based Measurement" [CEMP95b]
    Expansion of "6.2.6.2 Business".
*   "Benefits of Introducing GQM-Based Measurement" [CEMP95c]
    Expansion of "6.2.6.2 Business".

The following papers have been written in the context of the CEMP project and
published/submitted to various journals and conferences:

*   "Kosten-Nutzen-Analyse von GQM-basiertem Messen und Bewerten: Eine
    replizierte Fallstudie"
*   "No Improvement without Feedback: Experiences from goal-oriented meas-
    urement at Schlumberger" [Latum a]
*   "Shifting towards goal-oriented measurement: Experience of Schlumberger"
    [Latum b]

Detailed information on the CEMP project at the Schlumberger site can be found
in:

*   "Application of software measurement at Schlumberger RPS: Towards enhanc-
    ing GQM" [Solingen95a]
*   "Goal-oriented software measurement in practice: Introducing software meas-
    urement in Schlumberger Retail Petroleum Systems" [Solingen95b]

The dissemination actions of CEFRIEL include:

*   an external seminar to illustrate the results of the Digital experience
*   a brief paper submitted to a national IT magazine [Grigoletti96]
*   a scientific paper to be submitted to a major international journal [Fugetta]

Intermediate results from the period January 1994 – September 1994 of the
CEMP project are described in the Midterm Report [CEMP95a].

An important dissemination activity from the point of view of CEMP project
was its presentation at the CQS 1994 conference in Rome. The objectives and
preliminary results of CEMP were also presented at the second ISERN meeting in
Kaiserslautern by UKL/STTI-KL. Among the participants were representatives of
organisations as Daimler-Benz AG, Q-Labs Software Engineering GmbH, AT&T
Bell Laboratories, and European Software Institute Bilbao.

Furthermore, the partners disseminated first CEMP experience within their
companies resulting contributed to the very successful 3. STTI-Workshop (September 95 in Kaiserslautern), where a large number of German and European
companies has taken part.

Information on the CEMP project is also provided on the World Wide Web (WWW), including an overview on the CEMP project and a short introduction to the Goal/Question/Metric approach.

The performance, results and analysis of the measurement programs at the experimental sites are documented in detail for each of the industrial partner. Generalised results regarding cost and benefits of the introduction of GQM-based measurement are stated, as well as a complete description of the GQM process including guidelines and heuristics based on the experiences gained in the CEMP project. Further organisational information is also noticed here.

For Further Information on the CEMP Project, Please Contact:
Robert Bosch GmbH: Dr. Helmut Woda
Robert Bosch GmbH, FV/SLD
PO 10 60 50
70049 Stuttgart/Germany
e-mail: fvsld_wo@siiks_a1.bosch.de
Digital SPA Italy: Paolo Rivera
Viale Fulvio Testi, 280/6
20126 Milano/Italy
e-mail: rivera@varese.enet.dec.com
Schlumberger RPS: Erik Rodenbach
Industrieweg 5
5531 AD Bladel/The Netherlands
e-mail: rodenbach@bladel.rps.slb.com
CEFRIEL: Luigi Lavazza
Via Emanueli 15
20126 Milano/Italy
e-mail: lavazza@mailer.cefriel.it
http://www.cefriel.it/
UKL/STTI-KL: Prof. Dr. Dieter Rombach
University of Kaiserslautern
67653 Kaiserslautern/Germany
e-mail: rombach@informatik.uni-kl.de

6.2.8   Glossary

Abstraction sheet: summarises the main issues and dependencies of a GQM plan and represents this information on four quadrants of a sheet. The contents of the four quadrants is quality focus, baseline hypothesis, variation factors and their impact on the baseline hypotheses. The information of an abstraction sheet is applied for deriving GQM plans from interview results and for analysing measurement data within feedback sessions. For more detailed information see [Gresse95].

Experience factory: an organisation that supports project development by analysing and synthesising all kinds of experiences, acting as a repository for such experiences, and supplying that experience to various projects on demand. It packages experience by building informal, formal or schematised, and productised models and measures of various software processes, products and other forms of knowledge via people, documents, and automated support [Bas92]. See also [Basili94a].

Error: The difference between a computed, observed, or measured value or condition and the true, specified, or theoretically correct value or condition. For example, a difference of 30 meters between a computed result and the correct result.

A human action (a mistake), its manifestation (a fault), the result of the fault (a failure), and the amount by which the result is incorrect (the error) [IEEE91].

Experiment: a trial that is conducted in order to verify a hypothesis defined beforehand in a controlled setting in which the most critical factors can be controlled or monitored [Gresse95].

Failure: An incorrect result. For example, a computed result of 12 when the correct result is 10 [IEEE91].

Fault: An incorrect step, process, or data definition. For example, an incorrect instruction in a computer program [IEEE91].

Feedback session: meeting with the members of the pilot project team during which the collected data are presented in an easy to understand way. The measured data is compared to the initial assumptions (hypotheses) of the project team members and conclusions are drawn. For more detailed information see [Gresse95].

GQM plan: The GQM approach supports the operational definition of all kinds of measurement due to their top-down refinement into metrics via questions in a GQM plan. A GQM plan contains:

- a goal defining the object, purpose, quality focus, subject and the context w. r. t. the measurement program
- a set of questions refining the goal to characterise the object w. r. t. the selected quality issues from the selected viewpoint
- a set of metrics associated with the questions in order to answer them in a quantitative way For a more detailed description see [Basili94b].

GQM team/experts: persons who are responsible for the development and execution of the measurement program. It is a separate team, located in for example the quality assurance department, supporting the project team. The major task during the execution of the measurement program is the preparation and facilitation of the feedback sessions.

Hypothesis: A tentative explanation that accounts for a set of facts and can be tested by further investigation; a theory [Gresse95].

Measurement plan: states a concise specification of the data collection process in conformance with the project plan. For more detailed information see "Description of GQM process".

Mistake: A human action that produces an incorrect result. For example, an incorrect action on the part of a programmer or operator [IEEE91].

Model: A model is a simplified representation of a system or phenomenon with any hypotheses required to describe the system or explain the phenomenon, often mathematically [Gresse95].

Novice-user-test: Test method which uses inexperienced people to try and use the system and denote every deviation from the expected behaviour.

Project manager: is responsible for the budget of a single project.

Project personnel/team: are responsible for the development of a software product.

Project plan: describes the technical and management approach to be followed for a project. the plan typically describes the work to be done, the resources required, the methods to be used, the procedures to be followed, the schedules to be met, and the way that the project will be organised [IEEE91].

QIP: The Quality Improvement Paradigm (QIP) is an iterative, goal-driven framework for continuous improvement of software development. The QIP is a closed-loop process which includes steps for planning, executing, and evaluating improvements to software development environments, as well as for incorporating experience gained from improvement efforts into future development.

Quality assurance manager: is responsible for all activities ensuring the quality of the final product; she/he is responsible for ensuring that prescribed procedures and the defined process model are employed and that internal standards are followed.

Software: is the collection of computer programs, procedures, rules, and associated documentation and data [IEEE91].

Software measurement: the assignment of specified numeric values to software development activities, and/or products, in order to identify empirical relations.

6.2.9   References

[Basili92]
Victor R. Basili. *Software modelling and measurement: The Goal/Question/Metric paradigm*, Technical Report CS-TR-2956, Department of Computer Science, University of Maryland, College Park, MD 20742, September 1992.

[Basili94a]
Victor R. Basili, Gianluigi Caldiera, and H. Dieter Rombach. *Experience Factory*, Encyclopaedia of Software Engineering, volume 1, pages 469-476. John Wiley & Sons, 1994.

[Basili94b]
Victor R. Basili, Gianluigi Caldiera, and H. Dieter Rombach. *Goal Question Metric Paradigm*, Encyclopaedia of Software Engineering, volume 1, pages 528-532. John Wiley & Sons, 1994.

[Basili94c]
Victor R. Basili, Gianluigi Caldiera, and H. Dieter Rombach. *Measurement*, Encyclopaedia of Software Engineering, volume 1, pages 646- 661. John Wiley & Sons, 1994.

[Basili86]
Victor R. Basili, Richard W. Selby, and David H. Hutchens. *Experimentation in software engineering*, IEEE Transactions on Software Engineering, SE-12(7):733- 743, July 1986.

[Basili84]
Victor R. Basili and David M. Weiss. *A methodology for collecting valid software engineering data*. IEEE Transactions on Software Engineering, SE-10(6):728-738, November 1984.

[CEMP95a]
The CEMP Consortium. *Customised establishment of measurement programs*. Midterm Report, ESSI Project Nr. 10358, Germany,1995.

[CEMP95b]
The CEMP Consortium. *Cost of Introducing GQM-Based Measurement*. ESSI Project Nr. 10358, Germany,1995.

[CEMP95c]
The CEMP Consortium. *Benefits of Introducing GQM-Based Measurement*. ESSI Project Nr. 10358, Germany,1995.

[Fuggetta]
Alfonso Fuggetta, Luigi Lavazza, Sandro Morasca, Stefano Cinti, Giandomenico Oldano and Elena Orazi. Applying GQM in an industrial software factory. (submitted to the IEEE Transactions on Software Engineering).

[Grigoletti96]
Marco Grigoletti and Cristiano Gusmeroli. Software metrics, il paradigma GQM (in Italian). Informatica Oggi, January 1996.

[Gresse95]
Christiane Gresse, Barbara Hoisl and Jürgen Wüst. A Process Model for GQM-Based Measurement. Technical Report STTI-95-04-E, Software Technology Transfer Initiative, University of Kaiserslautern, Department of Computer Science, D-67653 Kaiserslautern, Germany, October 1995.

[ISERN95]
The ISERN Group. International Software Engineering Research Network, Annual Meeting October 1995. University of Maryland, 1995.

[Hoisl94]
Barbara Hoisl. A process model for planning GQM-based measurement. Technical Report STTI-94-06-E, Software Technology Transfer Initiative,

University of Kaiserslautern, Department of Computer Science, D-67653 Kaiserslautern, Germany, April 1994.

[Gresse96]
Christiane Gresse, Barbara Hoisl, H. Dieter Rombach and Günther Ruhe. Kosten-Nutzen- Analyse von GQM-basiertem Messen und Bewerten: Eine replizierte Fallstudie (in German), Conference on Empirical Research in Business Informatics, Linz, March 1996.

[IEEE91]
IEEE Standard Glossary of Software Engineering Terminology (Std 610.12-1990). Institute of Electrical and Electronics Engineers, Inc.USA,1991

[Latum a]
Frank van Latum, Markku Oivo, Barbara Hoisl and Günther Ruhe. No Improvement without Feedback: Experiences from goal-oriented measurement at Schlumberger. (to be submitted).

[Latum b]
Frank van Latum, Markku Oivo, Barbara Hoisl, Dieter Rombach and Günther Ruhe. Shifting towards goal-oriented measurement: Experience of Schlumberger (in preparation).

[NASA94]
National Aeronautics and Space Administration. Software measurement guidebook. Technical Report SEL-84-101, NASA Goddard Space Flight Centre, Greenbelt MD 20771, July 1994.

[Rombach91]
H. D. Rombach. Practical Benefits of Goal-Oriented Measurement. Software Reliability and Metrics, Elsevier Applied Science, 1991.

[Solingen95a]
R. van Solingen, F. van Latum, M. Oivo, E. Berghout. Application of software measurement at Schlumberger RPS: Towards enhancing GQM. Proceedings of the sixth European Software Cost Modelling Conference (ESCOM), May 1995.

[Solingen95b]
R. van Solingen. Goal-oriented software measurement in practice: Introducing software measurement in Schlumberger Retail Petroleum Systems. Master Thesis Report, Schlumberger, 1995.

6.3   Project 21323 – METPRO
Company Metrics Programme Introduction: A quantitative approach to Software Process understanding and improvement.

R. Barbati
Dataspazio S.p.A., Rome

6.3.1   Executive Summary

The objective of the experiment has consisted in understanding the software engineering practice (and then software quality and productivity) by measurement of the product and process. The goal was to start a company metrics programme in order to drive a software process understanding and improvement. The main goals of the metrics program were:

- to provide the quantitative information essential to identify opportunities for improvement;
- to verify the advantages of the implemented changes to the development process.
- The experiment has consisted on understanding and quantifying the shortcomings relevant to the following areas:
- software problem analysis and defects prevention capability;
- productivity and schedule estimation capability.

The experience gained with the execution of the experiment is fully transferable to all the companies developing software which decide to better understand and improve their development process.

The primary area/community of interest to which the experiment corresponds is:

- Industrial sector: Information Technology (any system and software supply company)
- Community of interest – System point of view: Technically oriented systems
- Community of interest – Technology point of view: any software application using high level languages, software product technology and an established process method.

The work done regards the definition of the metric program plan, described in the Annex A, the data gathering for the baseline projects, their re-engineering in electronic sheets designed by us and data validation respect to the established metrics. The results are complete for all the baseline projects and they are reported in the Annex B to the full final report.

The potential for replicating the results of the experiment is due to the fact that the proposed method and metrics framework present the following advantages:

- they are life cycle independent, so their use is not affected by various development methodologies which could be utilized;
- they are simple to understand and easy to apply.

6.3.2 Background Information

6.3.2.1 Objectives

Improving software product quality, product performance and development team productivity has become a primary priority for almost every organisation that relies on computers. This experiment describes a simple approach to improving software quality and productivity by measurement of the product and process.

To improve our software capabilities, we had to take at least the following steps:

- Understand the current status of the development process
- Develop a vision of the desired process
- Establish a list of required process improvement actions in order of priority
- Produce a plan to accomplish the required actions

The achievement of the objective above has required the following key actions for improving our products and development process :

- to establish a minimum basic set of process measurements to identify the quality and cost parameters of each process step (Process measurement);
- to establish a process database with the resources to manage and maintain it (Process database);
- to provide sufficient process resources to analyse these data and advice project members on the data's meaning and use (Process analysis);
- to assess the relative quality of each product and inform management where quality targets are not being met (Product quality).

6.3.2.2 Involved Companies and Their Roles

No other company was involved in the project, except Dataspazio and those involved during the external dissemination of the experiment results.

6.3.2.3 Starting Scenario

Since 1994 Dataspazio has established its own standard development process, based on the ESA Software Engineering Standards PSS-05-0, Issue 2. This process is documented in company procedures and Quality Manual and is widely understood and used within the organisation.

Deviations have to be documented and approved by an independent SQA function, who conducts reviews and audits at each phase of the software life-cycle and is an active agent in process implementation and in the evaluation of its effectiveness.

The Dataspazio software process maturity has been evaluated by two independent assessments based on the SEI methodology:

- the first one has been carried out in January 1994 by Metasistemi, an independent auditor, within the SIMTEST Application Experiment of the ESSI pilot phase; the Dataspazio process has been placed at a maturity level between 2 and 3 (repeatable/defined process);
- the second one has been carried out in February 1995 by the Software Engineering Process Group of the Motorola Satellite Communication Division, a qualified software supplier evaluation group; as result of this evaluation, Dataspazio has been qualified as software supplier, because its software process has been considered at the defined maturity level. The major opportunity of improvement identified during this assessment consisted in "developing a comprehensive metrics programme to drive process improvement". The detailed suggestions have been:
  - "create a project history database";
  - "define, collect and analyse metrics, including estimation accuracy";
  - "use existing data and translate into usable management information". The auditors have acknowledged that Dataspazio "has already collected useful data in the past (e.g. software problems reports) which provide excellent management information now and it is a good start to establish a project history database";
  - "communicate metrics to all, where appropriate, to promote self-improvement";
  - "use metrics to drive process improvement by defining where the problem areas are".

Motorola suggestions are fully compliant with the key steps identified in the literature, shown in the following table, required to improve a process at maturity level 3 (defined process):

Table 6.1 Improvement Steps vs. Current Situation

Improvement Step	Current Dataspazio Status
Establish a minimum set of process measurement to identify the quality and cost parameters of the process. The objective is to quantify the costs and benefits of each major project activity such as the cost and yield of error detection and correction methods.	The process is not measured in a quantitative way. Techniques of quantitative management are not used.

Improvement Step	Current Dataspazio Status
Establish a process database and the resources to manage and maintain it. Cost and yield data should be maintained centrally to guard against loss, to make it available for all projects and to help process quality and productivity analysis.	There is not a standard format for the project history database.
Provide enough process resources to gather and maintain this process data and to advise project members on its use. Assign skilled professionals to monitor the quality of the data before entry in the database and to provide guidance on analysis methods and interpretation.	There are not resources assigned to these tasks.

At the experiment beginning the company did not have any practice about metrics. Nevertheless all the project data were gathered, but they were not organised to execute an analysis. In this way, every time a new proposal was drafted for a new project, we could not apply objective valuation parameters derived from past measurements but personal and qualitative impressions deducted from feelings and subjective evaluations; besides at the end of a new project we could not know if we were better than the previous ones or not.

The organisational environment of the staff dedicated to the experiment comes from the Quality Department; nevertheless the staff skill is not only quality-specific, because its past cultural background is of technical type. This condition allows the staff to manage independently all the tools necessary for the experiment (Microsoft tools, programming with specific software language to develop the automatic data gathering program, etc).

The Quality Department is responsible for the Quality Assurance of the company. The Quality Department does not depend hierarchically from the Technical Direction to guarantee an independent quality work. The Quality Department is made up of Program Quality Engineers (PQEs) that perform the quality assurance and control activities for all projects. Their work is validated by the Quality Assurance Manager (QAM); in this way the control activity homogeneity at the company level is guaranteed.

6.3.2.4   Workplan

The experiment consisted of the following steps:
- Initial survey, research, and assessment
- Metrics programme plan
- Data gathering/ Existing data re-engineering
- Data collection/validation
- Data processing

- Data analysis/Metrics validation
- Dissemination of results
- Reporting

During the experiment Dataspazio provided the Metric Programme Plan, periodic reports, a mid-term and a final report, documentation about the data-set; internal meetings were made to disseminate the experiment results and to give suggestions to the management for the next projects.

6.3.2.5 Expected Outcomes

The experiment consisted in approaching the improvement of the software engineering practice (and then software quality and productivity) by measurement of the product and process. The underlying principles are :

- You can improve only what you can measure
- You need to measure if you want to manage

The adopted metrication approach is the AMI method (Assess, Analyse, Metricate, Improve). Starting from a defined and assessed software development process, with known strengths and weaknesses, those areas with the following characteristics have been picked out:

- improvement is most needed, both internally and by the customers;
- opportunity for improvement has been clearly identified by the previous independent assessments;
- data have already been collected for past work (of the baseline projects).

With these assumptions and criteria, the established metrics programme has to drive improvement in the software problems analysis, in the defects prevention and in the schedule estimation capability.

6.3.3 Work Performed

After a first activity to research data and information about the baseline projects, the experiment work was to define a standard collection of metrics that can be used to report productivity, quality, and profitability to the various levels of management. These metrics have been applied on a set of baseline projects.

Given the nature of the experiment, more than one baseline project have been selected, as shown in the following table. The baseline projects were representative and they have involved the 70% of the technical department of the company for six years. They belong to the Ground Segment for a non geostationary-low orbit satellite for x-ray astronomy. All the baseline projects are now in operational phase.

Table 6.2 Baseline Projects

Acronym	Description
SCS	Spacecraft Control System, conceived to support the mission during the pre-operational and operational phases
SIM	Real time simulator of the satellite for training and operation procedure testing
SDC	Repository of the scientific data acquired during the mission, providing also an environment for their analysis

The following categories of metrics were taken into account:

- size
- product quality
- process quality.

As suggested by the literature, the following global and simple metrics were defined:

Table 6.3 Metrics defined

Metric	Category	Note
Lines of code	Size	A unique definition of LOC has been applied to all the baseline projects
Software problems, Defect Ratio	Product quality	S/W problems have been analysed on the basis of: - severity - test curving movement and problem solution effectiveness - where, when, how, who found - where, when, how caused - where, when, how fixed
Effort	Process quality	Effort to develop the project and to solve the problems
Productivity Effectiveness during the life cycle Mean Time To Repair defects Process quality	Productivity has been classified on the basis of the source code characteristics ("C" source code, code generated by tool Motif Standard etc.)	

The measurement framework was defined and a standard collection of work-product, work-effort, productivity and quality metrics were prepared.

The metric format used includes:

- *Name*: the meaningful name of the metric
- *Purpose*: a summary of the use for that metric
- *Metric Formula*: the formula used to calculate the metric
- *Definitions*: any terminology specific to that metric
- *Source of Information*: the original source for information needed to calculate this metric
- *Frequency of Reporting*: the recommended frequency of use for this metric in reporting to the various levels of management
- *Audience Level*: the recommended levels of management for which it is useful to report this metric

The proposed Metrics Program Plan was distributed and explained to the program managers and the project leaders of the baseline projects, which were requested to provide the initial and final baseline projects planning, personnel time reports, overtime personnel allocation, source code, software problem reports and support.

At this point the data gathering/existing data re-engineering phase started.

The considered metrics were:

- Lines-Of-Codes (work-product metric),
- Work-Effort (work effort metric),
- Development Delivery Trends, (productivity metric),
- Application Support Rate (productivity metric),
- Defect Ratio (quality metric),
- Mean Time To Repair Ratio (MTRR) (quality metric),
- Phase Containment Effectiveness (PCE) (quality metric).

The objectives of these metrics were:

- to measure the baseline projects by the size-type metrics (Lines-Of-Codes, Work-Effort);
- to quantify the provided product quality by the raised problems analysis (Phase Containment Effectiveness, Defect Ratio, defect duration, effort to solve them, severity percentage);
- to measure the process quality by the analysis of the schedule, the effort and the productivity (Development Delivery Trends, Application Support Rate, Mean Time To Repair Ratio).

The proposed Metrics Program Plan was distributed and explained to the program-managers and the project leaders of the baseline projects, which were requested to provide the initial and final baseline projects planning, personnel time reports, overtime personnel allocation, source code, software problem reports and support.

The data collection/validation phase started.

An Excel work-set was designed to analyse data and to extract some technical evaluations. The work-set includes two input worksheets (*Activities* and *Software Problem Reports*) that contain in particular work product and work effort data related to the developed product and the found defects, and several output worksheets: *Development Delivery Trends Table* (that shows the results about the homonymous productivity metric), *Project Summary* (that shows besides the results about the Mean Time To Repair Ratio and the Defect Ratio metrics), *PCE Table* (that shows the results about the Phase Containment Effectiveness), *Line and Pie charts* about defect duration, effort to solve them and severity percentage.

Besides a code processor has been implemented to count the number of code and comment lines inside a text (C code, Fortran code, VAX assembler code, DCL command code, SQL code, Abstract Notation code, UIL code, Motif resource code). In this way we were able to evaluate the Lines-Of-Code metric for the baseline projects.

Then data about the defects and the activities of the baseline projects has been collected and processed; in particular we have measured the productivity of the single software tasks (detail design, code and unit test) by means of counting of the Lines-Of-Code and the effort data (deducted from the planning provided by the project managers), and the defect distribution along the project life by their duration, effort to solve them and severity.

By the analysis of these evaluations we were able to validate the considered metrics basing on the obtained results and on the evaluation between their cost/benefits ratio to apply them in the future.

Now the managers can use the metrics results as reference for the planning of their projects and the project leaders can identify those development process aspects or phases that need investments to improve the whole product.

6.3.3.1 Organisation

The experiment was:

- led by the Quality Assurance Manager and the Program Quality Engineer, so that a deep knowledge of the projects and the consistency with any other initiative on quality improvement were assured;
- supported by the senior management, because it aimed to have an impact on the entire organisation (Program Managers, Project Leaders, Team Leaders).

In accordance with the activities planned for dissemination purposes, the project results were communicated throughout the organisation by internal meetings. Its objective was to disseminate the technical results to the program managers and project leaders to obtain the improving of the quality culture (the metrication technique shall be widespread and understood in the company at all levels) and more investment in the weak aspects of the development process.

The responses of the internal dissemination have been positive: the whole technical and managerial staff involved in the baseline projects has demonstrated a large interest about the experiment and was available to provide every data and information relating to it. Besides it is going on a distribution of a final document that contains the technical results and suggestions.

6.3.3.2   Technical Environment

The technical equipment used for the experiment consists in a set of software office tools for all the publishing needs (Microsoft Word 7.0, Microsoft Power Point 7.0), an electronic sheets manager (Microsoft Excel 7.0) by which it was possible to define a database for the software problems, the electronic sheets related to the metrics defined in the Metrics Programme Plan, the graphs and the histograms derived by the results sheets. In addition to this equipment, used on a PC with Windows NT, we used a workstation Digital with operating system VMS, required to extract all the information directly from the source files of the baseline projects. For this reason a tool for the automatic counting of code was designed in DCL.

6.3.3.3   Training

Only a two days training course on "Software Best Practices and Scheduling and Management metrics" was undertaken at the beginning of the experiment.

6.3.3.4   Role of the Consultants

No consultant was involved in the experiment.

6.3.3.5   Phases of the Experiment

In the following the main phases of the project workplan and the associated key deliverables are described:

1. Initial Survey, Research and Assessment

The purpose of this activity was to perform surveys of the data collected by the teams of the three baseline projects up to that date. Meetings and interviews with the technical people and the project management were necessary to gather the information needed to prepare the detailed metrics programme plan.

Output: Meetings and interview reports and assessment results.

2. Metrics Programme Plan

The purpose of this activity was to identify the objectives for the metrics programme and to define the measurement framework. The quality assurance personnel prepared the plan on the basis of the output of task 1. The plan was agreed with the Technical Manager.

Output: Metrics Programme Plan.

3. Data Gathering/Existing Data re-Engineering

The aim of this activity was to obtain the data, identified in the metrics programme plan, needed to calculate measurements. We have re-engineered and properly completed data already collected for past work of the projects. For this step, a program for automatic data gathering was designed.

Output: Re-engineered data set (e.g. software problem reports, Gantt charts) and design document of the Automatic Data Gathering program.

4. Data Collection/Validation

The purpose of this activity was to validate the gathered raw data, verifying the correctness, and to collect them in a spreadsheet (Microsoft Excel).

Output: Validated data set

5. Data Processing

The aim of this activity was to process the validated raw data to obtain the metrics defined in the plan.

Output: Report of the metrics defined in the plan (quantitative results in terms of measurements, graphs, tables and histograms).

6. Data Analysis/Metrics Validation

The aim of this activity was to analyse the measurement data. The selected metrics have been validated by analysing the results. This has been the real key point of the experiment: from the results analysis we have understood that most of the selected metrics were correctly chosen and that Dataspazio will use the same metrics in the new projects, to conduct its continuous process improvement.

Output: Report of the results analysis and the metrics validation, with the suggestions to the management for the next projects and final considerations on the experiment. language; this tool works on all types of source files used in the baseline projects.

7. Dissemination of Results

For dissemination purposes, Dataspazio produced two technical papers on the experience gained to be submitted to relevant international magazines for publication. The task included the presentation of the experiment results to two dissemination events that Dataspazio, with the Commission approval, has considered as appropriate (CQS'97 in Rome and AquIS'98 in Venice).

Output: a Final Report has been issued to summarise the work performed and the results obtained.

8. Reporting

This activity covered the preparation of the contractually agreed documentation such as three Periodic Progress Reports (every 6 months), a Mid-term Report and a Final Report detailing all the work carried out and the results obtained under the contract.

6.3.3.6   Internal Dissemination

The internal dissemination mechanism has been based on the following initiatives:

- a seminar to present the metrics programme plan to all the technical staff (also to technical people not involved in the experiment);
- meetings with the technical staff involved in the experiment to report the progress of the data analysis and preliminary results;
- a final seminar to present the result of the experiment to all the technical staff;
- a questionnaire to collect impressions on the experiment and suggestions for further process improvement initiatives.

The current responses of the internal dissemination have been positive: the whole technical and managerial staff involved in the baseline projects has demonstrated a large interest about the experiment.

6.3.4   Results and Analysis

This section details the actual results of the experiment and our analysis from different perspectives and includes qualitative and quantitative results and how they were measured.

6.3.4.1   Technical

The adopted metrication approach was the AMI method (Assess, Analyse, Metricate, Improve) and the assessment was the key step:

- to understand the status of the company's current software practice and to show strengths and weaknesses
- to identify key areas for process and product improvement
- to facilitate the initiation of improvement actions by defining a metrics program plan.

Actually we have processed and analysed data about all the baseline projects. The obtained results are shown in the Annex B to the full final report. By the data analysis we can do the following comments:

- the total productivity of all projects is rather high for these type of projects: in part this is caused by the re-using of some software, inherited by a previous project;
- the comparison between the Project Phases Effort percentage of the three baseline projects shows that these values are very similar: it means that, following the same company standard process and software life-cycle, different products have similar project phases effort percentage;
- the mean time to close a software problem is rather high (due to some justifiable values extremely high); without those anomalous cases the distribution of the problem duration decrease drastically;
- analogous considerations can be explained for the mean time to solve a software problem;
- the short distance between the curve representing the open software problems and the curve related the close software problems during the project points out the tendency to carry on a system without bugs along the whole life cycle of the project.

6.3.4.2   Business

The experiment, led by the quality assurance personnel, involved program managers, project leaders and team leaders and it should have high relevance to the business of the participants because will increase customer confidence through seeing that Dataspazio faces up problems and acts to improve quality.

Particularly from this experiment we have obtained some reference values useful for the next projects. For new projects we are able, now, to establish some quality objectives such as:

- decrease the software problems number respected to the reference value, paying attention to those project phases that had a low PCE value for the experimented projects;
- increase the productivity aiming to re-use as much as possible the existent software and automatic tools for code generation;

Anyway the obtained results represent the visiting card of the company for the future customers.

6.3.4.3   Organisation

Besides the technical results analysis, it was evident that some changes in the technical organisation needed to be done.

Since we had some problems to compare data related to the same activities, starting from the Gantt diagrams, because each project manager used different and personal name activities for a specific project phase, the Quality Assurance department decided to create, supported by the technical director, a unique work breakdown structure, at macro activity level, for all the future projects that have to follow the company standard software lifecycle: each project manager can use specific and different names only at micro activity level.

To avoid any manual check on this procedure, an automatic tool can be designed for the Personnel Time Report forms. Furthermore this automatic tool can be integrated with the tools used for the project management, to obtain a more rigorous project data gathering.

When we tried to determine the metrics about the software problems, we realised that some necessary information were missing. Therefore we were constrained to ask for these information to the involved people afterwards. The information were dealing with:

- the effort to solve the problem (analysis, realisation, its testing and its configuration control),
- the involved subsystem,
- the project phase in which the problem arose,
- the phase in which the problem was solved (necessary data for the PCE metric).

After these considerations, we decided to update the form related to the SPR, in order to take all these information into account.

6.3.4.4   Culture

While we were carrying on the experiment, we noticed a large interest about it and about its results. This is contributing to feed a metric culture to quantify the provided product quality and the followed process quality. We consider a positive effect the particular interest shown by the project managers; this is a signal of a tendency to adopt rigorous measurement methods being applied in the further projects.

6.3.4.5   Skills

People working on this experiment are from the company's Quality Department; anyway they had technical experiences from previous works.

The analysis of the data and the assessment of the product and process quality have allowed the experiment participants to analyse their past technical work in a completely different aspect.

This allows the addition of new objectives to the project standard goals: to delivery the product within the foreseen schedule, in the respect of the foreseen costs, with a satisfactory quality level. This implies a quality assessment higher than the one assessed in the baseline projects.

6.3.5   Key Lessons

The key lessons of this experiment involve two different points of view: the technical one and the business one. From the technical point of view the lessons regard the way to organise the information, while from the business point of view they are indications about the benefits that we can obtain adopting a measurement practice in the company.

6.3.5.1   Technological Point of View

The key lessons from the technological point of view are the following:

* change the way to yield data to make them more useful and complete. In particular the definition of a new form to describe and collect the project activities will help us to check the time spent for each project phase; the updating of the SPR form to include all the missing information about a software problem required for the evaluations, will help us to locate the most critical project phase;s automatic tool can be integrated with the tools used for the project management, to obtain a more rigorous project data gathering.
* organise the project information during its development to perform the measurements while the project is on going: this will allow to control it run-time, to avoid loss of time in researching and organising project information after its conclusion and to wide a process history database to use in the future;
* minimise the time over-head necessary to the data gathering during the project; to this aim it is convenient to use automatic and distributed tools and simplify as much as possible the procedure to follow.

6.3.5.2   Business Point of View

From the business point of view the key lessons are indications about the short term benefits that we are obtaining adopting a measurement practice in the company:

* better estimating and project planning;
* improved management understanding;
* identification of those aspects of the development process where investment in improvements will give the best return;
* increased customer confidence through seeing that Dataspazio faces up problems and takes action to improve quality;
* improved quality culture (the metrication technique has been widespread and understood in the company at all levels).

The following medium/long term benefits are foreseen as the metrics programme continues:

* higher productivity and hence lower costs;

- early identification of problems, and so more time to correct them, reducing the impact of the overall time table;
- more effective control of product and process quality;
- steady and continued improvement;
- the availability of the trend indicators and measures during the life of a running project will improve the communication between the business managers and the technical managers, allowing better and shared visibility of the project and reducing incomprehension and delays in performing corrective actions.

6.3.5.3   Strengths and Weaknesses of the Experiment

The experiment has the following *strengths*:

- all the baseline projects are significant for the company because they involved most of the personnel for a long time;
- all the experiment results can be used as reference value for the next projects;
- all the metrics are applicable in the future because they are life cycle independent, so their use is not affected by different development methodologies which could be used;
- all the considered metrics are simple to understand and easy to apply.

Weaknesses of the experiment could be that:

- quality culture requires the highest level of senior management support in a structural and systematic way;
- the practice about metrics is not mandatory but it is left as a PM's personal decision and it could not be applied in further projects;
- the real assessment of the initial condition of the projects and the dissemination of their results are difficult but necessary steps to increment the process improvement.

6.3.6   Conclusions and Future Actions

The experiment has pointed out some problems during its execution: these problems were time-consuming and also caused the experiment delay. The future obstacle to apply continuously the improving steps pointed out by the experiment is to face this extra-cost.

For this experiment the European Community supported the whole project; but in the future, it will need to cut it, overcoming those problems and adopting the corrective suggested actions. This is one of the most ambitious aim of the experiment.

The following future actions are foreseen as the metrics programme continues:

- a training phase to incoming personnel about quality concepts and current quality level and objectives represents a good practice toward a mature company quality policy; in fact the consciousness of producing quality software is necessary to develop quality software.
- new projects will start with defined metrics and objectives since the beginning, so feedback and improvement will be possible inside the project life-cycle;
- increase the quality culture making everyone aware of the importance and convenience of the metrics approach; in this way this will be a systematic practice in the company;
- insert metric practice among the guidelines and recommendations in the company procedures standards;
- invest more time to perform internal project reviews: this will guarantee that the defined quality guidelines about the collection and the organisation of the project data are followed (for example by suitable check-lists).

6.3.7   Glossary

AMI	Assess, analyse, Metricate, Improve
DCL	Digital Command Language
ESA	European Space Agency
ESSI	European Software and System Initiative
LOC	Lines Of Codes
MTRR	Mean Time To Repair Ratio
PCE	Phase Containment Effectiveness
PM	Program Manager
PSS	Procedures Specifications and Standards
SEI	Software Engineering Institute
SQA	Software Quality Assurance
S/W	Software
SPR	Software Problem Report
SQL	Standard Query Language
UIL	User Interface Language

6.3.8   References

[Beizer90]
    B. Beizer, *Software Testing Techniques*, USA, 1990
[Humphrey90]
    W.S. Humphrey, *Managing the Software Process*, USA, 1990
[Salvatore97]
    C. Salvatore, R. Barbati, *"Process Improvement through metrics and stan-*

dards", Proc. of CQS '97 Conference on Exploiting Excellence in European Information and Communication Industry, pp.177-179, Roma, Italy, April 7-10, 1997

[Barbati98]
R. Barbati, *4th International Conference on Achieving Quality in Software*, pp.301- 307, Venice, Italy, March 30 – April 2, 1998

6.3.9   Annex A: Metric description

6.3.9.1   *Work Product and Work Effort Metrics*

Lines of Code (LOC)
Purpose: to measure the SW size of projects and applications

Metric Formula:
- way of counting lines of code: Logical delimiter, such as semicolons
- kind of lines to count: New, changed, and reused lines
- type of product: High level language, assembly code, data definition, and screen presentation

Definitions: lines of code are the adjusted LOC as defined above

Source of Information: LOC are determined from existing applications

Frequency of Reporting:
- when a project is completed, reporting can assess productivity and quality
- on request for an existing application
- for analysis of historical projects

Audience Level: the lines of code count is used in many different ways and can be reported to all audience levels. Lines of code can be reported alone as "LOC" or combined with different factors and reported as part of a ratio.

Work-Effort

Purpose: to measure the work-effort expended in application development, as well as in maintenance activities

Metric Formula: an established and consistent time accounting procedure based on work-hours accepted in the enterprise

Definitions: work-effort reflects the hours spent on development of an application, or the maintenance of an existing application

Frequency of Reporting: work-effort is collected as the work is done. For projects, it is accumulated to totals based on project completion. For application support, it is accumulated to totals at the end of specified time-periods, such as quarterly or annually

Source of Information: work-effort is collected at the individual project or application level, according to the time-accounting procedures of the enterprise. Work-effort is usually divided in the following general categories: Project effort, Application effort, Special assignments, Administrative (such as vacation and sick time)

Audience Level: work-effort can be reported at all organisation levels.

6.3.9.2   Productivity Metrics
Development Delivery Trends

Purpose: to show the trend in development productivity for development and enhancement

Metric Formula: (LOCs) / (Work-Effort) computed and plotted for each selected project group and time period

Definitions: Lines of Code are the sum of the delivered LOCs for the selected project group and time period; Work-Effort is the sum of the work-hours for the selected project group and time period

Source of Information: Lines of Code and Work-Effort are obtained from each project involved

Frequency of Reporting: this ratio should be reported at least annually

Audience Level: this ratio can be reported at all audience levels.

6.3.9.3   Quality Metrics
Defect Ratio

Purpose: the Project Defect Ratio is used by the project manager to measure the quality of the new development and applications enhancements delivered to the user. The defect ratio may be calculated for all defects or any class of defects

Metric Formula: (Number of Defects) / (Project LOCs)

Definitions: Project Lines of Code are the delivered LOCs of the project; Number of Defects are the number of reported instances where the application does not meet specifications

Source of Information: Number of Defects are taken from the defect log maintained by the quality engineering. Project Lines of Code are counted when the project is implemented

Frequency of Reporting: calculate the Project Defect Ratio after project implementation

Audience Level: the Defect Ratio is used at the project level. The value of this ratio decreases at higher levels in the organisation.

Mean Time To Repair Ratio

Purpose: to measure the average elapsed time needed to repair defects. This ratio shows how quickly defects are repaired

Metric Formula: (Elapsed Time) / (Number of Problems)

Definitions: Elapsed Time is the total number of calendar days between problem notification and problem resolution for all problems resolved in the month; Number of Problems is a count of the number of problems reported in the month

Source of Information: Elapsed Time and Number of Problems come from a review of the problem log maintained by the quality engineering

Frequency of Reporting: the Mean Time To Repair Ratio should be reported monthly

Audience Level: this ratio is used at the program level but it is valid at all levels in the organisation.

Phase Containment Effectiveness

Purpose: to measure how effective the project team has been in finding and solving defects in their origin phase

Metric Formula: (Single Phase Long Problems) / (Phase Problems) * 100

Definitions: Single Phase Long Problems is the total defects found and solved in any single phase; Phase Problems is the total defects originating from that phase

Source of Information: Single Phase Long Problems and Phase Problems come from a review of the problem log maintained by the quality engineering

Frequency of Reporting: the PCE should be reported at least at each phase end

Audience Level: this evaluation is used at project level but it is valid at all levels in the organisation.

6.4   Project 21443 – MOOD
OO Estimation – an Investigation of the Predictive Object Points (POP) Sizing Metric in an Industrial Setting

T. R. Judge, A. Williams
Parallax Solutions Ltd, Coventry

6.4.1   Abstract

The Metrics in Object Oriented Developments (MOOD) project 21443 is focused on the introduction of metrics to aid Estimation on Object Oriented (OO) projects at Parallax. This is in line with meeting Parallax Solutions' requirement to improve its estimating processes and the requirements of a Process Improvement Experiment (PIE) as defined by the European Systems and Software Initiative (ESSI), under whose auspices the project is being run. For more information on this initiative see http://www.esi.es/ESSI/.

Improvement is to be achieved by:

- The sound application of project metrics to 4 baseline projects.
- Improvement of the whole metric gathering lifecycle.
- Development of metrics that aids the estimation process.

This will lead, at a minimum, to the business benefit of greater confidence in delivering OO developments on time to the satisfaction of the customer.

The project will initially involve a period of study, primarily to review information and material relating to estimation and metrics.

The PIE will then enter a cycle of metric development and constant process improvement. This process improvement will be applied on 4 selected OO projects within Parallax.

As part of the evaluation of suitable metrics, Parallax has investigated the state-of-the-art Predictive Object Point (POP) software sizing metric with a view to its complementing the use of the well established Function Point (FP) software sizing metric at Parallax. This paper presents the results of an industry application of the POP metric. Results for the FP metric are also presented for comparison.

6.4.2   Introduction

It is important to be able to accurately estimate the time-scale for a project in order to improve the quality of risk analysis and planning within a business and also to build a reputation for delivering products within budget and on time. This can only be to the advantage to the customer who can be made aware of potential risks at the earliest opportunity and thus achieve a level of certainty as to the impact of the project schedule on their business.

This is perhaps much more the case when applied to a software project, which is a relatively new discipline, still immature in many ways and not easily open to accurate prediction. Parallax has sought to address this with an evolving system of software development consisting of well-defined processes and practices and has consequently accumulated a large amount of experience and project data. It is through such experience that one phase of the project cycle in particular has been identified as key to the success of estimation: that of providing an estimate for development of the build phase, that is the phase in which the code is written. The other project phases, Testing etc., appear to be more or less proportionately related to the build phase of the project.

6.4.3   Object-Oriented Software Sizing Metrics

6.4.3.1   The Search for a Better Metric

Parallax currently employs many different estimation techniques across its different projects, including Consensus, Weighted Average (WAVE) and FPs. However, none of these techniques is directly applicable to software written to object-oriented standards. Therefore New MOOD has concerned itself with investigating a recent development in object-oriented estimation techniques as part of its Process Improvement Experiment (PIE). Thus by application of such techniques to past Parallax projects it has been possible to compare the results with those from the techniques that were actually used at the time.

The technique under scrutiny in this paper is the Predictive Object Point (POP) software sizing metric, due to Arlene F. Minkiewicz of PRICE Systems [Minkiewicz]. POPs are intended as an improvement over FPs, which were originally intended for use within procedural systems, by drawing on well-known metrics associated with an object-oriented system. Price Systems market an estimation tool, ForeSight, that implements the POP technique.

6.4.3.2   The POP Metric

It is widely held that an object-oriented metric must measure three aspects of a system: raw functionality, inter-object communication and amount of reuse through inheritance. These aspects can then be used to give rise to a single metric in order to indicate the amount of effort involved in the production of a software system.

The POP metric is proposed as such a metric. This utilises several other popular metrics; the most important of which is the Weighted Methods per Class (WMC):

- TLC – number of top level classes
- WMC – weighted methods per class

- DIT – average depth of inheritance tree
- NOC – number of children per base class

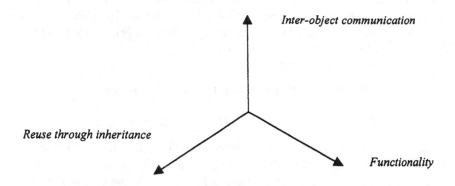

Fig. 6.6 Aspects of an Object-Oriented System

where a top level class is one which has no parents within the system and a base class is one which has at least one child within the system. The NOC and DIT provide a basis for the breadth and depth of the object-oriented system and also contributes to the reuse through inheritance dimension for the POP. In determining the WMC metric, the methods of a class can be conveniently categorised into five method types, according to Booch:

- Constructors – instantiation
- Destructors – destruction
- Modifiers – change state
- Selectors – access state
- Iterators – iterate parts

For the purposes of calculating the POP metric though, constructors and destructors are combined into a single type – the reason for this is that the project data analysed by Minkiewicz suggest that these two types are very similar in complexity. These metrics are then gathered to form the following equation, giving the number of POPs for a system (see Fig. 6.7), where f1 is a measure of the overall system size and f2 is a measure of reuse through inheritance.

$$f1(TLC, NOC, DIT) = TLC * (1 + ((1 + NOC) * DIT)^{1.01} + (| NOC - DIT |)^{.01})$$
$$f2(NOC, DIT) = 1.0$$

$$POPs(WMC, NOC, DIT, TLC) = \frac{WMC * f1(TLC, NOC, DIT)}{7.8} * f2(NOC, DIT)$$

Fig. 6.7 Equation: POP formula

6.4.4   Comparison of POPs and FPs

6.4.4.1   Overview

Both POPs and FPs rely on a corresponding metric for the Productivity Rate of the organisation for a given technology/programming language. The effort for a particular development can then be calculated by the formula below using either the FP count or the POP count:

Equation – Calculating Effort:

$$Effort = (Number\ of\ FPs) / (FP\ Productivity\ Rate)$$

$$Effort = (Number\ of\ POPs) / (POP\ Productivity\ Rate)$$

Actual effort can be obtained from historical project data, and the FP and POP counts can be calculated using their corresponding methodology. Therefore it is possible to determine the POP and FP productivity rates for an organisation for a given technology. The following sections describe the process for obtaining POP counts as applied to Parallax's historical project data and subsequently provide a criticism of the POP software sizing metric.

6.4.4.2   Method

Two projects were selected from Parallax's archives, project alpha and project beta. Both projects were written in Java. The following process was followed:

Step 1

The first step was to obtain the Source Lines of Code (SLOC) metric for both projects. This was achieved through the use of CCCC, an object oriented metric gathering tool. This is a free metric tool for C++ and Java (CCCC) developed by Tim Littlefair. The SLOC metric was used in the calculation of the FP metric by applying the "backfiring" technique.

Step 2

CCCC was once more used to obtain metrics necessary for the calculation of the POP metric for the two projects. Using the generated DIT metrics for each class it was possible to calculate the average DIT (one of the metrics required for POPs). Similarly the generated NOC metrics for each class were averaged to obtain the average NOC.

$$Average\ DIT = (Sum\ of\ Class\ DITs) / (Number\ of\ Classes)$$

$$Average\ NOC = (Sum\ of\ Base\ Class\ NOCs) / (Number\ of\ Base\ Classes)$$

Step 3

It was then necessary to determine for each project the number of methods of each method type for use in the WMC calculation. In order to achieve this, the average method count per class was found by dividing the class count (generated with CCCC) by the method count (generated with CCCC):

Average Methods per Class = (Number of Classes) / (Number of Methods)

The POP methodology suggests weightings that should be applied against this average in order to determine the average number of methods in each type, and so the following calculations were made:

Average Constructor/Destructor Method Count =
20% (Average Methods Per Class)

Average Selector Method Count = 30% (Average Methods Per Class)

Average Modifier Method Count = 45% (Average Methods per Class)

Average Iterator Method Count = 5% (Average Methods per Class)

This spread of method types can be seen as typical and arose from a manual investigation of source code by Minkiewicz. Bearing in mind that POPs are to be calculated at the object design stage of a project, the absence of coded methods necessitates the use of such estimated weightings. It needs to be stressed that the weightings discussed here are not the same as those giving the WMC metrics.

Step 4
The TLC metric for each project was then calculated and this was achieved through a combination of CCCC and a spreadsheet. The output of CCCC is a set of where each row represents the metrics for a particular class. The table containing the appropriate metrics (DIT etc.) imported into a spreadsheet, whereupon the rows were filtered so that only those showing a positive NOC count were included, i.e. the base classes. It was then trivial to find the average of this NOC column to arrive at a metric for the average number of children per base class.

Step 5
Next the FP metrics for each project were calculated using an estimation tool called KnowledgePlan. This software estimation tool took as its input the SLOC count and the language used (Java) and generated a pseudo FP count using a technique known as "backfiring".

Step 6
Before the POPs could be calculated, one final metric was required, the WMC. This was arrived at as follows.

First each method type was divided into three categories of complexity using weightings, which arose from a manual investigation of source code, by Minkiewicz.

Low Complexity Method Count = 22% Average Method Count

Average Complexity Method Count = 45% Average Method Count

High Complexity Method Count = 33% Average Method Count

This observation indicates that for a given method type, 45% of the methods are of average complexity, for example. At this stage, the average methods per class had been split into four categories according to method type and these four categories had been split into three further categories according to complexity.

It then remained to apply weightings to each of the twelve categories, again using values obtained from an examination of past project data (statistics again from Minkiewicz). These weightings derive from a study of effort and are summarised in the following table:

Table 6.4 Method Type Complexity Weightings

Method Type	Method Complexity		Weight (effort based)
Constructor/Destructor	Low		1
	Average	12	4
	High		7
Selector	Low		1
	Average	16	5
	High		10
Modifier	Low		12
	Average	48	16
	High		20
Iterator	Low		3
	Average	27	9
	High		15

This table indicates that out of a scale of 103 units of effort (the sum of the Weight column), 48 units of effort were spent coding modifier method types. This estimation was possible since the original developers of the historical project data had recorded effort data per class and were consulted in order to split this effort on a per function basis.

The weightings for the complexity categories were calculated by noting that those functions that took longer to write generally responded to more messages and affected more class properties, thus inspiring the following look-up table (see table 6.5).

It was then possible to establish into which complexity category a function fell and therefore assign its effort contribution accordingly.

Table 6.5 Complexity Categories

Message Responses	Number of Properties		
	0, 1	2, …, 6	7, …
0, 1	Low	Low	Average
2, 3	Average	Average	Average
4, …	Average	High	High

Finally these weightings were applied to the data from the two Parallax projects and a sample calculation is shown here:

Low Complexity Constructor/Destructor Weighted Method Count (CDWMC) =
    1 * Constructor/Destructor Average Complexity Method Count

Average Complexity Constructor/Destructor Weighted Method Count =
    4 * Constructor/Destructor Average Complexity Method Count

High Complexity Constructor/Destructor Weighted Method Count =
    7 * Constructor/Destructor Average Complexity Method Count

For each project, the remaining nine calculations were performed and their sum formed the corresponding WMC metrics, so that it was a simple matter to compute the POP count according to the formula.

6.4.4.3   Results

The following table illustrates the metrics gathered for project alpha and beta

Table 6.6 Summary of Project Metrics

Project Attributes	Project Alpha	Project Beta
Source Lines of Code (SLOC)	38854	20570
Total Number of Classes	404	147
Total Number of Methods	2412	833
Average of the Methods per Class	5.971	5.667
Average Depth of Inheritance	0.941	0.701
Average Number of Children	3.700	2.688
Top Level Classes	201	73
Constructors/Destructors (20%)	1.194	1.133
Selectors (30%)	1.791	1.700
Modifiers (45%)	2.687	2.550
Iterators (5%)	0.299	0.283
WMC	62.564	59.379
Number of POPs	10478	2566
Number of FPs	729	386

6.4.4.4   Comparison of Estimated and Actual Effort

At this point it is worthwhile to discuss some of the background behind the two projects and summarise the effort metrics that were originally estimated by the development team (using a Consensus approach) and the effort that was actually expended. These statistics are presented as ratios:

(Estimated Effort Project Alpha) : (Estimated Effort Project Beta) = 6.32

(Actual Effort Project Alpha) : (Actual Effort Project Beta) = 4.58

In other words, from the estimated efforts, project alpha would have taken 6.32 times as many days to develop than project beta, whereas project alpha actually took about 4.58 times as many days to develop than project beta. This information is useful for comparing with a similar ratio of POPs and FPs between the two projects. The ratio approach is applied here as the actual effort data is confidential (this does not affect the conclusions).

6.4.4.5   General Observations

A Consensus estimation technique was used to generate the original estimates, which is currently standard practice at Parallax. The developers who were responsible for building the system produced the estimates.

The actual effort data totals for both project alpha and project beta were higher than the original estimates, which is often the case for software developments. The initial estimate for project alpha is within the 10% accuracy range suggested by Boehm (1995) for an estimate performed at the detailed design stage of a project. Also the estimate for project beta is close to the 50% suggested by Boehm (1995) for an estimation produced at the requirements specification phase of a project. This would indicate that both estimates are quite reasonable by industrial standard for software development especially considering the initial estimates were actually produced during the requirements specification phase of the projects.

Project Alpha

Project Alpha forms part of a development program for a large insurance company. The program includes a number of integrated phases, which build on a set of core base classes. Project Alpha builds on the work performed in previous phases and has benefited from a more refined set of requirements. However, this refinement of requirements has resulted in expansion of and alteration to a number of the core base classes. A point of note for this project is the quality of the initial estimate, which was within 10% of the actual. This was performed by an experienced development team, which benefited from excellent development skills and experience of the client market.

Project Beta

Project Beta was performed for a large finance company and was a self contained development. The technology used for the project was cutting edge and the development tools were immature. There were a large number of change requests for a project of this size, which would indicate that the requirements were not stable. The change requests for Project Alpha (by contrast) were extensions to the requirements rather than alterations to existing functionality. The project was performed early in Java's evolution and development tools were still primitive. Experienced developers performed the project but this was Parallax's first experience of utilising Java in a commercial environment. These factors would suggest that the initial estimate was result of limited experience with the development language.

6.4.4.6 Function Point Observations

Comparing the FP count for the two projects reveals project alpha is nearly twice as large, in terms of the FP count, compared to project beta, using the following percentage calculation:

$$\frac{FP\alpha}{FP\beta} = \frac{729}{386} \approx 1.89$$

Fig. 6.8 Equation: FP Ratio

The closer this ratio to that of the actual efforts, the more accurate the FP technique. This is because Effort and FP count are proportional, where the constant of proportionality is the FP productivity rate for the mix of technologies in the system.

Predictive Object Point Observations

Comparing the POP count for the two projects reveals project alpha is approximately four times as large, in terms of the POP count, compared to project beta, using the following percentage calculation:

$$\frac{POP\alpha}{POP\beta} = \frac{10478}{2566} \approx 4.08$$

Fig. 6.9 Equation: POP Ratio

As with the FP technique, the closer this ratio to that of the actual efforts, the more accurate the POP technique. This is because Effort and POP count are proportional, where the constant of proportionality is the POP productivity rate for the mix of technologies in the system.

6.4.5   Conclusion

6.4.5.1   The Metrics Compared

The results show that using the POP metric, as an indicator of software size was considerably more successful than using the FP metric when applied to two of the projects. This is because the POP ratio of 4.08 was much closer to the actual effort ratio of 4.58. This compares with the FP ratio of 1.89, which indicates the projects were more similar in complexity than was actually the case and can perhaps be attributed to the fact that the backfiring technique for calculating the FP count was based on the lines of code (SLOC) metric:

(LOC Project Alpha) : (LOC Project Beta) = 1.89

which ignores the metrics available within an object-oriented system.

The POP ratio of 4.08 is actually smaller than the effort ratio of 4.58 and an analysis shows that the true ratio is probably smaller still (see Fig. 6.10).

So in order for the estimate to be better than the FP calculation, k has to be greater than 0.41, which is the POP ratio divided by the FP ratio. In other words, as long as the productivity rate for project beta was not less than half that for project beta, the POP count can be said to have been more accurate in this case.

$$f1(TLC, NOC, DIT) = TLC * (1 + ((1 + NOC) * DIT)^{1.01} + (|NOC - DIT|)^{.01})$$
$$f2(NOC, DIT) = 1.0$$

$$POPs(WMC, NOC, DIT, TLC) = \frac{WMC * f1(TLC, NOC, DIT)}{7.8} * f2(NOC, DIT)$$

Fig. 6.10 Equation: POP formula

6.4.5.2   POP Metric Concerns

The main concern is that the POP metric relies heavily on the availability of the object design, which is almost certainly subject to change during the course of a project. Therefore it is crucial that all system requirements, or use cases, are captured in the design at this stage in order to prevent feature creep. One way in which the design may change is by acquiring new top level classes (classes which have no parent within the system) and an inspection of the POPs formula (see above) shows this contributes significantly to the POP count. On the other hand, if such top-level classes are on average low in complexity, the WMC value will decrease, thus reducing the POP count overall. This is likely to be the case where the extra classes are not directly related to the system requirements due to a good requirements capture and corresponding object design.

- The methods were split into various types according to proportions taken from Minkiewicz. An organisation would benefit by using a split based on its own historical data. This also applies to the weightings used to further categorise the method types into complexity types. In fact this is perhaps more true when applied to a language which encourages a high number of pure abstract classes (for example Java, where interfaces might be thought of as pure abstract classes). The reason for this is that each additional interface contributes significantly to the top-level class count (and thus to the POP count), whereas the complexity is intuitively very low, which isn't reflected using a spread based on projects such as C++, which tend to use pure abstract classes less extensively. It might therefore be prudent to rate a top-level class according to its percentage of abstract functions, which an organisation would do by analysing its historical data.

- Use of the CCCC tool in this investigation brought to light McCabe's Cyclomatic Complexity metric (MVC) which is a system metric and is defined as the number of linearly independent routes through a directed a cyclic graph which maps the flow of control of a subprogram. This is an indication of system complexity and the POP technique could benefit by incorporating this metric for the analysis of historical code. The system might be divided into subsystems for the purpose of estimation. The historical data of an organisation could then be consulted in order to supply such an MVC metric on a per subsystem basis.

- As well as splitting a system into several subsystems, each subsystem could be divided into several stages according to time. For example, at the start of the project a developer would have a lower productivity rate due to time spent becoming familiar with the subsystem, and hence the POP formula could be applied at each stage assuming a corresponding productivity rate for that stage, using a particular technology. This isn't a suggestion for an alteration to the POP metric, but instead is a refinement of its use.

In conclusion, the POP metric when applied to historical data on two of Parallax's deployed projects gave a better indication of their size than did the FP metric. This is significant, since it is common practice to express the size of an object-oriented project in function points for the purposes of estimation despite the fact that it was not originally intended with object-oriented systems in mind. The possibility of a metric, which takes into account several well-defined metrics within an object-oriented system, is therefore very encouraging. However, it is important to realise that in an industrial setting an OO design for the entire system to be developed is seldom undertaken. OO analysis and design is often restricted to the more complex subsystems that need careful design. This suggests that the POP metric might be best applied to the estimation of the critical subsystems.

6.4.6   References

[Parallax]
Parallax Solutions Ltd.: http://www.parallax.co.uk/
[ESSI]
European Systems and Software Initiative: http://www.esi.es/ESSI/
[ForeSight]
ForeSight Estimation Tool by Price Systems: http://www.buyfs.com/
[CCCC]
CCCC Metric Tool by Tim Littlefair: http://www.fste.ac.cowan.edu.au/~tlittlef/
[KnowledgePlan]
KnowledgePlan Estimation Tool by SPR: http://www.spr.com/
[Minkiewicz]
Arlene F. Minkiewicz, "Cost Estimation Using Predictive Object Points", The Tenth Annual Software Technology Conference "Knowledge Sharing – Global Information Networks" conference proceedings, Salt Lake City, Utah, 19-23 April 1998.

6.5   Project 21476 – MBM
Management By Metrics

G. Sabbatici
Alenia, Rome
P. Panarono, S. Farina
Intecs Sistemi, Pisa

6.5.1   Executive Summary

Management by Metrics (MBM) experiment concerns metrics collection and exploitation in support of managers to gain an improvement in the software process. Alenia and Intecs Sistemi have already in place a defined process including the collection of many process and product metrics. However these metrics are often just thrown into a database for statistical purposes. Rarely they have a direct impact on the same process they are taken from. MBM intends to bring back those metrics into the process, for the benefit of the process.

The MBM experiment has the goal to provide a Software process and product indicators "Metrics" with a friendly user presentation. The indicators are depending on the company goals. Practised deployment of Management by Metrics is expected to move from actual level 3 (of both Intecs and Alenia) to perform a project working at maturity level 4. Inside the experiment execution, firstly technical and managerial aspects have been selected as related domain to be improved ("Company Business Goals" selection), then AMI method (Application of Metrics in Industry) rigorous approach has been applied and the detailed "metrication plan" has been derived. Automatic Support Tool(s) have been delivered and Metrics collection has started (and is currently running) to feed the "dashboard" in the two companies.

The metrics viewer "dashboard", is a highly intuitive, user-friendly presentation tool selected among commercial off-the-shelf (COTS) available solutions. The "dash-board" experimented on two quite different baseline projects, provide the managers (and quality managers), at a glance and graphically, all basic process indicators, including planned vs. actual vs. historical, flagging warning and alarm values. On a mouse click, basic process indicators show up into sub-dash-boards to provide more detailed indicators, up to the level of detail required. Management decisions (e.g. when to stop testing, increase the staff, postpone a release, improve inspections, trigger an audit on a subcontractor, etc.) are taken on a quantitative basis. Managers become familiar to read these dash-boards and to understand their dynamics. The "in action" phase for managers community has run: the benefits for involved people are therefore evident and valuable. The Alenia and Intecs dash-board are not identical – because each company has its own business goals, Software Architecture and development Platforms. The Priorities are different and different indicators are necessary; nevertheless the "harmonisation" of the two dash-boards has been pursued with a benefit for the projects. Partnership between Alenia and Intecs Sistemi optimises the overall experiment effort and makes a first generality attempt for the great potential of technology transfer to other organisations. Differences between the two MBM-experiment "implementation details" are identified in the rest of the document.

At the conclusion of the experiment the result of SPICE assessment can be summarised as follows: – for Alenia although the selected processes have not reached the capability level 4, their execution provides the opportunity to other process to be executed at level 4. – for Intecs Sistemi: the capability level 4 has been reached. This experiment is contributing at on going standardisation efforts, the Management by Metrics practice is intended to be institutionalised as part of both companies Quality Systems. The dash-board is near to become an integral appendix of all project progress reports.

MBM experiment is related to research carried out by Alenia as Prime and Intecs Sistemi as Associated Partner in the frame work of the ESSI Community Program with financial contribution by the Commission.

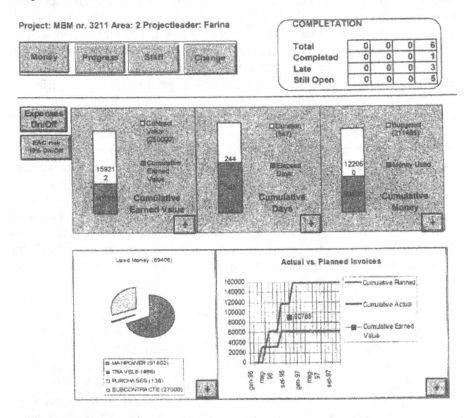

Fig. 6.11 The dashboard – an illustration kindly supplied by Mr. Paolo Panaroni, Intecs.

6.5.2 Background Information

6.5.2.1 Objectives

Alenia and Intecs Sistemi are intensive software producers within the air traffic control domain and space domain. Both companies have been formally assessed at a maturity level 3 (their processes are defined and enforced). The experiment objective is to reach, for both the participating companies, the capability to operate at level 4 (managed) by the systematic and institutionalised use of metrics to plan, manage and control the software process as for cost, quality and timeliness, in a phrase "Management by Metrics".

To improve the process measurement plan; the most important steps are:

- Establish a basic set of process measurements to identify costs and benefits of each process task (e.g. cost and yield of error detection and correction methods).
- Establish and maintain a data base of process metrics available to all projects.
- Provide resources to collect, verify, enter and maintain data in the data base and advise on analysis methods and interpretation.
- Designate an independent quality assurance group to track each project against its quality plan and targets, and alert management to deviations in the process.

The most important MBM activities are below shown :

Table 6.7 MBM Activity

Activity	Comments	Deliverables
Definition of "Business goals"	trade-off among possible improvement areas	Business Goals Document
Definition of "Metrics Dashboard"	breakdown: from selected "Business Goal" to "metrication plan"	Dashboard Definition
Automatic Support for the dashboard	tools selection glue software delivery	Dashboard tools
Collection of project metrics	metrics collection and validation	
Management By Metrics "in action"	prototype tuning metrics analysis	
Final Assessment	independent SPICE assessment	Assessment Final Report
Quantitative annotation	feedback of learned lessons in the whole company	Quantitative Annotated Process

The project progress is assessed through the milestones met and the issue of deliverables.

6.5.2.2   Involved Companies and their Roles

- Alenia, a company of Finmeccanica group, as prime user is responsible for the project.
- Intecs Sistemi is a software company with the partner role. Companies are both involved into Dashboards deployment to improve their (slight) different business goals. In fact each company emits different deliveries. Partnership between Alenia and Intecs Sistemi optimises the overall experiment effort and makes a first generality attempt for the great potential of technology transfer to other organisations.
- The Det Norske Veritas (DNV) international institute and Qualital institute have participated as subcontractor, their role in the experiment being the final assessment (SPICE conformant) for both Alenia and Intecs partners.
- Two international experts (Mrs. Combelles and Mrs. Pflegger) as subcontractors, with the consultancy role in the definition of the business goals and of the dash-board indicators and layout.

6.5.2.3   Starting Scenario

This investigation is not a formal but a pragmatic industrial attempt to explore improvements in the software development process. The experiment is NOT concerned with the injection within the development process of a particular tool or a particular design method or technique. Tools, methods and techniques "serve" the process and not the other way. The experiment addresses the overall process by attempting improving its maturity so that it can be "quantitatively" planned, monitored, controlled and assessed.

There is consensus that only once enclosed in the software a metric system, the "injection" of new technology (tools, methods) can be proposed and assessed within a rational and quantitative framework (e.g. in which activity I am spending too much where tool support could help?, which activity is originating too many defects where a new method could help?).

Too often there is the temptation to improve the process by the simple injection of the last fashion technology . But not every process "change" is an "improvement": determining that a change is an improvement requires analysis of measures. The objective of this experiment has been to provide a quantitative view of the process which is the only sound basis for further, controlled, process improvement steps. The dashboard tools have been necessary for proper and efficient collection, analysis and presentation of metrics, but not central to the experiment.

6.5.2.4   The Companies
Alenia

Alenia is a company with about 15.000 employees distributed in 41 plants in Italy and abroad, it is the Italian leader in aeronautics, electronics and space fields. Alenia can be characterised as a complete systems construction company that designs, develops and installs Software for high technology Embedded Computer Command and Control Systems for defence and civil market. Software development within the company is relevant to a variety of classes of systems such as:

- control software embedded within mobile vessel units and radar installations;
- information systems, control and communication software embedded in Command and Control systems;
- information systems, control and communication software embedded in Traffic Control systems;
- control and communication software embedded within ground and on-board equipment for satellites and spacecraft operations. Software has a central and critical role within such systems.

Status Scenario of Metrics Practices at Alenia

In February 1992 a large self-assessment exercise was performed on many companies and divisions of the Finmeccanica group. The self-assessment was integrated by an external survey conducted by Professor David Garlan of Carnegie Mellon University. Work was sponsored and co-ordinated by the Corporate Staff. Despite the differences among the various sites and divisions, yet the most advanced ones resulted to stay at level 3 of the SEI Capability Maturity Model. To assess the software weak area a "qualitative" approach has been conducted and with the results a Technology Report has been issued. From the high number of replies and comments, metrics was the area where improvement is perceived as most urgent and needed. Having identified hundreds of indicators and systematically collected many of them has not yet reached the goal to quantitatively and effectively manage the software development processes.

Personnel

The staff assigned to this project is software oriented and has sufficient skill to be fully confident with Software Metrics introduction activities. Mr Giorgio Cicerchia, key person of the project, has been the metrics initiator and he is head of the software of Project and Development department of Alenia Radar System Division, he act currently with the role of the ESSI Experiment project manager Mr Giorgio Sabbatini, metrics promoter and project contact, is an experienced metric specialist, he has a large experience as software project manager in the field of Alenia typical software development activities. Mr Giovanni Massara , with a large experience in the software development activity, has been involved developing the data base interface window in the software metrication program using the selected tools. The manager and software team leader of the baseline project, have been involved as advisers of reference in the "business goal" and "dashboard presentation" definition phases. Other analysts and programmers, as technical support (data collecting, storing, etc.): working to the project baseline and to the software metrics project of the experiment.

Intecs Sistemi

Intecs Sistemi is a software company with more than 200 employees distributed among the five sites of Pisa, Rome, Naples, Piombino and Toulouse. It produces high quality software for major customers such as the European Space Agency, MATRA, Alenia, Tuscany Region, Telecom Italia, in the domains of defence, space, electronic, telematics, geographical information systems and other public services. Facing so many demanding and varied projects a large experience and expertise on software engineering and software quality has been accumulated over the years and "institutionalised" through company standards and quality manuals. The high international calibre of its senior staff completes the picture and places Intecs Sistemi among the leading software companies in Europe. Beside its main mission to produce high quality custom software, Intecs Sistemi actively participates in main R&D programmes such as ESPRIT, Eureka, RACE, ESSI, etc. Provides consultancies and services (e.g. process modelling, independent V&V, etc.) and has developed and is commercialising all over Europe, a CASE tool supporting the HOOD method.

Starting Scenario of Metrics Practices at Intecs

A BOOTSTRAP assessment was performed in June 94 (sponsored by ESSI) and a SPICE trial is just terminated. Both concluded on a stable level 3. Moreover ISO 9001 certification was granted by Det Norske Veritas.

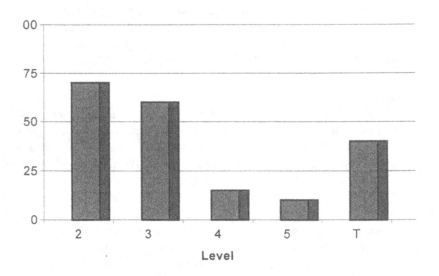

Fig. 6.12 Global Assessment

Personnel

Mr. Paolo Panaroni, key person of the project, acts currently with the role of Intecs Sistemi QA Responsible. He is an experienced metric specialist, with a long date specific knowledge. Mr. Sandro Farina, key person of the project, has a large experience in the field of Project Control. He acts as Program Manager in the "Command & Control" and "Surveillance" Company Area. Mr. Leslie Von Neumann, Mr. Sergio Ferri and Mr. Dario Citterico (respectively Technical Director, Contract Officer and Program Manager in the Company) have been involved as users of reference in the "business goal" and "dashboard presentation" definition phases. Other analysts and programmers are consulting to the project.

6.5.2.5 Phases of the Experiment

The Phases of the experiment with the delivered documents, identified in the Project Program Annex I [Annex95], are below described:

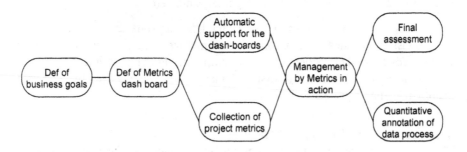

Fig. 6.13 Workplan Pert

Definition of Business Goals

The business goals, not exactly the same in Alenia & Intecs, have been formally identified and prioritised. Alenia and Intecs stated to focus to the following business goals:

- Project Status Monitoring (Alenia and Intecs)
- Increase understanding of testing phase (Alenia)
- Increase understanding and modelling of Software Engineering processes & products (Intecs)
- Business goals (Joint Alenia, Intecs) document delivered [MBM/T96a].

Definition of the Metrics Dash-boards

The "initial step" has been to study the Software Metrics techniques most suitable in the Alenia and Intecs application environment. Having decided to use the AMI method to put our measurement programme into place, areas of concern and problems have been first identified. With the AMI method the number of metrics that need to be collected is focused on those that correspond to the more important goals.

Goals have been further analysed to identify sub-goals yielding a goal tree. The detailed metrication plans have been delivered by the Dash-Board Definition (Alenia & Intecs) documents.

A goal/question/metrics approach, starting from business goals, has been adopted, as complemented by the AMI approach. – Dash-Board Definition (Alenia & Intecs) documents delivered [MBM/T96b].

Automatic Support for the Dash-boards

Once the dash-boards are defined, a tool is required to support them. Development of a new tool was out of scope of the experiment, though some "glue" software have been necessary to "connect" metrics collection tools with the dash-board.

- Metrics Interchange File Definition (joint Alenia, Intecs) document delivered [MIFDD96]
- Dash-board tool (Alenia & Intecs) documents delivered

Collection of project metrics to initially feed the dash-boards

This task is intended to start collection of metrics to be later visualised by the dash-boards tools. This collection is continuing during the experiment to keep up to date the collection metrics. A first dashboard validation has been reached using historical available project data.

Management by Metrics in Action

This is the core stage of the experiment; managers have the dash-board (properly initialised and configured) to "drive" their projects quantitatively. The dash-boards have been experimented on the a baseline projects (Alenia) and most of active projects in Intecs. The reaction of the manager is of paramount importance. Actually, managers have participated to the definition phase as well as for the design and tuning of the dash-board!

Mid-term Report (joint Alenia, Intecs) document delivered [MTReport96]

Final Assessment

A SPICE assessment will verify, close to the end of the experiment, actual achievement of a stable level 4 for both companies. Intecs and Alenia will profit from the new SPICE technology that, at the time of experiment completion, should have reached an industrial maturity. - Assessment SPICE Report (Alenia & Intecs) documents delivered [SPICE98]

Quantitative Annotation of Data Process

The quantitative processes annotation is a special (off-line) activity aimed at "improving" not directly the process but, rather, the process definition (e.g. company quality manuals, project standards, rigorous process models) by "attaching" quantitative measures to process elements.

6.5.2.6   Expected Outcomes

The relevance of the project to the business of the participants, and its likely impact achievement of the objectives of the experiment result in enhancement of the predictability and efficiency of the partners software process, of the company know how and of its image. These aspects all contribute to increase the overall competitiveness on the market. At the end of the experiment it is expected that Alenia and Intecs increase their contractor/sub-contractor relationship thanks to commonly understood and tracked project management indicators.

A process "dash-board" has been defined, implemented by COTS (Commercial Off The Shelf) tools and experimented on two quite different baseline projects to provide the managers (and quality managers), at a glance and graphically, all basic process indicators, including planned vs. actual vs. historical, flagging warning and alarm values. A final conformant assessment verify the achievement of level 4 for both companies on one or a set of projects.

6.5.3   Work Performed

6.5.3.1   Definition of the Experiment in the Context of a Baseline Project Baseline Project Overview

Alenia

The selected baseline project, to feed the dash-boards, has been the ModoS Radar, named SIR-S. The Modo S is the main functionality of the SIR-S Radar, a Secondary Radar implemented by Alenia – Divisione Sistemi Radar (Alenia/DSR). The Radar implements a bi-directional data link between ground and air. The ModoS implements the surveillance activity, consisting in the discovery, localisation and reception of the principal information related to the flight.

Intecs

The Dashboard has been experimented on the whole of the company projects (both in-progress and recently completed).Moreover detailed extra metrics have been collected for the MUIS (Multi Mission User Information Service) project from ESA/ESRIN. The project started on 1/96, its end is foreseen within 5/98. Its purpose is to provide earth observation users the following services:

- "Documentation and News Service"
- "Product Catalogue Service"
- "Order and Delivery Service"

6.5.3.2   Organisation

The work undertaken as part of this ESSI experiment has involved Alenia as prime user and Intecs as associated partner. The experiment conducted by Intecs mirrors (intentionally) the one conducted by Alenia, in spite of the fact that the two companies have different business goals, different processes and different application domains.

The project managers are Mr Giorgio Cicerchia (Alenia) and Mr Paolo Panaroni (Intecs Sistemi), which have been the main MBM Responsibility. The 2nd key persons are Mr Giorgio Sabbatini (Alenia) and Mr. Sandro Farina (Intecs Sistemi), which have been involved in the projects, starting from the initial phases as for requirements as well as for the implementation phases (glue software). The experiment has involved furthermore the following community of the both companies Alenia and Intecs:

- managers (for requirements, dissemination and the "in action" phase)
- clerical staff and quality engineers (for the implementation phases, the metric collection and data validation)
- technicians for technological contribution on specific aspects

Co-ordination between Alenia and Intecs has been achieved by periodical meetings

Alenia Dashboard

The dash-board is a data base interface-window for software metrics. A means for get in the project-data and then visualising and monitoring the project-condition.

The "dash-board" has been defined and deployed on the baseline project to provide indicators (metrics) that are not just the result of measurement but history and trends (within the project). The main indicators monitored are:

- Monitoring of Project Status :
  - total spent effort, effort to complete (for each life cycle phase)
  - evaluation of each life cycle phase completion
  - money used, cost to complete, estimated final cost
  - percentage of delivered products (code, documents, ...)
- Monitoring of test phase :
  - problems type distribution on the test life cycle phases
  - test phases cost
  - rate of detected, solved and remaining problems during test phases
  - analysis of problem fixing during test phase
    (cost, Type of effort, time to fix, ...)

The implemented dash-board is graphic-interface, executive-oriented and hierarchically-organised.

Windows reproducing the data-collection forms have been implemented to insert primitive metrics

- Project Characteristic Data window
- Development Status window
- Personnel Resources window,
- Test Phase Problem Tracing window

The hierarchical organisation of Alenia/DSR dash-board is as follows :

First level: Project –Project selection is allowed and the selected project budget data are shown, it includes the interactive session for budget data input

Second level: Measured Data – Actual and historical primitive data access is allowed. It includes the interactive sessions for the measured data input.

Third level: Processed data for trend and warning analysis are shown by printable numerical arrays

Fourth level: Data are presented by histograms, curves, pie diagrams, ... in order to give an immediate impression of trends. The graphical presentation can be selected to show both coarse data or fine data

The dash-board is also :

- the Data Base structure
- algorithms to check the data congruence and to store
- algorithms to make the computation of derived and statistical metrics.

Intecs Sistemi Dashboard

The "dash-board" has been deployed on most of the company projects to provide the managers the following main graphical information:

- Project Registry Form (NR, description, leader, open/close dates, type, customer, etc.)
- Work Packages Status Table(Total, Still Open, Late, Completed)
- Change Actions Status Table (Pending, Closed, Rejected, Total for NCR, RID, SPR,SEP)
- Cumulative Earned Value (CEV) "thermometer"
- Project Time "thermometer"
- Used Money "thermometer"
- CEV vs. Used Money comparison Graph
- Real vs. Planned Invoicing Graph
- Real vs. Planned Staff Effort Graph

Furthermore, each info can be requested to be detailed by available "more" push-buttons.

The same is for basic project data: Timecards, Travels, Purchases, Subcontracts, Work Orders, Initial Budgets, Historical Estimations To Complete (ETCs) and more.

Excel-based "Dashboard" could run on both PCs and Mackintosh desktops, nevertheless with company currently-available Macs the "Dashboard" is not adequately performing. That's why we decided to drive the experiment in two alternative options:

- Excel-based "Dashboard" with graphical and tabular data presentation (adopted for PC-Pentium minimum-platforms only): Projects Data are available as down-loadable files over intranet geographic network.
- "Dashboard-subset" by Intranet COTS Browsers with tabular data representation (adopted for MACs and PCs low-end but PC Pentium available too): Projects Data are already available as html pages ready to be seen

6.5.3.3   Technical Environment

Alenia

The environments utilised from the Alenia Radar System Division people in the software development systems are different for operating system, data base, tools, languages. The standard selected platforms make easy to interchange data between applications so no changes have been made to the technical environment in term of equipment. Technical solutions for Alenia "dashboard" selected for the MBM experiment are based on Visual Basic and Access Database toolset part of Office suite (by Microsoft).

Intecs Sistemi

A company-wide NT Intranet Server (from MS) is available. Its deployment has make possible intranet company metrics Dashboards publishing & browsing.

6.5.3.4   Training

Alenia

All the components involved in the experiment are people with long software experience, so the tools acquisition has been done without training courses.

Intecs Sistemi

Training on the Excel Programming Environment (Visual Basic – Microsoft Query) and Intranet Publishing and Browsing. It was done "on the job" with no formal training courses.

6.5.3.5   Role of the Consultants

Shari Pfleeger for Intecs Sistemi and Annie Combelles for Alenia

- understood clearly the context and environment of the software business (the part where metrics should be put in place)
- got a clear picture of the objectives and their quantification and time frame
- validated the business goals
- built the complete schedule of the mission

- worked on the goals tree
- COTS dashboard possible solutions
- meeting points with Intecs and Alenia
- provide extremely valuable references and examples.

6.5.3.6   Internal Dissemination

The Management by Metrics practice is intended to be institutionalised as part of the company Quality System; internal MBM presentation have been held as in Alenia (Rome & Turin) as in Intecs Sistemi (Rome & Pisa). A fair participation has come from company managers, as in the "business goals" definition phase as during the "in action" phase. We have verified initially and during the experiment that there was an internal high expectation from MBM work results.

Dissemination Plan (joint Alenia, Intecs) document [MBM/M96] describe how the project results were, or are to be, communicated throughout the organisations.

6.5.4   Result and Analysis

6.5.4.1   Technical

Dashboard means two main things: data collection and presentation tool. The first item seemed the more complex because of the amount and validity of data. Companion work-flow and database sharing needed to be "rethought" a number of times before the and of the experiment.

Data collection has been a critical activity because of:

- cost reasons. In fact data collection is a constant effort during the whole project (instead of "una tantum" ticket for Dashboard tool delivery)
- mismatching to be prevented avoiding redundant and useless data collection
- some workers resistance to give much more details on their work, which can result in late data or not valid (wrong data).

Metrics Cost

A program of measures has implementation cost, and management and use costs.

The objective to keep the implementation cost of the MBM experiment within 15% of the overall effort of the application project has been respected. The Costs of software measures management and use is function of amount of data to collect by means of the developed dash-board. The use of metrics require :

- Data collection of the primitive metrics which costs has been (nearly 1% over-cost maximum on development process)
- Costs – to load and to process data – to analyse and to distribute results

The data collection, loading and elaboration activities are tasks of the organisation charged of the data repository management. Total costs for data collection and data processing for the selected software project has been less than 2%

Measurement of Results

The metrics accumulated in the course of the experiment have been compared with old available historical metrics for the evaluation of : "productivity", "timeliness", "quality" and "predictability"; but historical data collection was carried out mainly for accounting purpose by Administrative Section. The metrics comparison has provided a "quantitative" basis to assess the software process improvement. To fully capture the benefits also a "qualitative" approach has been conducted. A specific investigation has been defined and circulated to collect directly from the (project manager, quality engineer, development team, test team) an assessment of the process deployed. Predictability is very important. Management by Metrics provides, from the very beginning, strong evidence that the process is more predictable, that deviations of actual vs. planned are kept under control much better. It is only a secondary objective to show that the baseline projects had actually improved the software development process, compared by previous projects.

The main measure of the success of the MBM experiment remain in the achievement of the new maturity level. This evaluation has been done according to ISO/IEC TR 15504 (SPICE) standard system [ISO/IEC97]. ISO (the International Organisation for Standardisation) and IEC (the International Electrotecnical Commission) together form a system for world-wide standardisation as a whole. The international organisation Det Norske Veritas (DNV) has conducted the SPICE conformant assessment. Det Norske Veritas is one of the organisation accredited within Italy for ISO 9000 certification for software organisation.

The DNV's task has been to assure that the assessed process was compliant with ISO 9000.

The Alenia evaluation in the SPICE model has been done selecting the software process more suitable for assess the implemented system of metrics. The attention of the assessment team has been applied to the following four processes:

- Project management: identifies, establishes, co-ordinates, and monitors activities, tasks, and resources necessary for a project to produce a product and/or service meeting the requirements.
- Quality management: monitor the quality of the project's products and/or services and to ensure that they satisfy the customer.
- Measurement: collects and analyses data relating to the products developed and processes implemented within the organisational unit, supports effective management of the processes, and objectively demonstrates the quality of the products.
- Problem resolution: ensures that all discovered problems are analysed and resolved and that trends are recognised. Although the selected processes have not

fully achieved the capability level 4, their execution at the level 3 provides the opportunity to other process to be executed at level 4.

Two are the aspects, following the assessors advises, that need a further development to reach the level 4 in the process of the life cycle:

- the metrics identified do not cover the quality of the product
- for the quality management of the software process and products is not enough to fix metrics but also to define target values and to control the software process so that can be possible to keep the measures into the range.

It is natural that this point of view has not been yet developed because the ESSI project has allowed the Management By Metrics process experimentation and so only a first "limited" set of metrics have been inserted in the software management. Moreover the lack of historical data make hard or impossible to fix target values.

The Intecs Sistemi evaluation in the SPICE model has been done and the capability level 4 has been achieved.

Finally, it has to be remarked that, running the (Intecs and Alenia) experiments in parallel, has allowed to compare results and exchange lessons learned even in the course of the experimentation.

6.5.4.2   Business

Much effort can be saved having the correct and in-time info from projects. Monitor and control becomes a quantitative activity rather than a qualitative one. Dashboard availability all along the course of the project provide managers the continuous stimulus to keep the project on track (budget, time, quality).

Even expert managers have often a feeling that software projects are very complex and dynamic "beasts", hard to understand, control, dominate. And this let them anxious or aggressive. They tend to react to events (fire fighting): they "defend" the planned budget, schedule and quality against the "beast".

The dash board becomes a powerful weapon to help the managers prevent the fire and, if needed, to shot at the right time and at the right target.

The impact of new approach on the business environment is leading to an effective competitive advantage.

Furthermore, an initial framework based on measures is the milestone for future improvement programmes.

6.5.4.3   Organisation

Main experiment impact on the companies organisation have been the institutionalisation of the dash-boards. Proper collection of metrics implies company mechanisms quite sophisticated to record worked hours, involved peoples ...etc. Hard copies of the dash-board become an integral appendix of all project progress reports. (passive data base of metrics become "active" data base for future projects). The MBM practice is reported within the quality manuals and procedures.

Alenia\DSR

The *Alenia* metrication program has adopted dedicated data acquisition procedures:

- Data collection happen in the same place where the metrics are produced, by the responsible of the process/product.
- Data collection is an integral part of the software process.
- "Primitive Metrics" collection scheme has been defined and implemented
- Data collection must be done at the start of the project and periodically (every week) during the implementation and maintenance phases.
- The "primitive Metrics" acquisition is performed by compilation of ad hoc "Forms" or using automatic tools, to have measures more reliable, homogeneous and accurate.
- There is a responsible of data input and correctness
- There are procedures for data access and protection.

Intecs Sistemi

Main experiment impact on the Intecs Sistemi organisation have been the need to publish company data on an Intranet company environment. Administrative and technical people is periodically publishing cost data to let the "Dashboard(s) browsing".

6.5.4.4   Culture

Company-wide quality & project indicators have improved a common feeling and language for the companies business managers. The quantitative approach make more rigorous and well-defined the companies managerial processes contributing to clear grey areas where not defined responsibilities / actions can be critical items.

A further culture improvement is in the attempt to synthesise the business environment in a numeric/graphical context.

6.5.4.5   Skills

Project staff has gained Metrics and Visual Basic additional skill. Moreover, for Intecs Dashboard, networking and internet/intranet solutions have been evaluated and relative experience gained.

6.5.5   Key Lessons

The Complexity of the software process is at the basis of the difficulties encountered by all project managers. Basic management techniques as WBS, PERT, GANTT though highly successful in other disciplines are not enough for the software managers. The waterfall model of the process seen as a pipeline of stages or phases is a painful "trivialization" of what the real process is: a complex dynamic system where continuously the process rolls back to previous steps, re-align results, or anticipates steps to investigate feasibility or to stress parallelism (concurrent engineering). All of that is common to all software projects, across all application domains.

The MBM experiment provides managers with basic and effective process indicators of great interest and high potential for transferability. It is not claimed that the very same indicators are directly available by all interested parties as these indicators may vary depending on the project/company goals, but it is deemed that most of them are and, especially that the global approach adopted, would be a good example showing the way ahead.

6.5.5.1   Technological Point of View

Alenia/DSR

- "Project Status Monitoring" help really to estimate and control the effort of each software phase (specification, design, testing, rework) during the software projects development. A project in the maintenance phase require a dashboard structure and layout rather different from a project during development.
- "Increase understanding of testing phase": controls the reliability (errors found and location, conformity to requirements) and requirements stability (change rate and error rate).
- The introduced metrication system has demonstrated the high cost of "Software Test", "System Integration" and "System Test and Evaluation" activities. All problems detected at System Integration and at System Test and Evaluation require software changes and therefore the Software Test repetition. The measurements analysis has showed that the high cost depends on:
  - Inadequate covering of all requirements verification during Software Test
  - Lack of compliance of the peripheral equipment interface characteristics with respect to the expected ones (normally discovered during System Integration).
  - Great amount of software changes required by the radar system specialists to fit the system functionalities/performances to the expected ones in the real environment.
- The Improvement of Embedded Computer System (ECS) Software Testing process, has to be reached reducing the overall software and system test cost; this result will be achieved:

- Improving the flexibility, capability and usability of the environment by which Software Test is performed.
- Extending the requirements verification coverage; which means trace all system requirements having any software impact during the whole life cycle software process. The tracing has to be expanded to all generally unexpressed requirements.

Intecs Sistemi

- There is a large offering of intranet solutions, that is a not yet consolidated "moving target": too many risky "announces" to be verified ("vapourware"). After an initial trade-off phase, the Intecs Sistemi "Dashboard" has been delivered with a moderate intranet profile (i.e. not too conservative but also not too much advanced and insecure!).
- Two experimental dashboard have been implemented: one is graphical but slower and the other tabular BUT faster with a better exploitation of intranet technology (htlm language). The result is impressive: almost all the users prefer the faster intranet data access w. r. t. . The preferred solution is that with 5 sec. response time w. r. t. to the other with the other. Look is important ... but faster is better!
- MBM chance suggested already-collected metrics reuse. The following lessons have been learned from MBM experiment:
- not anymore "private data" but rather "common data" with private operations
- it's mandatory to avoid proprietary ad-hoc data format to minimise future cost and time to share data
- common database has to be maintained with all comprehensive information. Data filtering has to be avoided not to loose original data.

6.5.5.2   Business Point of View

- An improvement in the company software process is of great benefit for the effectiveness and firms image.
- Effectiveness depends a lot from the quality of the data used by managers.

6.5.5.3   Strengths and Weaknesses of the Experiment

- A good presentation "look" make the users more convinced to participate to the experiment.
- Company innovation programmes are sometimes difficult to be "felt" by all managers. If the innovation is "funded" by the Commission the innovation gets more strengths and internal credit.
- Risks have been found in the data collection activity. Collection involves : organisational aspects (proper collection of metrics, such as re-work rate) implying company mechanisms quite sophisticated to record worked hours, involved peoples etc. as well as psychological risks (for example collecting met-

rics on defects at module level might be perceived as an evaluation of individuals rather than of the products).

- Some sort of resistance has been found to get "new" metrics data from the its suppliers (cost impact of data collection and processing).

6.5.6   Conclusions and Future Actions

Alenia\DSR

The software projects make use of advanced technologies and methods. Before the MBM experiment the "management" of such technologies were often completely manual and subjective; in some cases a simple management tool was used to plan the project at its start; in rare cases tool was used also to track progress and expenditures; but that was not enough to support the "driving" of a software process toward its goals. A software project is a very complex process and its "status" is also a Multi-facet complex information. Proper program management requires some means to readily determine project status.

The project control "Alenia's dashboard" has been implemented using Visual Basic and Access Database Toolset part of Office suite (by Microsoft) per Windows 95. The Data-base management is centralised and is relied to specialised staff. The implementation now running allows that the software manager detects whether the software activity converges to the end, shows the presence of obstacles to be removed, allows the estimate of the activity duration visualising and monitoring the condition of the project.

The software process is a complex network of different activities. Most of these activities suffer of a tremendous re-work rate so that when they are marked as completed, up to another 50% of the work is necessary to remove defects or accommodate needed changes.

Technical managers are aware of overall cost impact with no details about involved personnel, time, effort. Problems found and software changes request on the selected baseline project (the ModoS Radar named SIR-S) during the ESSI experiment showed that the software development and evaluation activities high cost depends on the Software Test phases (Software test, System Integration and System Test).

The future Alenia action will be to introduce a general improvement in the Software Testing as a relevant part of the Alenia software development life cycle. This improvement will be related to the following needs and goals: extending the requirements verification coverage and improving the environment simulator used for the Test of Software.

Intecs Sistemi

The project control "dashboard" is now fully operational. It has been implemented using Microsoft Excel, through its advanced programming facilities. A centralised Projects Information's Master Repository is kept in a server in Rome. Every project manager can access it through the web and get access, through the "dashboard" metaphor, of the up to date status of any project.

More details can be get by clicking on "zoom" buttons placed on the dashboards (e.g. how many travels, where, when, who, etc.) The decision to go through the web, though not originally part of the experiment, was deemed a necessary step. We now are regularly using it within our intranet infrastructure.

Major gained experience is relevant to the metrication plan. Before MBM project in Intecs environment the data collection was carried out mainly for accounting purpose by Administrative Section. Technical managers was aware of overall cost impact with no details about involved personnel, staff warnings and so on. Data was available only on paper and later, now it's timely and electronic. MBM has modified the centre of gravity of data collection toward vs. technical management. Data is not collected only for a centralised cost control BUT even for an effective and timely technical/managerial projects control.

Further future actions are foreseen in the field of "Dashboard" intranet profile, expected to be grown as available technology and performance.

6.5.7   Glossary

AMI	Application of Metrics in Industry
ECS	Embedded Computer System
CASE	Computer Aided Software Engineering
COTS	Commercial Off The Shelf
ESSI	European System and Software Initiative
ISO	International Organisation for Standardisation
IEC	International Electrotechnical Commission
MBM	Management By Metrics
MUIS	Multi Mission User Information Service
SEI	Software Engineering Institute
SPICE	Software Process Improvement and Capability Determination
WBS	Software Work Breakdown Structure

6.5.8   References

[Annex95]
    Annex I (Project Program) to project Contract No. 21476, Management By Metrics (MBM) version 3, November 21st, 1995
[MBM/M96]
    Dissemination Plan, MBM/MANAGEMENT_REPORT/ALENIA Issue 1, May 30th, 1996
[MTReport96]
    ESSI MBM Mid-Term Report Issue 1, December 20th, 1996

[MBM/T96a]
Business Goals, MBM/TECHNICAL_REPORT/ALENIA, Issue 1, June 30th, 1996

[MBM/T96b]
Dash-Board Definition, MBM/TECHNICAL_REPORT/ALENIA/2 Issue 1, July 30th, 1996

[MIFDD96]
Metrics Interchange File Definition Document, November 21st, 1996

[SPICE98]
Assessment SPICE Report (Rev. 0), January 22nd, 1998

[ISO/IEC97]
ISO/IEC TR 15504 (SPICE) – Software Process Assessment Standard,, Vers. 3.02, Nov. 1997

6.6   Project 21568 – CMEX
Configuration Management Experiment

Helge M. Roald
Sysdeco GIS AS, Kongsberg

Jens-Otto Larsen
The Norwegian Technical University, Trondheim

6.6.1   Executive Summary

This experiment aims to improve the efficiency in a software development department by introducing a new and advanced configuration management system. The aim of the experiment is to reduce the number of error reports by 10% and the time-to-market by 5%.

The experiment was done in the development department of Sysdeco GIS AS in Norway, developing software for the mapping industry or GIS sector (Geographic Information Systems). The experiment shows significant better results than originally aimed for. The errors have been reduced by 35,7% and the development effort has increased by 22%. The latter has contributed to bring the new products quicker to the market. The identified process improvement is not just a result of introducing a new system, but a result of many additional factors as general process improvement, product maturity and a focus on new development, to mention the most important.

Apart from the result above, the key lessons from the experiment have been:

To introduce the new configuration tool, ClearCase, was more difficult than anticipated. Careful planning and experimenting took more time than planned and caused more problems for the developers than expected.

Too little training using the new system made the introduction of the system difficult.

Well-established routines for handling errors and a well-experienced development group significantly contributed the success of the experiment.

Relevant background data to measure the improvement was harder to collect than anticipated. It took more time and required also more effort to analyse than expected.

The management of the project has gained valuable experience in how to collect and analyse data regarding process improvement. New ideas for further improvements have been identified.

The success of the experiment makes it evident to continue to use the new system in our development and maintenance of our products. Further improvements can and will be done. We have also identified new areas for improvements and we plan to do a similar experiment introducing automatic testing tools.

This experiment is relevant for SMBs planning to introduce new tools in their development department, especially configuration management tools. The European Commission through the ESSI/PIE program has financially supported this project.

6.6.2   Background Information

Sysdeco GIS A/S (SGIS) is a company developing mapping applications for the international marked. The company has subsidiaries in Europe (England, Norway, Germany, Sweden, Italy) and in Asia (Singapore and Malaysia). All together there are about 150 employees, whereof about 40 are employed at the headquarters in Norway, 40 in UK and 40 associated with the Singapore office.

Using Sysdeco's own development tool-kit develops mapping applications. The development department in Norway is responsible for developing this. The department has existed in some form for almost two decades. It currently consists of 13 people, mostly core developers as well as some doing documentation, production and support personnel. The development department has little direct involvement with customers and deal mostly with Sysdeco subsidiaries, which in turn handle the marketing, sales, first line support etc. This ESSI project is done in the development department of SGIS.

6.6.2.1   Objectives

The overall objective of the project is to measure the effect of introducing a formal configuration management and version control system in the software development process. The introduction of the system is successful if the experiment shows that we achieve a:

- 10% reduction of error reports for the software products.
- 5% shorter time-to-market.

Both of these objectives will contribute to significant costs saving. Estimates shows that a typical error reported from customers takes about 80 hours to fix and costs over 5000 ECU. This involves first line support of the customer, second line support (verification in support team), third line support (correction, testing, upgrade in new release, testing of release, production and shipment). Reducing the number of errors will not only save significant costs, but definitely increase customer satisfaction with the existing products and bring new products quicker to the market.

There is a possible correlation between reducing the number of errors and getting new products quicker to the market. Less effort spent on error corrections in the development department can free resources to be used to development of new products. More resources on development should decrease the development time of new products and therefore shorten the time-to-market.

We also intend, in line with one of the main objectives of the ESSI program, to share the result of the experiment with the European software community.

6.6.2.2   Involved Companies and their Roles

There is one participant and one subcontractor involved in the experiment. The participant is Sysdeco GIS AS (SGIS) and the subcontractor is The Norwegian Technical University (NTNU) in Trondheim Norway. SGIS will collect background data, introduce the new configuration management system, adjust procedures using the new system, collect data from the experiment, be responsible for dissemination and administer the project.

NTNU will provide expertise in training using the new configuration tool, define metrics to be used, analyse the existing and the new data collected, report and contribute to the presentations of the results. Both are involved in writing reports and dissemination activities.

6.6.2.3   Starting Scenario
Organisation

The CMEX project is done at the development department of Sysdeco GIS AS (SGIS). SYSDECO GROUP ASA wholly owns SGIS. Sysdeco Group ASA also owns Sysdeco Tools AS and Sysdeco Health AS (see figure below). SGIS is situated in Norway and is the owner or partly owner of a number of sister companies in Europe and Asia. Each of these companies has one or more product groups. A product group serves a defined market, for example national mapping authorities or electricity companies. A product group makes special applications for the end-user customer.

The development department at SGIS makes a tool-kit that is used by a product group to make the end-user products. In this way the development group at SGIS only have contact with the product groups in the different Sysdeco companies and not directly with the customer buying the end-user application.

The advantage with this organisation is that each product group can specialise on an application area using a common tool-kit developed by the company. Since the applications are made with the same tool-kit, the different product groups can share both knowledge and modules.

Business

The company makes end-user systems for different mapping areas such as topographic mapping, utility mapping, systems for power plants, fleet management (GPS), WEB solutions, etc. The customer database consists of national mapping organisations, power plants, local authorities, utility companies, insurance companies, the military, software houses, etc. The different Sysdeco companies offer consultants making end-user applications. These are made by using SGIS's GIS tool-kit. The main business of the company is to make end-user applications.

However, Sysdeco also sells the tool-kit to other companies. This puts strong requirements on the tool-kit regarding robustness and documentation.

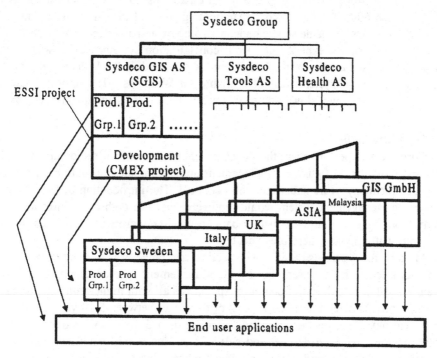

Fig. 6.14 Organisation of Sysdeco

Technical Environment

The development department delivers two main products; Tellus and Tellus Vision. Tellus, which was originally developed for various UNIX environments in the late 1980's, provides developers with a hybrid raster and vector tool-set for layered colour maps and includes a proprietary programming language (TCL) for application dependent code. Tellus is currently in version 2.4 and is supported on several different UNIX platforms (HP/UX 9.05, HP/UX 10.3, DEC Ultrix, DEC OSF/1, SUN Solaris, SunOS and IBM AIX) with four database connections (Oracle, Sybase, Mimer and Ingres).

The newest product is Tellus Vision, which offers the Tellus mapping technology on MSWindows NT/Win95. Several releases has been produced, TV1.0, TV2.0, TV2.3, TV2.4, the first in 1995. We have currently sent out the beta version of TV 3. TV1.0 was a port of the existing UNIX version to NT. Gradually the new releases adopted more and more of mainstream components for handling databases, programming language and GUI. TV3 is based on Microsoft object technology, COM, and can be used by main development tools such as Visual Basic, Visual C++ and of course Sysdeco's own development tool QBE Vision. In addition to adopting the new mainstream technology, TV3 also offers a wide range of new functionality compared to the original UNIX version.

The Tellus family of products consists of more than 20 different variants depending on platform (UNIX, Windows) and database system. The system consists of more than 600.000 lines of code. The management of the different variants of products based on the same source code is a complex and an erroneous process.

At the start of the experiment an old configuration system, SCCS, was used. This worked satisfactory for the UNIX products, but when the Windows products was introduced, the system was not available for Windows NT. The development was depending on manual procedures that easily led to errors and inconsistencies.

Culture and Skills

The project was performed in the development department of the company. The existing tools for configuration management and accompanying routines had been in place for many years and were well accepted. The introduction of a new configuration management system would require changes in both procedures and the daily working environment. On this background scepticism and even resistance would be naturally and therefore expected.

Another, more serious reason for expecting resistance, was that the new system was not selected by the users, but by the management. The development department consisted of a dozen of computer specialists all with higher education (engineers, computer scientists, Ph.D.). Most of them had between 5-10 year of experience and have been in the company for more than 5 years. All procedures and tools have earlier been defined and selected by this highly qualified team. The decision to choose ClearCase as the new tool was based on a study by another development group in the company, which used a similar tool to ClearCase.

To document the user acceptance of the system before, during and after the system was introduced a questionnaire was worked out. The results are shown later in this report.

6.6.2.4   Workplan

The project was divided into 5 workpackages. The first workpackage, WP1, is a preparation phase for the experiment. Sysdeco's experience data base would be studied and analysed. The existing data was planned to form the basis for the experiment. Metrics based on the data were to be defined.

The preparation phase of the project also includes installing a new configuration management system. The experiment will be done after the preparation in WP1. The experiment is two folded. In the first phase data is collected developing the next version of the software. Based on the experience of phase 1, the process will be improved and another experiment will be done during the development of the next version of the software.

The remaining workpackages, WP 3,4 and 5, deal with analysing, preparing and presenting the data from the experiments. Key milestones and deliverables for the project was:

- Document defining metrics and procedure
- Install Configuration management tool
- Collect and analyse data on phase 1 of the experiment
- Collect and analyse data on phase 2 of the experiment

6.6.2.5   Expected Outcomes

In "Objectives" of this report, the aims for the introduction of the new configuration management system was described to achieve a 5% shorter time-to-market and a 10% reduction in error reports for the software products. We expected this to be achievable.

Another expectation from this experiment was that the development department successfully will start to use a better and safer configuration management system. This would hopefully put less pressure on the developers, especially on the system administrator and improve the working environment in the department and last but not last increase the customers' satisfaction.

6.6.3   Work Performed
6.6.3.1   Organisation

The involved staff in the project was from the development department of Sysdeco and the consultants from the subcontractor NTNU. The figure below gives an overview of the involved staff and how these interact.

The thin lines in the figure show the reporting structure. The thick lines show the workflow in the department. The workflow is the same as being used in the experiment. The project manager is also the manager of the development department and is therefore responsible for the day-to-day operation of the development.

The Support Responsible receives customer requests. These come indirectly from Sysdeco customers via one of Sysdeco's sales offices. The request can be an order of a product, a support question or an error report. The order by-pass the development co-ordinator and goes directly to the person responsible for shipment. A support question usually does not involve developers, but might do in difficult cases or when the question initiates an error report. Error reports goes to the Development co-ordinator, who gives the report to a developer. When the problem is solved, the system administrator takes over, includes the corrected code in the official version and generates the new official release. This is sent to the QA responsible for testing. When the new revision is accepted an official version is produced on the appropriate media and shipped to the customer.

The processes described are followed by a number of forms and procedures. Each involved person fills out the forms. The data from these forms are some of the sources for data collected in this project.

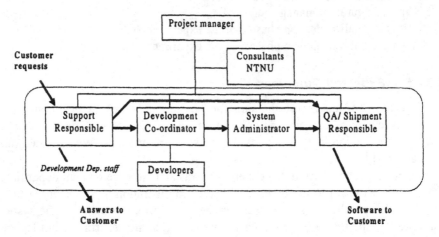

Fig. 6.15 Organisation of the CMEX project

6.6.3.2 Technical Environment

The purpose of the project was to observe any change in the productivity of software by introducing a new configuration management tool, ClearCase, to replace SCCS, an old UNIX based system.

Originally 5 licences were purchased for the experiment to be used by 8 developers. It soon turned out that each developer needed a software licence and that sharing significantly slowed down the productivity.

The use of ClearCase also required more computer resources than expected. A dedicated PC-server with 8Gbyte disk and 160Mbyte RAM had to be allocated, together with at least 80Mbyte of RAM for each PC-workstatuion. The latter was not only triggered by ClearCase, but perhaps mainly by the development tool Microsoft Visual C++. Also, some upgrades of the UNIX server had to be done (disk and memory) to host the ClearCase system in order to be able to use the system both for the NT/Win95 products as well as for the UNIX versions.

6.6.3.3 Training

Originally training courses were planned for both the developers and especially for the system manager. However, the scheduled training courses arranged by the vendor were cancelled. We had to build up the competence in other ways, since we had no time to wait for new courses to be scheduled.

The training was done by:

- The system manager studied the ClearCase documentation.
- The system manager interviewed other using the system.
- The system manager made a prototype on a machine that did not effected other developers.

This gave him time to get acquainted with the system and carefully plan the final implementation.

- One developer integrated the system in his development environment (Visual C++) and gained experience with the system
- The system manager and the involved developer trained the rest of the developers.

As we can see, a significant burden was put on the development manager. The vendor gave very good support during the process, but there is no doubt that the introduction phase of the system required more resources and took more time than originally planned. This is also clearly reflected in the user acceptance questionnaire answered to the developers, see the "Annex A:". The conclusions in this Annex are:

Conclusions:

- The team was motivated to change to old CM system to a new system.
- The team did not get enough training to use the system
- The team lost a lot of time in the introduction period, but not more than expected.
- The team has accepted the system.

Fortunately, the team has accepted the system, in spite of too little training. This is due to the good work of the system manager and the positive attitude of the developers. *However, we strongly recommend to other introducing ClearCase to get formal training by the vendor and plan for some months experimenting and introduction time!*

6.6.3.4   Role of the Consultants

The project has one external consultant organisation, NTNU, The Technical University of Trondheim. Their main role of the project has been to define a set of relevant metrics, identify data sources, collect and analyse the data in the project.

In order to fulfil these tasks, it has been required to study the organisation, procedures and the workflow of the organisation. Through this, relevant data sources have been identified and based on these, a set of metrics was defined.

The data sources were then studied in detail and validated against the originally defined metrics. Some of the metrics were left out since there were not enough relevant data available.

Another significant contribution to the project from the consultants has been to write reports and contribute with dissemination activities.

6.6.3.5   Phases of the Experiment

The project was divided into 5 workpackages:

- WP 1 Analysis of current situation and preparation
- WP 2 Experiment: Change Control
- WP 3 Analysis of final situation
- WP 4 Dissemination and administration
- WP5 Administration

Of these workpackages the first 3 concern the experiment and will be enhanced here.

WP 1 Analysis of Current Situation and Preparation

The overall objective of this workpackage was to do the required preparation for the experiment. This was done through the following activities:

- Installing ClearCase (Configuration Management and Version Control system)
- Measure before situation for the PIE
- Decide metrics to use; how to measure
- Prepare for actual experimentation (infrastructure)

Installing ClearCase was relatively easy due to good installation procedures and an experienced system manager. To organise the source-code under the system was also easy, but to get the system operational and well configured should turn out to be difficult (See WP2 following).

Sysdeco has built up an experience database over many years. The different data sources were identified and the different processes for handling errors and making new releases were documented.

Based on the different data sources a number of metrics were defined, all together 16 different ones (see Annex C, Original metrics proposed and used). At this stage of the project, no evaluation of the data had been done. We were prepared for that some of the defined metrics could not be used because of lack of sufficient data. The data sources being used were:

- *SAM* is a database containing customer information, licenses issued, and defect reports.
- *Defect logs*: The development group maintains a list of external (SQR) and internal (RPR) defect reports. All defect reports regarding the Tellus/Tellus Vision product family are recorded in this log and are being updated during the maintenance process. The log is one large text file with a number of programs to extract data for management and status reporting.

- *Delivery logs*: The personnel in the 2. line support organisation is responsible for handling orders and deliveries. Some orders may be delivered directly, while others require production of a specific delivery revision or even porting to new platforms. Orders for new revisions are also placed routinely when customers with maintenance agreements report problems that need to be corrected (or are already corrected). All open and closed deliveries are maintained in a log.
- *Time sheets*: All employees report resource usage using a set of project numbers. The spreadsheets used are collected bi-weekly and entered into a database.
- *Source code*: The source code has up till now been managed with SCCS. We have found some product and version specific characteristics for Tellus 2.2 in the period April 1994 to February 1996 from an analysis earlier in the project. This analysis was based on revision logs extracted from SCCS.

This workpackage made the following deliverables:

- D1-1 Document defining metrics and procedure
- D1-2 Installed Configuration management tool

WP 2 Experiment: Change Control
- The objective of this workpackage was to:
- Train team in the Configuration Management system
- Use the Configuration Management system developing new releases of a product
- Collect process data during experiment
- Provide services to team

A formal training was planned both of the system manager and the users of the system. The vendor cancelled the planned training courses and new courses were too late for the project. The system manager therefore took the responsibility to learn the system by studying the documentation, getting help from other users and by using the support system of the vendor. This has proven to be possible, but it took much more time than planned. More training should have allocated for the users, which is clearly expressed in the user questionnaire (see Annex A).

Data were collected for the two phases 95/96 and 97 and documented in two deliveries. By analysing the sources described in WP1, a final set of metrics were selected. We ended up with 5 of the original 16 defined. They were sufficient to study the main objectives of the project. The results are presented in Annex B: Results of measurement. This annex is a part of delivery "D2-2 Data on phase 2 of the experiment" and contains also the conclusions of the analysis.

This workpackage made the following deliverables:

- D2-1 Data on phase 1 of the experiment
- D2-2 Data on phase 2 of the experiment

WP 3 Analysis of Final Situation

The objective is to summarise the findings in the experiment and draw conclusions. The results and conclusions are shown in Annex B: Results of measurement. This activity had one deliverable:

- D3-1 Preliminary report of the experiment

6.6.3.6 Internal Dissemination

All developers in the company have been involved in the experiment and they are perhaps the most important target group for this project. They have contributed to the reports, results have been presented at internal meetings and all reports and data have been available for them.

The awareness of the project and the results has been published in Sysdeco's internal newsletter. This is sent to all GIS associated companies in Sysdeco in UK, Germany, Sweden, Italy, Singapore and Malaysia.

6.6.4 Results and Analysis

Measurement of the effects of the project on product quality and business operation is an important part of the experiment. At project mid-term we performed a thorough measurement of quality and process parameters for the initial process, resulting in a good basis for quantifying improvement results at the end of the experiment. Towards the end of the experiment we processed data collected during the second phase of the project, i.e. 1997. We discovered that data for some of the metrics initially defined were not consistently recorded. As a consequence we have used 5of the originally 16 metrics to identify the quantitative results (see Annex C, Original metrics proposed and used). The following metrics were used:

- M01 – Defect arrival rate
- M03 – Defect priority
- M07 – Defect fix time
- M13 – Resource usage
- M14 – Maintenance effort

In addition to the quantitative results measured by the metrics above, a questionnaire to the users was distributed to get an impression of the human factors by introducing a new system in a well-established development department. (See Annex A: Human factors, User acceptance).

The overall aims for the CMEX project was stated in the application to the European Commission (Annex 1, Project summary):

"Introducing a formal change control system is believed to improve the process, resulting in 5% shorter time-to-market and a 10% reduction in error reports for the software products."

The measurement results show a significant improvement, higher than what was planned. In the following these results of the data analysis will be elaborated and discussed.

6.6.4.1   Technical

"Annex B: Results of measurement" contains an extract of the results of the different metrics used in the project. The two metrics "M01 – Defect arrival rate" and "M13 – Resource usage" gives results that are directly relevant for the overall aim of the project as referred to above. There are two observations that show:

The aim of the CMEX project to reduce the number of reported errors from customers (SQR) by 10% has been achieved. The SQRs errors have been reduced by 35.7. (ref Conclusions M01 and see table *Error reports received externally (SQR) and internally (RPR)*.

Development work has relatively increased by 22% and maintenance relatively decreased by 33.3%, leading to bring the product quicker to the market. (ref Conclusions M13 and the graph *Relative change of work areas*)

Further studies of the reported errors show that both high priority errors and low priority errors have been significantly reduced (ref. M03). The above results are for external reported errors (SQR). We have also observed the development of internal reported errors (PRP), which are errors reported on non-released products (alpha and beta versions). These have significantly increased. This is a most wanted development since the costs associated with correcting and external error is much higher than those associated with internal errors. The earlier an error is detected the less effort and costs are used.

However the reduction of SQR errors is not a result of the increase of PRP errors since the RPRs and SQRs are reported on two different products (TV2 and TV3). What we can conclude is that we are currently spending more time on testing (ref M13) and finding more errors before we release a new product.

We have also observed that the time to fix an error has decreased both for internal and external errors. There has been a decrease in fix time of serious external errors by more than 5.5% (for some half time) and for internal reports a reduction of more than 56%. *We are getting less external errors and we use less time to fix an error!* In terms of qualitative improvements we will mention:

The process modelling activities at the start of the project resulted in a better understanding of the maintenance process, and, following a discussion, a number of process changes, mostly concerning responsibilities and use of report forms. Sysdeco GIS has been following a quite formal maintenance process for some time, and this experiment activity played an important role in clarifying some of the loosely defined parts of the process.

When installing ClearCase, Sysdeco GIS also revised its Make-based production and delivery systems and this activity resulted in improved quality of the production and delivery services of Sysdeco GIS.

The introduction of ClearCase has resulted in an increased ability of reconstructing previous product revisions.

The measurement activities have resulted in an increased knowledge about the performance of the maintenance processes and the costs involved.

The reported improvements can not only be attributed to CMEX and the use of ClearCase, but is also results of a number of other factors. We should also state that 1996 was an exceptional year in terms of changes: in addition to work on introducing ClearCase, the company was restructured, and a number of product versions were released on new platforms.

6.6.4.2   Business

The major business outcomes of the experiment has been a significant improvement of the quality and efficiency (cost and time) of the maintenance services and process. There has been a 33% decrease of maintenance effort (from 22% to 15% of total human resource usage in 1996 and 1997 respectively), mostly corresponding to the fewer defect reports. As a result, significant resources have been made available for development activities, an increase of 22% from 48% of the total human resource usage in 1996 to 58% in 1997. Defining "time-to-market" in terms of available development effort, we have achieved an improvement much higher than the 10% that were expected. We have also saved significant maintenance costs.

ClearCase is expensive compared to a simple version control system. The costs of purchase, training, installation and administration are high. A mature company with a well-founded change process will need to spend 100-200 KECU to acquire ClearCase and get the system up and running. ClearCase by itself can not be expected to improve the product quality, but accompanied by a formal change management process improvements might be expected.

One way to calculate the return of investment is to compare the costs mentioned over with the reduced costs for correcting errors. This can be done by using the formula $R = I/(P*N)$, where R = number of months to regain the investment I, I = invested capital, P = price to correct an error, N = reduction in number of errors/month.

In our case we have reduced the number of errors by 4.3/month (=N), from 12.1/month to 7.8/month. The cost for correcting an error (P) has been estimated in average to be 5000 ECU. This might sound high, but be aware that this involves not just the development department. It involves first line support of the customer (usually abroad), second line support (verification in support team in Norway), third line support (correction, testing, upgrade in new release, testing of release, production and shipment). By applying the formula above, we regain an investment of 100-200 KECU in 4.7-9.4 months.

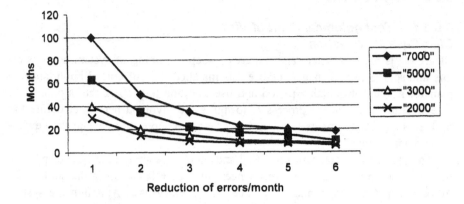

Fig. 6.16 Return of investment of 200.000 ECU

6.6.4.3   Organisation

The experiment has so far only had a very small impact on the organisational environment. The maintenance process has undergone some changes in terms of more clearly defined responsibilities and tasks, and introduction of some additional forms to support the change process.

The reason for this might be that Sysdeco GIS is a mature organisation with a long experience in product change management and using simpler version control and production systems. The process changes connected to the experiment have been perceived as a natural part of the continuously ongoing discussion of the company's processes.

6.6.4.4   Culture

As mentioned earlier the company's culture is in favour of a clearly defined process and the involved personnel largely developed the revised change control routines. All parties acknowledged the need for a revision of the change control routines before the start of the experiment.

There was some initial scepticism towards introducing a large and complex system as ClearCase, but when exposed to the functionality of ClearCase the system was acknowledged as superior to the alternative of keeping the existing system.

At the end of the project all personnel involved in the project answered a questionnaire about various aspects of the process of introducing ClearCase. The general opinion was acknowledged need for a new CM-system, some dissatisfaction with the process of selecting ClearCase, and a very positive reception of Clear-Case once in use. The detailed results are available in Annex A. 4.5.

6.6.4.5   Skills

A large part of the organisation has acquired skills in using ClearCase.

6.6.5   Key Lessons

6.6.5.1   Technological Point of View
ClearCase Introduction

ClearCase is a large system and requires in-depth training of system administrators and source code managers before it is installed. It is of crucial importance to plan for a long introduction period and use the time to prepare the organisation. One possible introduction process is to make the involved personnel define the problems and requirements to the new process and support tools, and then evaluate candidate tools.

Training of the users is also required and more time should have been spent on this. Also the number of software licences must be relevant from the start of the introduction. Our experience is one license for every user. Although the system allows sharing of licences, it makes the system unusable.

It has also become evident that the management of product changes is far more dependent on a rigorous and accepted work process than on the tools used to support the process. The success of the experiment so far is largely dependent on the fact a work process was already in place. In another setting, the experiment might have failed or taken considerably more effort.

We believe that it is important that the ClearCase system administrator is given enough time to get acquainted with the system so that the installation is stable when other personnel start using the system. Otherwise, the attitude towards the new system could quickly have become negative.

A related issue is that the management of defect reports and other change-related items is equally as time-consuming than the management of file versions. The lesson for this issue is that support tools for managing defect reports, orders, and product revision availability lists might have been a more cost-effective investment, and that early versions of tools supplied by the CM system vendor are not necessarily the best choice.

Process Modelling

Defining the work process is a time-consuming task, which should be paid much attention to. It is important to assure that one ends up with an agreement on how the work is going to be carried out.

The different groups involved in the work process might have quite different views on what is done at each process step and whose responsibility it is. The process modelling activity is an excellent opportunity to discuss these views and arrive at an agreement or even revised process definitions.

Measurements

The measurement activities have required far more effort than originally planned. This is due to the facts that existing data do not lend themselves to direct use in measurement, and that parts of the data required to measure success are not present. To get a relevant data basis one has to measure the process over a period of time.

We have also learned that new measurement efforts are useless unless the data collection is an integral part of the ordinary work process. In our case we have solved this by extracting data from new and existing lists and databases used for managing defect reports and orders.

6.6.5.2   *Business Point of View*

The major business outcomes of the experiment has been a significant improvement of the quality and efficiency (cost and time) of the maintenance services and process. As a result, significant resources have been made available for development activities and we have been able to bring new functionality to the market earlier than expected. The configuration management system is not expected to improve product quality by itself, but the increased focus on maintenance (costs and resource usage) has lead to fewer product defects.

From a business point of view, ClearCase, would not have been the obvious choice since this system is more expensive than other systems. The obvious alternative would have been Sourcesafe from Microsoft that cost about 1/7 of ClearCase's about 4500 ECU/lisence. ClearCase is a complex system to understand and it takes time to understand the advantages over simpler systems. This was not obvious at the beginning of the project, but is clear now. The cost of the system has proven to be insignificant compared to the potential for improvements.

There seem to be few managers in a company that understand the importance of configuration management and even less that heavy investment in tools is required. This project has set the focus on the complexity of the problems and therefore the need for investing in good tools to secure efficient development as well as securing the investment in the software.

6.6.5.3   *Strengths and Weaknesses of the Experiment*

The most obvious strength of the experiment has been the maturity of the organisation and the fact that the involved personnel had acknowledged the need for a new change control system. The process of motivation the personnel for using ClearCase was a distinct phase, but it was simplified by these facts.

The most obvious weakness has been the lack of background statistics over the last few years. This has lead to much effort being spent on data collection and analysis. Another issue has been the extraordinary events during the experiment: a company restructuring, change of primary development and supply platform, along with unusually frequent product releases has left small and fragmented timeframes for training, installation and deployment of ClearCase.

6.6.6   Conclusions and Future Actions

The overall objectives of this project were to successfully introduce a new configuration management system and through this improve the performance of the development department. The overall objectives are met, but this is not just a result of introducing a new system, rather more a result of the entire process around changing to a new system and a natural maturity of the existing products.

Perhaps the most important result of the experiment is that the users have accepted the new system. Through the funding of this project has been given the opportunity to go through the entire development process and introduce a more advanced tool than a SMB like Sysdeco GIS naturally would choose.

Sysdeco will continue to use the new system in its development and maintenance processes and will further improve and enhance the established routines. It has become evident that there is a need for tools to support the management of change requests and defect reports parts are important and we will consider introducing such tools along with ClearCase.

Sysdeco will continue to improve its development process and the next area that we plan to focus on is software testing. This is motivated by the experience that the earlier an error is found, the less costs is associated correcting it. Sysdeco already have systems for software testing, but new and modern tools are available that we believe significantly can make testing easier and more efficient. This project has already given a set of valuable background data that will be used to measure the effect of further process improvements by introducing automated testing tools.

6.6.7   Glossary

SCCS	Source Code Control system (comes with UNIX OS)
ClearCase	Configuration management tool from Rational Software Corporation
Tellus	Sysdeco GIS's 4GL development tool-kit for making mapping applications. Available for Windows NT/95.
Tellus Vision	Sysdeco GIS's 4GL development tool-kit for making mapping applications. Available for Windows NT/95.
Windows	Microsoft Windows
DEC	Computer from Digital Equipment
HP	Computer from Hewlett and Packard
SUN	Computer from SUN Microsystems
IBM	Computer from IBM

6.6.8   References

[Basili88]
    V.R.Basili, and H.D.Rombach, *The TAME project. Towards improvement-*

orientated software environments, IEEE Transactions on Software Engineering 14(6), pp 758-773, 1988

[Humphrey89]

W.S.Humphrey, *Managing the Software Process*, New York, NY, Addison-Wesley Publishing Co. 1989.

[Chillarege92]

R.Chillarege, I.S.Bhandari, J.K.Chaar, M.J.Halliday, D.S.Moebus, B.K.Ray, and M-Y. Wong, *Orthogonal Defect Classification– A Concept for In-Process Measurements*, IEEE Transactions on Software Engineering, 18(11), pp 943—956, 1992.

Annexes

To be found at the VASIE web site. Very recommendable for the reader interested in getting a thorough metrics approach.

- Human Factors, User Acceptance
- Results of Measurement
- Original Metrics Proposed and Used

6.7   Project 21670 – PRIME
A Practical Strategy for Industrial Reuse Improvement

Anthony Powell
Rolls-Royce University Technology Centre/University of York

Duncan Brown
Rolls-Royce plc, Derby

6.7.1   Abstract

Rolls-Royce plc have first-hand experience of delivering systematic software reuse in the production of real-time embedded control systems for civil aero engine applications. Reuse levels of 80% have been achieved between control system developments giving substantial economic savings, along with reduced cycle times and assured software quality. But since these early savings were aided by intrinsic similarities between projects, there has been no room for complacency. Faced with new and more diverse applications the reuse process will increasingly be a major determinant of business performance. A continuous search for reuse improvement has therefore become a strategic necessity.

This paper presents some results of the PRIME project in the form of a six-step reuse improvement strategy. It is notable for the concept of improvement paths – the effective "policy levers" that a project manager can use to control the reuse process. The improvement framework and lessons learned will be of interest to practitioners interested or actively involved in reuse and to researchers engaged in reuse technology transfer.

6.7.2   Introduction

The last decade has seen a significant body of research aimed at unlocking the economic potential of systematic software reuse. However, the transfer of research principles into industrial practice has been more problematic than the seductive simplicity of reuse ideology has led us to believe. Pragmatists are acutely aware that successful reuse depends on cultural and organisational issues as much as supporting technology.

The evidence that systematic reuse can have a significant impact on business performance is now compelling. Hewlett Packard divisions have used reuse to double productivity, halve defects, and dramatically reduce time-to-market [Lim94]. Motorola's 86% reuse level provided a tenfold increase in productivity [Joos94] and Rockwell International experienced benefits lower project bids and of responsiveness to customer needs [O'Connor94]. These and other published studies stress that achieving successful reuse requires a large amount of foresight, investment and, above all, commitment. But for those inspired to embark on a reuse programme the route to successful reuse is by no means clear; experience from a wide variety of domains and development environments all suggests that *there is no one right way to perform software reuse.*

The absence of an objective definition of *"best practice"* means that companies must determine for themselves the effectiveness of alternative reuse approaches from the bewildering array of tools and techniques available. A lack of comparative data to establish *"what – works – where"* means that effort is being focused on techniques to support a quantitative understanding of reuse within an individual organisation. These quantitative techniques allow organisations to evaluate the effectiveness of their reuse processes, identify process improvements and, to a certain extent, share reuse experiences at a common level of understanding. As reuse increasingly becomes a significant determinant of competitive performance, this capability for continuous process improvement becomes vital.

The Rolls-Royce BR700 team began a formal programme of systematic software reuse in the development of a new generation of Full Authority Digital Engine Controllers for civil aero engines in 1992. A FADEC is a control system responsible for managing engine thrust, temperature, pressure, communication, and maintenance functions. Whilst the embedded software is relatively small (typically 200,000 lines of Ada code) the process required to produce flight-critical real-time software is inherently expensive. Hence, by viewing FADEC development as a product-line with instantiations of a "generic architecture" the company hoped to exploit the potential benefits of formally reusing engineering products and processes. Software reuse was therefore considered key to producing the most cost effective, high quality systems in the shortest possible timescales.

During the introduction of the original reuse programme, management were keen to measure the levels of reuse achieved and evaluate the impact of reuse on bottom-line business performance. A first-cut reuse measurement process was introduced with the goal of *demonstrating cost savings due to reuse.* The calculation was based on the component development cost, the additional cost of making a component reusable, the cost of reusing the item, and the percentage reuse level achieved. The metrics collected demonstrated impressive results. The target project achieved a level of *82% source code reuse* and *cost only 20% of its predecessor.*

Whilst the baseline reuse metrics confirmed the significant benefits of systematic software reuse, there were still problems. The high reuse levels had been aided by the intrinsic similarities between the target project and its predecessor. Furthermore, the reuse measurement process itself was onerous, a considerable overhead on development, and insufficient for meeting business goals. The metrics demonstrated that the reuse process was successful (in cost terms) but failed to indicate exactly where improvements could be made, nor how we might accurately estimate for future projects. There could be no room for complacency.

Faced with new and more challenging applications, we needed a measurement and improvement process by which we could ensure that our reuse processes are consistently aligned with business objectives.

6.7.3   A Strategy for Continuous Reuse Improvement

In partnership with the European Systems and Software Initiative, the Practical Reuse Improvement MEtrics (PRIME) project has sought to deliver "best practice" capability in reuse management and continuous improvement within Rolls-Royce. The remainder of this paper describes some of the results of this work captured as a six-step reuse improvement strategy which is used to present our lessons learned as a set of practical guidelines for improving a reuse process.

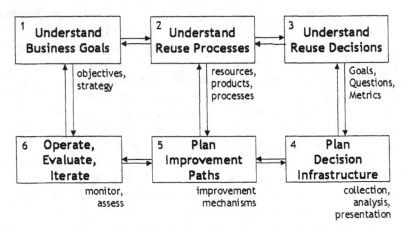

Fig. 6.17 Six-step Reuse Improvement Model

6.7.3.1   Step 1: Understand Reuse Business Goals

Identify Your Business Goals

A major factor in the success of the original reuse programme had been a continuous focus on business results. Reuse provided a means to reduce production costs and lead-times whilst meeting the exacting demands on software quality. Demanding but realistic targets had been identified for the reuse programme based on engineer assessments of potential system reusability. A persistent focus on these targets made sure that participants were aware of their responsibility in meeting them.

A major failing of the original reuse programme, however, was an assumption that meeting our reuse targets implied that the reuse itself had been successfully introduced into the organisation. As targets were met, the push for reuse declined and team members settled back into old patterns of working that saw reuse levels falling well below our full reuse potential. We realised that (to use Myers' frame-work Fig. 6.18) the reuse process had been adopted but we had failed to fully inte-grate or internalise reuse into the process. Faced with a new engine application that was significantly different to its predecessor we needed to ensure that our reuse pro-gramme was capable of meeting challenging new business targets.

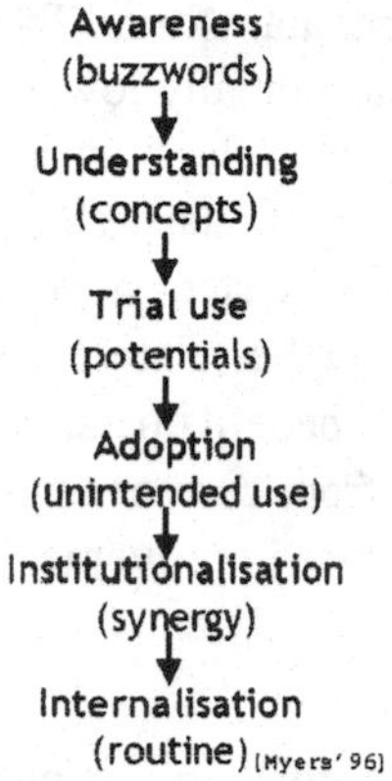

Awareness
(buzzwords)
↓
Understanding
(concepts)
↓
Trial use
(potentials)
↓
Adoption
(unintended use)
↓
Institutionalisation
(synergy)
↓
Internalisation
(routine) [Myers' 96]

Fig. 6.18 Maturity of Technology Adoption [Myers97]

The PRIME project was therefore established to ensure that our reuse pro-gramme was measurably in-line with business objectives and continuously im-proving in the context of our changing environment. This process had to start with a thorough re-evaluation of our business goals. Reuse had now become a *strategic necessity* for producing the most cost effective, high quality systems in shorter timescales. Moreover, to meet our goal of internalising the reuse process we had to convince participants that the reuse problem had not yet been solved. Reuse was not the end in itself, but an ongoing means to achieve business goals.

Identify Your Reuse Goals
The rationale for elaborating business goals was an important part of the reuse improvement process: business objectives and constraints determine viable reuse strategies that affect both the nature, and degree, of the reuse solution to be em-ployed. These goals were captured as a vision of the target process over the short, medium, and long-term, expressed against a baseline assessment of the current capability.

The *short-term objective* was to deliver incremental process improvements in the reuse process. These improvements would contribute to a reduced cost of software development, increased product quality (by the use of mature trusted components), and further reductions in project timescales that were essential to meeting delivery targets. Furthermore, reuse would result in less tangible benefits by, for example, providing a route for managing the growing complexity of the control system by standardising on well-documented existing components.

The *medium-term goal* was to encourage a shift in our perception of the product-line by providing the required incremental changes in our reuse processes. The aim was to capture requirements in a reusable way and effectively turn the process "on-its-head." The focus on producing a stable product-line architecture would enable core engine functions to be provided "off-the-shelf" with alternative system configurations being costed as optional extras. To our customers this would mean systems of proven maturity for substantially lower costs.

The *long-term goal* was to develop the *"generic engine controller."* A generic control system demands more revolutionary changes to product architecture than possible with traditional methods of system development. The high initial costs of the generic system would however be relatively small compared to bespoke development costs and the potential benefits of an assured marketplace. A prerequisite for such a radical departure from current approaches would have to be a permanent organisational focus on reuse improvement.

Articulate Your Goals

The clear articulation these reuse goals in our business context helped secure the commitment of all participants. Their clarity supported the reuse team in enacting the necessary changes to business and reuse processes.

6.7.3.2   Step 2: Understand Reuse Processes

The evaluation of business and reuse goals had established the context for the reuse improvement programme and the criteria for an appropriate reuse process. Our next step was to identify the current and desired reuse process in order to optimise reuse within each development stage and across the process as a whole.

Identify Reuse Products, Resources, and Processes

The original reuse process had been derived from a combination of traditional reuse and domain engineering techniques [Lam97]. However, we were aware that the actual process had migrated some way from that originally planned, for a number of reasons. These included both changes in the underlying development process and "fixes" introduced to make the reuse process practicable. Moreover, we recognised that individual perceptions of the reuse process were sometimes inconsistent between team members. We therefore sought to model the processes, architecture, assets, tools and roles, of the actual reuse process compared to our planned and perceived processes. Re-engineering of the process would provide a defined reuse process that, once understood, could be more effectively aligned with process goals and later quantitatively evaluated.

The planned reuse process itself was considered to be best practice of its time [Hill94]. Software reuse was primarily achieved by the reuse of software requirements – each requirement being tagged as either generic or specific to a project. This led to cascaded reuse of designs, code, and tests from previous applications along with the development of new bespoke components as required. Reuse was also achieved at a low level by the use of library functions specified in the requirements using specific symbols and coded as reusable functional blocks (Ada procedures). This process proved to be a considerable advance over the informal "cut-and-paste" reuse of earlier developments.

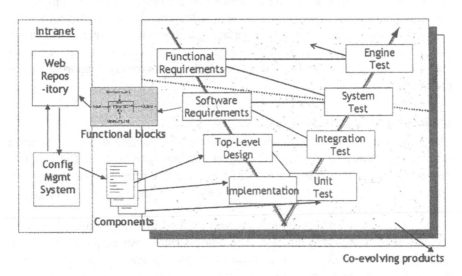

Fig. 6.19 Cascade Reuse Process

The modelling process revealed some characteristic features of the actual reuse process employed.

Project concurrency: A distinct feature of the process was the co-evolving nature of products. Reuse occurs between two or more simultaneous product developments "live" from the more mature development into the following project. The result can be reduced project timescales and benefits of dynamic design for reuse (i.e. information flow between the two projects to improve overall reuse levels). A damaging side effect of this concurrency, however, was the potential to introduce generic problems that necessitate fixes to all affected products.

Process Infrastructure: The reuse process was heavily dependent on the systems for configuration management and change control. The reuse process had become an integral part of the development process itself. Improvements to the reuse process thus implied changes to quality management systems including appropriate standards and procedures.

Reuse Communication: The manner by which reuse is communicated in the development process was seen to have a major impact reuse performance. Formal communication routes included product representations, product traceability, design meetings and the intranet-based reuse library. Equally important however were the informal communication routes such as informal conversation, and unwritten assumptions about system architecture and design practices. Problems in both formal and informal communication channels were seen to be limiting achievement of our reuse potential.

Architectural Control: Fundamentally, the reuse process was being driven by limitations in the system architecture that had been inherited from a history of bespoke development. Consequently, the product structure was highly sensitive to external change – with damaging consequences for process cost and timescales. This change, however, was viewed to be largely avoidable by producing a more appropriate architecture that used interface partitions to isolate the effects of change. The necessary transition from legacy to generic architecture would demand a higher degree of architectural control than currently supported by the present reuse process.

Identify an Evolution Plan

The insights obtained from the modelling activity were used to identify a more detailed evolution plan for both the product and the reuse process. The coupling between business and reuse process was a product-line strategy based on predictions of the number and type of future applications and anticipated changes in market and technology.

The actual reuse process experienced was typified by a small number of large projects of relatively long duration. The high outright costs of producing flight-quality software meant that development of reusable assets must be funded under the auspices of commercial projects. Product evolution therefore required a planned gradual migration of current "legacy" products at all process stages towards our target generic control system architecture to maximise reusability. Determining the focus and level of reuse investment to maximise returns was hence a critical part of the reuse process.

6.7.3.3   Step 3: Understand Reuse Decisions

The analysis of current reuse processes simplified the identification of reuse decisions; critically, it was observed that the effectiveness of our reuse process depends on our ability to *set realistic reuse targets, and our ability to meet them*. A quantitative understanding of reuse was therefore prerequisite to evaluating and improving reuse performance.

The problems of our original reuse measurement programme had taught us some important lessons. First, reuse measurement should preferably be via a few simple and well-understood metrics applied in anger. Second, the metrics must be purposeful with clear objectives on how the data will be used in process decision making. Third, both the metrics and their value should be clearly explained to their users. Fourth, metrics collection should be automated where possible to minimise overheads and improve data accuracy. Finally, the objectives of the reuse programme must be expressed in a measurable way.

The next step was to understand reuse economics at each stage in the development process. We isolated three generic decision processes that affect reuse process performance; namely reuse evaluation, reuse investment and reuse prediction.

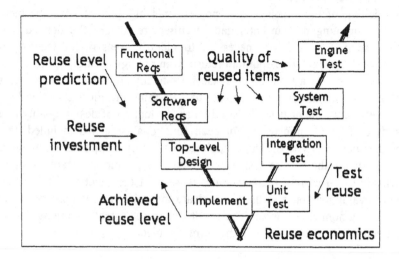

Fig. 6.20 Reuse Process Economics

Support Reuse Evaluation

Understanding reuse economics in our environment required evaluation of the effectiveness of the reuse process at each stage of development and across the process as a whole. This required accurate measurement of across four dimensions:

Effort: the effort of developing and modifying system components. This supports evaluation of the costs of development for reuse and the eventual return on reuse investment.

Time: the elapsed duration of process activities. This supports evaluation of the contribution of reuse toward improvements in product lead-time.

Quality: the number, type and root causes of defects in reused components along with their introduction/detection profiles. This supports evaluation of the effect of reuse on process and product quality.

Quantity: the level of reuse achieved across development projects and stability of system components. This supports evaluation of the impact of product changes on reuse profiles.

This evaluation capability served two purposes. First, it was used to identify specific questions that could be used to make improvements in our reuse process. For example: "Does system level reuse map down to code and test level reuse?" "What is the usage profile of components and how can it be improved?" "Does the architecture localise change to a minimum of system components?" and "What are the desirable size and quality characteristics of reusable components?" Second, it was used as a baseline of performance for reuse investment and prediction decisions.

Support Reuse Investment

The modelling of the existing reuse process had highlighted the importance of gradually migrating the current legacy architecture toward the desired generic control system. Hence, it was necessary to identify areas of the legacy system architecture that would give optimum return from re-engineering.

The outcome was a team-based reuse investment process that combines both qualitative and quantitative assessments to determine the most effective level of reuse investment. The decision is based on an evaluation of design quality and the demands of future applications. For each functional area this included: the expected number and type of future applications, component size, maintainability and testability of the current design, the potential for a more reusable design, and the availability of current reuse modules to support the function. This capability for reuse evaluation was also used to indicate the point at which partial reuse was no longer economically viable. The result was a hit list of functions that could cost-effectively be reengineered in the current project.

Support Reuse Prediction

The introduction of reuse had meant that business performance was now dependent on our ability to make accurate predictions of reuse levels and resultant costs savings. It was necessary to introduce a reuse estimation process based on a structured analysis of system reusability using evaluative data of past reuse performance.

The reuse prediction process assigns predictions using a variant of the commonality analysis technique developed at Lucent Bell Labs [Weiss96]. Essentially this approach formally divides a function into its constituent sub-functions that are then assigned weightings as a percentage of the overall function. This process uses the identification of likely changes in system components to predict a reuse level for the function in the future application. The cost of developing the component afresh and the potential cost of reusing are then used to identify an expected effort taking into account the expected benefit of reuse investments. A prediction of overall reuse levels across for the system can then be made along with the anticipated savings due to reuse.

As projects progress, the spend per function is measured against targets and used to monitor and control the reuse process. The measured level of estimate accuracy is factored into the prediction process to improve estimate quality next time around.

Identify Goals, Questions, Metrics

The investigation into both business and reuse processes was distilled into a traditional set of Goals, Questions and Metrics [Basili92] required both to support the current reuse process and provide feedback for continuous improvement. We believe, however, that the insights from our more wide-ranging investigation led us to a different GQM set than would have been achieved from direct analysis. In particular it identified the critical gap between perceived, current and desired reuse processes. As a result we were more equipped to measure those factors important to achieving the desired reuse process.

6.7.3.4   Step 4: Plan Decision Infrastructure

The improvement of reuse decision-making must be accompanied by an appropriate infrastructure to support effective data collection and analysis.

Automate Metrics Collection

The problems of our earlier metrics programme had encouraged us to put a large emphasis on automated collection of product and process metrics. Automation would increase data accuracy and allow manual effort to moved from data collection and concentrated on the value-added work of identifying and implementing process improvements. Three key in-house tools supported this metrication effort.

PRIME Cost Booking System (PCBS). PCBS is a powerful cost booking system that enables collection of effort information at a level of detail unachievable with current cost collection systems. The technique supports collection of activity effort, timescale, and resource data, based on the concept of a generic work-breakdown structure. The use of a Process Engineering Language allows expression of activity plans and results in natural language. This allows users to query the information in a myriad of different ways, many of which may not even have been anticipated at the project outset, with no additional overhead.

Rolls-Royce Change Control System (RoCCS). RoCCS is an advanced change control system that supports the management of multiple projects within concurrent phased-delivery lifecycles. It was adapted to collect information on the number, type and root cause of in-process problems and their introduction, detection, and removal profiles. The impact of reuse on trends in product quality could then be tracked without additional overhead.

Automated Reuse Measurement Tool (ARMT). The ARMT tool was developed to provide analysis of low-level code reuse and modification between software products and deliveries. The tool captured various size and complexity characteristics of software modules as well as the percentage black-box and white-box reuse of modules, subsystems and overall products.

The remaining metrics data was collected from the configuration management system and existing development and testing tools.

Support Decision Analysis

The use of automated metric collection helped us to standardise our analysis to support specific reuse decisions. This analysis took the form of decision-based spreadsheets that could be populated from the collection tools. By configuring these spreadsheets it is possible to capture decisions themselves to be and improved along with the reuse process itself.

We have also experimented with more advanced models of the software process that are more suited to incremental staged-delivery lifecycles of this type. Research work has investigated the use of system dynamics to model the impact of reuse and other improvements on process effectiveness [Powell98]. The preliminary results of this approach indicate its valuable potential in understanding of the effects of reuse on process lead-times. The comprehensive metrics infrastructure introduced by the PRIME toolset provides the prerequisite capability for these more advanced long-term improvement models.

6.7.3.5   Step 5: Plan Improvement Paths

The main contribution of metrics in the improvement process comes from their use to either support or contradict our perceptions of process behaviour. Only rarely, in our experience, do metrics point to unexpected process problems and their causes. The tendency for metrics programmes to trust on the latter may explain the common disillusionment with metrics processes and their frequent abandonment. Where metrics programmes have managed to collect meaningful data, the improvement programmes are frequently derailed by the gap between analysis and improvement action.

A key aspect of the PRIME six-step model was its concentration on how analysis would lead to actual changes in both reuse decisions and our modus operandi. The mechanism was the creation of *improvement paths* – the effective policy levers that decision-makers could use to affect changes in the target process. These included:

Reuse Education and Training. Despite reuse being still an essentially human activity, few engineers have had any formal education or training in its principles. In particular, more inter-discipline understanding is required of the effects of designs at one process phase on the architectural reusability at other stages. One such route to improved understanding was the use of internal reuse seminars. The level of investment and type of training on reuse principles has a significant impact on reuse performance.

Reuse Team Structure & Communication. Preliminary analysis of reuse metrics supported our observation that systems level reuse was not being mapped down to equivalent software level reuse. Such results suggested the use of dynamic team structures to combine systems and software engineers on a function-oriented process. Both formal and informal routes of communication could also be given greater support; for example, by improved use of the departmental intranet and lessons learned database to capture and share best practice.

Reuse Motivation. A successfully internalised reuse process would make reuse the norm, with bespoke development occurring only where absolutely necessary or more cost-effective. A number of policy levers were available to motivate higher levels of reuse; such as devolving responsibility for reuse improvement further down the team structure.

Reuse Investment & Architecture. A major policy lever is the level of investment applied to the reuse process. As explained earlier, analysis could identify the stability of the system architecture and point to areas that could cost-effectively benefit from redesign. The investment process was supported by a measured relationship between level of reuse and project savings, to provide quantifiable justification for sanctioning future initiatives to improve the reuse process. This encouraged a long-term approach to reuse investment since initiatives rarely pay back investment within the timescales of a single project. If reuse is to succeed then it must be properly funded.

Reuse Decisions. The decision-making process was itself a determinant of reuse performance. The concept of continuous reuse requires results of analysis to be used to improve the reuse decision-making processes; thereby closing the improvement loop.

Reuse Guidelines & Procedures. Analysis is used to affect changes in the technical performance of reuse. The use of reuse guidelines provided one way to feedback experience as process improvements. For example, analysis had shown the desirability of black-box reuse due to savings in re-testing of changed components (over £1000 per component). Evidence also supported the enforcement of basic design principles; the goal was to create small, simple, cohesive and loosely coupled requirements, designs and code objects. These steps helped to minimise the amount of change whilst making functions easier to understand and reuse. The reuse process is institutionalised when it is stable enough to be incorporated into operating procedures. This creates a defined reuse process that itself is subject to review and improvement.

The major benefit of identifying improvement paths was to make clear the link between reuse analysis and organisational changes that might result. It also served to keep the measurement process focused on end-results in the minds of all participants.

6.7.3.6   Step 6: Operate, Evaluate, Iterate

Whilst our description in this paper has been sequential, the improvement process is an inherently iterative model requiring gradual refinement at each stage. It is necessary to operate, evaluate, and iterate the process as inevitable changes occur in the engineering process and the business-operating environment. Hence, periodic reviews are a necessary part of managing a reuse-based process.

6.7.4 Resulting Improvements

The initial reuse programme had highlighted the commercial significance of systematic reuse in this organisation. The reuse from project A to B achieved a level of 82% code reuse with a corresponding 80% cost saving. For this application, a 1% improvement in the level of reuse achieved meant a saving in excess of £100,000. Reuse was therefore capable of providing convincing returns on investment.

The target project for PRIME improvements was known to be significantly dissimilar to the earlier applications. Our short-term goal, however, had been to maximise reuse levels on this project (project C) whilst implementing the improvements described in this paper. The resulting profile of package reuse levels achieved from project A to B, and from projects A & B to C, is shown in Figure 6.21 below.

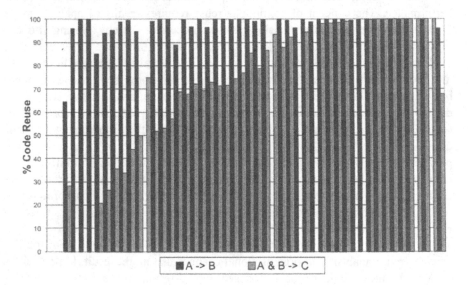

Fig. 6.21 % Code Reuse by Ada Package

A level of 42% system reuse had been achieved on the new project – a considerable achievement when the changes were taken into account. These changes included a new engine application, a different operational environment, and a mid-project shift to new controller hardware. This reuse level and corresponding cost savings were assisted by incremental process improvements introduced during the PRIME project.

The majority of improvements in reuse maturity introduced by PRIME will mostly impact future applications. But early results are providing evidence for its expected effect on business performance. The reuse-based process is now delivering some of the most rapid aero engine FADEC developments to date. The BR715 engine controller has been certified after just over two years of development despite a change in hardware standard and consequential software re-design. It is possible that such timescales could be improved beyond this level but controller development must ultimately compliment the engine and airframe programmes. Hence, reuse improvement can now be focused on efficiency rather than overall timescale reduction.

The reuse-based process is also increasing the speed at which systems achieve their required maturity giving earlier confidence in product quality. Furthermore, measuring the actual levels of reuse at the first build provides an early warning to project managers as to the final project costs giving a valuable improvement in project manageability.

6.7.5   Conclusions

This paper has described some experiences and lessons learned from the introduction of a continuous reuse improvement process within Rolls-Royce plc. Contrary to belief, successful reuse is seen to depend as much on organisational and cultural issues than to those of technology. Nevertheless, a significant and continuous effort is required to make reuse part of the organisation's culture and maintain reuse momentum.

The outcome of the process is a target-led reuse process in clear alignment with business objectives. The collection and analysis of a small set of well-understood metrics supports our emphasis on practical solutions to reuse measurement. Whilst the addition of "improvement paths" keeps participants focused on end results of this improvement process.

The improvements introduced by PRIME have resulted in a significantly improved measurement and management capability for both the reuse process and the process incorporating reuse. Moreover, they have provided a critical capability for further improvements in the future.

6.7.6   References

[Lim94]
   Lim, W. C. *Effects of Reuse on Quality, Productivity and Economics*, IEEE Software pp. 23-31, September 1994.
[Joos94]
   Joos, R. *Software Reuse at Motorola*, IEEE Software pp. 42-47, September 1994.
[O'Connor94]
   O'Connor, C. and Mansour, J. Turner-Harris, G. Campbell, *Reuse in Command and Control Systems*, IEEE Software pp. 70-79, September 1994.

[Myers 97]
   Myers, C., *A Framework for Technology Adoption,* Software Engineering
   Symposium, Software Engineering Institute, Pittsburgh PA, June 1997.
[Lam97]
   Lam, W., *Achieving Requirements Reuse: A Domain-Specific Approach from
   Avionics,* Journal of Systems and Software, 1997.
[Hill94]
   Hill, J. Harper, K. Rimmer, R. McDermid, J. A. Whittle, B. R. and Yates, M.,
   Reuse of Engine Controller Technology, presented the Avionics Conference
   "Systems Integration is the Sky the Limit?", Heathrow, 1994.
[Weiss96]
   Weiss, D.M., *Family-Oriented Abstraction Specification and Translation: the
   FAST process,* Proceedings of the 11th Annual Conference on Computer Assur-
   ance, Gaithersburg, Maryland, IEEE Press, New Jersey, pp. 14-22, 1996.
[Basili92]
   Basili, V.R., *Software modelling and measurement: The Goal/Question/Metric
   paradigm,* Technical Report CS-TR-2956, Department of Computer Science,
   University of Maryland, College Park, MD, September 1992.
[Powell98]
   Powell, A.L., Mander, K.C. and Brown, D.S., *Strategies for Lifecycle Concur-
   rency and Iteration – A System Dynamics Approach,* Process Modelling and
   Simulation 98 (ProSim'98), Silver Falls, Oregon, 22-24 June 1998.

6.7.7   Biography

Antony Powell is a Rolls-Royce Research Fellow in the Rolls-Royce University
Technology Centre at the University of York, UK. His research encompasses the
measurement, modelling and management of software development projects. He
provides active support for various intra- and inter-organisation collaborations as
well as maintaining responsibility for a number of process improvement initiatives
across the Rolls-Royce group of companies.

Duncan Brown MBCS CEng graduated in 1987 from Queen Mary College,
University of London, in computing systems and microelectronics. He spent two
years at British Aerospace Military Aircraft Division working on real-time systems for both data acquisition and stimulation, and manufacturing control. Since
1989 he has worked on flight-control software within Rolls-Royce plc and is currently software manager for the BMW Rolls-Royce 700 series of aero engines.

6.7.8   Acknowledgements

The authors would also like to thank the following people for their contribution to
the PRIME project: Andrew Nolan, Steve Kerr, Paul Essam, Stuart Hutchesson,
Keith Harper and Eddie Williams.

6.8   Project 21718 – MMM
Metrics, Measurement and Management

Gerd Eickelpasch
KoDa GmbH, Würzburg

6.8.1   Executive Summary

KoDa GmbH, a small business software developing enterprise has conducted a process improvement experiment (PIE), that is financially supported by the EU within the ESSI programme. This PIE was targeted to introduce measurement in the software engineering of the company. The chosen approach was the Goal Question Metric method after the first preparatory steps of the PIE.

Following this methodical approach lead to the discovery of insufficient process descriptions, to the refinement of the process and the introduction of additional process steps. This forced our focus on the guideline to keep things simple and the target to allow for measurement activities in the future not more than 4% of project effort.

The conclusion of the PIE is that measurement is possible even in a small company but care must be taken with the first difficult steps in order to control effort and cost. We had no difficulties with regard to personal objections but a lot of engagement of our engineers due to the open cultural climate of our company. But in the longer run we recognised that additional measures have to be taken to keep the motivation and attitude to support this PIE and the goals behind it.

The strategy to rely on good consulting in parallel with our own studies of literature and the approach to first try to manage our task by available means and organisation and then look for tool support was right for us but we were aware of the high costs of doing so and now we desire to have simple tools for our needs available at the market.

Measurement is not only possible in a SME but also worthwhile. The investment can be controlled and the value can directly be related to the goals. There are also – in our case at least – unintended advantages if you promote and maintain a measurement culture, keep an open mind, allow for flexibility and support responsibilities and competence of your project leaders and engineers.

Available within our company is now an environment for effort collection and the various GQM and measurement plans according to GQM as well as a history database to store the main results and support estimations.

6.8.2   Background Information
6.8.2.1   Objectives

We wanted to establish an integrated measurement organisation and introduce metrics based on some basic goals of our business in order to understand our process better and identify clearly and objectively the next steps of improvement of our software life cycle. We also wanted to be able to better estimate the effort and schedule of our projects.

In more detail we wanted to have metrics concerning the size and complexity of the various software elements (i.e. for the major deliverables of our life cycle steps), the effort to conduct them, the amount and categories of detected errors during the different lifecycle steps, the effort needed to correct them, the performance of changes and the workload that is coming from change requests.

Also we wanted to find out the costs for introducing and maintaining our measurement organisation. We had to define them and to answer the questions when and where to collect the figures that are necessary by their definition.

With respect to size and complexity of the software and their relation to estimation of a project we had in mind an approach, that adapts function points and the results of the structured analysis phase for the early guesses and for benchmarking. We wanted to have a deeper knowledge of the applicability of function points.

We wished also to have a history database of our projects available for comparison reasons and to support estimation.

With respect to errors we wanted to have a methodical way to find the reasons and avoid them. In order to define precisely quality targets we had to derive statements about the quality of our products.

All this implied the necessity to define and fix interfaces and work flows to collect the data. Partly we wrote scripts, that scan our existing tool databases partly we developed software to support time collection. Also we needed means to produce and to present reports and methods to analyse them for process improvement reasons.

In order to see the progress, we had to make sure that the required tools and methods are introduced, the mentioned different interfaces and activities are established and the procedures are documented in an intermediate state at the beginning of the experiment, where perhaps alternatives are tested and in a final version at the end. (see annex 6.8.9.6 for achievements).

6.8.2.2   Involved Companies and their Roles

There is only one company, which conducted the experiment, and therefore it is the so called Prime-user: KoDa GmbH (Kommunikations- und Datentechnik GmbH). Contact Person: Mr. Gerd Eickelpasch.

KoDa GmbH makes use of the following subcontractor: Fraunhofer Einrichtung für Experimentelles Software Engineering: Prof. Dr. Rombach, Dr. Bomarius.

6.8.2.3   Starting Scenario

Technical Viewpoint / Environment

Most of our software development is customer driven and ordered. On our site we have a net with different UNIX- and Windows-Systems. We have introduced the methods of structured analysis, structured design and structured entity relationship modelling making use of a Case-tool set called "Innovator" from MID GmbH in Nürnberg, Germany. This client-server type tool box is running in our net on UNIX-Motif machines and on Windows machines. We export the results of this tool box for creating tables and so on within our relational database environment (Oracle, Sybase). Based on the latter entries we build a repository in our graphical user interface builder (JAM of JYACC, New York), which serves us for both: rapid prototyping and real product development. Integrated in JAM is a 4th GL. A certain amount of software is nevertheless written in C.

For the GUI we have developed our own style guides, based on Motif/Windows Standards. All the output of this work is version-controlled by means of RCS with a supplement of self written shell scripts and Perl scripts giving us easy access to the files needed for editing. We are actually supporting configuration-management by making use of RCS together with Make and Perl scripts.

Project management is supported by MS-Project. We have used it almost only for planning in former times and intensified its usage to control a project during the duration of the PIE.

Business Viewpoint

KoDa GmbH is a small house with 10 employees and about the same size of free-lancers. We dealt mostly with software development of commercial systems. Up to 1994 our business was dominated by order driven development with an average project size of about 250 person days. A strong focus and dependency on few customers and the recognition, that requirements in terms of quality, schedule and costs were growing as well as the effort to get and the risks to fulfil contracts urged us to change our strategy. This change was also necessary because some of our big customers reduced the size of the projects. (Often this was and is only a matter of business terms and internal commitments and allowances meaning the real project consists of several contracts i.e. projects are split due to available or allowed budgets of customers. But this has consequences for the administration and for our planning of resources.

There is a tendency of the Damocles sword over every project since our customers and hence we depend more on customer internal politics.) In addition we had to notice, that SME type customers were hesitating. (The latest projects had a meantime from 18 months from first contact with the customer with respect to his needs to the real contract.) Price negotiations were tougher and quality no argument in the negotiations. Very often customers do not have any knowledge what quality is about and only see additional costs when introducing to them the ideas of our lifecycle. Some of them urged us to develop along their poor model or restrict the allowed time and schedule in such a way that it is more than difficult to follow our whole life cycle. Fix-price offers were more often required because the customers need to control their costs.

"Selling" is more important. This is the point we – and we think a lot of SMEs – are quite weak. We are only good in selling, if we are convinced the products or services we offer are good – meaning that they are nearly excellent and therefore probably oversized in terms of quality. (What we needed beyond improvement of our process was support in getting orders.)

In this situation we decided in 1994 as a strategy to develop also products for the market (about one per year), to focus on getting more customers (2 per year) and in addition to try to get larger contracts (>350 person days). Also we decided to offer consulting in the field of software engineering based on our own experience.

During the PIE (June 1996 to January 1998) we had to experience that software development for the market bears additional risks in the sales phase and our first two products could not be considered successful. We had difficulties with respect to our revenues and were forced to switch the baseline project during the PIE, because it was a project for our own purposes and usage and was thus of less importance than one paid by customers (see also annex 9.8). The chosen baseline project was a subset of a larger one (600 person days), a fact that was not seen as a severe obstacle although nevertheless this took some time for adjustment of our measurement and we will perform all of our tasks and measurements for the whole project in the future beyond the scope of the PIE.

Organisational Viewpoint

Up to now KoDa GmbH is developing software following essentially the V-model. Our process was revised and documented during the PIE. Also our procedures with respect to quality assurance and especially ISO 9000 certification is still pending.

Testing and all other quality assurance activities are up to now not done by a special group within our company but by colleagues, that are not actual involved in the same project or part of the project (peer reviews). Normally there is a procedure within our customers organisation at least for system integration testing we have to follow. Responsible is the project leader. There was also no tool support for testing nor was there a specified way of problem tracking and release planning. The latter has improved during the duration of the PIE (i.e. there are regulations within our process model) but it is too early to report a real success.

Two of our engineers are assigned to form our software engineering process group, a duty they have to fulfil in parallel of other tasks. The responsibility changed from one of them to another one since the former was fully involved in a development project completely under control of a customer and with rather small time of work within our own site.

We did not have measurement incorporated in our life cycle, except some manually done collection of daily spent people hours for projects. Now we have it.

Cultural Viewpoint

KoDa GmbH depends on its staff and all over the history of the company their motivation, co-operation and the willingness to improve were fundamental. The employees have the opportunity to hold a share of the company. One third of them used this opportunity but all of them feel responsible for the existence and growing of the company. The working conditions (except the earnings) and management attitude are considered as excellent.

As e.g. with regard to our configuration management all engineers follow the rules we have given ourselves. These rules are "lived" and we were convinced we will do so with regard to measurement. But we have to state that in comparison to our midterm experience this attitude is not running by itself and the first motivation has carefully to be maintained and sponsored. This means you (the sponsor of the measurement movement) have to have on one hand a closer look on details to make sure the necessary activities are done in a suitable way and on the other hand you have to raise and maintain the awareness of the benefits of measurement for the involved people.

Available Skills

Most of our engineers are graduates of a Fachhochschule (which translates roughly to advanced technical college). With regard to the technical environment they all have the skill to work with our case tools and our GUI builder. Of course the methodical background with this respect was available in a sufficient way. Partly this was achieved in former times by their general education, partly by external courses as well as by internal lessons and studies.

There was no very deep understanding of the role and advantages of measurement before writing the proposal except with the our promoter of measurement – the general manager. Of course this has changed during the PIE

6.8.2.4   Workplan

Our workplan was structured according to the following work packages.

WP1: Preparation

The target was to get the necessary knowledge, have tools available and fix the goals and scope.

WP2: Direct Metrics

The objective of this package was to have operational definitions of direct metrics available and the tools for data collection and storage concerning these metrics.

WP3: Derived Metrics

We wanted to have the theory i.e. a model of relationships between attributes, that we are going to measure. Special issues were concerned with measurement of errors, change and product metrics, where we wanted to have a quality model available. We also wanted to have the software to build the figures, store them (and make them available by queries) and have software for producing and presenting reports. A document of organisation of access rights, reporting lines and responsibilities was also planned.

WP4: Analysis and Reaction

We wanted to have documents and checklists about how to read the reports, assign possible actions on the results of the reports and limits of figures to trigger actions.

WP5: Comparison

The objective was here to have the first steps done for a prediction system including algorithms to be used for prediction. We changed our opinion with the latter respect to an approach that is more reasonable for us and more practicable (see annex). We wanted to have documented estimations, software for future comparisons i.e. for making use of our database as a history database.

WP6: Evaluation

In this step we wanted to validate the chosen measurements and document conclusions of improvements or corrections. We also planned for a documentation of results i.e. benefits versus cost and effort.

WP7: Dissemination
WP8: Management of the Project

Remark: Although the content of the planned work packages was worked out during the PIE a different perspective was introduced by the GQM-method because we did not know GQM when proposing the PIE.

6.8.2.5   Expected Outcomes

We wanted to have measurement as an integrated part of our process. This leads to a better knowledge of our process and products. Software development has to make use of the given possibilities for estimation of the whole effort and the effort of the various steps.

Quality goals can be given in different but numerical descriptions.

We longed for an organisation ready to handle changes, i.e. to derive short term and mid term goals [based on most objective numbers] and to control the influence of new methods and techniques.

We expected to have indicators of how we can best reduce the effort without disturbing our quality level and without paying a price for this reduction, that is too high (in terms of money and reorganisation effort). In other words how can we produce, construct quality rather than test errors out.

We can precisely in a better founded way see next improvement steps and focus on the latter (e.g. answer the question of cost benefit ratio of the very expensive test tools we are offered).

We intended to have metrics for products (size, complexity, quality), process and documentation. They should be simple and precisely defined, objective, easily obtainable, valid and robust. The ability to recognise misbehaviour and react on them partly supported by automatic triggers was another objective, e.g. the ability to see the dynamics of occurring problems and errors and their solutions in general and the distribution of their occurrences with regard to their category, their severity, the time and activity of their detection, the time and phase of their implementation, the activities for their corrections and the effort needed to do this.

We expected a better knowledge about the number of reused modules and can work on this result. As we could not afford a special team for required tasks within our development process (a group for quality assurance, measurement, ...) we had to find a way to assign these roles to persons within a project.

Remark: Most of our expectations became true (see chapter results and annex 9.6) but again a different point of view was added during the PIE . We know now that metrics for products as all other metrics have to support a goal and hence we could cancel some academic debate.

Also the precision of the definition and the ease of obtaining the metrics have to be seen with relation to the goal. The mechanistic view (automatic triggers) was relaxed and we came to the conclusion, that we can act on problems on a more case to case way supported by organisational means also in the next future.

6.8.3   Work Performed
6.8.3.1   Organisation

The Pie started with a core team of 3 software engineers, that worked together with the head of the company, Mr. Eickelpasch in this PIE, two of them had to be replaced because of external reasons. Mr. Eickelpasch is also responsible of quality management in general. Two of the above mentioned engineers were in former times assigned to form the Software Engineering Process Group (three if one takes the switch into account, that took place during the experiment). Some of the other engineers were partly involved in the PIE, some were performing the baseline experiment.

In total there was an average of 26 working days of additional labour per month planned for the PIE actually done were about 24 per month in a longer than planned duration (20 instead of 16 months).

Some supportive and administrative work was done by the secretary of Mr. Eickelpasch using emails, meetings, spreadsheets, editors and since its availability our effort collection environment.

6.8.3.2   Technical Environment

In addition to the existing environment, a tool for developing, maintaining and presenting the workflow and processes of our lifecycle was introduced. This helped us to control the responsibilities, deliverables and exit/entry criteria for our process steps and supports us with regard to a sufficiently clear definition about the objects to be measured.

The GQM-tool of IESE was evaluated but not used because it was not sufficiently complete and in a prototype stage.

We were evaluating tools, that could help us to present results in a suitable form, that can be easily understood and are simply to manage and to configure. As we did not find one (except a report writer) we solved these tasks by our own available tools, self written scripts (Perl, shell and Tcl) and organisation.

The same is true with regard to possible benefits of function point analysis. Nevertheless the topic of function point itself was and still is worth a deeper consideration although the reason we did mention in our midterm report is less important for us now. This reason was: we were working with definitions of size in various contexts, that are chosen for practicability reasons and are not satisfying a more rigorous approach. (For more details see 6.8.3.5 and annex 6.8.9.4)

We developed and use a history database together with an effort collection and evaluation environment (see chapter 6.8.4). The development was essentially based on our own development environment.

6.8.3.3   Training

In the beginning of the experiment we were taught about the Quality Improvement Paradigm, the concepts of the experience factory and especially the Goal – Question – Metric approach. The lessons were given by IESE.

During the work of the consultants special emphasis was given on the aspect of "Training on the Job", since we not only wanted to have one special metric effort conducted but want to be able to perform the whole procedures of the GQM-method ourselves in the future.

One 1day course and 2 day seminar on function points were attended by two people. Additional experience was gained by joining the DASMA (a German function point user group). These activities were not accounted to the PIE but are of course closely related to it.

Internal training was given on how to use our tools. Especially with respect to our effort collection tool this training is meanwhile a part of the briefing and instruction of new personnel.

Further additional training was not regularly conducted but the engineers in charge had to build their knowledge by their own studies and work, e.g. with the process management tool.

Not charged to the experiment but in general relevant and related to our improvement effort were external courses on Spice and basics of CMM.

6.8.3.4   Role of the Consultants

FhE IESE supported us with two main foci:

- To provide us with knowledge about the experience factory concept, the QIP and especially the GQM (see also training).
- To give us guidance in our first introduction of measurement and the whole GQM cycle.

In the very beginning of our PIE we had to realise, that some requirements for introducing GQM in a solid way had to be fulfilled and worked out with regard to our processes. There was not enough unique understanding of the details and even the naming of our process-steps. So we were forced to describe our processes with more detailed activities, giving the responsibilities, deliverables, entry and exit criteria of these activities. During this process we were also well supported.

6.8.3.5   Phases of the Experiment

From an ex post perspective with a slight different point of view than a project planner we can recognise several different phases of the PIE partly done in parallel.

General Preparation

At first we had indeed a preparation phase. But the content of this phase was broadened by the necessity to clarify our process and to define some notions and entities we deal with. We did this (guided by IESE) in several steps. First we attempted to describe it as plain text. This approach was improved by using a formal way i.e. a special syntax and finally with the help of a tool. Also we developed templates for various deliverables of process steps in order to keep the work simple. Our project plan template contains now more then 100 project steps. A lot of activities, responsibilities and products are new (more then 40% of new deliverables). We also reorganised the file structure of new projects and thus in total we improved the visibility of our process and the ability to have a precise knowledge about the attributes of entities we are going to measure.

In this phase we were also taught by IESE about the principles of the experience factory, the quality improvement paradigm (QIP) and especially the goal question metric (GQM) approach. We also learned from literature about the pros and cons (see 8. References) and decided to follow the GQM approach. In essence 4 people took part in this learning period. The preparation work package was with respect to the schedule shortened by the delay of the planned function point method evaluation and general tool evaluation.

Guided Set-up of Measurement

Together with IESE we fixed 6 goals from various perspectives or roles, developed the necessary abstraction sheets, which mainly gave information about basic quality aspects, assumed influencing factors and quantitative hypotheses. Thus both a starting point for the development of GQM and a measurement plan and a base for interpreting the collected figures was provided. We also took care to learn how to do it alone in the future. The goals were derived in interviews and recorded. The core of the measurement plan was held as an spreadsheet file. It contained 104 metrics to be calculated or collected. Within this phase were covered the main contents of what was planned as work pack 2 and 3 (direct metrics and derived metrics) As a general remark these work packages have been planned with the approach of looking for metrics that somehow make sense with respect to some general targets. Within the original plan was also made some provision for

Software Support of Metric Collection and Analysis

This can be considered as a phase in its own, though its activities covered the period from the set-up of our measurement to the end of the PIE (and we will work on its improvement in the future). There were besides some smaller pieces of tools two main components developed: our effort collecting and analysing environment and the history database. The concept of the former one stayed valid but the development was done iteratively. At first the functionality was provided as soon as possible and then recognising the difficulties with the acceptance improvements in terms of ease of use were done.

In general software support stemmed mainly from our consideration that some of the goals and metrics will be of a longer lasting, strategic relevance than for only the baseline project and hence especially worthwhile for support. The general ideas were "keep it simple" and "have the tool at hand, when you need it".

Metric Collection and Analysis/Provision for Flexibility and New Ideas

During this part of our PIE we learned by practice, that we will not need sophisticated statistical packages and we cancelled our original mechanistic approach to have software for triggering actions on special results but took care to provide for organisational improvement. We also experienced in the earlier time of this phase new ideas (e.g. new smaller goals, see annex 6.8.9.7) and allowed to follow them. We also recognised that despite our strong effort during the preparation and set-up phases some of the hypotheses or better some of the relations between quality and productivity and influencing factors were simply wrong or without deeper sense. We also had to struggle with the fact that some tasks of our design phase were delayed and reached into the implementation phase i.e. with this respect our planned life cycle was changed beyond the tailoring allowances we had given ourselves in the definition of our lifecycle and causing trouble for our analysis. (There are sound reasons for this fact as well as for the fact we had not seen it in advance).

Another aspect in the analysing stage was the detection, that during the configuration of our effort collection tool some severe mistakes can be done. The various tasks of a project must be made known to the tool (responsible was the project leader). It was obviously not trivial to decide for the necessary granularity of tasks and our decision not to annoy ourselves by measuring activities of a short duration (e.g. configuration and version management activities) lead to a too relaxed handling of measurement in some cases pointing to a motivation and awareness problem. Thus this period is partly to be seen as covering also unplanned task of a meta analysis of our approach. Nevertheless it provided for additional organisational results with respect to measurement as well as it did deliver nearly all of the figures we wanted. As a whole this phase covered the work package 4 (analysis and reaction) and parts of 6 (evaluation).

Function Point and Estimation Improvement

The original plan to introduce the function point method at the beginning of the PIE and adjust some of its parameters in work package 6 (comparison) in order to have a means for prediction was changed due to our GQM approach (see above). Because the objective to be better prepared for estimation stayed valid and because we did not know enough about function points when fixing our goals to introduce them as a supporting metric we had to work out this topic partly in parallel. The work was done in the second half of the PIE. Again we decided against a former claim to have a prediction software system. Instead we document various influencing factors and also the estimates of effort for tasks, lifecycle phases and projects and make use of our history database. This provides for sound arguments for future estimates, which will be done in a separate process step under the responsibility of the project leader. Within this phase we had a closer look to the tool "Knowledge Plan" but rejected it because of our changing attitude with respect to prediction algorithms and because of the hidden assumptions and statistics of this tool (see annex 6.8.9.9). But we learned about the benefits of function points beyond the estimation task (see annex 6.8.9.4 Function Points of the Whole System).

The Evaluation of the PIE

Provided for the facts that form the base of this report.

6.8.3.6   Internal Dissemination

Internal dissemination of the results was provided within regular meetings and by doing on the job.

The meetings were scheduled based on achievements of results. In this way e.g. the new process steps were already introduced in other projects as well as some goals and hence metrics were applied. Because of the size of our company a lot of informal dissemination provided for actual information and response e.g. the idea to measure not only our software processes.

6.8.4   Results and Analysis
6.8.4.1   Technical

From a closer technology point of view we have gained the following achievements:

- a software system – internally called EVA – to collect and store effort data, analyse and report them including file interfaces to other software packages;
- a software system to store and present condensed history data;
- a defined file structure for every project;
- a system to manage and analyse software processes (especially the V-model; i.e. the Innovator Workbench of MID GmbH in Nürnberg; the structure of spreadsheets used for various purposes, e.g. to keep the measurement plan);
- various script like software modules;
- a deeper knowledge of other already used software together with minor improvements (e.g. our own version and configuration management and RCS, MS-Project, the Innovator tools for structured analysis, design and entity relation modelling).
- EVA is used by the project manager to introduce the project, its tasks and the project related staff, by the project people to configure it to their convince and to store the start and end time of work on a special task. (We reported during the mid of our PIE our effort to reduce annoyance of usage of the tool and stated a reduction of mouse clicks and overall effort necessary to perform this task.

Qualitatively this is still valid but the given 5 seconds turned out to be wishful thinking of the general manager who tested it in optimised situations. While the molestation is no more a great obstacle felt by the engineers, they reported to need about 15 to 20 seconds for such an activity. We have now – not only for projects within the PIE – collected more than 4000 working blocks (thus is our name for the time between start and end of an activity), documenting the acceptance of the tool. In this way we provided for collection of most accurate and sufficiently granular effort data. These data can be analysed by the tool by means of aggregating them in various perspectives, most importantly by grouping the tasks to domains, which are most naturally the life cycle phases. This assignment of tasks can be done at every time and multiple assignment is possible (e.g. a review of the application concept can be grouped to the whole cycle of application concept development and also to all quality assurance activities). To provide for additional statistics and analyses export of data is also possible. The history database system has undergone different versions and is actually a system with high abstractions of data on projects to be stored including type of project, artefacts generated during the projects, involved people and of course the condensed or even elementary metric results. Because of its abstraction it is not as easy to handle as we wanted and we have beyond the PIE to work on improvement with this respect to reduce experience packaging effort.

The complete file structure for every project and a meta structure containing general documents of KoDa GmbH is predefined. It consists of 21 directories 28 compulsory files. This provides for a means to find information and organise and relate them with each other. With this respect we have also improved our configuration management system. E.g. it is now possible for us to assign symbolic release names to all deliverables that consist of many isolated documents (e.g. the application concept may consist of output of our case tool (structured analysis graphs), plain text, prototypes,...).

The technical results from a methodical point of view can be listed as:

- documented life cycle and available project plan templates;
- the GQM method;
- the function point method (counting procedures);
- better definitions of notions;
- a baseline characterisation of processes and product.

Not only do we have our own life cycle documented but have also gained knowledge about how to document one that is only partly documented or not at all. This covers practical hints for detection of artefacts, processes that build them and resources that are used as well as the advantages and disadvantages to control and synchronise the steps by semaphore like means or messages. Within our life cycle we introduced the principle of self similarity meaning that the principle tasks and their sequence is the same for the major life cycle phases. This was a helpful means in order to avoid to produce shelf ware but have the processes always in mind. It refers especially to the phases requirements specification, design and implementation. Our process model formed the base for general project plan templates for in-house product development and customer driven projects. They contain more than 100 activities. At every major life cycle phase a planning process was introduced to decide among other aspects which of the tasks of our process in an actual project are compulsory and which of the document parts must exist. Also measurement activities are predefined.

The GQM method is known in its whole. This means we have practised the steps from expressing goals, developing abstraction sheets, GQM plans, measurement plans and evaluating the results(for literature on this topic see references). We also learned to recognise and consider difficulties in advance as well as to handle them during the measurement process and can provide enough flexibility. Thus we are able to conduct the next measurement programmes without external guidance and can even help other companies. Also we know about the integration of GQM into the Quality Improvement Paradigm and its relation to the Experience Factory approach we partly support by our history database.

With respect to function point we are capable to count them precisely enough for our purposes but doubt its usefulness for benchmarking (see annex 9.4.3). We also learned about its value in negotiation phases, project control and planning of work load in the maintenance phase but did not implement this so far. Parts of these useful aspect will require a revision and confirmation of the correctness of our counting procedures. In essence we make only use of a spreadsheet tool for calculating the function points.

Our notions are better defined (e.g. error, fault, failure; application concept). This was necessary at the beginning of our PIE to recognise the entities and attributes of them we wanted to measure.

Some results and characterisations of our process and the baseline are given in the annexes.

The six goals lead us to 120 elementary metrics to be collected (normalised: 104 meaning some of them are identical). Of these 104 figures 56 are covered by the usage of our effort collection environment, 11 by scripts calculating results with regard to various documents and 37 manually. 19 of the manually derived metrics are only collected once in project.

6.8.4.2   *Business*

Several aspects of this PIE influenced our business and will do so in the future:

- the effort for conducting the experiment as whole;
- the measurement programme (introduction, performance and maintaining measurement);
- the new life cycle developed within the PIE;
- the tools we developed for us;
- the knowledge we gained with respect to the used methods;
- the findings of our measurement;
- the internal dissemination of result and
- the motivation of our engineers

Although the effort for the PIE is funded by the EU commission the resources bound for the PIE were lacked in other projects. Without the funding this work and thus our Software Process Improvement Activities in the future would only be bearable with a quarter of the effort. We used about 24 days a month. Because we know about the pitfalls and benefits of our activities we feel able to help other companies to achieve a lot of our results in significantly less time. We believe that to introduce measurement and conduct a first GQM cycle gaining also the ability for future measurement programmes in a smaller SPU will need a minimum investment of 100 days.

For future activities with respect to measurement we experienced, that we can manage it with 2 – 4 % of project effort depending on the goals (and hence comparable to the benefits) and the size of the projects. In general the percentage is decreasing with project size and "reuse" of goals and tool support for data collection. When proposing our PIE we have had a target of less than 8% so the actual numbers are motivating (for a hint in literature refer Watts Humphrey pages 304ff) and approving the respective information we were given by IESE.

Our new life cycle introduced a lot of new activities and up to 40% new (usually small) deliverables. The additional effort was estimated with 25 days meaning about 10% of our average project size.

This does not seem to be related linearly to the project size (we spent actually about 28 days for the most of these activities in the whole project of about 600 person days) and we are able by tailoring of our process to reduce the effort for smaller projects. Nevertheless we were forced to perform them in a slim way and had to recognise that at first hand the cost benefit ration was becoming worse.

Tool development for our own purposes was extensive and can perhaps be avoided by other companies or at least be reduced depending on their priorities and culture. We are convinced, that we have gained and maintained acceptance by our engineers significantly by the ease of data collection and analysis. It might probably turn out in other companies that smaller steps and a longer period (with success stories) are more suitable.

The knowledge we gained about the methods is already used earning additional revenues. We held one seminar on measurement and quality assurance, give consulting service for a first customer and are negotiating other contracts.

The findings of our measurement are a not only a valuable but also indispensable help for rationalising the debate on future strategic steps and on the focus of next improvement activities with the result to care for our conceptual phases, make profit of our available assets i.e. our actual development environment and experience (which were recognised as a measurable asset during the PIE) and introduce OO techniques in a more controlled and less enthusiastic way. We have also a baseline for estimations and more solid arguments to support it and thus we are in a better position for fix price offers and product development decisions (including a better standing in negotiations of financing with our banking institute).

Some not so much or not at all intended findings provided for saving of effort of about 3,5 person months a year. This was strongly supported by the information flow in our company and the motivation of the staff – not only the software engineers.

As a whole our approach might seem to be oversized for a small company like ours. But we keep our strategy in mind that we also want to offer consulting in software engineering. Therefore a great part of our knowledge is wanted to be based on practical experience as well. Actually we have strong indicators, that our strategy is possible and helps us to exist and to grow.

6.8.4.3   Organisation

The refinement of our software process was the most noticeable change in our software engineering organisation. This includes provisions for new measurement activities e.g. the decision to support an existing goal or introduce another one at the beginning of a project. No additional separate job was created but 3 members of our company have a deeper understanding of GQM. The engineers have to be aware that they might slip into different roles during projects. One result was, that we are now aware of our process and have our organisation documented and the respective notions are clear. With this respect we have overcome the situation, that because of our order driven history and the involvement in process chains of our customers we had different meanings when using the same words.

6.8.4.4   *Culture*

In our climate of confidence and trust we did not expect and have not experienced any difficulties in applying measurement neither against the introduction of a measurement organisation as additional workload nor against measurement and the possible misuse to measure people. On the contrary many suggestions came from the employees to make optimal use of it beyond the scope of software engineering. The effort collection environment was also instantly used by the engineers to try to derive some personal metrics they find useful for themselves and their personal process.

Other key factors for this good situation are the involvement of all people, the most practical approach with the principle to keep procedures simple and the common opinion, that we are following the right strategy. Part of our practical approach is, that people are not only allowed but asked to introduce improvements by themselves (e.g. the development and improvement of templates of documents, of scripts for supporting the work on a task). With regard to their involvement their is inherent support by the GQM method itself. The sessions of presentation and interpretation of the data and of our procedures showed the decline of the motivation to support measurement. This was recognised while considering details of the implementation of our measurement environment.

Obviously a measurement culture needs longer and closer support and supervision to become a self running process that is considered in the same way as essential as configuration management is within our company. (For details see chapter "key lessons"). We want here to mention, that a part of the culture is or sociological aspects is how people feel about their job and it was another unintended benefit of the PIE that our engineers simply felt proud to take part in a ESSI project.

6.8.4.5   *Skills*

There is now more awareness and knowledge about the software process in general and in the way we handle it. This applies e.g. to the strict usage of our new project file structure and the small changes of our configuration management that were introduced during the preparation stage of our PIE as well as to the rules with regard of our process steps.

Special skills with regard to metrics are developed and the ability to set up and implement a GQM based measurement program is available. This is considered as a major advantage. We already deploy this giving consulting services to other colleagues. It is to mention that our approach is strictly oriented to practical needs and in some sense this might not be sufficient from an academic point of view. But this is the only way to introduce and maintain measurement programs in SMEs. With respect to function point we have in principle the skill for counting and learned how to deal with it in negation phases of projects, asset (developed software) management and workload estimation for maintenance.

Of course there is to mention also the ability to use the purchased and developed tools and the knowledge about the reason we use them.

Also to mention is a considerable improvement in presentation skills caused by the participation of international events.

6.8.5   Key Lessons
6.8.5.1   Technological Point of View

To build the fundament for measurement it is necessary to have a stable process and a precise knowledge about what attributes of entities you are going to measure. But these attributes need not to be theoretically sophisticated and generally agreed upon but should be chosen in a methodical way. E.g. we do not debate whether an attribute like number of layers or processes in a structured analysis graph is belonging to the category of size or to complexity. In this way we will work on our own purpose and it might be that our results are not directly transferable to other companies or worthwhile to be stored without comment in any statistical database. This implies difficulties for bench marks. But we advise other companies to work as well with strict focus on their own needs and peculiarities. Only if you feel the need to apply commonly used concepts of measures – like we did with respect to function points – you should apply them. But this is better to be done if you have already prepared and conducted the easier approach and thus seen some positive effects that help to maintain the effort.

One has to follow the principle to keep things simple. We have managed this by means of templates with regard to process step deliverables, by introducing a complete file structure we use in all projects and be means of self similarity of our life cycle phases. We learned that this all could also be summarised under the topic of reuse. With regard to our measurement organisation we tried so far successfully to avoid manually to be done work. This applies for iteratively to be done work. With respect to one time collection of data there is always the choice to do this manually or with support of available basic tools.

We believe despite contrary arguments in literature (see Bache and Neil in Fenton, Whitty, Iizuka), that to work under the guidance of a method i.e. of the GQM approach is much more worthwhile, than the naive search for metrics, that are available in literature and are somehow related to your work. With this respect and in general we can state that good consulting is worthwhile as well and we advise to invest here before you invest in tools. Tool support should be considered a step after you are sure about your needs anyway, i.e. after you have understood why you want to perform a special task and what the principles are that guide the performance of this task.

When you have understood the principles of a method it is your turn to tailor it to your needs and your responsibility not to act in a way, that makes the method worthless. You should make explicit why you need an adaptation and why you think the results are still valid and valuable for your company or your software engineering group. To make it explicit means also to document it and documentation is really a critical factor (We agree here with ISO9000). The way you organise your documentation and support it by tools is a secondary matter though by far not neglectable. But you need your ideas documented, since you will not learn them by heart and loose a lot of information e.g. in evaluating the results and drawing the correct conclusions. It is also helpful to have these documentations available to make use of them in evaluation schemes of new tools and methods.

6.8.5.2   *Business Point of View*

To introduce measurement even in a small company is possible if it is part of the strategy of the company and people commonly share the vision of software process improvement and if the necessary funding and managerial support is available because improvement is not for free.

Especially settling the starting point (baseline) may take more effort than originally planned (strictly following a method leads to discovering deficiencies).

Measurement in a company pays back. One may find it difficult to count the financial aspects but it is a good advice to try to quantify the main aspects to keep the momentum. In our case some minor goals or even unintended benefits became visible and only a part of them provide for annual savings of at least 5% of all labour costs (for details see annex 6.8.9.9). In reporting these benefits one may think that a part of the results could have been achieved by common sense. But we believe this is the same truth as with other ideas that are costly to work out and easy to understand once you have done the work. Awareness of problems and benefits of solutions can be rationalised only by measurement and in fact by measurement in a methodical way in order to detect as much as possible (also in an economic sense) the principles and relations of various factors that contribute to the results.

To keep it simple is of course not only a principle to overcome complexity and support motivation but it is absolutely necessary in terms of spent effort and costs. We have done a lot of work for us to handle things in a lean way (and experienced some draw back when on the other hand we tried to generalise some approaches to save effort in the future e.g. with our history database) and we had and have carefully to keep track and analyse what measurement will cost us in the future. But we are now able to quantify it (see annex 6.8.9.5). Nevertheless we have to state, that the planned 26 days a month for SPI within a company of 10 employees is near the upper limit or beyond of it.

6.8.5.3   *Strengths and Weaknesses of the Experiment*

To perform this experiment proved an excellent means for process improvement. We achieved most of the results we wanted to have and even more. We are able to organise measurement and gain profit from it.

When writing our proposal, we were not able to decide for a methodical approach. This proved to be an obstacle since we first had to learn about the method had to judge and decide for it and then were confronted with preliminary tasks we had not seen in advance i.e. with fixing our own processes.

GQM itself was helpful beside the already mentioned advantages to work out different perspectives and views on our process and goals for our measurement activities depending on the different roles of project leaders, software engineer, quality assurance responsible and manager of the company.

If we could start again we would propose a longer period for the experiment (18 month instead of 16) but the effort itself seems to be quite correctly estimated if one takes the difficulties during the project into account, that cannot be planned for (change of processes, change of baseline, notice of employee) and if you take into account that the funding of the EU provided for an intensive work on essential topics (e.g. ease of use) that we feel able to reduce significantly for those companies that contact us. We thankfully want to mention that during the negotiation phase of our PIE contract we were helped by our project officer to focus our approach so that we dropped some originally planned aspects and saved time for our main target. Also the work packages would be formulated more tightly according to the chosen method although in general their content remained valid. We would plan more time for a meta analysis of obstacles within our methodical approach and how to circumvent them in a valid way (compare 3.5 collection and analysis).

We feel satisfied with our approach to try improvement first without considering too much tool support. It helped us to understand better our needs. With this respect we did not need all the proposed money for software licences and advise other companies strongly to resist any temptation of merely buying software funded by EU programs but to acknowledge the benefits of a deeper insight into problems based on own work and experience.

6.8.6   Conclusions and Future Actions

In general we are convinced that we have chosen the right path for improvement. We recognised a considerable amount of work to be done and it would not have been possible to conduct such an intensive improvement step without external help (IESE) and without the financial contribution of the EU. Other companies of our size will not be able to undergo this learning path and we will offer our experience to them and thus make it affordable for them to catch the opportunities. But we know already, that we are able to start similar measurement programmes to that we performed already. This ability is an important asset provided by our PIE. We have got the baseline information on how we perform our process with respect to quality and efficiency. One challenge in the future will be its adaptation to a changing environment, because we are going to object oriented development and have to select our own way with this respect.

The results of our experiment give us a realistic view but also an optimistic mood for the future.(see annex 6.8.9.5)

We will work on further improvement of our history database or experience packaging to decrease the time and effort needed to store the (condensed) data and to make better use of it in future estimations, comparisons and decision support. Also some details with respect to our effort management will be improved by better integration of our project planning tool and our configuration management. All this can be summarised under the topic of improvement of our measurement abilities for those goals and metrics we recognised as worthwhile to support for a longer period.

The results on the other hand gave us more than a hint to focus on some general phases of our life cycle (and to postpone the priority of others e.g. of considering configuration and version management, see annex). We will especially deal with our analysis phase and the still unsatisfying status of our design phase. This can be considered as parallel to our future OO activities or better as a specialisation of it, because we are interested in the benefits of UML and use cases to understand customer problems deeper and more easily. It goes along with considerations of a more iterative development based on prototypes. In general this can be summarised as deploying the current results of measurement. An additional component with this respect is the relation of measurement to assessment activities which will be documented for our own purposes as well as for our consulting branch.

Our motivation for measurement also provided for some new ideas to support longer lasting goals and controlling of our achievements. E.g. we will implement and improve some new features within our software to get product data out of life experience i.e. some modules to count their usage and the occurrence of faults. And the success of our measurement experiment lead to the idea to apply it not only to our software development but also the various other activities we perform (e.g. selling of products and services).

Also we are negotiating with Fraunhofer IESE, whether we should develop software for the market to support the whole GQM and QIP methodology.

With respect to the results of the PIE we want to mention our plan to prepare an improved report of our findings, when the baseline product and its additional functionality, that is required by our customer are long enough in use by our customer.

Last but not least we will take care to maintain the contact to the various companies dealing with SPI in order to make proper use of new experience of the ESSI community and to offer the results of our next steps in a similar or even improved way to them. We have done so in the past within the ESPITI project establishing a software quality association in the regional area and will contact in the future the ESPInodes. These contacts are seen as a value of its own for us offering opportunities in our business and – to allow ourselves a more political statement – promoting the idea of really European Community we work and live in.

6.8.7   Glossary

Table 6.8 Glossary

ESSI	European Systems and Software Initiative
EU	European Union
GQM	goal, question metric;
IESE	Institute of Experimental Software Engineering, a Fraunhofer institute in Germany
PIE	Process Improvement Experiment
QA	quality assurance
QIP	quality improvement paradigm
SME	small or medium sized enterprise
SPI	Software Process Improvement
SPICE	Software Process Improvement and Capability Determination – an assessment model
SPU	software producing unit
WP	work package

6.8.8   References

[Basili94]
Basili, Victor R.; Caldiera, Gianluigi; Rombach, Dieter H.: *The Experience Factory*, Encyclopaedia of Software Engineering – 2 Volume Set, John Wiley & Sons, Inc., 1994.

[Bröckers96]
Bröckers, Alfred; Differding, Christiane; Threin, Günter: *The Role of Software Process Modelling in Planning Industrial Measurement Programs*, Proceedings of the 3rd International Metrics Symposium, Berlin; IEEE, 1996.

[Crosby80]
Crosby, Philip B.: Quality is free – *The Art of making quality certain*, Mentor (Penguin Books), USA, 1980.

[Dumke94]
Dumke, Reiner; Zuse, Horst (Ed.): *Theorie und Praxis der Softwaremessung*, Deutscher Universitäts Verlag, Germany, 1994.

[Fenton95]
Fenton, Norman; Whitty, Robin; Iizuka, Yoshinori (Ed.): *Software Quality – Assurance and Measurement*, International Thomson Publishing Company, UK, 1995.

[Humphrey89]
  Humphrey, Watt S.: *Managing the Software Process*, SEI series in software
  engineering, Addison-Wesley, USA, 1989.
[Jones97a]
  Jones, Capers, *course papers and slides: becoming best in class* (1997), held in
  Munich 1997
[Jones97b]
  Jones, Capers, *The Impact of Project Management Tools on Software Failures
  and Successes*, Article of Software Productivity Research Inc., March 23, 1997
[Jones91]
  Jones, Capers, *Applied Software Measurement*, McGraw Hill 1991
[Melton96]
  Melton, Austin: *Software Measurement*, International Thomson Computer
  Press, UK, 1996.
[Pulford96]
  Pulford, Kevin; Kuntzmann-Combelles, Annie; Shirlaw, Stephen: *A quantita-
  tive approach to Software Management* – The ami Handbook, Addison-Wesley,
  UK, 1996.

6.8.9   Annexes
6.8.9.1   Example of One of the Six Goals

Analyse the software process (object) with respect to effort (quality aspect) from
the point of view of management (viewpoint) within the project ODIN of KoDa
GmbH (context) for the purpose of characterisation (purpose).

6.8.9.2   About the Measurement Plan

In essence our measurement plan has the structure:

Metric-Id, name, reference to goal and GQM-plan, reference to other metrics in
plan, object to be measured, type (scale) of metric, time of data collection, way of
collection (e.g. tool, questionnaire), collector, validator, reference to documents
containing the detailed results;

We have derived – guided by the method – 120 metrics (104 different elementary metrics) to support the above mentioned six goals.

Remark to table 6.9: Line one (number of metrics) counts all of the 120 metrics, the other lines exclude those, that are identical to an already collected one.

Whether the average of 20 metrics per goal is a general size we cannot judge
but we will see it in the future. The same applies for an average of about 15 % of
these elementary metrics occurring more than one time within a measurement
programme. This will at least depend on the number and similarity of the goals.

Table 6.9 Goals vs. Metrics

	goal 1	goal 2	goal 3	goal 4	goal 5	goal 6	sum
#of metrics	14	47	12	16	20	11	120
1 time collection	2	6	2	12	5	6	33
event triggered	0	0	0	2	11	2	15
iterative	12	37	6	0	1	0	56
tool supported	12	37	6	6	1	2	67
manually	2	3	2	8	16	6	37

6.8.9.3   Project Plan Templates

The complete templates for product development and customer driven development can be made available on demand (German language only). Here is to mention, that these templates include now also tasks in the major lifecycle phases for the implementation of a measurement programme related to the project.

6.8.9.4   Some Results Concerning the Baseline Project Analysis of Structured Entity Relation Model

Table 6.10 Types

	Number	Average number of attributes	Maximum number of attributes
Entity type	15	7	15
Entity relation type	63	7	25
Relation type	19	3	6

This corresponds to a total number of 97 Oracle tables to be implemented. Because we know that we are working with quite abstract models the reader should be aware, that in a "normal" application the figures would be reasonably higher (up to 100%). As an example we deal with the concept of a "partner", who can be e.g. a customer, supplier or even an employee or any combination of them.

Modules of the Baseline Project

Without going into the details of our development tool and hence without detailed definition of the following notions of type of a module but a roughly interpretation we present the following figures (in brackets numbers of the baseline part of the project):

Table 6.11 Modules classified

1. total number of modules :	242	(149)
2. algorithm type (implemented as C-functions)	27	(27)
3. JAM / prolific type (implemented in a 4GL)	195	(112)
4. complex ones	116	(60)
5. templates of modules + global modules	19	(19)
6. list modules	20	(10)

The prolific type modules consist normally of two files, one responsible for the GUI one for the behaviour in case of events. They can be separated as screen overviews (lists), management of objects, simple info screens, dialog screens and parameter input screens. For these types the templates are developed, partly in two different kinds depending on the number of involved entities. These templates will be used (or are used in case of baseline part) in 104 (79) of the prolific type modules and saved effort of about 50 % in those cases. The advantages in general of our templates are not only performance increase but also easier maintenance and the provision for quality in terms of avoiding errors. The mere implementation of these templates took us 30 person days. Test effort was difficult to count since it was booked on the tests of the first modules that used them. The same applies to the design of the templates because some principles were dealt with before our effort management tool set was in place. Partly these templates can be used without or with only minor modifications in other projects.

We remind the reader, that because of our strong abstraction (see 6.8.9.4 Analysis of Structured Entity Relation Model) together with the usage of parameters we save a lot of modules to be written. The modules themselves consist of various procedures representing the actions on special events. Partly to mainly the adaptation of the templates consists in amending the modules by additional procedures.

Function Points of the Whole System

Table 6.12 Function Points of the Whole System

first determination	2358 FP
Re-evaluation	3958 FP
for the baseline part of the project	2154 FP

Comments

Capers Jones states that 1000 function points are the starting level for commercial system. [Jones97b]. This figure is conformant to our calculation of FP but the performance of the TOP-performers is given by Capers Jones with 50 to 100

FP/month [Jones97a] and the average in the US with 8FP/month in 1990. ([Jones91], page 139 ff.) in the management information system domain of evaluated projects with 1000 and more FP and he guessed a productivity average of 12 FP/a in 2000). This together with our development time for the baseline part of the whole project and the project itself (600 person days) leads to the conclusion, that we belong to the best in class. Although some arguments and elements for this statement like our usage of structured methods, CASE tools, high level languages and skilled people [Jones97a] support this, we have until now serious doubts about this fact and hence about our ability to figure out the function points correctly or doubts with respect to the function point approach as a whole. The latter one was and is under discussion within our company given the difficulties that arouse because of various notions of the FP method, its former and most strict relation to Cobol oriented development environment and problems. E.g. to determine what is a list (output) caused difficulties: we have introduced – as we suggest is common practice now – general list programs each capable to be controlled by the user with respect to sorting and filtering, so that the user can produce lots of different lists with one module. Again we decided not to take part in a general debate but make our own use of it knowing, that we can not go for reasonable benchmarking with our figures but that we can measure improvement and make use of our figures for estimation.

Effort for Configuration Management

One of the short term goals that came up during our PIE (but are related to the above mentioned goal 1, because the management wants a closer look to the overall costs of a project) was to find out what amount of effort has to be done for configuration management. There was a first shocking calculation of about 4%. This implied a deeper survey with techniques outside of our general effort management approach since we had an agreement not to measure every very short activity like the check in of a file into our version control system (another example of the mentioned flexibility). Instead we took a sample of activities and measured the average time for a check in or check out operation (15 seconds), surveyed our configuration and version control system for existing versions of all included files belonging to the baseline project and the behaviour of our engineers (they check out a file more often than in for evaluation purposes and hence not for editing the file). An average of 11 check in or out activities per engineer and file was found. This leads together with some set-up activities to the knowledge, that we spend about 2% of project effort for configuration management. We present this here because we have never seen a figure for this fact in literature and because it is a not neglectable figure but an example of the value of measurement. We know now that improvement in configuration management performance of 50% will earn money of about 1% of a project and can thus prioritise special actions.

6.8.9.5   Cost Estimation of Introduction and Maintaining Measurement

To introduce measurement as a solid, ongoing movement in a small software producing units (following figures for 30 engineers) will need an effort investment of about 100 days minimum:

Table 6.13 Steps of introducing measurement and estimated effort

Step	Effort
inform and train people about the basic principles	1 day per employee
educate (see 6.8.9.12 additional remarks) and train specialists	20 days each (2 recommended)
provide for environment and organisation	depending on goals (30–150 days)
provide for management support	depending on company size (0,5 days per month of senior management in the first year at least)
there is also most probably need of external support	at least 10 days

Current estimation for a new goal (in person days and percentage) depending on project size (also in person days) within KoDa GmbH:

Table 6.14 Current Estimation

project size in person days	300	200	100	50
1 reasonably precise definition of goal	0,25	0,25	0,125	0,125
2 Abstraction sheet development depends on involved people	2	1,5	1	0,5
3 GQM-Plan	1	1	1	0,5
4 Measurement-Plan	2	1,5	1	0,5
5 Implementation of measurement: Writing forms, spreading them, collecting them (project)	1	1	0,5	0,5
6 Collecting any effort data 2 minutes per day and engineer	1,3	0,8	0,5	0,25
6a Preparing the environment project, tasks and involved people have to be introduced to our effort collection system	0,25	0,25	0,125	0,125
7 Collecting other data	1	1	0,5	0,5

project size in person days	300	200	100	50
depending on necessary provisions / environment				
8 reporting-evaluation	1	1	0,5	0,5
1 hour per duration in months				
9 inclusion in history database	2	2	1	0,5
will be improved in the future				
estimated total measurement effort:	11,8	9,925	6,125	3,75
rounded total measurement effort	12	10	6	4
in % of project size	3,93%	4,96%	6,13%	7,5%
percentage based on rounded effort	3,67%	5,00%	6,00%	8,00%

The figures change if measurement is done in larger projects with the result of a decrease of percentage.

They also change if only effort related metrics are involved to:

Table 6.15 Current Estimation – Changes for effort related metrics only

rounded total measurement effort	8	7	4	3
percentage based on rounded effort	2,67%	3,50%	4,00%	6,00%

And if in addition the goal is already given, current estimates change to:

Table 6.16 Current Estimation – Changes if goal is given

rounded total measurement effort	4	3	2	1
percentage based on rounded effort	1,33%	1,50%	2,00%	2,00%

As our general opinion about the above figures can be given, that we believe they are achievable but we also believe that they are not significantly reducible.

Remarks with respect to other costs and effort during the PIE that can be avoided by other companies:

A considerable amount of time of the overall nearly 490 days was spent on:

Table 6.17 Current Estimation – what could be avoided

the definition of our processes	about 110 person days
provision of environment support	about 190 person days

Including evaluation of tools of the market, development of our environment with respect to effort collection, development of our history database and other tool support. There is still some work going on beyond the PIE.

This intensive work can probably not be done in another SME without funding. Of course we have the advantage of a better insight by trying some approaches and doing this job by ourselves but we also do know now a lot of possibilities to introduce measurement in a less extensive way (with smaller steps and perhaps longer duration to reach our level). And in addition we have available a very suitable environment for us.

6.8.9.6 *Comments on Some Objectives and Results*

Table 6.18 Objectives and Results

Nr.	Objective	Achievement	Comment
1	Establish measurement organisation	Fully	methods and environment available; improvement in details possible;
2	Ability for estimation	Strongly improved	doubts in function point or our knowledge about it; further improvement desired.
3	Availability of metrics	mostly	Depending on goals; some goals and hence the related metrics longer lasting than the project;
4	Availability of history database	fully	up to now still too inconvenient and effort prone usage, reconsideration of approach going on (less abstractions)
5	Availability to find reasons of errors	organisation available	not much practical experience
6	Integration into process and assessment activities	mostly	by project plan template; relation to assessment activities and results to be specified
7	Knowledge about introducing GQM	good	already applied to customers

6.8.9.7 *List of Some not Intended Additional Benefit*

• Our organisation or better our attitude has changed in more than the intended ways, even if you take the first steps of our PIE into account that tried to fix our actual life cycle. We distinguish better between strategic and tactical goals and have a better background for discussing it. Lots of the arguments were not implications of our measurement activities alone but also of findings of colleagues presented in literature. E.g. the findings of Capers Jones ([Jones91], page 142 ff), that the adequacy of using various tools is dependent on the size of the project.

- We were told about the usefulness of function points during the maintenance phase especially with respect to the assignment of work for a product in maintenance. This will more closely be investigated in order to be used for our product development branch and for the decision making process there.
- We are now in a position to discuss performance targets. Although this topic has to be handled carefully in order not to fall into the mistake to measure people there are some motivating possibilities for a project team if they are given enough means i.e. budget and time in their on responsibility to improve. These performance aspects lead to another benefit:
- The re-evaluation of strategic plans with respect to used tools and methods (object orientation).
- Especially with respect to "visual basic" we could rationalise the debate in our company whether we should move to the Microsoft world. Within the evaluation scheme of a switch to this development environment there is not only to reflect the requests of the market, the de facto leadership of Microsoft in several respects, but also the quality and dependency on the quality of MS software as well as our actual degree of ability to provide interfaces for Microsoft tools or integrate them in our products and all the assets we will loose in case of dropping our old environment. These assets consist among others in our in depths skills and experiences and in our development guidelines and templates leading to fast implementation cycles and the available sources ready for reuse in other projects.
- This relates also to an approach to evaluate (with figures) our experience and environment in terms of our guidelines, scripts and templates, which we can really consider now as an asset, that we have invested for and that needs to be reinvested in case of a methodology or technology shift. In short this delivers us a special view of reuse.
- We found some "data mining" possibilities and ideas e.g. we (re-)assured our template success. It was not a primary goal to analyse it but could easily be implemented and raised the motivation of the involved people considerably. With respect to the results of this approach, we could spend some time on the design of the templates and reusable modules. We have a more precise internal knowledge about reusability based on concrete needs.
- Some changes took place within KoDa GmbH based on the awareness of our measurement approach in general and some findings according to the effort measurement: We have now a schedule (supported by some organisational means), where customers are allowed to contact engineers by a phone call – a benefit of about an hour each day, that is nearly 1,5 person month a year. With respect of studying newspapers or journals we detected a too open attitude and could save 2,5 days a month or nearly 2 person months a year!
- Findings about our environment where detected and made conscious, that are influencing our quality or at least performance, e.g. the noisiness of some

hardware components. These and similar soft factors must be known in some way and pointed to, because if you are not aware of it you will not go and measure it (or simply avoid the obstacles without in depth measurement). In our case we became aware of this by studying the literature and thinking about our environment.

- If people otherwise were asked about hindering aspects in our environment they would not have mentioned it, because of personal feelings about it.
- New ideas of expressing to our customers what quality is for us came up. Partly this can be done by providing them with a glimpse to our process (e.g. project plan template) partly by presenting them figures related to our products.

6.8.9.8   Most Severe PIE External but Probably Common Difficulties Encountered

We had to deal with the fact, that one of our leading participants in the project quit for an excellent other job opportunity. Another member of our PIE group was in the last half of its duration extremely bound by another customer project. Also we were forced to switch the baseline project during the PIE. This caused additional labour and implied three extra months of duration of the PIE.

6.8.9.9   Remarks About the Usage of Tools

We planned to introduce tools to support the whole GQM-process. There have been available only tools in prototype stage and they supported only parts of the process. We had e.g. a closer look to the GQM-tool of IESE but since the former statement applied also to them and IESE is not focussed on development, delivery and maintenance of tools but on further improvement of the methods we decided not to use it. Reasonable support could be provided by the use of spreadsheets and organisational means.

Also we had in mind to use a statistical package like SPSS for deeper investigation of our findings. We delayed it for the time being, because the facts and conclusions we have to deal with can also be supported by spreadsheets and we recognised, that on one hand we will not have enough sample data in the near future and on the other we will follow an approach to support our most important goal of estimation of effort and schedule by informed discussion based on well presented singular experiences of past experiments instead of deriving a strict formula that delivers us a number and is influenced by various factors. Within this discussion during the negotiation phase of a project we will also get aware of possible performance enhancement possibilities.

With this respect we also evaluated "Knowledge Plan" of Software Productivity Research Inc., which seems to be suitable for large organisations with no possibilities to compare future projects with some similar already performed ones. The main obstacle for us was, that the algorithms of

"Knowledge Plan" are not known and the documentation as a whole was to flat. We repeat our statement, that first you have to understand the task well enough before you decide for a tool.

6.8.9.10 Additional Remarks

We take the opportunity for the following statement. We feel it necessary that in formal education i.e. within the universities or similar institutions the topic of measurement has to be included and that with this respect supporting activities of the EU and on national level are required.

7 Lessons from the EUREX Workshops

Lars Bergman
SISU, Kista

Workshops were used by the EUREX project as a principal means for collection and processing of PIE experiences. The workshops were organised by regions in order to facilitate PIE participation both from a travelling point of view and from a language point of view. The partners arranged the workshops in order to develop the common themes in accordance with the EUREX taxonomy. SISU, the Nordic EUREX partner arranged four workshops on Configuration and Change Management, Metrics and Lifecycle, Object Orientation, Components and Reuse, Requirements and Testing, all in Stockholm. The participating PIEs were Norwegian, Finnish and Danish as well as Swedish. An additional metrics workshop was organised and conducted in the UK.

The following sections of this chapter present the metrics workshops in Spain, Stockholm and London. The first two workshops followed the standard EUREX structure, whereas the London workshop was organised in to profit from the experience of Prof. Fenton. Finally, a summary of the conclusions reached by the various metrics workshops is given.

7.1 Metrics Workshop Spain

"Software Metrics as a Support in Business Management" was the theme for the introductory presentation made by José D. Carrillo Verdún of the AEMES (Spanish association for Metrics). This presentation is to be found in chapter four (Perspectives). The workshop was well populated by around 70 participants. The level of experience seems to have been mixed. But a very engaged discussion was the result of a well prepared and conducted group discussion session. The workshop was arranged by EUREX Spain partner SOCINTEC.

7.1.1 Conclusions of the Working Groups

7.1.1.1 Description and Aim of the Working Groups

Four areas or layers have been established in the work methodology of the EUREX project for the discussions in the Regional Workshops. These layers group together the findings and conclusions related to the positive as well as negative aspects of the Presentations made by the different PIE speakers.

The four areas of interest used for the exchange of ideas and opinions are the following:

- Methodology and Process area
- Technology area (tools used/implemented)
- Change Management area
- Business area

The Work groups were made up of approximately 8/10 people.

Previous to the Workshop, the people responsible for the organisation (SO-CINTEC), with the collaboration of an Expert in the area (José D. Carrillo, Caja Madrid, and Secretary of AEMES) analysed and processed the information received from the PIEs. Their aim was to obtain the preliminary conclusions and findings which would serve as discussion topics and dynamizers in the Work group meetings.

On the other hand, a person from the organisation (SOCINTEC) and one from each of the four PIEs joined the Groups with the aim of helping discussion.

Summaries of the conclusions presented by each of the Groups after a work session of approximately 75-90 minutes can be found below.

7.1.1.2   Group A – Methodology and Process Area

Starting point: The definition of metrics should be based on business objectives and therefore the implementation programme should be supported by the company's top management.

The method should assure that the metrics are defined according to the business objectives. The implementation of a metrics programme in a company is not exclusively a technical problem, it should also be promoted by the top management in order to improve the organisation of the Information and Technology Systems.

Excessively ambitious objectives should not be established at the beginning.

An excessively ambitious measurement or value programme that does not precisely define the variables should not be established at the beginning. The measurement programme should only be started once the objectives are clear.

Function points: The positive experiences are verified.

In many cases (and it is a growing tendency to use the automatic code generation) the code lines are not appropriate volume metrics.

The function points metrics are of no use unless used as a software volume measurement.

Two of the companies that participate in the discussion of this work group report their positive experiences on implementing the function points metrics. The figure of two hundred points measured per day and per functional analyst is given. An objective is considered adequate if there are measurements in function points in the "live" applications.

Function points: It is important to adapt them and to define the way of measuring them in each organisation.

Each organisation should define a way of measuring the function points according to the kind of software they carry out. The definition should be validated and then kept stable allowing for the comparison and measurement of the development of the ratios. Some of the criteria used to measure function points are qualitative which makes the definition of the standards based on these measurements difficult.

Function points: It is a limited tool when carrying out benchmarking.

This is a result of the previous point. Each organisation will differ on important points when calculating the function points. This hinders carrying out consistent comparisons with a certain level of precision.

The automation of the measurement collection process is very important.

This is the way of minimising costs (which obviously exist in all processes, including metrics) and of obtaining more precise and detailed information. The manual handling of information generates errors and is more expensive.

A function that appropriately manages the metrics programme should be implemented.

A group of experts should be responsible for the standardisation and dissemination of the information collected on the measurements carried out in the company as well as for applying the appropriate techniques homogeneously.

There is great interest in metrics on a technical level in companies. Nevertheless it is not easy to implement a programme due to the existing culture in technology management.

A great interest is detected in many companies on certain technical levels but the top management's lack of means and knowledge on how to demand that the technology be managed makes implementation difficult.

7.1.1.3   Group B – Technology Area

The implementation of a software measurement programme is not a tool problem.

The technology will help to collect, analyse and disseminate the information but the acquisition of a tool does not necessarily lead to the implementation of a metrics programme.

It is necessary to have clear ideas before choosing the tools, but – tools can also help to clarify ideas.

The fact that an exclusively technological solution will not usually solve the problem is applicable here. Nevertheless, one cannot ignore the fact that tools used for a specific use can be useful in suggesting aspects that have not been contemplated at first. What they won't usually do is substitute the lack of ideas.

Selection criteria: platform, integration, open, technical support, etc

It must be taken into account that the tool should be integrated into a technological context previously. To ignore this aspect could lead to disappointments.

Estimation tools: although not a panacea, they constitute an important support.

Tools do not avoid decision-making, but help to systematise some kinds of criteria. Positive experiences in the field of estimation have been confirmed, although each organisation should learn how to adapt the value proposed by the tool to its real needs.

Precision vs. tendency: more relevance is given to the tendency analysis.

The real use in this case comes from the study of the relative magnitudes rather than the absolute. It is fundamental, in everything, to highlight the importance of consistency in the criteria followed to analyse the tendencies.

Is the construction of a complete tool interesting (and justifiable)? – Main opinion: generally difficult to justify.

The market is considered to offer interesting metrics tools that are often founded on a strong base of experiences.

7.1.1.4   Group C – Change Management Area

Assess people with metrics: Apart from not being ethical, it is not very intelligent.

The people being assessed lose confidence and therefore ruin the metrics system

It should be known beforehand.

Unless people know beforehand that they are to be assessed and against what criteria

Resistance to change: To avoid it or to lessen the effect, the management and the technical team must work together.

The management plans, channels and manages the means for change but always starting from the experience gathered from the technical team on what needs to be changed: what doesn't work, how can it be improved

Improvement groups: They should be integrated into all the represented parties.

In particular, it is not advisable to use specialized groups foreign to everyday problems (e.g. improvement groups made up only of quality personnel). It is recommended that the best technical personnel and engineers participate (on a rotary and part time basis).

They should have assigned resources.

The technical team should have a certain amount of time reserved for the improvement group (e.g. two hours per day), the task should not be an overload for people working to 120%...

Software techniques: They seem to be on the edge of the business.

They should be involved in the present and future objectives of the business. An equilibrium should be established between the professional worries and preferences (e.g. the latest methodology, the latest tool), and the interests and possibilities of the company within its environment.

Do they own the project.

The rate of change in new technologies and the high level of specialization necessary to dominate them means that some members of the management team (even those with a more technical profile) find themselves almost completely in the hands of their technical team. Only the very careful management of the project resources, avoiding the dependency of concrete people in key tasks, can lessen this "power investment".

One of the basic sayings in software engineering is: "If you have somebody in your employment who is indispensable, give him the sack".

7.1.1.5   Group D – Business Area

It is difficult to align metrics with business objectives. A methodology is required that will make this alignment easier.

Due to the fact that in general they have been established as measurements for technical aspects rather than measurements of the achievements of the business objectives that the technology provides.

In general, companies do not know how to tackle a metrics project: A structure is lacking that would bring the metrics closer to the different management levels.

Mainly due to the lack of maturity existing in companies. As this increases the need will arise and the structure will be implemented.

Implementing metrics helps the computer personnel gain credibility.

It is a mechanism that gives visibility to the real situation and allows the realistic proposals to be fulfilled.

The structuring of the metrics should be made top down, its development, on the other hand should be carried out bottom up.

In fact if the management do not provide a real commitment, the metrics will not be implemented. In the same way, if the people implied are not involved in the metric establishment process, they will not work either.

It is important to take into account the information necessary to use the value analysis technique when collecting data.

The use of investment analysis techniques for the selection of projects requires data that should be collected during the development and exploitation of products and should allow the analysis of the value they provide for the company.

A metrics programme based on a short term investment return should never be established.

In fact successful programmes are established as a series of changes that provide improvements that lead to excellent work in the corresponding environment. These will produce investment returns on a long and medium term; but a metric will never be established as an investment return unless that is what is to be implemented. In other words, the investment return is usually the excuse used when a metrics programme is not wanted.

7.1.2   Lessons Learned

It is evident that there exists great interest in this subject, but the level of use of metrics continues to be very limited. In many cases it is made known that this is carried out by personal initiative or by a group, rather than by the implementation of structured programs promoted by the company Management.

- Its use has been analysed in different fields
- Software maintenance
- Reusability of the software components
- Project development
- Management concerned with the productivity, quality, cost and development activity of the software

Quality of the Source Code

Quality of the design and development of the software orientated to objects

The use of metrics has been shown in all cases, and in the majority they have resulted to be essential in obtaining concise results from the experiments carried out.

It is necessary to define a metrics policy in the company so that an adequate balance can be obtained between the measuring cost and the benefits in mind.

We should not be ambitious in the collection of the measuring data. Only the information related to the variables with which you are going to work should be collected as the validity of the data and its tendency is more important than its precision.

Metrics make it possible for the clients to change their perception of processes and services on a long term. The information used should be part of the culture of the organisation.

Metrics have served to increase awareness of the measuring objectives and to transmit the priorities to the organisation.

The measuring objectives should be taken into account during the whole iden-tification and metric implementation processes. The use of the GQM methodology has been of great use.

The human factors which are linked with the obtaining of measurements should be studied in great detail. The measuring objectives should be clear and respected by all those that use them. The involved agents should agree with the use of the measurement for the improvement processes and agree that data is not to be ques-tioned afterwards.

When metrics were used in the software maintenance processes, the size / com-plexity metrics permitted us to check that the defects also increased with the size and complexity of the affected function. There is no evidence that its use permits us to improve this process. The use of a workflow tool was also proved for collect-ing measuring data in this process.

In relation with the software quality and design orientated towards objects, the traditionally denominated (basic) metrics are not valid by themselves to measure quality and development. The selected metrics should measure three key aspects: capsulation, inheritance and polymorphism. Also the necessary viewpoints were fixed to select a tool for the metrics in this area.

The metrics should be used in a OO software development project: during the design and development stage to validate the quality of the software architecture and of the code. They should be calculated at the same time as the corresponding elements are going to form part of the configuration management.

7.1.3 Overall Conclusions

The following conclusions can be reached as a result of this workshop:

The large number of people who assisted as well as the participation in the workgroups and debates that followed, show the interest of this subject in many companies. This is also confirmed by the high percentage of company inscriptions and in the participation of the activities of the Spanish Metric Software Association (AEMS)

In spite of this interest, existing experience is very limited. In many cases it refers to its use in very specific applications especially in project estimates, and not to implementation projects with clearly defined management objectives, supported by the company's top management.

All the cases presented by the participating companies, showed positive results demonstrating the use of metrics in different fields. However, all companies except one, had no specific plans to continue metric development and application.

The use of metrics in determined areas still finds itself in an immature stage. In general, an existing gap has been verified between the world of research and the final user to easily use these techniques.

The interest in metrics is centred mainly on tactical applications whereas the Information System and Technology Management is still carried out with qualitative and technological criteria without applying common use techniques with other company resources that require specific measurement utilisation.

Because of this lack of experience and market interest suffered until recently, there are only a limited number of consultancy companies that can offer experience, knowledge and products within this area.

Metrics are considered very important as a means to align the technological objectives with those of the business. They also help to determine the value that Technology adds to the company and to improve the credibility of the technicians.

The introduction project in the company measuring program is a strategic project, and should not be planned exclusively as a classical investment benefit analysis. If the implementation is to be successful there must be an adequate plan, organisation and the necessary resources.

It is not possible to improve software quality without quantitatively knowing the level of progress of the process improvement with the correct metrics.

In general, we can confirm that this workshop has permitted participating companies to become more aware of the need for the introduction of metrics to improve the Information Alignment Systems management and to permit a better Technological Information with business objectives.

7.2 Workshop on Metrics & Process Improvement Stockholm

"Metrics Based Process Improvement" was the theme for the workshop as well as the introduction given by Mr. Otto Vinter, Bruel & Kjaer. This workshop gathered PIEs on a Nordic base and had around 20 participants. It turned out that the external participants were interested but brought rather little experience. The following report is done by Mr. Antonio Macchi III, who is a doctor student at the Stockholm University.

7.2.1 Introduction

This paper presents the workshop in the theme Metrics & Process Improvement, held in Stockholm at March 30th, 1998. The number of Nordic PIEs initially classified to belonging the theme "Metrics" were few, and in order to attract more PIEs, the theme was broadened to include also "Process Improvement". The underlying assumption we made was that collecting measurement data with the bare objective to assess does not make the most of the metrics approach. Instead, a further objective, e.g. for building prediction models based on the measurement data, or to initiate an improvement program based on the measurement data indications, ought to be necessary, if not for other reasons, then for getting a top management commitment. At the other hand, a process improvement effort without any measurement is like a ship without a target: the concept of improvement is meaningless unless there is a measured baseline and comparison of the actual to the baseline after the improvement effort.

Below, the invited PIEs will be listed according to the following coding: ACRONYHM(NO,XX,YY), where ACRONYHM stands for the short name for the project, NO is the project contract number within EC, XX is ND for no documentation, DR for documentation in a report form, DS for documentation as slides, YY is P for participating, NP for non-participating.

- AMPIC (24099, ND, NP) (Terttu)
- ESTEX (21569, DS, P)
- GRIPS (23887, DR, P)
- PET (10438, DS,P)
- PREMISE (10255, ND,NP) (Lars)
- PRIDE (21167, DS,P)
- PROMM (10616, DR,NP)
- SCERA (10147,DR, NP)
- TELMET (21780, ND,NP) (Terttu)

For various reasons, AMPIC, PREMISE, PROMM, SCERA, and TELMET could not participate. All but AMPIC are completed projects, some with the end date in 1995, or earlier. AMPIC was at the time of the workshop involved in a certification process, with assessors at the work place, and therefore, the key person could not leave the company.

The group of other participants consisted of eight participants of software companies, one technology student, and the SISU- EUREX workers Lars Bergman and Terttu Orci. The moderator of the workshop, Mr Otto Vinter, also represented two of the invited PIEs. The majority of the industrial representatives work in large software companies in Stockholm area.

This Report is Organised as Follows

In Section 2, the PIEs above, both participating and non-participating (if documentation available), will be shortly presented. In Section 3, the talk of the moderator will be overviewed and commented. In Section 4, the discussion at the workshop will be shortly reviewed, and Section 5 presents the conclusions arrived at during the discussion, and comparison with the conclusions presented from the Spanish workshop in Metrics.

7.2.2   Presentation of the PIEs

AMPIC – Application of Metrics for Process Improvement for Safety Critical Software

The partner is Normarc-Garex AS. The problems of completing projects within time and cost limits, the common software engineering problems, are the basic trigger to this PIE. The underlying reason for the experienced problems is an increasing amount of software in the products, in particular the safety-critical software. Development of safety-critical software does not only demand the time and costs being within the budget, but also the quality of the product to meet the special criteria. A quality improvement of the development process and its compliance to very strict certification standards are the backbone of this experiment.

The objectives of the PIE are to develop adequate metrics in order to

- improve estimation.
- identify problem areas.
- improve the quality and productivity of the development process.

The methodology used in the PIE is the AMI approach. The project will be in end in August 1998.

ESTEX – Project Estimation Experiment
The Business and the Baseline

CRI Space Division is the partner performing the PIE. The main objective of the PIE is to develop reasonably formalised, yet simple, bottom-up based estimation techniques. The reason for the this starting point is the hypothesis that in the environment of the PIE owner, it is difficult to establish historical data over a large number of similar projects. Thereby, the algorithmic cost models like COCOMO data, are discriminated. The organisation is reported to be at CMM level 2 and attempts to further improve their software process. The estimation problem is believed to be one of the major obstacles in improvement. The project was ended in October 1997.

The core projects can be characterised as including activities from design to specification, they are performed according to Waterfall process model, representing the diversity of projects in the organisation. There have been a number of changes in the space market, currently it is more competitive, the focus is on price, the contracts are fixed price contracts, cost overruns lie with the contractor, and therefore, reliable estimates are paramount.

Goals of the PIE
The objectives of ESTEX were to

- improve estimation capabilities
- support proposal calculations, contract negotiations, baseline change management, in-process re-estimation
- provide access to historical project data

An estimation model was developed with the following characteristics: it supports estimation by analogy, still leaving room for professional judgement, it allows estimating and measuring size and effort consistently across projects, and recording and using assumptions, risks and uncertainty, and obtaining historical productivity factors.

Table 7.1 ESTEX key activities and work products are as follows:

No	Activity	Work Product	Size Metric
1	User and system requirements analysis	Software requirements document	Individual requirements are counted
2	Architectural design	Architectural design document	All nodes in all design trees are counted
3	Detailed design, coding, and unit test	Deliverable Code	Lines of code
4	Test description, planning, set-up, execution, and reporting	Test specifications and reports	Test cases, scripts and sessions are counted
5	Handling of problem reports from analysis through closure	Error fixes	Software problem reports are counted
6	Conception, writing and issuing of documentation	Other project documentation	Pages are counted
7	Project management		
8	Quality control		
9	Other work		

Basic Productivity Equation

$$P = size/effort$$

Total Project Effort Equation

$$EP = sum(size/productivity) + sum(effort)$$

where size/productivity is counted for all work products, and effort is counted for all other activities

Productivity is calculated at a team level, not at individual level. Productivity data assumes the participation of an expert in the team, as without experts, the productivity will (most probably) decrease.

Assumptions, risks and uncertainty are handled by recording the assumptions, flagging the risks when high probability is significant and impact of an assumption failing. Worst-case calculations is done for all affected key activities, and there is no quantification of risks.

Further characteristics of the estimation model is that it

- uses own organisational data
- is easy to use, intuitively understandable
- covers all project phases and activities
- allows measurements to be easily collected
- can be supported by automated tools but it is not a requirement
- not bound to specific tools or development methods

The model validation is done as follows:

- initial application (two operational projects, and their preliminary results, three completed projects – data collection, model refined)
- second application (five operational projects, project tracking, baseline change procedure)
- accuracy of estimates (goal is to be within 5% of the actual)

Table 7.2 Results Deviations of estimates from actual effort

Project	Normal	Worst case	COCOMO
1	33%	18%	11%
2	26%	9%	N/A.

Table 7.3 Time requirements

System overhead	Man-days	User project overhead	Man-days
Set-up of procedures and database	5	Introduction	1/2
Start-up	5	Initial application	2
Support	2-7	Re-estimation	1/2
		Measurement	1/2

Comments

From a metrics perspective this was the most consistent presentation at the workshop, although we did not obtain a more exact picture of how certain measures are defined and used. The measures are associated with products and activities at different phases of the development process, and they concentrate at simple measures like the number of requirements, LOC, number of defects, simple complexity measures.

For many of these measures it is fundamental to have the stability of a clear application domain as well as stability of their development process. This stability helps to keep consistency of the measures across the organisation. For instance, there is a known criteria of how much one requirement implies in terms of functionality, so that the number of requirements can be used for estimations of size. Regarding the analysis of software defects it was not clear how the measurements are defined, although there is consciousness on the classification of defects since the customers are surely very aware of dependability issues. The speaker was not directly involved in the improvement program, and more detailed information could not be given to the audience.

GRIPS – Getting the Grip on Software Product Support Through Error Prevention Measures
The Business and the Baseline

SimCorp has moved from developing specially tailored systems for customer to the development of standard systems, currently a treasure management system and a standard pension fund system. The new market direction puts new demands on the quality of the products, both from the current and from the potential future customers' point of view. It is experienced as an urgent business need to be able to give adequate product support, achieved by minimising the number of changes required, by controlling the introduction of side-effects when changing, and by reducing the number of errors in the baseline project release. The project will be in end in August 1998.

It is not surprising to get convinced about the lack of stability of the development process when we heard that the projects had no documents for specifications and project plans. Projects were managed by informal contacts between marketing, developers, and management. Their development process shows an incredible lack of stability of requirements during the product development life cycle. Requirements were never frozen but kept changing during the development phase and even after product release. After release the change requests kept growing mainly due to reports of software defects found by end users. There is very much noise in the requirement handling process since one third of requests generated by the developers themselves are rejected. Approximately a year after release there were three times as many change requests (about 3000) than upon product release. The causes of problems were very general and not specific, and there was no control of the development process since the picture keeps changing very fast all the time. Ideally they recognise that most defects should have been detected before release of the product instead of the current practice with the product practically tested on the field.

The Goals of the PIE

The goals for the improvement program are to achieve increased credibility in the market and to reduce the workload imposed on developers due to the need for support of previous releases of their products.

The objectives for the improvement program were to reduce the number of defect reports by 20%, to reduce the ratio of "unnecessary" change requests by 5%, and to reduce the rate of rejected features of new releases to no more that 10%. All these measures considered within three months of the release of a product.

Measurement has been introduced for the reasons of tracking the progress against goals, and for understanding better how the work is actually performed. Inspections have been included in the work. The qualitative sign of progress so far is that the developers report significantly reduced number of distractions by outside calls, the management has started to see the change specification process as their tool, and test cases are now documented.

Inspections in Order to Devise the Specification Process

Gilb & Graham: Software Inspection, has been a significant source of inspiration.

Individuals have been responsible for managing changes. There are many new work products available for review:

- Project plans
- Requirements specifications
- Design detail specifications
- Integration specifications
- Test specifications

Decision to start specifying all larger changes to one of the products before they were implemented was made. It made it necessary to find a way to organise, support and guide change specification groups. It was achieved by building on a number of key ideas from Gilb style inspection process – or by turning inspections inside out to produce documents. Inspection groups should include 3-7 persons. Expected life-time should be 2-6 months. The first groups started in April/May 97 and should deliver first results in June/July and final results in August 97. About 30% of the staff are involved.

Basic ingredients of the process are to organise a kick-off meeting, to assign the roles and responsibilities, to define the deliverables, develop checklists and templates for the different review types, to monitor progress monitoring, to perform post-mortem analysis, to define the scope of the project, by using existing know-how, keeping the critical dates, and to organise a reference group. The roles and responsibilities include chief editor, process moderator, project manager, editor, developer, and document responsibilities.

The deliverables are project plan, requirements specification, design details specification, integration specification, and test specification. Other deliverables are being defined through checklists and guidelines. Checklists and guidelines are gradually being improved and new templates defined. Review types are steering group meetings, walkthroughs, inspections.

Progress monitoring requires that the project plan is to be kept updated at all times, and that it includes a special section, namely action item log. The issues raised at reviews are also tracked to closure. Post-mortem evaluations are aimed to continuously improve the process.

The methodology used is to define error prevention measures by analysing the weaknesses of the current practice. The effect of the introduced measures will be studied during the 12 month period over consecutive product releases. Root-Cause-Analysis technology will be used to identify the weaknesses of the process, based on error reports from the past.

The findings obtained so far are as follows:
- causes of errors are general rather than specific
- workload is too high leaving insufficient time for each task
- requirements and/or expectations are not stable and known prior to opening the development of new versions
- there is too much noise in the process

Situation Now

Experience from inspections made it possible to successfully build a process around the specification groups, and it actually worked

Feed-back from users of the process is very positive

The inspections were introduced and the prospects of improving their effectiveness are very promising as on process further matures

In inspections they have achieved logging rates of 1/2 issue per min, which is said to be extremely good for the business.

Quantitative improvements, as defined for the objectives have not yet been achieved, but most figures are reported to move on the right direction. Most improvements achieved are of qualitative character:

Problems with Showing Return On Investment

Mr. Elvang remarked that if the motivation for the software process improvement program counts on showing a return on investment, there might be difficulties to prove that ROI for management, especially if the organisation focuses their measures on single projects. He points to the fact that the return on investment figures may only show improvements in a longer time scale (for instance three years) while immediate results are expected by management already during the project. He states that a commitment from the management for the improve program shall be achieved through a consensus that quality and process improvement are important for the business.

Lessons Learned

- KISS – not too ambitious; when starting, it is all about people, not numbers
- only measure if you have a clear purpose (failed attempt to introduce err-type)
- obtain buy-in before starting any new measurement (side-effect)
- feed back statistics a s a p (to maintain buy-in)
- experiment with a build on what you already go to understand what it is that you want
- it might take longer than you think
- as long as you believe in it it will work

Comments

The project gives the impression that the goals and objectives have been formulated with a clear focus on the immediate business goals by management, with little influence from methodology professionals. It is possible to see an attempt on reducing the symptoms of low process maturity, instead of addressing directly the causes of problems experienced by the company. But anyway, this is the way the organisation experiences the problems and therefore it is good that at least they recognise the existence of those problems and search for solutions. The reason for the remark is that it would be good to see more technical substance regarding Software Engineering and Metrics on the formulation of the goals and objectives.

From a Metrics perspective the presentation was weak since the connection between goals and objectives to measures was loose, and the measures were not well defined. But it is at least interesting to see that the organisation is now committed to a process improvement effort. After all there was an attempt to measure important parameters for the development process and these measurements will hopefully be corrected and refined.

PET – The Prevention of Errors Through Experience-Driven Test Efforts

Bruel & Kjaer Measurements A/S and Danfoss A/S are the partners of the PIE. The project ended in May 1995.

The objectives of the PIE were:
- to extract knowledge on frequently occurring problems in the development process (embedded software)
- to change the development process by defining the optimum set of methods and tools available to prevent these problems reappearing, and

to measure the impact of the changes in a real-life development project.

The project underlying the experiment was a seven man-years project, and 1100 bugs were analysed from the error logs, bug reports covering a period until 18 months after the first release.

The definition of a bug is said to be anything between a serious defect and a proposal for improvement. Bug reports, to be analysed in the project, start to occur in the integration phase. Defect analysis from error logs was performed by bug categorisation according to the scheme by Boris Beizer, including the following categories:

- requirements and features
- functionality as implemented
- structural bugs
- data
- implementation (standards violation, and documentation)
- integration
- system and software architecture
- test definition or execution bugs
- other bugs, unspecified

Each category was detailed to a depth of up to four levels.

The results of the analysis were as follows:
- no special bug class dominated embedded software development
- requirements problems, and related problems was the prime cause (36%)
- problems due to lack of systematic unit testing was the second largest cause (22%)

Management Attention to Software Process Issues

Actions to improve unit testing were the introduction of static and dynamic analysis, by host/target tools, and by defining a basic set of metrics.

For the bottom-up perspective they emphasized the importance of starting with already existing information as the only realistic solution for measurement. Therefore the focus has been on the analysis and quantification of software defects and on testing. We have been told that about 200 out of 1200 defect reports were selected and analysed carefully by a team of process consultants and developers. At least half of the defects observed after product release have their origin in erroneous requirements or on erroneous interpretation of requirements. The analysis of software defects helped them to point at candidates for improvements, mainly on the requirements process and on the software testing phase.

Comments

From a pure Metrics point of view the presentation was weak, since many basic principles have not been considered carefully. For example there is a lack of consistency when describing software failures.

The expression "bug" is used for errors, faults, failures, and bugs in the software. Here the conventional use of the terms could have been applied, as in Software Engineering and Metrics literature. It is also good to point out that defect density measures have several pitfalls. It would be good to consider carefully those issues in the continuation of the improvement program.

Strengths of the Experience: But the strength of the presentation is on the fact that the organisation has successfully implemented a process improvement program, and is now likely to further develop their skills in Metrics towards a higher maturity level on their development processes. From a management point of view this achievement is very important. The fact that the theoretical foundations for the work are initially weak may be considered as less important, as long as the organisation has started to work explicitly with quality improvement issues. The usage of concepts on Metrics may be improved on the next phase of the project.

PREMISE – Productivity in Software Engineering of Electronics Based Equipment

The partners of the PIE are Bang & Olufsen A/S, P.I.V. Eldutronik (NL) and Sextant Avionique (F). The main objective for the embedded software engineering community is time to market and control of complexity of the embedded software, associated to the users' demands for advanced functionality, communication features, and unique quality. The PIE objectives were to verify the possibility of increasing both productivity and quality using the following methodologies/techniques in an integrated fashion: SA/SD-RT methodology, state/transition technique, automatic logical check functions and direct code generation. The project ended in June 1995.

PRIDE – A Methodology for Preventing Requirements Issues from Becoming Defects

The methodology would be integrated in the ISO 9000 Quality Management System of the partner, Bruel & Kjaer A/S. The project ended in October 1997.

The main objective of the PIE was to

- extract knowledge on frequently occurring problems in the requirements engineering process
- change the development process by defining the optimum set of methods and tools available to prevent these problems reappearing

measure the impact of the changes in a real-life development project

The project was based on the results of PET project, namely that requirements related problems were the main cause of bugs (33%).

Requirements related bugs are caused by

- missing requirements (1/3)
- misunderstood requirements (1/3)
- changes to requirements (1/5)

Error logs were analysed, involving 900 bugs. Bug categorisation was based on the same classification scheme as in PET. Analysis of requirements issues gave that the following attributes should be available for the bugs:

- error source (forgotten, misunderstood, tacit, wrong ...
- interface where the bug occurred
- quality factor (functionality, reliability, usability ...
- complexity of bug (correction cost)
- what could prevent the bug

The result was that 51% of the bugs were requirements related. Major requirements issues were:

- usability (64%)
- external software (3rd party & MS products) (28%)
- functionality (22%)
- other than above (13%)

It was also found that 92.5% of the requirements issues were easy to correct, even if found late in the project, and the most "difficult to fix" problems (7.5%) were mostly related to external software. To find and fix the difficult problems takes 45% of the time. Empirically it could be stated that McCabe's complexity measure was correlated to fault intensity for their class of products.

The importance of throw-away prototyping of user interfaces was also discussed. In average about 40% of the functionality of prototypes is discarded during the product development life cycle. It is obvious for me that in these circumstances the handling of requirements may be very critical for the development process.

Examples of techniques identified to prevent requirements issues are demand analysis, usability techniques, external software, tracing techniques, risk analysis techniques, formal specification techniques, inspection/checking techniques.

Some 40+ techniques were considered, some well-known, some from check lists, and some invented when needed. The proposed methodology includes techniques for requirements elicitation and validation, and verification of requirements specification.

Requirements Elicitation and Validation
Requirements elicitation and validation was done by presenting scenarios (related demands to use situations and describing the essential tasks in each scenario. Another technique was usability test concerning the daily tasks, by means of a navigational prototype of the user interface.

Verification of Requirements Specification
The verification was performed by

- stress testing the external software (to test that the external software fulfils the expectations in the requirements, with special emphasis on extreme cases),
- orthogonality check (check of requirements specification to see whether an operation or feature can be applied whenever it is useful,
- performance specifications (check requirements specification to see whether it contains performance goals for the requirements).

Static Analysis
- data flow anomalies (undefined by referenced variables, variables redefined with no use in between, variable defined but not used in scope)
- complexity measures (code size, McCabe, Halstead, loop nesting analysis),
- source code visualisation (static flow graph, static call tree, identifies unreachable code, and programming standard violations)
- dynamic coverage analysis (statement, branch, sub condition, test-path)
- dynamic coverage visualisation (dynamic call tree, dynamic flow graph, execution trace, cross references statements to test cases, identifies redundant test cases)

Qualitative Results
- scenarios gave the developers a clear vision of the user needs of the product
- user interaction with the product was totally changed as a result of the usability tests
- demo versions of the nearly finished product created more positive responses from potential customers
- product was released in December 1997 and orders could be shipped before the end of the year

Quantitative Results
- error logs were analysed and compared to a similar project (same team, same platform person hours within 10%, 5 times increase in screen)
- total number of error reports -27%
- requirements related reports -11%
- non-requirements related reports -37%
- requirements issues

- usability issues +5%
- other requirement issues -36%
- 46% improvement in testing efficiency
- 75% reduction in production-release bugs
- 70% requirements bugs in production-release

General Conclusions
- scenarios capture the most important user needs
- usability tests on early prototypes verify these needs
- the impact on the perceived quality of the product is much greater than on the prevention of bugs
- the benefits of focussing the scenario and usability test techniques will have a major impact on our business
- the requirements elicitation techniques are rapidly being adopted by other projects by the contractor
- the requirements verification techniques will be tried out in another experiment
- defect analysis is a simple and effective way to assess and improve the software development process

Conclusions on Static/Dynamic Analysis
- it is an efficient way to remove bugs
- marginal delay on trial release date
- marginal increase in the testing resources required
- immediate payback on tools, training and implementation
- remarkably improved test coverage
- increased quality
- reduced maintenance costs
- increased motivation
- applicable to whole software development industry, including embedded software

Defect analysis from error logs is a simple and effective way to assess the software development process. The analysis of bugs has had a significant impact on the way we now look at our software development process, has established a basic set of metrics for test activities, and is a starting point for process improvement programmes in companies.

The organisation considers usability to be an important issue for product quality. What is observed by the end user is fundamental for the product image. To improve usability the activities for collection of requirements use extensively prototypes of user interfaces (paper prototypes!) as a help for producing requirement specifications. Compliance to specifications has therefore a large weight on quality. About 64% of the defects analysed by the improvement program could be classified in this category. Improvements in the requirements process and on software testing are considered to provide large enhancements on product quality.

PROMM – Software Engineering Project Management and Metrication
Background and Problems
Partner Irish Life, a company providing life insurance and pensions products. The
software development life cycle model is Waterfall – well-defined and documented. Systems development is supported by established methods and techniques
for analysis and design in a main-frame development environment. The main
problems were exceeding delivery dates and budget limitations. The main reason
to the problems were believed to be lack of formal methods for project management and control.

Project Objectives
The main objectives of the PIE are to evaluate the PRINCE1 project management
methodology and Function Point metrics in order to improve the attributes productivity, quality and time-to-market within the framework of a well-defined and
established systems development life cycle. Further estimation techniques will
also be included in the experiment. The project ended in July 1995.

Starting Scenario
The customer opinion about Irish Life was that the business systems developed by
IL were expensive, the on-going maintenance efforts are due to poor quality in the
development process, and that late and over-budget delivery had become an accepted norm. Independent audits have confirmed the facts above, and the specific
numbers were given: the projects were 70% late, 150% over-budget and required
often 30% additional effort in implementation rework after delivery.

The causes were identified to be:

- lack of formal estimation techniques
- insufficient attention to cost-benefit justification and risk assessment
- inadequate advance planning of project phases, tasks and detailed activity
  scheduling
- poor management and utilisation of project resources and skills
- no formal tracking or reporting of project schedules, costs and expended effort
- no defined framework for user participation, leading to a lack project ownership, control and commitment
- no separation of responsibility for project content and execution processes
- unbalanced or excessive effort directed towards delivery of marginal functionality, reflecting inadequate project control
- patchy implementation of quality assurance procedures

Expected Outcomes
The expected outcomes are the reduction of development and maintenance costs
to be obtained by improving productivity and quality, an increased credibility

among the clients regarding the quality of the products, delivered on schedule and within budget, and by shortening time-to-market to gain competitive advantages.

Benchmarking

Two benchmarks (databases with other organisations using FP) were conducted: against financial institutions only in the external database, and against all organisations in the database. The benchmark results were that the company was close to industry average, especially on medium size projects and delivery rate was below average (Delivery rate is defined as function points delivered per elapsed week, measuring responsiveness, the speed at which software solutions are made available to clients.) The key factors were found to be: lack of control on delivery dates, spreading resources too thinly, and client delays.

PRINCE – Projects in a Controlled Environment – is a project management methodology, tolerable to a user organisation, but intended to be used with the SSADM systems development methodology. MicroMan, a multi-project, multi-user, LAN-based project planning and control software package was selected for its capabilities for project planning, time recording, project control, management reporting, and cost accounting.

Estimation Methods and Tools

The evaluation concluded that most of the methods and tools required low level design specification to be useful, while early estimation was required, based on business functionality at a high level. Also, a few of the tools/methods evaluated supported FP. An estimation framework was developed which would lead the project manager through a number of steps to a more objective estimate, with a documented assumptions and quantified risks. The framework is not only useful in planning, but during the life time of the project. The idea is that project management, risk management and estimation should be integrated.

Experimental Phase

In each of the experimental five projects, the new methods and techniques were applied:

- establishing project management board, review and control mechanisms
- applying estimation methods and tools to determine the project resource requirements, duration and costs
- performing detailed project planning
- conducting FP counting during project execution
- record actuals and compare with estimates
- conducting post partum project review with the clients and its production staff to assess performance against quality, delivery and productivity attributes

Evaluation Phase

- The evaluation phase included the following work on each of the experiment projects:
- collecting and summarising: quality, productivity, delivery, FP, resource utilisation metrics
- analysing the data by: project type, size, complexity, and evaluating against baseline performance as well as against industrial benchmark.
- Summarising the final conclusions and experiences and highlighting implications for the systems development life cycle.

Key Metrics

Productivity showed 3.4% improvement against the baseline, which is assumed to be low because of the initial difficulties and learning curve for introducing new methods. The increased focus on delivery had a positive influence on productivity. Delivery rates showed 200% improvement, the majority of it to be counted to the new methods and control procedures. Schedule variance improved 78%, an encouraging result contributed to the increased focus on project planning and control. The average rework for experimental projects was 8.2%: 0.4% for reviews, 5% for acceptance testing, and 2.8% implementation support. The baseline quality metrics were lacking, which means that the figures are not comparable with the actual before the experimental projects.

Metrics Definitions

There are the following metrics:

- *Productivity* is the number of FP developed per work hour. It is calculated by dividing the system size in FP by the amount of effort invested in the project, P = size/effort
- *Delivery rate* is defined as the number of FP developed per elapse week. It is used to determine how fast the system has been delivered. It is calculated by dividing the system size in FP by the number of elapsed weeks spent on the project. DR = system size/elapsed weeks
- *Cost variance.* The cost variance metric is used to track how much a project is over/under its allocated budget, both original and final. Final budget is based on any re-planning exercises during the project life cycle.
- Original = (Actual Cost – Original Budget)/Original Budget
- Final = (Actual Cost – Final Budget)/Final Budget
- *The schedule variance* metric is used to determine how much a project deviates from its schedule (in planned elapsed weeks). It is calculated as:
- Original = (Actual Elapsed Weeks – Original Planned Elapsed Weeks)/Original Planned Elapsed Weeks
- Final = (Actual Elapsed Weeks – Final Planned Elapsed Weeks)/Final Planned Elapsed Weeks

- *Quality, Rework effort.* Total rework on a project expressed as a percentage of overall project effort. Rework arising from QA Reviews, Acceptance Testing, Implementation Support

Table 7.4 Summary of Results

	Baseline Count	Benchmark	Experiment Results	Difference
Productivity	0.1483	0.16	0.1534	+3.4%
Delivery Rate	2.62	8.69	7.98	+204%
Cost Variance	24.97%	19.68%		21.2%
Cost Variance	9.93%	9.71%		+.2.2%
Schedule Variance	86.21%	32.13%	5.54%	+78%
Quality Rework	8.2%			

Estimation and Risk Management

Risks are identified, quantified and controlled. The total risk is translated into a potential budget/time scale variance and agreed with clients. If the figures are not acceptable, some risks are addressed before the project commencement. The risk management implies that the clients have more realistic expectations regarding delivery. The project board quantifies and presents the figures of risks at project initiation meeting. Occurred risks are reported to the project board by the project manager.

FP Function Points

FP was found difficult, requiring external expertise. Also, when knowing the technique, FP includes some subjective measures, and sometimes it is difficult to know what to count. The observation was also made that FP is not adequate for object-oriented systems. OO projects were measured by drawing ER diagrams of the system and interpreting the objects as entities.

The major idea of the project initiation was that commitments should not be made until there is an understanding on both producer and client side about what is to be delivered and how it is to be delivered. The past mistakes were of making too early commitments, resulting in unrealistic and incorrect client expectations. The key deliverable of the initiation phase is Project Initiation Document including project objectives, deliverables, quality criteria, budget and time scales, quantified risk factors. The client participation is emphasised by the IL-PRINCE methodology. The client reactions have been quite positive, except in the early beginning some time commitment was difficult. Now there seems to be an understanding by the client that the participation gains their own sake. To prevent the overruns in time and budget were the basic objectives. By better estimates, the clients now have more realistic expectations.

The new methods and tools were adopted quite well with the people concerned. In the beginning, there was some doubt to need to employ full methodology in the experimental projects, e.g. formal sign-offs were forgotten, becoming better once the project progressed and understanding of the benefits was gained. FP counting was problematic though. FP was difficult, but also difficult to understand the reward of it. The reasons for it:

Failure to gain full benefit of FP as there was not enough historical data for supporting the calibration of the model

- Lack of support tools, making a CASE tool with FP a wish
- Lack of expertise
- Consequences like doubt of the FP consistency because lack of expertise

Key Lessons
Technological Point of View

- Project management experience combined with an effective project management methodology is critical to delivering on client expectations.
- Support tools are only effective if they support the methods and procedures in use.
- FP counting requires commitment and expertise to implement.
- Metrics is an extremely powerful and necessary aid to the management of a software engineering function.

Business Point of View

- Project participation and ownership by business people is critical to the delivery of business benefits.
- Project management is not just an IT discipline, it is just as relevant to business projects.
- Quality is something than can be built into a project. There is an associated cost which needs to be realised and justified.

Strengths and Weaknesses

The experiment being in a real life situation was a strong point. Ideas for the further development have already been raised. The weak points was the time duration of the project, over two years including the time of commitment by EC. During that long time, objectives and the organisation can radically change.

Conclusions and Further Actions

Overall positive impact on quality and delivery. Productivity is believed not to suffer of introducing the new methodology but it is too soon to tell. A very objective measure of the performance has been reached and it will help to identify and quantify further process improvement initiatives. The IL-PRINCE is now used in every project – it is a standard.

Within a few months it is believed to extend the coverage to all business areas through the appropriate IT Account Managers.

SCERA – Integrated Software Cost Estimation and Risk Assessment in Industrial Companies

The Information Technology Development Centre (TIEKE) together with Finnish companies developed the LaTuRi (La – from Laatu, Quality in Finnish, Tu – from Tulos, Result in Finnish, Ri – from Riski, Risk in Finnish) tool for project estimation and risk analysis. Function Point method has been implemented in LaTuRi. A risk analysis method, RiskMethod, and an associated tool, RiskTool, were developed by the Technical Research Centre of Finland (VTT). The objective of the PIE was to integrate RiskTool to LaTuRi. The project ended in December 1994.

The target was to enhance the estimation of effort and duration to achieve average prediction accuracy PRED(80) = 0.15. Cost estimation integrated with risk calculation is important to make a commitment to a customer.

The results of the experiment including 14 baseline projects were as follows:

Target for effort estimation was PRED(60) = 0.15. With only Laturi PRED(58)=0.15, and with Laturi and the RiskTool, the result of PRED(90)=0.15 was obtained.

Target for duration estimation was PRED(70)=0.15. With only Laturi PRED(40)=0.15, while with Laturi and RiskTool, PRED(78)=0.15 was obtained.

The business changes during the experiment were that more formality was introduced to the estimation, and more project used estimation. The partners involved were in average half-way to reach level 2 in CMM maturity model.

Conclusions
- Methods and tools for effort and duration estimation are valuable support.
- Project personnel needs expert support.
- If not qualified support is available, the resistance of project managers grows.
- Company and project specific background data is outmost valuable.
- Estimation must be planted to project management practice to keep alive and grow.
- Better integration of the tools still needed.
- Project manager attitude towards experiment was more positive than expected.

Lessons Learned

The participating companies were novices in using tools. That might be a possible interpretation of the fact that the results of using the estimation tools were not significantly better than expert opinions.

The targets were made unrealistically high. That might be the reason for the positive attitude project management had to the experiment.

If project can be decomposed to a detailed enough level, e.g. three months duration, there is no need of estimation tools.

The disciplined and standard way to estimate project effort and duration makes communication and understanding between management and project specialists easier.

7.2.3   Metrics Based Process Improvement

A talk of the moderator Otto Vinter.

The topics covered by the talk of the moderator were the following:

- why measure?
- data driven vs. goal driven metrics programmes

The reasons for measuring were said to be to know where you are, to decide what to do, and to stay on track.

- *To know where you are:* If you don't know where you are, a map won't help (Humphrey)
- *To decide what to do:* If you don't know where you're going, any road will do (Chinese)
- *To stay on track:* If you can't measure it, you can't control it (Lord Kelvin / Tom DeMarco)

To know where you are is essential as a starting point for a measurement program. However, a measurement programme is not a means to an end, but a supporting technique for an improvement of the current practice in one or another way. To know where you are can be made by performing an assessment, e.g. CMM, Bootstrap, SPICE/ISO, or by analysing existing data, e.g. error reports, progress reports, by performing interviews.

To decide what to do is naturally important, otherwise you can choose whatever action. There are principally two types of improvement programs: bottom-up or data driven and top-down or goal driven.

The bottom-up alternative uses existing data (if any), analyse problem areas, so called hot-spots, decide on changes and start new measurements where needed. The top-down approach starts by goals, breaking down goals to operational actions, start measurement and evaluate and revise. Measurement for staying on track is necessary, otherwise there is no possibility to control the line of actions.

To stay on track requires measurement. The "things" than can be measured are processes, products, or resources. Process measurement may concern attributes like time, effort, cost, efficiency, benefits, defects, and changes. Product attributes are size, complexity, modularity, test coverage, reuse, and a number of quality factors, e.g. functionality, reliability, usability, efficiency, portability, maintainability. Resources are persons, tools, techniques, and methods. Their attributes may be productivity (persons), experience (person), environment and context for tools, and performance and price for tools, techniques.

Data driven metrics programs starting from data may consider a study of the error reports (time history, classification of errors, change requests), study of the code (size in terms of KLOC, complexity, structure, degree of reuse). Tests can be analysed by collecting test cases, defect finding rate, test coverage, releases. Documents can be measured in terms of pages (size), revisions, requirements, design elements, modules. Project schedules are measured by comparing the plan with the actual, change requests, progress. Project accounting is measured in terms of phases, activities, actual vs. budget.

Goal driven metrics program is based on the Goal-Question-Metric Paradigm (GQM), developed by Basili and Rombach.

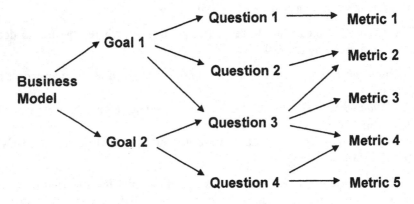

Fig. 7.1 Goal-Question-Metric Paradigm

The business model involves a number of goals, which might be needed to break down to sub goals until it is possible to formulate a question, the answer of which states whether or not the goal / sub goal is satisfied. For each question, a number of metrics is defined, which when instantiated by a value, answers the question they are associated to. Examples of applying GQM were given.

Goals are formulated in a template:

- *Purpose:* characterise, motivate, improve, evaluate, predict, monitor, control, increase, reduce, achieve, maintain
- *Focus:* particular characteristics of study
- *Object:* process, product, resource
- *Viewpoint:* participant, group, stakeholder
- *Environment:* project, department, company

Textually: Analyse the [Object] for the purpose of [Purpose] with respect to [Focus] from the viewpoint of [Viewpoint] in [Environment]

Application of Metrics in Industry (AMI) method was briefly presented. It includes the steps: assess, analyse, metricate, and improve. In each of the steps, a number of actions is taken.

Mr. Otto Vinter remarks the importance of having in the improvement process leaders that have power to affect the organisation. Methodology professionals shall be actively engaged on the improvement work.

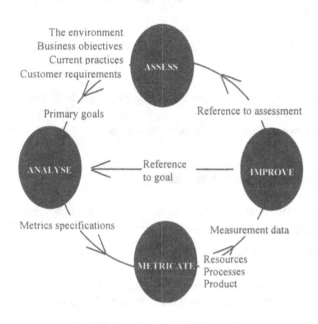

Fig. 7.2 Application of Metrics in Industry (ami)

References

[ami92]
ami Consortium: *Metric Users' Handbook*, ISBN 0 9522262 0 0, 1992
[Fenton97]
Fenton N. and Pfleeger S.L., *Software Metrics: A Rigorous and Practical Approach*, ISBN 0-534-95600-9, 1997
[Grady92]
Grady R.B., *Practical Software Metrics for Project Management and Process Improvement*, ISBN 0-13-720384-5, 1992

[Kaplan95]
Kaplan C., Clark R., Tang V., *Secrets of Software Quality, 40 Innovations from IBM*, ISBN 0-07-911795-3, 1995
[Basili88]
Basili V.R. and Rombach H.D., The TAME Project: Towards Improvement-Oriented Software Environments, *IEEE Trans. on Software Eng.*, June 1988
[IEEE91]
IEEE Software: *Special Issues on Measurements*, March 1991, July 1994, and March 1997
[IEEE92]
IEEE: *IEEE Standard for a Software Quality Metrics Methodology*, IEEE Std. 1061-1992
[IEEE94]
IEEE Computer: *Special Issue on Product Metrics*, September 1994
[IEEE96]
IEEE Software: *Special Issue on Software Quality*, January 1996.

7.2.4   Discussion at the Workshop

The intention of structuring the discussion at the workshop was to use the predefined set of question groups:

- Purpose of metrics action
- Pie Experiences – advice to metricians
- Points to cover in presentations (Why metrics? For whom? What to measure? How to measure? Actions based on Metrics? Results of actions?

However, the workshop participants from Swedish industry, had very little knowledge of these questions, almost no experience at all but a great interest. The participants presenting PIEs were only two at the discussion. The moderator Otto Vinter had to leave before the final discussion.

Because of the state of the participants, no experience, little knowledge but great interest, much of the discussion was on the question: where to start? Should the starting point be metrics, in order to assess the current state of practice, or should the metrics program support an improvement effort and measure whatever needs to be measured for the improvement program. It is obvious that there must be some kind of process defined before it is meaningful to start measurement activities. Otherwise there is a risk to use the measurement data as it might be inconsistent, and we could end up doing statistics on faulty or inconsistent data, or to compare apples and oranges.

On the other hand, if we first start an improvement action, we must assess the current state in some way, by measurement. Otherwise we cannot argue that there is a change to the better.

Top management commitment was also discussed in this context. If the measurement/improvement program is started by top-down, top management commitment is natural to get as they decide about the new line of process. However, if the engineers are given an order to start measurement or doing practice in a new way, it is determined to fail, or to be met by un-enthusiasm.

One way to start a metrics programme is in the context of a technology shift, e.g. within a PIE, introduce a tool or methodology and in order to know whether it is a success or fail, to measure.

During the presentations many questions have been raised and many discussions took place regarding on different aspects of Metrics and Process Improvement.

Some important questions have been collected by consulting all participants of the workshop on which issues they considered to be of immediate significance. It was a consensus that it is important to consider the whole perspective before, during and after a Metrics and Process Improvement program. The questions from the participants have been reformulated to fit the classes of Why to measure, How to measure, What shall be measured, and Who shall measure:

- *Why measure?* There is need for examples and business cases. Important issues are return on investment, and typical figures for activities, for instance the amount of rework.
- *How to start a Metrics program?* Which preconditions shall be observed for organisations that intend to start a Metrics and Process Improvement program.
- *How to find practical guidelines, figures, statistics, and form templates to easily start a Metrics program without the "burden" of theoretical implications on the subject?*
- *How to know if the figures obtained are consistent?* Is the improvement effort meaningful without a solid theoretical base? The theoretical foundations for the Metrics programme must be solid, there is no easy way out!(This is somewhat the opposite of the previous issue)
- *How to define a standard accounting plan for software projects?*
- *How to define what shall be measured? What can be easily measured? What is difficult to measure?*
- *What shall be analysed? What is meaningful for feedback to the organisation?*
- *What to measure regarding ad hoc processes?*
- *Who owns the Improvement Process and guarantees its continuity? Who shall be the actors of an improvement effort?* Shall high management be involved? Which are the critical success factors? In which way the organisation manages its human resources?

7.2.5   Conclusions

There has already been one EUREX workshop on the Metrics theme, held by the Spanish partner. In order to get the maximal effect of the metrics workshops to the

EUREX consortium, instead of presenting Stockholm conclusions explicitly, we present the Spanish conclusions and comment them by the Stockholm experiences directly. Under each bullet, the Spanish conclusion and explanation is given, followed by the Swedish comment in italics. Some of the Spanish conclusions have been left out because their semantics was not clear.

Methodology and Process Area

- Starting point: the definition of metrics should be based on business objectives and therefore the implementation programme should be supported by the company's top management.
  The conclusion is not difficult to agree with. Without a top management support a metrics programme has very difficult to survive, but also to get started. No metrics programme should ever be started without knowing the reason for the metrics collection. A GQM approach is a reasonably way to establish the accommodation to the business goals.

- Excessively ambitious objectives should not be established at the beginning.
  This conclusion is not difficult to agree with – everything can not be changed over one night.

- The automation of the measurement collection process is very important.
  The data collection that can be automatic, should be automatic.

- A function that appropriately manages the metrics programme should be implemented.
  A function i.e. an organisational group, is important for the reasons given: to apply the appropriate techniques homogeneously and for being responsible for the standardisation and dissemination of the information collected.

- There is great interest in metrics on a technical level in companies. Nevertheless it is not easy to implement a programme due to the existing culture in technology management.
  One way of proceeding is to tell success stories with numbers like ROI, defect density decrease. As long as you cannot show figures, it is hard to convince managers of the extra costs of introducing metrics programme or any improvement effort.

Technology Area

- The implementation of a software measurement programme is not a tool problem. It is necessary to have clear ideas before choosing the tools. But tools can also help clarify ideas.
  The conclusion applies not only to metrics programmes, but to any improvement programmes.

- Estimation tools: although not a panacea, they constitute an important support.

No estimation tools give other than estimations as result, and estimations can be wrong, more or less. Estimation tools should be calibrated to local data. Moreover, no estimation tool should be used without an expert judgement as a complement.

- Precision vs. tendency: more relevance is given to the tendency analysis
Unclear if estimation or measurement or both are meant. Sure it is better to observe the trends than to get fixed with precise values, which, after all, might only be approximations anyway.

Change Management Area

- Assess people with metrics: apart from not being ethical, it is not very intelligent.
The question is what the metrics etiquette tells. In US, assessing individuals is said to be a bad etiquette. In Sweden, the etiquette is one thing, and the law is another. A company is not allowed to register on an electronic medium individual assessments unless they have allowance from an authority.

- It should be known beforehand
The individuals, if assessed whether or not it is good or according to the law, should at least be aware of the assessment.

- Resistance to change: to avoid it or to lessen the effect, the management and the technical team must work together.
This is the meeting point when approaching from both top-down and bottom-up. The explanation tells that "The management plans, channels and manages the measurement actions for change but always starting from the experience gathered from the technical team on what needs to be changed: what doesn't work, how can it be improved." Both parties, the technical groups and top management, should be aware of the needs of improvement and metrics, as well as of the possibilities of gaining in many aspects like business goals, profit, customer and personnel satisfaction, etc.

- Improvement groups: they should be integrated into all the represented parties and they should have assigned resources. They should be integrated into all the represented parties, not only quality personnel.
The conclusion is easy to agree with.

Business Area

- It is difficult to align metrics with business objectives. A methodology is required that will make this alignment easier.
By the approach of top-down, e.g. using GQM, the suitable metrics would follow from the analysis.

- In general, companies do not know how to tackle a metrics project: a structure is lacking that would bring the metrics closer to the different management levels. The main reason is said to be the lack of maturity.

Every company, mature or not, should have business objectives. Starting from the objectives, an improvement programme including metrics could be defined.

- Implementing metrics helps the computer personnel gain credibility
This conclusion applies to the company as a whole as well.

- The structurisation of the metrics should be made top-down; its development, on the other hand should be carried out bottom-up
Yes, as already indicated earlier.

- A metrics programme based on a short term investment return should never be established
This conclusion is difficult to agree or disagree, depending what is meant by short term. In PIE experiments, return on investment in 18 months have several times been reported. Usually such experiments are improvements of specific processes, e.g. configuration management process. For climbing on the maturity levels of CMM, two years might be a long enough time for next level achievement.

General Conclusions

- There is a great interest in this subject in companies – Spanish Metric Software Association got new members.
In Sweden, the workshop resulted in the creation of a metrics and process improvements network.

- Existing experience is very limited.
The experience in practice field is very limited. The theory is ahead of the practice in Sweden.

- Positive results but still no plans to continue
Also in the presented PIEs at this workshop, the results were overall positive. However, some of the presented PIEs were definitely going to continue with the improvement efforts.

- Use of metrics in immature stage – there is gap in research and practice
The conclusion was already stated earlier.

- Interest centred on tactical applications
This might be evidence of that the top management is not aware enough of the possibilities yet.

- Limited number of consultancy companies offering experience, knowledge and products in the area
This is also true in Sweden.

- Metrics needed to align the technological objectives with the business objectives – determining the value of technology adding to the company and improve credibility of technicians
  This conclusion has been stated earlier, and agreed to.

- Strategic project to introduce a project, and should not planned exclusively as classical investment benefit analysis, there must be a plan, organisation and necessary resources.
  The same comment as above applies.

- It is not possible to improve software quality without quantitatively knowing the level of progress of the process improvement with the correct metrics.
  Yes, process improvement necessitates measurement in order to get quantitative data of the progress.

- Participating companies are now more aware of need of the introduction of metrics to improve the information alignment systems management and to permit better technological information with business objectives.
  The PIE participants were determined to continue with the improvement efforts. The other participants showed a great interest, and very likely will go back to their business and let the metrics ideas grow and hopefully be implemented in the near future.

7.3   Metrics Workshop in London
7.3.1   Introduction

The following report is done by Mr. Antonio Macchi III, who is a doctor student at the Stockholm University.

Professor Norman Fenton was invited to give an presentation of his views of Software Metrics in relation to Software Process Improvement as well as to participate and monitor the following discussions. The presentation is to be found in chapter 4.1.

Mr. Fenton is Professor of Computing Science at the Centre for Software Reliability at the City University, London and Managing Director of Agena Ltd. He is an active researcher with wide industrial experience, and has written several books on software metrics.

The experience presentations were:

- "PRIME, Practical Reuse Improvement Metrics" by Anthony Powell, Rolls-Royce & University of York
- "MEFISTO, Metrics Framework for Improving SME Total Operations" by John S. Keenan, Defence Evaluation and Research Agency
- "The Basic Steps in Setting up a Successful Measurement Programme" by Kevin Daily, Improve QPI Ltd.

Discussions *were to a large extent intermingled to the presentations.* A couple of issues were covered like economy of metrics and culture.

7.3.2   PIE Presentations and Discussions

7.3.2.1   *PRIME, Practical Reuse Improvement Metrics*

Anthony Powell
Rolls-Royce & University of York

Introduction

PRIME, "Practical Reuse Improvement Metrics" is a process improvement project at Rolls-Royce for deployment and management of systematic software reuse in the organisation.

A substantial part of civil aero engine product development at Rolls-Royce is software-related. Modern flight engines require an advanced digital control system for managing thrust, temperature, pressure, communication, and maintenance functions. The embedded control system comprises hardware and software for an extremely safety-critical real-time application., and has high development costs. It is strategically important for Rolls-Royce to optimise development times and costs, as well as to assure high levels of dependability for the software.

The intrinsic similarity between products together with specific business and dependability requirements demanded improvement efforts to introduce software reuse.

The project was successful and software reuse became a business critical issue, essential for meeting business goals.

The Model: Six Improvement Steps

The introduction of systematic reuse in the organisation is more than a pure technical issue. Successful reuse comprises also organisational and cultural issues, in addition to strong connections with strategic and business goals. Therefore, a well defined strategy for continuous reuse improvement was created and put in action .

The model emphasises management issues and has six steps:

1.   Understand Reuse Business Goals
2.   Understand Reuse Processes
3.   Understand Reuse Decisions
4.   Plan Decision Infrastructure
5.   Plan Improvement Paths
6.   Operate, Evaluate, Iterate

The main activities are commented in the following sections.

Understand Reuse Business Goals

The business goals are identified.

Different time-scale for the reuse business goals regard short-, medium-, and long-term goals for reuse.

For Rolls-Royce, the business goals are production of real-time safety critical embedded control systems with Ada, having constraints on compressed timescales for projects and low unit costs. Reuse was essential for meeting business goals. Targets were 80% reuse, with short-term goals to maximise current reuse, medium-term goals to have continuous reuse improvement, while in the long term the goal is to create a generic engine controller.

Lessons learned are that reuse is not an end in itself, and the improvement work has to be clearly linked to the business goals regarding cost, time, and quality. Reuse requires a continuous improvement process, to guarantee its successful and efficient use by the organisation.

The outcome of this improvement phase was the ensured senior management commitment, a demonstrated value, and clear objectives for all participants.

Understand Reuse Processes

The reuse process, domain, and product family are identified. Many lessons can be remarked for this phase. Particularly, the actual processes may differ from the planned and perceived processes, as well as individual perceptions of the reuse process can be inconsistent between team members. Thus, the reuse process has to rely on good communication and good decision making, in addition to understanding of the processes and a grasp of the economics of the organisation. Considering a top-down view of reuse, the process handles issues in domain engineering toward a common architecture. For the bottom-up view, the common denominator are component libraries. Reuse management involves planned migration from a legacy architecture, where the product and process evolve side by side.

Understand Reuse Decisions

The reuse decisions are identified.

This involves definition and measurement of performance at all levels, for instance regarding reuse prediction, investments, test, and quality. A measure of break-even must also be considered. Once measurements are defined, a baseline can be established for reuse performance , and the measurements will help to identify improvements. The focus shall be on a few simple (and meaningful) metrics, with simple (and meaningful) measures of reuse.

Reuse decisions are led by the targets and involve both individual and team decision making processes. The ability to meet targets depend on the ability to set realistic targets and the ability to meet them. A Goal-Question-Metric methodology was used, and the results were wider than if GQM would have been applied to the previous process (without reuse).

Plan Decision Infrastructure

The objective of this phase is to provide an infrastructure to support effective data collection and analysis. Examples for data collection are a booking system for cost and duration of activities (per function), a tool for evaluating reuse level (bottom-line percentage of code reuse), and a change control system with data on defects per function.

The analysis mechanisms have also to be defined, remarkably the reuse prediction model and the architectural reuse analysis. The infrastructure is critical, and collection and analysis overheads have to be minimised.

Plan Improvement Paths

The collection and analysis of measures does not provide solutions to all problems. It is also necessary to find improvement paths. The reuse management levers have to be identified, such as reuse training, communication, guidelines, and investment issues. The focus on results has to be persistent and improvements to the reuse process have to be funded.

Operate, Evaluate, Iterate

Even though the improvement process is described as sequential, this process is inherently iterative, requiring gradual refinement. It is necessary to operate, evaluate, and iterate the process, making suitable corrections and improvements along the way. Hence periodic reviews are a necessary part of the reuse improvement process.

Lessons and Business Benefits

The results of the improvement project were convincing:

Historically, zero defects are reported for reused components. Due to a better system structure, the number of components was reduced by 30%, providing memory and performance improvements, while the number of requirements was reduced by 50%.

The predicted level of 76% reuse allowed cost savings in the order of 80%. This produced a stimulating business impact, since 1% of reuse improvement represented savings on the order of ECU 140K . Software is no longer on the critical path of engine development and there has been a significant increase in system maturity, with fewer defects. Additionally, the manageability of the improvement programme was significantly increased.

Conclusions

The main conclusions are:

- The reuse capability has been increased significantly at Rolls-Royce,
- The six-step model guided the improvement process
- The process is consistently aligned with business goals

- Questions on Discussion

Several questions and issues for further discussion have been raised by participants:

- How to account for cost savings? What has to be considered?
- Reuse is an added cost, it has to be seen as an investment.
- Which are the effects of extensive reuse on innovation?
- What is the ideal level of reuse? Maximal?
- For how long can the level of reuse be sustained?
- Which assumptions have to be made on human resources? Reuse also involves issues on human resources, since a medium- or long-term stability of staff and products is required.
- Which reuse issues are generic and which are domain-specific?

Most answers are actually in the kernel of the proposed improvement model, but asserting the questions helps to emphasise the need for management and careful consideration of the reuse improvement process.

7.3.2.2 MEFISTO, Metrics Framework for Improving SME Total Operations

John S. Keenan
Systems and Software Engineering Centre
Defence Evaluation and Research Agency

Introduction
The MEFISTO project runs at the SEC DERA, aiming to spread best practices and demonstrate the benefits gained from introducing a metrics framework into organisations.

The framework covers three aspects:

- Cost estimating techniques
- Process assessment and improvement techniques
- Mechanisms for experience capture

The Defence Evaluation and Research Agency, DERA, is Britain's prime provider of research, development, and independent advice to the UK ministry of defence. This organisation employs 12K people and has a budget of about ECU 1.4G (one billion pounds), of which 40% to 50% are software-related.

The SEC, Systems and Software Engineering Centre collaborates with industry and other organisations, providing services on implementation, project management, technical assessment, advice, and training related to systems & software engineering.

Capability Assessment Techniques

The main assumption is that the quality of a software system is highly influenced by the quality, or maturity level, of the process. Immature software processes are improvised, not rigorously followed, very dependent on the current practitioners, and present low visibility into progress or quality. Furthermore, immature processes have compromises in functionality, unreliable schedules, higher maintenance costs, and quality that is difficult to predict.

Mature software processes are defined, documented, and consistent with the way work actually gets done, creating a well controlled environment for continuous improvements, supported by all levels of management. There is a constructive use of product and process measurement, as well as a disciplined use of technology.

The benefits from a mature process are that people develop their potential more fully and effectively, since most of the problems are created by the system, not by the people.

An effective change programme requires an understanding of current status of the systems and software development process. This is accomplished with assessments and evaluation. Assessments are normally internal, for self improvement, while evaluations (audits) are external., for contract monitoring. The techniques used for assessments and evaluations are SPICE, the Software Process Improvement and Capability Determination, and CMM, the Capability Maturity Model.

Techniques for Process Improvement

The process improvement in MEFISTO focus on business drivers for maintaining customer satisfaction, meeting the contents of specifications, as well as on-time, and on-cost delivery, prioritised on this order. The Goal-Question-Metric paradigm is used to identify metrics with relevance for the business aims.

The DERA was initially found to be at CMM level one, Initial, the same level that almost four fifths of the UK software industry are reported to be. After about two years, the organisation is reported to be mostly in a transition between levels two and three of the CMM, that is between repeatable and defined levels.

Estimating Techniques

The work with estimating techniques aims at improving the accuracy of cost estimates. The starting scenario is estimating by experience ("guesstimates") . Several techniques are used, depending on the type and nature of work SEC undertakes.

Estimating by experience and analogy is very dependent on in-house experience and is not always repeatable. Models like COCOMO have tuning difficulties in the SEC environment and results were no always repeatable.

Other techniques used are Delphi, that collects estimates by individuals and then a consensus of estimates, before iterations for further improvement. This technique has drawbacks of being slow, but has a spin-off application for risk estimates.

Function Point counting is used as a sizing technique for software systems. It is relatively new for SEC, a full training programme has been implemented, tools are in place and the technique is reported to produce repeatable results. The technique can work based on requirements specifications, and the improvements reported ranges from plus or minus fifty percent to plus or minus twenty percent of the actual project effort. The tool in use is CHECKPOINT. The outcomes of the FP estimating technique are a skilled estimating group, the systematic use of the technique, tool, and measurement practices, as well as the ability to offer external services in the area.

Conclusions and Free Discussion

Here are very short excerpts from free discussions after the presentation:

Function Point count is useful on environments where there is no total, true control over what the application can be. The FP "creep" is also a useful measure on a project (an analogy to feature "creep"). Considering estimations, a word of warning has to be issued, since fixed-price contracts are self-fulfilling prophecies. Alignment with business goals is fundamental. At the same time, a metrics program has to be as invisible as possible, in order to reduce overheads on projects.

Culture issues are fundamental in process improvement. The use of metrics is reported to be more accepted now, but there are negative reactions to assessments, especially to audits. Sometimes a classic "blame" culture may offer resistance to change and improvement. Process improvement projects has to create organisational structures to assure that individuals feel that they can prosper and develop together with the organisation.

7.3.2.3 The Basic Steps in Setting up a Successful Measurement Programme

Kevin Daily
Improve QPI Ltd.

Introduction

This presentation discusses a series of recommended basic steps for establishing a measurement programme. The main idea is to use measurement as a management tool, by connecting software measurements and business goals. The measures contribute to increased visibility in the process and convey channels for communication. The material was originally developed by Brameur Ltd for use by the MAST project in a series of workshops on "Measurement as a Management Tool".

Please observe comments by the audience at the end of the notes, since some of the recommendations on this presentation seem not to be in harmony with a more rigorous approach to metrics.

Basic Steps in Setting up a Successful Measurement Programme
Some Fundamental Questions to be Asked: There are many fundamental questions to be asked when setting up a measurement programme. It is necessary to reflect upon the current capability of the organisation, which improvements are required, how to achieve the improvements, and how to know if the goals have been met. In addition to working with the organisation's own goals, it is also important to benchmark the organisation, comparing performance to the competition.

Potential Problems and Barriers
Some of the potential problems and barriers that can cause the failure of a measurement programme are: resistance to change, unrealistic management and staff expectations, poor communication, lack of management commitment, imprecise or inappropriate definition of objectives, lack of alignment with business goals, and lack of feedback.

Suggested Steps for Setting up a Measurement Programme
An iterative approach for the establishment of a measurement program involves the following activities:

- Appoint an Executive Sponsor
- Establish Scope and Goals
- Define Key Performance Indicators, Process Measures and Models
- Establish a Data Collection Infrastructure
- Explain the Programme
- Devise Success Criteria
- Set Baselines and Targets for Key Performance Indicators
- Develop a Feedback Mechanism

Appoint an Executive Sponsor
The measurement programme requires executive support of a leader that is committed to change, and moreover, a leader that is committed to the results of the change. The sponsor must be a strong motivator and a dynamic leader, that will set challenging, but realistic, targets. The leader must also commit to monitor if the organisation is on track.

Establish Scope and Goals
The scope of the measurement programme and of goals have to be defined. The time perspective shall also be observed, that is short-, middle- and long-term goals are defined. Examples of practical goals are to identify trends in defect counts, determine the effort spent on rework, etc.

Define Key Performance Indicators, Process Measures and Models.
Key performance indicators (KPIs) are defined according to the business goals and needs. A set of questions relating to the KPIs is developed, metrics are defined to capture relevant data., and models for combining the metrics that enable the questions to be answered. KPIs must allow the establishment of baselines for tracking improvements.

Establish a Data Collection Infrastructure
The data collection requires an infrastructure. Responsibilities for data collection, storage, analysis, and presentation are required, as well as definitions of when, where, and how the data is collected, and how it is validated.

Explain the Programme
The goals, support, commitments, and consequences of the measurement programme must be communicated clearly for all people involved. Feedback, incentives, and recognition must be ensured.

Devise Success Criteria
The measurement programme must be reviewed periodically to check correctness and consistence of the information being generated. The measurement results must be checked against baselines and goals.

- Decisions, and actions must be tracked to closure.
- Set Baselines and Targets for Key Performance Indicators
- Establish baselines and targets, derived from quantifiable information.
- Assess performance against baselines and targets.
- Develop a Feedback Mechanism
- Good mechanisms for feedback of the collected information have to be devised. For instance, mechanisms for reporting project status or degree of goal fulfilment.

Comments
Free List of Success Criteria. This is an excerpt of suggestions from participants on success criteria:
- Causal analysis (root cause analysis) must be performed on identified problems.
- Customer satisfaction, effort, and rework are important to be tracked. It is necessary to distinguish the improvement process from the measurement process.
- Processes should have an owner.
- Unintended bad effects on the organisation have to be evaluated.
- Beware of side-effects.
- Blame culture must be avoided.

- Links between models and measures are difficult issues. Assumptions and definitions have to be made with care, with a warning for simplistic solutions.
- There must be a balance between people-based and management-based improvement approach.

Strengths

Many professionals in the software and system industry require concise information on establishing a measurement program.

Weaknesses

The measurement programme is presented as a separate entity from process improvement. Measurement is not a goal in itself. It is more useful to track goals, questions, measurements to improvement actions in the same framework.

The sequence for the basic steps is not uniquely defined according to the presentation and the paper copy of the slides. The author of the notes would recommend a different sequence for the basic steps. Additionally, the process would be easier to grasp if the number of steps is reduced, and the flow is made straightforward.

The expectations on one executive sponsor as a driver of the process may be unrealistic. It would be more suitable to speak in terms of roles associated to the sponsorship, leadership, and management of the measurement programme. These roles do not necessarily have to be assigned to one person, but can actually be shared by different individuals, as long as they have common goals and coordinate their actions.

The basic steps for establishment of scope and goals, definition of key performance indicators, follows the patterns of a Goal-Question-Metric paradigm. Apparently it would be useful to align these steps with GQM, that is a widely recognised framework.

Several "key performance indicators", questions, and measures provided as examples contain inconsistencies, if analysed from the perspective of a rigorous approach to software metrics. Therefore, examples have been omitted from the notes.

7.3.3   References

[Fenton99]

Norman Fenton, *Metrics for Software Process Improvement*, Agena Ltd & City University, UK, 1999

[Powell99a]

Antony Powell, *PRIME – Practical Reuse Improvement Metrics*, Rolls-Royce Research & The University of York, UK, 1999

[Powell99b]
  Antony Powell and Duncan Brown, *A Practical Strategy for Industrial Reuse Improvement*, Rolls-Royce Research & The University of York, UK, 1999
[Keenan99]
  John Keenan, *MEFISTO – Metrics Framework for Improving SME Total Operations*, DERA Systems and Software Engineering Centre, UK, 1999
[Daily99]
  Kevin Daily, The Basic Steps in Setting up a Successful Measurement Programme, Improve QPI Ltd, UK, 1999

7.4 Conclusions from the Workshops

The first Swedish workshop on metrics centred on issues concerning the initiation of new metrics programmes. Then the Spanish and second Swedish workshops discussed more systematically methodology and process, technology, change management and, business. Following a presentation of the state-of-the-art, the UK workshop debated the culture and economics of metrics. Sustainable improvements were a topic in the UK as well as in Sweden.

The first Swedish workshop raised a number of questions about starting to use metrics in an organisation. The concerns raised in this workshop were considered and revisited in the other metrics workshops, and it seems safe to say that the collected knowledge presented in this book answers many of those questions.

- *Why measure?* There is need for examples and business cases. Important issues are return on investment, and typical figures for activities, for instance the amount of rework.
- *How to start a Metrics program?* What are the preconditions to be observed by an organisation that intends to start a Metrics and Process Improvement programme?
- *How to find practical guidelines, figures, statistics, and form templates to easily start a Metrics program without the "burden" of theoretical implications on the subject?*
- *How to know if the figures obtained are consistent?* Is the improvement effort meaningful without a solid theoretical base? The theoretical foundations for a Metrics programme must be solid – there is no easy way out! (This is somewhat the opposite of the previous issue.)
- *How to define a standard accounting plan for software projects?*
- *How to define what shall be measured? What can be easily measured? What is difficult to measure?*
- *What shall be analysed? What is meaningful feedback to the organisation?*
- *What to measure regarding ad hoc processes?*
- *Who owns the Improvement Process and guarantees its continuity? Who shall be the actors of an improvement effort?* Should upper management be in-

volved? What are the critical success factors? How does the organisation manage its human resources?

The areas of methodology and process, technology, change management and, business were more thoroughly discussed in the Spanish workshop the conclusions of which were in turn compared to a Swedish context from the second Swedish workshop. Those are fully documented by the workshop presentations earlier in this chapter but the main points should be mentioned here. There is a growing interest in industry but experience is low. And there is a clear gap between metrics in academia and the deployment of metrics in industry.

7.4.1   Methodology and Process Area

As a starting point, the definition of metrics should be based on business objectives and therefore a company's top management should support the implementation programme.

Automation of the measurement collection process is very important.

There is great interest in metrics on a technical level in many companies. Nevertheless, the existing culture of technology management often impedes the implementation of metrics programmes.

7.4.2   Technology Area

The implementation of a software measurement programme is not a tool problem. It is necessary to have clear ideas before choosing the tools. But tools can also help clarify ideas.

7.4.3   Change Management Area

There have been attempts to assess people with metrics; however, this is not terribly ethical and it doesn't work very well.

Resistance to change: to avoid it or to lessen the effect, management and the technical team must work together. This is the meeting point when viewed from top-down and bottom-up. The explanation is that "The management plans, channels and manages the measurement actions for change but always starting from the experience gathered from the technical team on what needs to be changed: what doesn't work, how can it be improved." Both parties, the technical groups and top management, should be aware of the needs of improvement and metrics, as well as of the possibilities for advancement in many areas such as business goals, profit, customer and personnel satisfaction, and so on.

Improvement groups should be integrated into all the represented parties and appropriate resources must be assigned. They should be integrated into all represented parties, not just quality personnel.

7.4.4 Business Area

It is often difficult to align metrics with business objectives. A methodology is required that will make this alignment easier.

By the approach of top-down, e.g. using GQM, the suitable metrics would follow from the analysis.

At he UK metrics workshop, Professor Fenton's discussion of the evaluation of improvement methods was complementary wisdom to the other workshops. The culture and economics of metrics were otherwise the two topics for debate in London. (The economics discussion is taken further in chapter 8, and gives some additions to the points mentioned from earlier workshops.) There is an obvious difficulty in establishing business objectives and to relate those to PIE metrics. Business goals tend to be formulated in qualitative rather than quantitative terms. For instance "satisfied customer" is an often used but vague term, with weak correspondence to metrics goals, as is the presumed relation "A x % satisfied customer gives y Euros renewed sales per year". Still the general economic conclusions on the benefit side are favourable for the introduction and use of metrics. There is also some quantification on the costs of introducing and running metrics programmes.

Culture represents an inconclusive and somewhat confusing area when it comes to concepts, interpretation and conclusions both regarding the workshops and the PIE documentation. There seems to be one line of thinking which regards culture as the extent to which metrics is a normal part of the work in a software organisation. If the organisation is mature, then metrics is established and used routinely. A distinctive other use is connected to "resistance" as key word. The differences in views seem fairly obvious when comparing the Spanish top-down approach to introduction of metrics to some of the German approaches. The Germans seem to have a more team-oriented style.

A quote from the final report of the PITA project gives an experienced and insightful view on the different cultures and their relation to the area of software process improvement. This message should be of value to most PIE organisations:

Measurements on both the process (lead-time, effort) and the product (fault density) have been introduced in the past and some of those measurements were being institutionalised before PITA. Such measurements reflected mainly a high-level management perspective, indicating general and long-term trends. However, these were not tuned to specific project and software developers' concerns and viewpoints. Therefore, these provided only a superficial view of the underlying process and had no real value in areas considered as potential sources of problems. These measurements, because of their generality, did not provide significant help in achieving general objectives set, neither were of much use in supporting improvement activities.

7.4.5   On Sustainable Improvement

Of great interest to every organisation setting off on a metrics programme is of course to reach a state that can be called sustainable improvement. The following is a short discourse on this issue.

The duration of the normal PIE is one to two years. This means that the organisations involved usually complete the experiment but do not achieve broad deployment within the same period. As a result, there is very little evidence to illustrate the beginning of sustainable improvement. In several cases, though, there are declarations of the intention to deploy to a broad base within the software development organisation and even outside it in some cases.

On the other hand, the reality meeting in workshop organisation gave another view that was not very encouraging. Persuading finished PIEs to participate in the workshops turned out to be difficult, and increasingly so in proportion to the time elapsed since the PIE was completed. The problem was not one of unwillingness to be philanthropic but rather of contacting someone able to relate the PIE experiences from the organisation. Very often the one person who was the driving force for the PIE had moved to other work, another department or to another organisation. And no one else felt competent to report on the PIE experience. In many cases there had been a reorganisation ending the processes to which the metrics were applied, or a merger or a sell off. This situation leads to the need to discover a solution to the "lost competence" problem. One method is to plan to keep the effort alive, as explained by the MMM PIE:

But we have to state that in comparison to our midterm experience this attitude is not running by itself and the first motivation has carefully to be maintained and sponsored. This means you (the sponsor of the measurement movement) have to have on one hand a closer look on details to make sure the necessary activities are done in a suitable way and on the other hand you have to raise and maintain the awareness of the benefits of measurement for the involved people.

Another possible action is to plan for making metrics part of everybody's job. This was given as one of the tactics for implementing Configuration Management by one of the industry participants in the Swedish CM workshop, but should be equally useful in a metrics setting.

A third possibility would be to take an investment perspective to the PIE and the subsequent wider deployment. This is also the approach used by a number of the PIE representatives as given in final reports. In summary, it takes longer than the typical PIE lifetime to achieve the full benefit of a metrics programme.

8 Significant Results: Benefits, Costs, and Processes

Lars Bergman
SISU, Kista

In this chapter, we examine several issues that were raised in virtually all of the measurement PIEs: business and technological benefits, measurement related costs, and measurement processes. In each case, we give several examples from the PIEs themselves to illustrate the issues.

8.1 Business Benefits

In considering deployment of a measurement programme, the benefits to be gained are of course central. In this section the business benefits reported by the measurement-focussed PIEs are surveyed.

Generally in the case of measurement PIEs, quantification is poor when compared to cost issues presented. In some cases direct business generated by the measurement PIE is indicated. More commonly, indirect variables are presented (usually not quantified) with opinions or hypotheses on outcomes and outcome values.

In cases where the measurement program is part of a technologically domain oriented PIE for instance testing, configuration management there seems to be more quantified outcomes. However, these are not really business benefits as seen in this context but technological benefits.

It seems to be difficult to find a business motivation for measurement programmes and it may be that measurement systems should be viewed in a fashion similar to accounting systems. You know you need one but you cannot assign a value for the benefit of having it. But you certainly can have some thoughts on how much to invest in it and how much is reasonable for operating it.

8.1.1 New Business Won

The ultimate benefit of a PIE is to generate business. Encouragingly there are some such cases. The following quotes from PIE reports support this argument.

8.1.1.1   ENGMEAS

Some large customers have started to assign big software development contracts, in which payments are related to the number of delivered function points and suppliers are requested to declare their productivity indices and associated price per function points.

So far, the company was reluctant to tackle such kind of tender due to the difficulty to correctly evaluate productivity indices. The ENG-MEAS results revealed extremely useful: e.g., in the last months, company productivity baseline data and associated predictive model gave significant inputs in the formulation of the offer for some tenders, with positive feedback (the acquisition of a large contract).

8.1.1.2   MASLYD

Bespoke Development being an area where cost estimation in particular was very poor in the past is now much more predictable and delivering projects on time and within budget. As a result of this improvement, this area of business will continue for the foreseeable future whereas if it had not started to make a positive contribution, it would have been discontinued. As a result of these improvements, it is now making a positive contribution towards profitability.

The review of Work in Progress helped us to identify a number of activities which, had they not been tackled, would at least have failed to be profitable, and in some cases, would have caused the department to make a significant loss. Addressing these as a result of the project has meant that we were in a position to take corrective action in sufficient time to prevent these becoming major problems or drains on resources.

8.1.1.3   APPLY

The global improvement effort has provided visible effects on the hard numbers. The product sales revenue 96/97 growth (which is a major business goal) has been of +40%. On three consecutive releases of the same product (the latest with the APPLY process running) the overall improvement in terms of project control capability and reliability have been dramatically improved.

The numbers cannot be directly compared to each other because contexts were different (content of the release, related effort and competitive position).

Anyway, for a business perspective, it is indubitable that the benefits are invaluable. They can be classified in the following way:

- Direct financial benefit. Better forecast and control of the initial budget.
- Better control of the release content. A better competitive position is expected.
- Customers have a better image and confidence in the product and in the company.

- The development team is placed in a winning position which is much better for the motivation.

8.1.2 Business Enabling Outcomes

There is a group of variables common to many PIEs that are not directly business win variables but nevertheless represent increased likelihood of winning business. These variables are:

- Customer satisfaction
- Customer trust
- Delivery precision
- Product quality

Several PIEs reported results that addressed these issues, including MEFISTO, METPRO, MBM and INCOME, which are quoted below.

8.1.2.1 MEFISTO

An underlying assumption of the MEFISTO project is that improved effort estimates lead to:

- improved customer satisfaction
- more reliable profitability
- competitive advantage

It is still too early to say categorically whether the methods and tools used for this experiment strand have lead to improved estimates. Although a subjective measure, confidence in effort estimates is much stronger among staff involved with bid preparation. The new techniques now being used are relatively low cost, though there is a considerable investment required in training if function point counting expertise needs to be gained. As part of the bid review process, at least two estimation procedures are used. Any significant discrepancies between estimates are then discussed and the final estimate constructed from the outcome of those discussions. The investment is likely to be cost effective as there is a large multiplier attached to improvements in areas such as improved customer satisfaction.

8.1.2.2 METPRO

It should have high relevance to the business of the participants because will increase customer confidence through seeing that Dataspazio faces up problems and acts to improve quality.

Anyway the obtained results represent the visiting card of the company for the future customers.

8.1.2.3   MBM

The impact of new approach on the business environment is leading to an effective competitive advantage.

8.1.2.4   INCOME

The main impacts on the business operation have been the following:

- communication with the baseline project's clients: a better insight in progress towards objectives and towards impact of changes in requirements was acquired;
- increased predictability of the process performance and then enhanced capacity of delivering in time and on cost;
- increased effectiveness of testing activities and decreased post-release defects.

8.1.3   Organisation Enabling Outcomes

Competence and capability to meet the future is another group of outcomes mentioned rather frequently by the PIE reporters. The following excerpts from the respective PIE reports illustrate these outcomes.

8.1.3.1   CEMP

- Better understanding of the products/processes related to the software process at all experimental sites was achieved.
- All experimental sites could derive quantitative baselines for all stated questions/topics of interest.
- Increased awareness of strengths and weaknesses to the products or the processes (w. r. t. to the respective quality foci) could be identified.
- Suggestions for improvement with medium/high impact on the SW development process could be formulated.
- The measurement programs further provide quantitative support for project planning, sound proposals/requests to higher management, tasks of quality assurance people.
- Improved SW measurement know-how of the project people. Improved measurement capabilities and a better understanding on the application of goal-oriented measurement could be identified. This was used to customize the measurement program in the second projects, resulting in decreased efforts.
- More detailed information about the application of the GQM method and tool support are available.

8.1.3.2   MIDAS

Values perceived by the management:

The development of a *process model* was perceived by the management as a valuable opportunity to gain a deeper insight into the actual process and product organisation. The process model allowed management and consultants to reach a common understanding of the process, of the improvement actions and constraints.

As opposed to the process model, which provides a qualitatively understanding of the process, *metrics* provided a quantitatively view of the process and product, resulting in a valuable decision support tool.

8.1.3.3 METPRO

Particularly from this experiment we have obtained some reference values useful for the next projects. For new projects we are able, now, to establish some quality objectives such as:

- decrease the software problems number respected to the reference value, paying attention to those project phases that had a low PCE value for the experimented projects;
- increase the productivity aiming to re-use as much as possible the existent software and automatic tools for code generation;

8.1.3.4 MBM

Much effort can be saved having the correct and in-time info from projects. Monitor and control becomes a quantitative activity rather than a qualitative one. Dashboard availability all along the course of the project provide managers the continuous stimulus to keep the project on track (budget, time, quality).

Even expert managers have often a feeling that software projects are very complex and dynamic "beasts", hard to understand, control, dominate. And this let them anxious or aggressive. They tend to react to events (fire fighting): they "defend" the planned budget, schedule and quality against the "beast".

The dash board becomes a powerful weapon to help the managers prevent the fire and, if needed, to shot at the right time and at the right target.

The impact of new approach on the business environment is leading to an effective competitive advantage.

Furthermore, an initial framework based on measures is the milestone for future improvement programmes.

8.1.3.5 MMM

Several aspects of this PIE influenced our business and will do so in the future:

- the effort for conducting the experiment as whole;
- the measurement programme (introduction, performance and maintaining measurement);
- the new life cycle developed within the PIE;

- the tools we developed for us;
- the knowledge we gained with respect to the used methods;
- the findings of our measurement;
- the internal dissemination of result and
- the motivation of our engineers

In our case some minor goals or even unintended benefits became visible and only a part of them provide for annual savings of at least 5% of all labour costs.

8.1.3.6   QUALIMET

The impact of QUALIMET on the business operation that was expected at the beginning of the project seems to be valid:

- The statement of a formal methodology for covering the quality assurance of the results of the programming phase. It has been obtained a way of quantitatively knowing what is the quality of the source code, which means that we know where we are and where we want to go. So we are in the way to increase the productivity and quality of the developed systems. Both terms will produce the improvement of customer satisfaction.
- QUALIMET has helped us to reinforce the application of the ISO 9001 that will introduce the company in the list of accepted suppliers of many organisations in which having this certification is a requirement for accepting vendors.
- Professionals involved in software development projects feels more confidence with the improved methodology by making their work better.

8.2   Technological Benefits

In this section we turn our attention to the reports of technological improvements, which include the methods and tools used by a software-producing organisation. In several cases, process definition is performed and some observations on this activity are presented here as well.

While the descriptions of the business aspects of measurement PIEs (see 8.1 above) are rather terse, the technology presentations tend to be considerably longer as well as more concrete. This often means that the results are more useful. The selection of results quoted below gives glimpses of the use of many different technologies and processes, including AMI, GQM, SPICE, CMM and Function Points.

8.2.1   ROAR

"What is measured tends to improve" is a saying that Informatique CDC hopes to be able to verify.

The only way of doing that, which is neither subjective, nor too expensive to be put into general use, is to measure automatically. Measuring quality also means giving awards (even if it is only the honour of receiving a good mark) to people who respect the standards and who place priority on writing well-written code.

The work accomplished behind this report will lead to the certification of quality by measurements, described as step 4 on the SEI scale of maturity.

8.2.2 ENGMEAS

The top-down, systematic approach enforced by GQM is effective in helping to achieve an internally consistent measurement program. To define our measurement program fully, we included a specification of the GQM "metrics" that identified the entity, attribute, unit scale type and counting rules and the measurement aspects implied by the GQM questions.

Function Points

Our internal discussion about the measure of software size and project productivity and its relationship with software project estimation (product-based estimation versus activity-based estimation) was very intense and without definitive and complete answers.

However, despite the yet strong internationally-wide debate on Function Point based metrics, technical and commercial considerations have suggested the adoption of Function Points as software sizing metric (minor dependence on the methodology, technology, or development tools used to create the software; standardisation by an international organisation – IFPUG; forecast for a steady increase of its adoption throughout the decade, reaching adoption at about 50 percent of large enterprises by 2000 – source: Gartner Group [GG95]). For estimation purposes (Advanced Function Points) we have considered keeping the raw counts of each FP element as well as the total value. The raw counts may be available earlier in the lifecycle and may be less subjective than the weighted FPs.

Main conclusions

A measurement program should be defined and evaluated focusing on the following viewpoints:

- Internal consistency of the analysis. This involves considering whether there are aspects that have been overlooked and whether or not any questions and metrics are unnecessary in terms of the goals.
- Data collection feasibility. This involves considering whether or not the identified measures will provide reliable data (i.e. whether the measures are defined well enough to be repeatable and comparable). Subjective metrics should be avoided as much as possible.
- Analysis feasibility. This involves considering whether or not the identified measures can be analysed in a way that allows the basic goals to be achieved.

8.2.3   MEFISTO

Cost Estimation Strand. The results of this strand of the experiment record the performance of one of the quantitative methods (*function point* counting using CHECKPOINT) against a) actual and b) expert estimates. The correlation results were sufficiently encouraging to warrant the inclusion of function point counting into the SEC bidding process. Risk assessment using @RISK produced results that were not intuitive and added significantly to the estimation process.

Process Improvement Strand. A SPICE assessment (see Annex E) of the SEC was undertaken which was generally satisfactory but indicated weaknesses in customer reviews and contract management. A generally accepted rule is that a period of eighteen months is required before the impact of enacting process improvements identified by a SPICE assessment can be measured objectively. A follow up SPICE assessment has been undertaken using recently recruited experienced SPICE assessors and the results are also included in Annex E although, in fact, this second assessment was outside the timeframe of MEFISTO. Metrics collected in this strand produced mixed results but have impacted on the SEC recruitment process.

Experience Capture Strand. The analysis of questionnaires (the source questionnaires are defined in the Experiment Definition Document in Annex C) highlighted further improvements in knowledge management within the SEC. The SEC Intranet was established.

8.2.4   PITA

Usability of Metrics

Measurements had been introduced at the SWDC, in the past, in an ad hoc manner, as an attempt to support overall monitoring and the implementation of certain improvement initiatives. However, their value to the software developers was limited due to the fact that these measurements were largely reflecting the viewpoint and the objectives of higher management only. On the contrary, the GQM approach and AMI are both based on the integration of various viewpoints (during Goal Analysis), while the supporting measurements provide useful information to all those viewpoints involved and especially the software development practitioners and the software project managers. In this respect, the GQM plan for PITA addressed the viewpoints of various personnel (managers and practitioners) involved in the baseline project who participated directly in its definition.

The introduction of AMI methodology provided thus process visibility to the baseline project software development team, by adopting goals that could be tracked through measurement data which were fed back to the development team periodically, during the project progress. In this way, the AMI method enhanced motivation and buy-in of the metrication initiative for the baseline project personnel. This motivation was established in the feedback meetings and ensuing discussions.

Long term measurements in the GQM plan for the baseline project were included to provide conclusive evidence about product quality and overall development process effectiveness / efficiency. At the same time, short-term indicators and estimates were also introduced to support baseline project planning and tracking/monitoring; this was especially important in the case of a relatively long development cycle such as the one in the baseline project. Short term indicators, were selected to support process performance evaluation and decision making per development phase (and overall).

AMI can Help as a Backbone of SPI

AMI was verified as a strong aid to plan, perform, monitor and support SPI activities, based on baseline project experience and CMM assessment (and reassessment).

Particularly important, is the linking of GQM analysis to the CMM paradigm and CMM assessment results.

As explained before, this lesson has been indirectly validated in the recent CMM full assessment, showing an increase in maturity level (from Level 1 to 2). To this last achievement, AMI contributed by offering training and a model for setting up and measuring goals related to CMM Level 2 key process areas.

These goals were piloted at the baseline project and were then copied in several newer projects (in a more limited way).

PITA enabled baseline project personnel (and then personnel in other projects) to visualise the CMM related goals in relation to their particular circumstances and to measure their performance in relation to such goals (or even fix goal performance). AMI provided a consolidated and consistent framework of short- and longer-term improvements. In the case of rather immature processes (as it is the case with the PITA baseline project). In this respect, since the use of measurements is scant and recent or just beginning, it was necessary to approach SPI by adopting mainly "knowledge" goals rather than "change" goals.

According to GQM, "knowledge" goals focus on establishing the current behaviour of used processes while "change" goals focus on the improvement of the used process. Based on the establishment of relevant historical data (currently being effected), it is expected that "change" goals, could be set in the future. Still, relatively good performance was achieved in several indices at the baseline project, reflecting higher focus, attention and motivation (like a Hawthorn effect). Overall, PITA has generated great interest in using AMI/GQM to support current and future SPI activities.

Reuse of Existing Goals and Measurements

In applying AMI at the baseline project, a crucial step was the identification and collection of all existing goals and metrics (from past or ongoing SPI activities). Such information can and should be reused when establishing the Goal Tree, to reduce overhead and improve consistency with overall operations, policies and targets. In addition, reuse of established goals and measurements, reduces resistance and provides additional buy-in of the new approach.

Validity of GQM Analysis

Intracom's limited experience with goals and metrics prior to PITA, caused some concerns that had to be addressed during AMI implementation in the baseline project as well as in other applications that were attempted later. This situation still prevails in general, albeit gradual experience and maturity is gained as AMI is repeatedly being applied. In order to make possible the establishment of a relatively stable and reliable process measurement baseline, special care was placed on the analysis and validation of measurement results at the baseline project. At the time when we expect AMI to be fully institutionalised, such issues should have matured to a significant extent. As a word of caution, where there is yet no statistically significant and systematic historical data available, one should avoid quick conclusions and judgements from analysing GQM data.

In immature situations (regarding the processes and goals involved as well as historical data available), it is difficult to establish acceptable measurement ranges for goal performance. Tentative hypotheses are made in order to provide some guidance, but they require validation and review when subsequent conclusive data become available. Maturity in planning and analysing at a statistical process control level can only be achieved based on sound relevant historical data being available (this is normally achieved in a general sense at CMM Level 4). In the case of some particular goals (e.g. improved design, better project planning), several repetitions / cycles of AMI application, at different projects, will be necessary to obtain a validated GQM model. At that time, a valid GQM model could be used to provide better process control (in the statistical sense), at least with respect to some established goals. It is estimated that this could be realised after 2-3 years of repeated applications of AMI in an institutionalised way.

Combining AMI with other SPI Methodologies and Tools

AMI is used together with other SPI activities, to support their implementation and measure their results. Its flexibility and adaptability is once again being validated. This also has potential for other interested parties, external to Intracom and is a point raised in various dissemination presentations.

8.2.5 METPRO

The key lessons from the technological point of view are the following:

- change the way to yield data to make them more useful and complete. In particular the definition of a new form to describe and collect the project activities will help us to check the time spent for each project phase; the updating of the SPR form to include all the missing information about a software problem required for the evaluations, will help us to locate the most critical project phase;
- organise the project information during its development to perform the measurements while the project is on going: this will allow to control it run-time, to avoid loss of time in researching and organising project information after its conclusion and to wide a process history database to use in the future;
- minimise the time over-head necessary to the data gathering during the project; to this aim it is convenient to use automatic and distributed tools and simplify as much as possible the procedure to follow.

8.2.6 MBM

Dashboard means two main things: data collection and presentation tool. The first item seemed the more complex because of the amount and validity of data. Companion work-flow and database sharing needed to be "rethought" a number of times before the and of the experiment.

Data collection has been a critical activity because of:

- cost reasons. In fact data collection is a constant effort during the whole project (instead of "una tantum" ticket for Dashboard tool delivery)
- mismatching to be prevented avoiding redundant and useless data collection
- some workers resistance to give much more details on their work, which can result in late data or not valid (wrong data).

8.2.7 MMM

To build the fundament for measurement it is *necessary to have a stable process* and a precise knowledge about what attributes of entities you are going to measure. But these attributes need not to be theoretically sophisticated and generally agreed upon but should be chosen in a methodical way. E.g. we do not debate whether an attribute like number of layers or processes in a structured analysis graph is belonging to the category of size or to complexity. In this way we will work on our own purpose and it might be that our results are not directly transferable to other companies or worthwhile to be stored without comment in any statistical database. This implies difficulties for bench marks. But we advise other companies to work as well with strict focus on their own needs and peculiarities. Only if you feel the need to apply commonly used concepts of measures – like we did with respect to function points – you should apply them. But this is better to be done if you have already prepared and conducted the easier approach and thus seen some positive effects that help to maintain the effort.

One has to follow the principle to keep things simple. We have managed this by means of templates with regard to process step deliverables, by introducing a complete file structure we use in all projects and be means of self similarity of our life cycle phases. We learned that this all could also be summarised under the topic of reuse. With regard to our measurement organisation we tried so far successfully to avoid manually to be done work. This applies for iteratively to be done work. With respect to one time collection of data there is always the choice to do this manually or with support of available basic tools.

We believe despite contrary arguments in literature (see Bache and Neil in Fenton, Whitty, Iizuka), that to work under the guidance of a method i.e. of the GQM approach is much more worthwhile, than the naive search for metrics, that are available in literature and are somehow related to your work. With this respect and in general we can state that good consulting is worthwhile as well and we advise to invest here before you invest in tools. Tool support should be considered a step after you are sure about your needs anyway, i.e. after you have understood why you want to perform a special task and what the principles are that guide the performance of this task.

When you have understood the principles of a method it is your turn to tailor it to your needs and your responsibility not to act in a way, that makes the method worthless. You should make explicit why you need an adaptation and why you think the results are still valid and valuable for your company or your software engineering group. To make it explicit means also to document it and documentation is really a critical factor (We agree here with ISO 9000). The way you organise your documentation and support it by tools is a secondary matter though by far not neglectable. But you need your ideas documented, since you will not learn them by heart and loose a lot of information e.g. in evaluating the results and drawing the correct conclusions. It is also helpful to have these documentations available to make use of them in evaluation schemes of new tools and methods.

8.2.8   INCOME

The combined use of SPICE and *ami* was effective because both techniques are complementary in nature:

- *ami*'s first step requires an assessment to take place; it recommends the SEI CMM, but the method can very easily be adapted to the use of SPICE instead;
- *ami* can be easily used, and provides great help, within the context of a software process improvement initiative, i.e. an initiative which has the objective to add or change practices; while the method originally focuses on measurement and addresses improvement as a follow-up activity, this experiment shows how

ami can be used to define an "improvement goal tree" which enables to measure the contribution of ongoing process improvement actions to the achievement of primary management goals;

- *ami* does not explicitly address planning issues in software process improvement, and this is where the SPICE process improvement guideline can help (Part 7 [3]); a measurement plan and an improvement plan can be effectively produced together.
- The "plan" phase of the improvement is essential and may take more than expected for a number of reasons:
- improvement of a high-visibility project requires more buy-in from management than usual because the fear to miss short-term deadlines is very hard to overcome;
- to understand the scope of the change and to motivate people involved at various levels, from managers to technical staff, may also take more time than expected;
- to organise for the measurement of improvement actions may be more time-consuming than their respective implementation, but the importance of quantitative data is such that in the absence of data no improvement can be effectively sustained;
- a medium to large project has a strong need for developing excellent planning and tracking procedures and tools that will allow for on-time reporting of meaningful data to key persons in the project.

Other general not less important lessons learned are the following:

- to establish a current performance baseline is very useful when old data can be easily accessed and interpreted, if this not the case improvements can be monitored by observing a trend in well-chosen indicators from the first day on which the improvement action starts;
- new technology plays a role, but only where a new process definition shows clear fit and emphasises its benefits (define first your process an then select the most adapted tool which can support it);
- senior management leadership is strongly required to launch and sustain a change effort and to provide continuing resources and impetus, as middle management is often largely concerned with meeting project commitments in the short term;
- staff motivation to achieve goals for improving the software process, is strengthened, if the goals are understandable, challenging and pertinent and progress is made regularly visible through proper reports.

8.2.9 QUALIMET

It is important to follow a certain methodology for selecting the interesting metrics for a certain purpose. In the PIE, we started with the definition of a set of metrics selected from those available in the literature and that were estimated useful for ensuring the quality of the Object Oriented Products.

But we missed something that allowed us to establish the relation between what is wanted to be measured (quality goals) and what is going to be measured (software elements). When the GQM was discovered, as a consequence of the participation in an EUREX workshop, it was decided to apply the methodology to refine the metrics selection. The result is that this systematic methodology is very helpful to decide what software elements can be measured in order to evaluate if quality goals are achieved or not.

We think that any try to know the quality of an Object-Oriented design must take into account three aspects: encapsulation, inheritance and polymorphism. These aspects must be measured from three points of view: the whole system, the classes and the methods.

One of the most difficult points in this project has been the definition of the quality thresholds and associated corrective actions. Due to the lack of literature and experience on Object Oriented Software Quality metrics thresholds and corrective actions definitions, it has been made a great effort in order to define both of them for those metrics included in the metrics program. These thresholds and corrective actions have been determined based on the literature, on the information provided by LOGISCOPE, on Object Oriented software developers experience and on the effort to respect all the mechanisms provided by the Object Oriented Paradigm.

We consider of great importance the process of validation of these thresholds. This has allowed to increase the confident of the people involved in the development of the baseline project during the application of the metrics model to the baseline project. The results obtained from its application have made more credible the presentation of QUALIMET inside the organisation.

When selecting a measurement tool, it was discovered that most of Object Oriented measurement tools apply only traditional metrics to Object Oriented software skipping measures in the use of Object Oriented Paradigm mechanisms.

Due to the fact that it is not useful to collect data just because it is available but at the same time data must be collected based on the metrics program, the selected measurement tool must allow to define those metrics that are not directly implemented by the tool.

For this reason, it is believed that any software metrics tool must support the selected metrics, allow the user to define new metrics, must be user-friendly, and easy to integrate in the development environment of the company.

8.2.10 MASLYD

The main lessons learned from a Technological point of view are as follows :

- Lack of skills in one area of technology or process will not compensate for shortcomings in any other e.g. ICE's Software Department was very strong on specific skills – particularly Programming, Program Design , Support etc. However, this was coupled with weaknesses in the areas of defining user requirements, and estimating etc.

- Any specific area in a Software Lifecycle cannot be defined in isolation – many options exist as to how to achieve a goal by having complementary features in each phase of the lifecycle.
- Change in process must be reinforced regularly – just because a change is seen to yield benefits will not ensure it is followed forever after.
- While the feeling that "small is beautiful" may be used as justification for the informality of a smaller organisation, it is clear that even small software development organisations can develop a very significant body of work, even over a relatively short period. Therefore, lack of formal methods will very quickly impose a ceiling on the organisations capacity to tackle new business.
- When evaluating Formalised development lifecycles / cost estimation models, it is essential to evaluate these in the context of what the actual problems within the organisation are. Otherwise it is possible to implement elements of formal models which are not appropriate to the specific issues within the organisation. It can be very easy to quickly grasp a solution but it is essential to examine.

8.3 Costs

To get a handle on cost/benefit tradeoffs, we examine several PIEs that reported on efforts to introduce measurements. The CEMP PIE stands out in rather meticulously reporting well thought out results. The QUALIMET PIE reported some data on a more ad hoc level. The MMM PIE presents a thorough summary of efforts completed as well as projected. The scope of each PIE differs, which leads us to consider the results more in the way of examples rather than standards *per se*. They provide some hints to an organisation that wants to make an estimate of the effort and cost of introducing a measurement program. The CEMP PIE is very thorough and is built on introduction of GQM in three organisations and several projects within each organisation. This provides a good basis for getting at relevant data with some representative value. The organisations concerned are large on the PIE organisation scale. The QUALIMET PIE is limited to an OO programming environment and thus is more technically focussed. The GQM approach was used which makes possible a comparison with the CEMP PIE. The MMM PIE represents a small organisation introducing GQM. This allows an interesting opportunity for comparison with the CEMP PIE.

8.3.1 Overall Cost for Introducing Measurement Program

Since the reports use different metrics, a simple conversion has been applied for making comparisons. 1 person year is taken to be approx. 220 person days and 1 person month as 20 person days. Using these assumptions, the overall effort for introducing GQM-based measurement is as follows:

- CEMP – 1 person-year
- QUALIMET – 1 person-year (incl. guideline development)
- MMM – 1 person year (based on data reported in appendix 9.7. Out of 490 days total less definition of processes (110 days) and less provision of environment support (190) days, 190 days seems to be the effort for the GQM metrics PIE).

Based on these three examples there seems to be an "inevitable" threshold level of 1 person year for the introduction of GQM-based metrics connected to software process improvement, independent of organisational size. One interpretation of this result is that even in the larger organisations, the PIE is performed by a smaller part of the organisation and with one or two baseline projects. This means that the organisations actually conducting the experiments are roughly equal in size, regardless of the overall size of the respective organisations.

8.3.2 CEMP

Cost of Introducing GQM-Based Measurement

In this section the most important results of the analysis on effort w. r. t. the GQM-based measurement generalized from the parallel analysis at the companies are reported. All values are averages of the results of the different sites and projects, where support activities are excluded:

- The total effort needed for introducing GQM based measurement is about 1 person year.
- The total effort needed for introducing GQM of about 1 person year comes to 1/3 from the project team and to 2/3 from the GQM team.
- The relation of the effort of the set-up and execution phase for the first projects is about 2/3 (set-up phase) to 1/3 (execution phase).
- The total effort of set-up and execution phase is about 6 PM in the second projects compared to 11 PM in the first projects.
- The project overhead due to GQM-based measurement (project team only) for the first projects was less than 3% at all experimental sites.
- The total effort for GQM-based measurement (for the set-up and execution phase, including project team and the GQM experts) in percentage of the total project effort is about 17%.
- In the CEMP project, the total effort for GQM-based measurement per month of execution is almost the same in the first and second projects with about 0.4 PM.

8.3.3   MMM

To introduce measurement even in a small company is possible if it is part of the strategy of the company and people commonly share the vision of software process improvement and if the necessary funding and managerial support is available because improvement is not for free.

Measurement in a company pays back. One may find it difficult to count the financial aspects but it is a good advice to try to quantify the main aspects to keep the momentum. In our case some minor goals or even unintended benefits became visible and only a part of them provide for annual savings of at least 5% of all labour costs. In reporting these benefits one may think that a part of the results could have been achieved by common sense. But we believe this is the same truth as with other ideas that are costly to work out and easy to understand once you have done the work. Awareness of problems and benefits of solutions can be rationalised only by measurement and in fact by measurement in a methodical way in order to detect as much as possible (also in an economic sense) the principles and relations of various factors that contribute to the results.

To keep it simple is of course not only a principle to overcome complexity and support motivation but it is absolutely necessary in terms of spent effort and costs. We have done a lot of work for us to handle things in a lean way (and experienced some draw back when on the other hand we tried to generalise some approaches to save effort in the future e.g. with our history database) and we had and have carefully to keep track and analyse what measurement will cost us in the future. But we are now able to quantify it. Nevertheless we have to state, that the planned 26 days a month for SPI within a company of 10 employees is near the upper limit or beyond of it.

8.3.4   QUALIMET

At the mid-term assessment, the results of the project were presented to RO-BOTIKER's Quality Department. They were satisfied with the results of the project and were interested in having at the end of the project real values related to:

- Effort necessary to define a metrics program.
- Effort necessary for introducing its use in a project.
- Possibility of extending its use to all types of C++ projects independently of the application's domain.
- Possibility of re-using part of the quality model for C projects.

None of these points were initially taken into account in QUALIMET, but as were suggested at the mid-term assessment, those points have been addressed in order to extract valuable conclusions for the future usage of the methodology developed.

Concerning the Effort necessary to define a metrics program it is divided in the following points:

- Effort devoted to training: 39.5 person-days.
- Effort the define the Programming Style Guide and the Measurement Process: 57 person-days.
- Effort to select the Metrics Tool: 26 person-days.
- Effort to implement and validate the Measurement Process: 122 person-days.

Moreover, these values will be much lower in case of defining a measurement program for other types of project apart from the Object-Oriented ones, due to the QUALIMET experience.

8.3.5   Summary of Cost Data

As can be seen in table 8.1 below, the activities are not expressed in the same terms, requiring some interpretation for meaningful comparison.

Table 8.1 Comparison of cost data reported by the projects – in person days

Activity	CEMP	QUALIMET	MMM
Definition of processes			110
Provision of environment support			190
The core Measurement implementation			190
Set up phase	130		
Execution phase	65		
Training		40	
Defining Progr. Guide & Measurem. Proc.		57	
Select Metrics Tool		26	
Implement & Validate Meas. Process		122	
TOTAL	200	245	490

With respect to QUALIMET, it seems that activity 7 contains part of what MMM represents as definition of processes and that activity 8 is contained in activity 2 of MMM. Assuming that activity 7 is split 50/50 would allocate approximately 30 days to measurement process and 30 days to process definition.

Table 8.2 Interpolation comparison of cost data – in person days

Activity	CEMP	QUALIMET	MMM
Definition of processes		30	110
Provision of environment support		26	190
The core Measurement implementation		*192**	190
Set up phase	130		
Execution phase	65		
Training		40	
Measurem. Proc ·		30	
Select Metrics Tool			
Implement & Validate Meas. Process		122	
TOTAL	200	245	490

Table 8.2 illustrates the result of adjusting activities 6, 7 and 9 according to these assumptions. The result is a similar level of effort.

The QUALIMET experimenters also expressed the opinion that subsequent efforts would be more efficient as a result of experienced gained.

8.3.6   Project Costs

There are two main examples of project cost in the PIE context. The first is the PIE project during which a measurement effort is used for the first time on a more or less experimental basis. The second occurs when a measurement activity is fairly established and the measurement program is used routinely.

8.3.6.1   The First Project

CEMP reports above (see 8.3.2 bullet point 6) that the total effort for GQM-based measurement (set-up and execution phases, including project team and the GQM experts) in percentage of total project effort is about 17%. The range varies between 3 and 41 percent depending on differences between projects.

Additional information is given by CEMP about measurement overhead (see bullet point 5). The project overhead due to GQM-based measurement (project team only) for the first projects was less than 3% at all experimental sites.

In MMM the goal given in the PIE proposal was to limit measurement effort to less than 8% of total project effort.

8.3.6.2   The Second Project

CEMP reports (refer to 8.3.2 above, bullet point 4) the total effort for set-up and execution phases is about 6 person months in the second project compared to 11 person months in the first projects. This indicates significant movement along the learning curve: the cost is almost halved between the first and second projects. It would be very interesting to have information on the third and fourth projects to understand the learning curve better.

According to CEMP (bullet point 7), the total effort for GQM-based measurement per month of execution is almost the same in the first and second projects: about 0,4 person months.

This seems a little disappointing, as one would also expect reduced effort in the second project. A possible explanation is that there is an ongoing learning phase in the second project. New people are being introduced to the measurement technology and new situations are being encountered, while at the same time the organisation's competence base remains small. It is also possible this could be a "standard value" for a stabilised measurement program.

MMM states that they expect future measurement activities will require 2-4 % of project effort depending on the goals (and hence comparable to the benefits) and the size of the projects. In general, the percentage decreases with project size and "reuse" of personnel.

8.4   Processes

The MMM PIE reported that substantial work was necessary to define and establish the affected company processes in order to have a sound basis for the establishment of a measurement programme. Out of a total effort of 490 person days, 110 were used for defining the processes.

The need to define processes as a prelude to PIE experimental work seems to be a general experience for the metrics PIEs as well as the PIEs in other domains.

8.4.1   MARITA

The MARITA PIE is a good example. In this PIE the need for process definition was recognised only after the PIE had begun. So it seems in some of the other cases as well. This leads to a definite "lesson learned" from the total PIE experience: The need to define processes is an integral part of process improvement.

MARITA's goal was to identify the configuration management processes needed to support component-oriented development and to automate as many of these processes as possible through the use of tools. It was discovered to be more difficult than anticipated to adopt existing commercial tools to the component-oriented process. During the experiment a number of project organisational

changes had to be made. *Even the development model had to be redefined.*
MARITA does not claim that the measures taken are the only possible approaches
or even the best approaches – there are still improvements to be had – but it has
improved the maturity of the MARITA experimenters as a software supplier.

8.4.2 MIDAS

The relations between PIE work and Metrics application is nicely illustrated by the
MIDAS report. It also shows the process definition (modelling) activity as a base
for other parts of the Process Improvement effort.

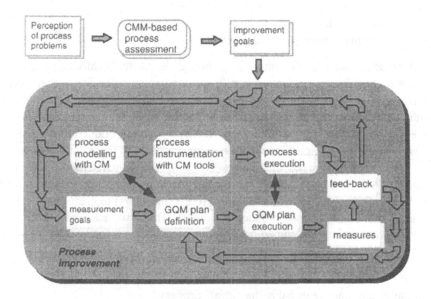

Fig. 8.1 The process modelling, execution and measurement flow

The process-related activities concerning the controlled establishment of CM
are summarised in figure 8.1 (where thin solid arrows indicate consistent views, or
even integration, while thicker arrows indicate the operations flow). Note that
Figure 8.1 accounts only for the pilot project: the collection of information for the
redeployment of CM in other projects and departments is not considered. The
results of the process assessment and the process improvement goals indicated that
a process model was needed, to understand both the current practice (the actual
process) and to formalise the target process, integrating development activities and
configuration management.

In the formulation of goals the process model was a constant reference, suggesting the product components and process activities to measure, highlighting

variation factors, indicating the roles responsible for carrying out measures or to validate them, and showing how the development process could have been enhanced with measurement activities. In particular the model allowed a strict control on the mutual consistency of the process model, the metrics, and the current practice (regarding CM as well as other development activities and measurement). *Process monitoring and evolution.*

The CM process has to be monitored and evolved (in order to cope with the natural evolution of the production process) and to be adapted to fulfil several needs that emerge after the first release of the CM system has been put in place.

Establishing a CM process involves the following phases:

- modelling of the production process,
- selection of the tools to support the CM process,
- customisation of these tools,
- monitoring the process and let it evolve.

All these phases present some critical points. In particular modelling the production process is very critical especially for companies – like SIA – that were at the first level of the Capability Maturity Model, and did not have a model of their production process (or, saying better, they had an "official" one not representing the everyday practice). It was found that in SIA the actual production process was different from the "official" one and, in some cases, even the team managers did not have a clear perception of the procedures effectively performed by the team members. As a consequence, it was necessary to interview all the people directly involved in the production process (not only the managers) to create a model that correctly describe the actual production process. This last statement can be valid in every organisation, and should be taken into account even for assessments.

The work was made further hard by the necessity to produce a model satisfying several constraints:

- it had to approach reasonably the "ideal" process,
- it had to be feasible (for instance, it was considered unfeasible to change radically the way people was currently working),
- it had to be easy to implement through the CM tools available.

Also this consideration is very significant to evaluate the effort required to introduce, or even only to modify, a software production process.

8.4.3   ENGMEAS

Metrics can be collected in a consistent manner only if the organisation of theme assured/involved activities obeys a defined company-wide procedure. The level of detail (maturity) of the software development process constraints the granularity of the metrics.

An issue for all efforts on defining the processes of the organisation is the level of detail (granularity) of the processes to establish. There are some trade-off decisions concerned. A more detailed process will be easier to measure and to give measures which are more easily interpreted and thus to act on.

There seems to be a likelihood of binding the process map to existing technologies by detailing.

Also an increased granularity should lead to a corresponding increase in measuring cost. This might not be a problem to the extent the data collection is possible to automate, but the effort to take care of measurement data might lead to an increased demand on person time. A cost which is important to take into consideration when deciding on measurement and granularity of processes to base those measurements on. From a motivational point of view it is not good to make measurements and collect data which you are not then using. So the conclusion is that you must strike a balance between the precision you may gain by granularity and the workload you are able to accept in the organisation for taking care of the results.

An other aspect of process granularity is that there is some level of description (granularity) which leaves the processes rather independent of the technology used in execution of the process. On this level you may find opportunity for making measurements for extended time series. You will have data which are comparable from before, under and after technology shifts.

Part III

Process Improvement Experiments

9 Table of PIEs

Table 9.1 below lists each of the PIEs considered as part of the EUREX taxonomy within the problem domain of Metrics and Process Modelling.

Table 9.1 Table of PIEs

Project No	Year of CfP	Acronym	Project Partners	Country
21757	1995	ACIQIM	DENKART NV	B
10965	1993	AERIDS	SAIT DEVLONICS	B
10146	1993	ALCAST	VOLUNTARY HEALTH INSURANCE BOARD	IRL
21415	1995	AMETIST	R.O.S.E. INFORMATIK GmbH	D
24099	1996	AMPIC	NORMARC GAREX AS	N
21511	1995	APPLY	VERILOG	F
23981	1996	ASAMETRICS	SCHNEIDER AUTOMATION GmbH	D
24331	1996	ASPIDE	SOCRATE SISTEMI S.A.S	I
21820	1995	AUTO-DOC	DATACARE Computers Ltd	IRL
21362	1995	AVAL	OBJECTIF TECHNOLOGIE	F
21284	1995	BEPTAM	NOKIA TELECOMMUNICATIONS OY	SF
21545	1995	BESTMM	HYPTIQUE	F
10841	1993	BEST-PM	INTECS SISTEMI SPA	I
24198	1996	BUSYSHOES	GABOR SHOES AG	D
21610	1995	CARERRAS	BRITISH RAIL BUSINESS SYSTEMS	UK
10358	1993	CEMP	ROBERT BOSCH GMBH	D
10358	1993	CEMP	Schlumberger Industries S.S.	F
10358	1993	CEMP	DIGITAL EQUIPMENT SPA	I
10702	1993	CET-IN	PORTUGAL TELECOM S.A.	P
21465	1995	CLEANAP	LABEN S.p.A.	I
21568	1995	CMEX	SYSDECO INNOVATIONS AS	N
21573	1995	COMPRO	DI SYSTEMER AS	N
23891	1996	CONFMANAG	VALMET AUTOMATION INC	SF
24187	1996	COQUIS	IGA mbH	D
10361	1993	CSSC	AEG HAUSGERAETE AG	D
10451	1993	DARE	MATRA MARCONI SPACE	F
21265	1995	DATM-RV	FAME COMPUTERS Ltd	UK
23699	1996	DECO	ENGINEERING INGEGNERIA IN-	I

Project No	Year of CfP	Acronym	Project Partners	Country
			FORMATICA S.p.A.	
23696	1996	DSP – ACTION	NOKIA MOBILE PHONES R&D	SF
10542	1993	EASIER	CMA SPA	I
10056	1993	ECO	CETE	F
10024	1993	EMS	VOEST ALPINE STAHL LINZ GMBH	A
21162	1995	ENG-MEAS	ENGINEERING INGEGNERIA IN-FORMATICA S.p.A.	I
21307	1995	EPOTEST	SKELTON GmbH	D
23901	1996	ESPRIT-ESSI:PIE	ROHDE & SCHWARZ	D
21569	1995	ESTEX	COMPUTER RESOURCES INTERNA-TIONAL A/S	DK
24266	1996	EXOTEST	DASSAULT ELECTRONIQUE	F
21622	1995	FAMPIX	FEGS Ltd	UK
21367	1995	FI-TOOLS	TT TIETO TEHDAS OY	SF
24189	1996	GEARS	MASMEC	I
21741	1995	HEMATITES	CRUZ ROJA ESPANOLA	E
10001	1993	IAS	RACE ASISTENCIA S.A.	E
21379	1995	ICONMAN	EVENT AS	N
23833	1996	IDEA	ISTITUTO NAZIONALE PREVIDEN-ZA SOCIALE	I
10312	1993	IDIOM	NYNEX MEDIA COMMUNICATIONS LTD	UK
10974	1993	IMPROVE	AEROSPATIALE Aeronautique	F
21733	1995	INCOME	FINSIEL S.p.A.	I
24395	1996	INDEED	SCHEIDT & BACHMANN	D
24395	1996	INDEED	TEBODIN CONSULTANTS & ENGI-NEERS	NL
21746	1995	INTOOAPP	A.I. SYSTEMS	B
10882	1993	INTRA	THOMSON-CSF	F
10189	1993	IPTPM	MATRA MARCONI SPACE	F
21603	1995	ISOTOPO	IBERMATICA S.A.	E
21405	1995	ISPI	IBERMATICA S.A.	E
21358	1995	ISUC	KNAPP LOGISTICS AUTOMATION	A
10549	1993	MARITA	ABB ROBOTICS PRODUCTS AB	S
24287	1996	MASLYD	I.C.E. COMPUTER SERVICES Ltd	IRL
21476	1995	MBM	ALENIA un' Azienda Finmeccania	I
21294	1995	MEFISTO	SOFTWARE ENGINEERING CENTRE DEFENCE RESEARCH AGENCY	UK
21323	1995	METPRO	DATASPAZIO S.p.A.	I
10594	1993	METQUASEP	CIM TECHNOLOGY TRANSFER CENTRE SUHL, bas GMBH	D
21244	1995	MIDAS	S.I.A. S.p.A.	I
23602	1996	MIFOS	INASCO Hellas C°	GR
21718	1995	MMM	KODA GmbH	D
21443	1995	MOOD	PARALLAX GROUP plc	UK

Project No	Year of CfP	Acronym	Project Partners	Country
23819	1996	MOODS	OPENLAKE	I
21547	1995	MSI-QBP	GEPIN ENGINEERING S.p.A.	I
10628	1993	NICE SPACE	ALCATEL ESPACIO S.A.	E
10196	1993	OASIS	TOTAL PERSONALSYSTEMER A/S	N
10995	1993	ODAGUI	VTKK REGIONAL GOVERNMENT SYSTEMS LTD	SF
21814	1995	OOSA	PRODATA N.V.	B
21292	1995	OOSD	TERMA ELEKTRONIK AS	DK
10738	1993	OPROB	MOTOMAN ROBOTICS AB	S
24176	1996	OUTSOURCE	ATB Institut für angewandte System-technik Bremen GmbH	D
21322	1995	PARI	PLLB ELETTRONICA S.p.A.	I
21550	1995	PIOREC	KT-DATACENTER	SF
21305	1995	PITA	INTRACOM S.A.	GR
21531	1995	PITA	AMT-SYBEX (Software) Ltd	IRL
23983	1996	POSE	THOMSON – CSF	F
23983	1996	POSE	THOMSON TRAINING & SIMULA-TION S.A.	F
23983	1996	POSE	THOMSON – CSF AIRSYS S.A.	F
23983	1996	POSE	SIGNAALAPPARATEN BV	NL
23983	1996	POSE	SYSECA Ltd	UK
10836	1993	PRAMIS	LABEIN	E
10836	1993	PRAMIS	CCL	UK
21670	1995	PRIME	ROLLS SMITHS ENGINE CONTROLS	UK
21188	1995	PROMIS	NOKIA MOBILE PHONES Ltd	SF
24149	1996	PROMISED	CSTB	F
21275	1995	PROSA/OM	ICL EDACOM OY	SF
21417	1995	PROVE	CAD.LAB S.p.A.	I
24060	1996	PSP – NC	FIDIA S.p.A.	I
21630	1995	Q-PRIME	PRODACTA GmbH	D
23982	1996	QUALIMET	ROBOTIKER	E
24256	1996	RECOMPOSE	SOFTWARE INNOVATION	N
21513	1995	REPRO	PROVIDA ASA	N
10714	1993	REQUITE	DATACEP	F
10714	1993	REQUITE	MARCONI RADAR AND CONTROL SYSTEMS LTD	UK
21649	1995	ROADS	THOMSON-CSF SA	F
10645	1993	ROAR	INFORMATIQUE CDC	F
21618	1995	SCOOP	ESBI Computing Limited	IRL
10937	1993	SECU-DES	DALCOTECH A/S	DK
10491	1993	SENC	FIDIA S.p.A	I
10218	1993	SMETOSQA	INFOGEA SRL	I
21424	1995	SPIKE	SHORT BROTHERS Plc	UK
23750	1996	SPIP	ONYX TECHNOLOGIES	ISR
21799	1995	SPIRIT	BAAN COMPANY N.V.	NL

Project No	Year of CfP	Acronym	Project Partners	Country
21271	1995	SQUEME	IBERIA AIRLINES	E
23855	1996	SWAT	TELECOM SCIENCES CORP. Ltd	UK
21780	1995	TELMET	NERA AS	N
21385	1995	TEPRIM	IBM SEMEA SUD s.r.l.	I
10665	1993	TIKE	MINISTRY OF AGRICULTURE AND FORESTRY / INFORMATION CENTRE TIKE	SF
24091	1996	TOPSPIN	TEDOPRES INTERNATIONAL B.V.	NL
10920	1993	TPDMP	NEW MEDIA PRODUCTIONS LTD	UK
24388	1996	TTM	NEDGRAPHICS B.V.	NL
24247	1996	UNCODE	CAS Software GmbH	D
10573	1993	WORKSHOP	CONSORCI HOSPITALARI DE CATALUNYA S.A.	E

10 Summaries of PIE Reports

10.1 ACIQIM 21757

Automated Code Inspection for Quality Improvement
Expected Impact and Experience

By setting up the automated framework for code reviewing and selection Denkart will not only have build a mechanism useful for every development process, but we will also gain understanding in metrics (automatically and manually collected) and their relation towards software quality. Furthermore it will raise the quality issue to the level of developers and management which is important regarding the culture change needed to build a quality conscious company.

Business Motivation and Objectives

Since the cost of repairing faults in software is considerably higher later in the development process, it is essential to obtain as small as possible fault tolerance throughout the complete development cycle. Denkart's objective is to reduce the workload by automating and streamlining the code inspection process. Our goal is to build an automated frame-work which can be used in any software development cycle.

The Experiment

To achieve the above mentioned objective, we will design and build an automated system which gives the biggest benefit, meaning reduced workload and smallest fault tolerance. During the baseline project we will concurrently do manual code reviews and run static and dynamic code analysis tools to determining the software quality factor. The results of the reviews and the resulting metrics will be combined to find a correlation. Out of this correlation report we will be able to make an automated selection of sources which have to be manually reviewed. By using the metric tools we will already exclude part of the faults while the automatic selection system will make sure the critical sources get reviewed.

Though the framework must be applicable to any software development project we will use one of Denkart's typical legacy business application migration projects as baseline project.

Denkart employs 35 people of which 7 will be involved in the ACIQIM PIE.

Contact Information

Denkart NV, Belgium

10.2   AMETIST 21415

Adoption of Methods, Engineering Techniques, Inspection & Software Tools

This experiment was performed by a small software company being in the transition from a research bound development style with very few developers to a professional software house with a defined software development process. The objective of the PIE was to achieve this higher level of maturity whilst retaining the support for the creativity of the developers. It was achieved by the following five measures which were applied to a baseline project typical for our development:

- Definition of a deterministic software development process tailored to our environment,
- Introduction of a quality assurance function,
- Introduction of quality engineering,
- Support by a scalable documentation system and
- Control by objective measurements.

Results achieved: At the beginning and the end of the experiment SynQuest assessments were performed and they showed an improvement of about 200% towards a process oriented company. For the related baseline project the number of the delivered errors was 60% lower than for our other development activities. The baseline project was completed before the planned end date and with fewer effort than originally planned. Extrapolating these effects to our other development we expect an increased customer acceptance and satisfaction for the future.

Lessons learned: There is a considerable gap between the leading edge experiences concerning software engineering and the stuff which is actually mediated to computer scientists during their education. Thus the cultural change from a research bound single developer environment to a systematic and process oriented team development took longer than originally expected. The effort invested in systematic software engineering activities at the beginning seems to delay the progress of a project but in long term pays off due to fewer iterations, earlier error detection and reduced correction and maintenance effort.

Next actions: The methods and tools applied during the baseline project will be consequently extended to all our development activities. According to the capability maturity model we thus hope to achieve the maturity level 2 in the near future. As a next formal step we expect the results of AMETIST to lay the foundation for a quality system which bears an ISO 9001 certification thus being ready for this certification should any customer or the market demand it. Acknowledgement: AMETIST was an ESSI project funded by the European Commission (Project Number 21415). It supported our transition from a research organisation to a professional software house. We appreciated this support very much.

R.O.S.E. Informatik GmbH, Germany

10.3   AMPIC 24099

Application of Metrics for Process Improvement for Safety Critical Software
Expected Impact and Experience

More accurate estimates and improved control of risk explosion, leading to better decision making. A more cost-effective development process, hence an increase in net margin. A common database of experience data, probably built upon existing release database at GAREX. Metrication defined as a standard activity within a Common Development Methodology (CDM). A better ability to prove quality towards customers, hence an increase in market share. A significant reduction in reported errors during system tests.

Business Motivation and Objectives

We experience problems with completing development projects within time and cost limits, and this is mainly caused by an increasing amount of software in the products. The amount of safety-critical software will increase in new development projects. Hence the quality for customers, and development process itself must be improved in order to demonstrate the quality for customers, and also in order to comply with very strict certification standards.

The Experiment

Objective: We want to develop suitable metrics for software development projects in order to improve estimation, expose problem areas, and also in order to improve the development process itself in respect of quality and productivity.

Methodology: The planned methodology for the project is to follow the AMI approach as described in the AMI handbook, which was developed in an earlier ESPITI project. Baseline projects: The experiment will be linked to two baseline project parallel in time, at former Normarc and GAREX respectively. The first one being a project for landing of aircraft based on satellite navigation, and the second one will cover two new releases of software for a voice communication system used in air traffic control.

Experiment plan: Assessment and development of metrics for both baseline projects and also for the PIE project itself. Metrication of a limited number of software modules in both baseline projects Assessment and evaluation of results from phase 1 Improvement of metrics and development of new ones Metrication of a new set of limited software modules in both baseline projects Assessment and evaluation of results from phase 2 Final evaluation and conclusion.

Contact Information

NORMARC GAREX AS, Norway

10.4   APPLY 21511

Amplified Process Performance Layout

VERILOG is a manufacturer of software and system engineering tools. VERILOG was looking for an improvement of its internal practices to deliver better products to its customers and for an increase of its experience to help external organisations to plan and implement its technologies.

The APPLY project is the experiment of the combined application of recommendations coming from a global Process Improvement Program initiated after a CMM self assessment. The main objective of APPLY was to implement the recommendations on a real size project in order to validate them and to obtain a quantitative project profile (cost break down and benefits) to facilitate internal and external replication.

The main achievement of APPLY are:

- Definition of a Project Control Panel capturing metrics on process performance, quality of the final product.
- Implementation of new practices supported by tools in the areas of:
  - Requirements Management.
  - Project Planning and Tracking.
  - Configuration Management.
  - Test and Validation.

APPLY results are:

- A better project control:
- Initial budget respected,

- delivery time managed within a 5% window (but the initial date is not respected).
- A higher reliability of the final product:
- Remaining bugs are divided by 2 for the same test effort

Economical consequences have to be evaluated on market side rather than on the internal productivity benefits. For instance, VERILOG has had 40% product sales growth and an increase of maintenance contract renewal.

The description of this experiment could give to other organisations ideas and facts in order to replicate such improvement.

This work has been financed by the European Commission as part of the ESSI program

VERILOG, France

10.5   ASAMETRICS 23981

Implement Metrics with Best Cost/Benefit Ratio
Expected Impact and Experience

After the PIE there will be a well established metrics system all over the software life cycle. The knowledge of the PIE and on metrics widespread in the company. The created experience database will help to develop future products with higher quality and reduced development time.

Business Motivation and Objectives

The overall goal of the PIE is to strengthen the competitiveness of Schneider Automation GmbH (ASAD) by improving continuously our software development and maintenance process. The technical objective is to define, implement and evaluate a metrics system for our software development process with the best cost/benefit ratio.

The Experiment

The PIE will be performed on a baseline project. In addition one or two other projects will be used for verification purpose. In the first step we will apply and test distinct metrics approaches on different phases of the software process of the baseline project. Next we will select those types of metrics with the best cost/benefit ratio and practise them in other projects. The results of these experiment swill be carefully recorded, analysed and evaluated to find our best choice.

Finally the experience and knowledge learned form the PIE will be disseminated both within our organisation and to external audience. In order to assure an efficient approach for the PIE we will involve appropriate consultancy.

Contact Information

Schneider Automation GmbH, Germany

10.6   CARRERAS 21610

Case Study of Analysis and Reengineering of Railway Resource Allocation Systems

CARERRAS is a Process Improvement Experiment to establish metrics, standards and processes to support re-engineering legacy systems. The experiment is being carried out by BR Business Systems(BRBS). The work has mainly been carried out by the PIE project manager and the re-engineering project manager.

Prior to the experiment, BRBS's Quality Management System provided support for standard projects with technically based metrics. The experiment is to produce additional processes for re-engineering projects together with process based metrics. The experiment covered 4 project stages, analysis, development, testing and installation along with the overall project management.

The main results and findings are :

The attempted technical re-engineering did not prove successful due both to technical problems and the customers business changing during the lifetime of the experiment. On the reporting of this change the commission carried out a project review to ensure that the project would still fulfil the purpose for which it was chosen and funding allocated. Additionally the review recommended extending the project timescales but not the effort for the PIE to take account of the delays incurred in the baseline project to allow proper completion of the experiment after baseline project implementation. The need for the experiment to focus on the means of re-engineering taking into account business change made it all the more worthwhile.

Customers are very supportive of the move to re-engineer their legacy systems based on the logical re-engineering model. This has resulted in a 25% increase in customers and a 5 fold increase in revenue from this customer base to fund the ongoing re-engineering. This is due to the re-engineering process underwriting BRBS's long term plans for the customers business area, planning for and supporting business change, the development of a controlled process and a recognition of the business, its pressures and its changing requirements.

The development structure proposed in the experiment was introduced on the baseline project and has successfully been reused on projects in other business areas within BRBS. This has allowed the Development phase to be very similar to that in standard lifecycle developments with a different overlying organisation and technical structure including the breakdown of large projects into smaller ones with their inherent decrease in risks..

The overall expected divergences from the standard lifecycle have come at the start of the project, in the analysis phase, rather than in the development phase, as originally predicted.

As a result of the experiment, we have a recommended process for analysis and development for re-engineering projects. We also have metrics for estimating the analysis stage of future re-engineering projects

British Rail Business System Ltd, UK

10.7   CEMP 10358

Customised Establishment of Measurement Programs

The Goal/Question/Metric (GQM) approach to measurement of software processes and products has been used successfully in selected industrial environments. This report summarises results and lessons learned from its application in three European companies: Robert Bosch, Digital, and Schlumberger.

Project Goals

Main objectives of the CEMP ("Customised Establishment of Measurement Programs") project were (i) to introduce and perform measurement programs based on GQM related to quality aspects of reliability and reusability in all three companies, (ii) to compare and analyse their results and experiences, and (iii) to derive replicable cost/benefit data as well as guidelines and heuristics for wide-spread establishment of GQM-based measurement programs in European industries.

Work Done

To increase validity of results, the project was organised as a synchronised and co-ordinated parallel case study. All application experiments performed the following main steps:

- Characterisation of the application environment.
- Definition of GQM-plans for reliability and reusability.
- Planning of measurement programs.
- Realisation of measurement programs.
- Company-specific analysis and interpretation of collected data.
- Packaging of results.

Additionally, comparison of results across companies were done to analyse commonalties and differences. Dissemination of experiences gained in the project was organised. All information on the CEMP project is also available on the WWW-server.

Results Achieved Including their Significance

Measurement programs for reliability and reusability were successfully introduced and realised in all three companies. Additional pilot measurement was included during the 22 months of CEMP project. After careful analysis of measurement results an improved understanding of software development with an increased awareness of strengths and weaknesses of products and processes was achieved. Based on established baselines for all topics under considerations, suggestions for improvement with high impact on quality of software development were derived. As an additional deliverable, tool support for performing goal-oriented measurement was developed by Digital. Across the replicated pilotprojects at the experimental sites a comparative analysis was done w. r. t. the introduction of GQM-based measurement programs. Commonalties and differences of all results and experiences were related to specific application domains and project characteristics to better enable transfer and application of the overall CEMP project results in other environments and organisations.

From the CEMP experiment it was shown that total effort for introducing GQM based measurement is about one person year. Project team effort devoted to GQM was proven to be less than 3% of total project effort. Taking into account achieved benefits, effort was considered to be an efficient investment even for the first measurement project. Reuse of experiences and results in the second pilot projects resulted in improved cost-benefit ratio. From a methodological point of view, CEMP-project experiences in performing goal-oriented measurement were summarised in a detailed process model which is accompanied by guidelines and heuristics for its implementation. This considerably facilitates the application of the approach by other organisations.

Next Proposed Actions

All three companies achieved a higher maturity in software measurement. They will introduce GQM for an increasing number of projects or even for all software projects as in the case of Schlumberger RPS. Results and experiences of CEMP-project initiated improvement programs for participating companies and will enable other companies to learn when starting with goal-oriented measurement.

Contact Information

Robert Bosch, Digital, and Schlumberger

10.8   CLEANAP 21465

Cleanroom Approach Experiment
Expected Impact and Experience

At the end of the PIE, results shall be matched with the traditional software process by means of quantitative metrics on both product and process. Impacts are expected in the following process area:

- Software testing: reduction of the 25% with respect to the development process; testing coverage measured and focused on the most critical modules;
- Code Validation: MTTF equals to mission extent Statistical 95% confidence level on the software correctness;
- Product and Process Quality: usual monitoring of process and product metrics variance on committed delivery time: ± 1 month

People Issues and Future Plans:

At the end of the Experiment, the software development process shall be provided with organisation-wide quality procedures for a cleanroom development able to target the required reliability level of the final product with reference to the level of safety of each project. Project-managers shall be able to use data coming from other similar projects to make more accurate predictions on resulting reliability level and needed resources.

Business Motivation and Objectives

In the aerospace market, mastering the development effort with respect to the desired reliability level allows a sharp commitment toward the final customers needs. The project is aimed at achieving a process improvement on software development in safety-critical domains with special regard to better qualification of the software reliability of the final product through: better efficiency and rigorous statistic measurements on the software testing process; development of intrinsic low-defective software (Cleanroom).

Measurable objectives shall be identified among process metrics related to time and efforts spent to detect single defects as well as time and efforts spent to design, execute and report tests. Also product metrics related to code physical properties like resulting complexity and size shall be considered and correlated to failure severity classes. With reference to the actual process some yardsticks are considered.

The Experiment

Context of the Experiment. The experiment shall be performed in the context of the European Photon Imaging Camera (EPIC) Project to be flown in the next

XMM/ESA spacecraft. The software for OnBoard Data Handling units is considered the Application Experiment.

Description of the Baseline project. The software for the OnBoard Data Handling shall assure the tele-command and telemetry link between the payload low-level controller and the spacecraft central data handling. As the payload is intended for an operational life of at least 2 years with extension up to 10 years, the requirement for high reliability is very important for the software as well.

In compliance to PSS-05, the software process is ruled by a Software Project Management Plan (SPMP), referring to a Software Quality Assurance Plan (SQAP), both appointed by ESA. Accordingly, a Waterfall Process is set up through 4 main phases: SW Requirement phase (SR), Architectural Design phase (AD), Detailed Design phase (DD) and Production, Transfer phase (TR). Incremental deliveries are not explicitly stated, though several issues on EM, EQM, and FM are planned. Different levels of testing are planned but not by means of a separate Validation Team, although reviews are managed by Q.A. Personnel separated from the Development Team.

Process Improvement Experiment Steps. Introduction of a Cleanroom Process implies many impacts on a traditional software development area as Engineering Process, Quality Assurance methods and Configuration Management, which shall be set as a rigorous, but not heavy-weight, process tool. Beside a first assessment and a final results evaluation, two main steps shall be performed by the experiment:

Introduction of a Cleanroom Process in the software development where the Software Life cycle shall be thought for incremental development and followed by a suitable Quality Assurance Reviews plan, able to support the increasing complexity of the released software. Metrics shall be introduced to monitor progresses

Cleanroom Experimentation Software is incrementally developed starting from the most critical components as kernel or operating system, in order to achieve an early control on the trending reliability and a monitored reliability growth from the software releases for EQM up to the last release for Flight Model (FM).

Contact Information

LABEN S.p.A., Italy

10.9   CMEX 21568

Configuration Management Experiment

This experiment aims to improve the efficiency in a software development department by introducing a new and advanced configuration management system. The aim of the experiment is to reduce the number of error reports by 10% and the time-to-market by 5%.

The experiment was done in the development department of Sysdeco GIS AS in Norway, developing software for the mapping industry or GIS sector (Geographic Information Systems). The experiment shows significant better results than originally aimed for. The errors have been reduced by 35,7% and the development effort has increased by 22%. The latter has contributed to bring the new products quicker to the market. The identified process improvement is not just a result of introducing a new system, but a result of many additional factors as general process improvement, product maturity and a focus on new development, to mention the most important.

Apart from the result above, the key lessons from the experiment have been:

To introduce the new configuration tool, ClearCase, was more difficult than anticipated. Careful planning and experimenting took more time than planned and caused more problems for the developers than expected.

- Too little training using the new system made the introduction of the system difficult.
- Well-established routines for handling errors and a well-experienced development group significantly contributed the success of the experiment.
- Relevant background data to measure the improvement was harder to collect than anticipated. It took more time and required also more effort to analyse than expected.
- The management of the project has gained valuable experience in how to collect and analyse data regarding process improvement. New ideas for further improvements have been identified.

The success of the experiment makes it evident to continue to use the new system in our development and maintenance of our products. Further improvements can and will be done. We have also identified new areas for improvements and we plan to do a similar experiment introducing automatic testing tools.

This experiment is relevant for SMBs planning to introduce new tools in their development department, especially configuration management tools. The European Commission through the ESSI/PIE program with project # 21.568 has financially supported this project.

Sysdeco GIS AS, Norway

10.10   COMPRO 21573

Component and Object Oriented Maturing Development Process through Use Organisations

DI Systemer AS develops and supplies economy management systems in the fields of accounting, orders/invoices and salaries to small businesses in Norway.

DI Systemer AS has a total of 24 employees, of whom 7 work in the development department.

The main objectives of COMPRO were: to implement development procedures and roles where reuse is an important element, to build libraries of reusable components and hence improve quality, increase productivity and reduce time-to-market. The plan was to reach maturity level 2 (and parts of level 3) of RMM – the "Reuse Maturity Level" (akin to the well known CMM – Capability Maturity Model).

Various technical and organisational problems arose in the course of the project, leading to delays and difficulties. It became clear that it would not be possible to carry out all of the work of the project as planned, and so it was decided (in consultation with the commission) that it would be best to terminate the project.

The premature termination of the project meant that not all of the objectives of the project were achieved in full. Despite this, the project was useful and some important lessons were learned. These were useful to our own organisation and – we hope – may be of assistance to other organisations considering similar process improvements. Development procedures and roles were introduced, and led to benefits within the organisation.

A reuse oriented approach to software development was introduced, and some reusable components were produced. Our general conclusion is that this work showed some promise – but that the benefits of reuse remain so far unproven. We worked at a detailed level with RMM, analysing the requirements imposed by RMM and drawing conclusions regarding the consequences for our organisation. We did some work towards implementing steps to take account of this, but our general conclusion is that RMM in its current form is not suitable for application in an organisation as small as ours.

In the course of the project, object-oriented programming techniques were introduced, together with a number of advanced tools. These will continue to be used. All in all, the project has had a positive impact within our company. Awareness of the importance of process improvement, quality assurance and reuse has increased considerably. Specific skills have been acquired and applied, and the organisation is more mature and effective than at the start of the project.

DI Systemer AS, Norway

10.11   DSP-ACTION 23696

Improving DSP Software Documentation Process to Promote Reuse

The efforts invested in the development of digital signal processing software are increasing dramatically, especially in telecommunication applications. Design of optimised mathematical algorithms has dominated research and product development, but as the size of software has grown, a need for improved software development practices has emerged. DSP-ACTION is a joint-project of Nokia Mobile Phones (NMP) and Finnish Technical Research Centre/VTT Electronics. The project was funded by the European Union under the ESSI program. The objective of this process improvement experiment was to improve DSP software development process in order to promote reuse of every level of design documentation. The experiment was piloted in a real product development project aiming at solving practical problems in everyday design and development work in industry. Effective review practice was introduced by defining elements of DSP software quality after analysing the customer needs of both forthcoming and current projects. Current revision management system was hierarchically restructured to intuitively reflect every domain of the pilot project's DSP software. Creation and collection of process documents into a single location founded a base for continuous process improvement. The expected impact of the experiment was faster cycles of high-quality product development with the use of collective base of design level experience. Quantitative measurements were used to guide current and future process development activities.

The experiment indicated that DSP software process can be improved using systematic approach and taking into consideration practical needs of the pilot project. Measurements also indicated significant reusability improvements in many aspects compared to the previous situation. We believe that efforts required for this kind of process improvement are biggest in the beginning, but after the organisation has gained experience on process improvement less effort is required to continue with next steps of process improvement. Our next steps will include continuation of the follow-up with most interesting metrics, gaining more experiences from project, and replicating proven best practices in other DSP software development projects.

Nokia Mobile Phones, Finnish Technical Research Centre/VTT Electronics, Finland

10.12 ENG-MEAS 21162

Introduction of Effective Metrics for Software Products in a Custom Software Development Environment

Measurement is an integral part of total quality management and process improvement strategies. We measure to understand and improve our processes. A software measurement programme allows organisations to improve their understanding of their development and support processes, leading to rational, planned improvements. Measurement programs also provide organisations with the ability to prioritise and concentrate their efforts on areas needing the greatest improvements. Motivated by such considerations, the ENG-MEAS Process Improvement

Experiment – conducted by Engineering Ingegneria Informatica S.p.A with the support of the Commission of the European Communities within the European Software and Systems Initiative (ESSI) – dealt with the definition of a company wide software metrics database. The project started in January 1996 and ended in June 1997, lasting 18 months.

As a large Italian software house, Engineering Ingegneria Informatica S.p.A. experiments all problems typical of software organisations involved in large turn-key projects for custom software products in rapidly evolving technological environments. Concerning this scenario, the definition and implementation of a measure programme was aimed to increase the company's capabilities in predicting and controlling software projects and in ensuring objective assessment of both the developed software and the software development process.

Since the most successful way to determine what we should measure is to tie the measurement program to our organisational goals and objectives, the PIE selected the "Goal-Question-Metric" (GQM) method for tying the measurements to the goals. The experiment was intended to characterise the company's process productivity and defectiveness in terms of some technological, methodological, organisational and cultural factors, chosen for their relevance (i.e., that might have a significant effect, typically those that are not restricted to a small part of the lifecycle).

Main choices included:

- introduction of new software sizing techniques, based on Function Points analysis,
- systematic definition of the measurement plan through the GQM method,
- adoption of adequate statistical procedures for data analysis:
- a procedure for analysing unbalanced datasets that include many nominal and ordinal scale factors. It is adequate for obtaining company statistical baselines. In our context, a statistical baseline comprises the average values and variance of productivity or defect rates for projects developed by the company, allowing for the affect of significant variation factors,
- an anomaly detection analysis. We used it in identifying those projects that deviate significantly from other projects either by being extremely good or extremely bad.

Engineering Ingegneria Informatica S.p.A

10.13   ESTEX 21569

Project Estimation Experiment
Expected Impact and Experience

CRI hopes to demonstrate that useful estimation procedures can be based on an approach which is reasonably formalised, yet still based on a bottom-up approach. This has been identified as the estimation approach that is most likely to be useful in the long run in a contractor environment where it is difficult to establish historical data based on large numbers of similar projects.

The CRI Space Division is actively pursuing process improvements that will allow the division to qualify at level 2 of the SEI Capability Maturity Model. A successful outcome of ESTEX will help to overcome a major roadblock towards that goal.

Business Motivation and Objectives

In the Space and Defence markets, there is a clear trend towards software development contracts based on detailed requirements, fixed price, and fixed schedule. This trend implies that the contractor bears an increasing portion of the risk involved in balancing requirements, risk, and schedule.

The process improvement involves introduction of a well-defined program of development process measurement, definition of an estimation model that integrates measurements from earlier projects in the estimation process, and implementation of an organisational memory that allows this loop to be closed.

The result of the experiment is determined quantitatively in the regularly recurring assessments of the software development process. Also, the result of the experiment is determined more subjectively through the quality of the estimates actually produced in the baseline project as well as through a demonstration that the measurement program involved is operationally feasible.

The Experiment

The experiment is performed on the ERA project that delivers part of the on-board software for the European Robotics Arm as a subcontractor to a prime contractor that in turn is under contract with the European Space Agency. The project has incremental delivery stages, which allow the experiment to close the loop from measurement of an early stage to estimation of a later stage. Other projects with similar characteristics are being considered as supplementary baseline projects.

Contact Information

Computer Resources International A/S, Denmark

10.14   ESPRIT-ESSI-PIE 23901

Implementation of a Metric Based Quality Management System for Software Development Process
Expected Impact and Experience

The definition and analysis of the software development process by the introduction of metrics, including the creation of a comprehensive data dictionary for collection and evaluation of data, will allow to improve the software development process utilising measurable criteria. The acquired capabilities concerning the development of high quality software will be utilised to improve software development practice and the software development process.

Business Motivation and Objectives

The motivation for performing the experiment was to improve the status of the engineering practice. With respect to process engineering, measurement and control of the software development process is not sufficient. Errors in the software development process are often found too late within the product development or its life cycle. This significantly affects the time and costs for product development itself.

The objective of the experiment is to develop and establish a metric system to be implemented in the software development process in order to improve the quality (i.e. reliability, performance, maintainability and safety) of our products. Additionally, the transfer of the results within the wider European Community will be achieved by appropriate publications.

The Experiment

To achieve the objective above, the following methods and tools will be applied in the experiment: Data collection plan. This will be used for comparison, evaluation and verification of metrics. Metric tools. Tools which are suitable to collect metrics for evaluation process quality and software product characteristics. Quality management. Quantitative measurement of the quality of the software development process. The metric system will be designed module scaleable for projects of different size and complexity. The experiment will be performed around a baseline project, in this case a measurement equipment for general purpose measurement of components for advanced digital communications systems. The baseline project team consists of 12-15 engineers involved with the development of hardware and 15-20 engineers developing the associated software.

Contact Information

ROHDE & SCHWARZ, Germany

10.15   GEARS 24189

Gaining Efficiency and Quality in Real-time Control Software

Company & Project Overview

MASMEC is an industrial enterprise that designs, develops and builds machines for functional and final tests; these machines are used to test automotive OEM equipment (such as alternators, fuel injectors, braking elements, clutches, steering system) lighting lamps, pumps, House appliances, air conditioners, etc.

Masmec integrated systems are built to: perform leak tests in low and high pressure; verify the reliability and functionality of pieces; execute run-in, calibration, assembling, manipulation; control load, stroke, pressure, couple and temperature; fulfil pneumatic, electric and mechanical tests. The ESSI PIE – GEARS (Gaining Efficiency and quAlity in Real time control Software), started in MARCH 1997 and was completed in November 1998.

Project Goals

The goals of the ESSI PIE GEARS project were both to better and formally structure the software system specification process, by easing the modelling of the real-time behaviour of MASMEC testing machines and its translation into software systems specifications, and to improve the degree of reusability of the company's standard software components, by revising and re-engineering them in terms of granularity, flexibility of use and access methods.

Relevance and Applicability of the Results to the Wider Community

The concern motivation of the PIE is common to many companies dealing in the market sector of testing machines for mechanical components (ex. automotive OEM equipment such us alternators, fuel injectors, braking elements, etc.). This PIE would origin a basic experience in the adoption of modelling-oriented method, to describe the behaviour of testing integrated systems in order to facilitate the translation of these schemes into software components and the use of an object oriented approach to the design and implementation of reusable software components.

The Work Performed

The main work steps performed concerned:

- SPICE conforming initial and final software process assessment;
- Definition of both the environment and the tools to support the software reuse methodology;
- Identification of the company's reusable components and set up of a related net-available library;

- Definition and application of a reuse oriented organisation model;
- Definition and application of a set of quality metrics;
- Intensive training focused on software reuse methodologies and tools;
- In deep evaluation of the achieved results.

Achieved Results

The achieved results are leading to a better acceptance of the system functionality and performance by the clients and to a more extensive reuse of base software components with reduced maintenance costs. In addition, the PIE allowed to improve the software process capability of the company, as determined by the process assessment results according to the SPICE capability model.

The New Process Improvement Perspectives

The experimented reuse oriented organisation model together with the technological apparatus set up during the PIE proved effective, so laying down the foundation for the transition of the entire MASMEC software development organisation towards a formally managed reuse approach. Follow-up plans have been defined in order to achieve this transition within 1999.

Contact Information

MASMEC, Italy

10.16   ICONMAN 21379

Implementing Configuration Management in Small Enterprises

This report is based on work performed in the ICONMAN project during the 18 months (June 1996-December 1997) of the process improvement experiment. The experiment was sponsored by the CEC under the ESSI Programme, project no. 21379. The project's main goal was to implement configuration management in three small software companies and assess the effect of this effort.

The main conclusion from the project is: Implementing configuration management is worthwhile in very small companies. This is based on both qualitative and quantitative measurements and observations.

The companies have with respect to their own judgement successfully implemented routines for configuration management. Even though the process has been more demanding than expected, the maturing of the system development process was a necessary step in developing the business processes in the companies as a whole.

The main lessons learned were:

- Configuration management is a complex activity with far reaching consequences for the business as a whole.
- Implementing configuration management is an iterative process, and requires continuous refinement.
- In very small companies the introduction of configuration management should be tested in a controlled, but real-life environment.
- It was difficult to identify quantitative data to measure process performance, but the defined simple metrics were essential for evaluation of the experiment.
- The existence of an operative configuration management system has shown to make a positive impact on customer relations.
- The existence of an operative change request database has proven to be valuable in planning product releases.
- The existence of an operative configuration item library has proven to simplify the process of reconstructing earlier releases, and led to a higher service level for the customer.

Event AS, TSC AS), Aktuar Systemer AS, Event AS, Norway

10.17 IDEA 23833

Improving Documentation, Verification and Validation Activities in the Software Life Cycle

The purpose of this report is to describe the contents of IDEA project with particular emphasis on achieved results and on final considerations about the experiment. It may be interesting for all organisations which, starting from a middle-low engineering level of the software processes, intend to introduce best practices in a gradual way.

Main goal of the IDEA Project was the introduction of software best practices concerning some limited, but critical processes of the software life cycle: documentation, verification and validation, in IT department of INPS, the main Italian public body providing social services.

The project defined standards for project documents, clear rules about the documentation flow and a Verification & Validation procedure. The application of defined rules has been also supported by a document flow application, named IDEA-FLOW, developed during the experiment.

An assessment activity, according to the ISO/SPICE [2] emerging standard, has been executed at the beginning and at the end of the IDEA project, in order to verify the impact of the improvement activities on the critical processes. A Measurement Plan has been defined and measurements collected to evaluate the project results.

Among the results gained from the experiment, we observed that people involved in the experiment, have realised that it's useful to work with quality standards, and that a clear definition of roles and responsibilities is necessary to improve the organisation of work. Defining people responsibilities is an important step towards the improvement of the company processes.

Further, the adoption of a software tool supporting the document management procedure which guarantees higher security and timeliness in documents distribution, has encouraged the application of the learned concepts also outside the experiment area.

The INPS management has shown a good attention level to the project, by promoting the adoption of its results, in other software development projects in some peripheral sites. It has been started a review of the software development process, taking in account the lesson learned trough the IDEA experiment. For the future, a stronger integration between these revision activities and the results of IDEA project has been proposed.

With regard to Publicity and Information relating to this project, the European Commission shall be entitled to publish general information on the IDEA project, but all reports shall remain confidential. In addition, INPS shall grant the Community to translate, reproduce and distribute all Project Deliverables.

Istituto Nazionale della Previdenza Sociale, Italy

10.18   INCOME 21733

Increasing Capability Level with Opportune Metrics and Tools

This final report illustrates the results of the ESSI project n. 21733, a Process Improvement Experiment (PIE), named INCOME (Increasing Capability Level with Opportune Metrics and Tools). The Project started in January the 15th 1996 and had a duration of 21 months.

The goal of the experiment was to demonstrate how the use of an assessment method such as SPICE [1] and a goal-oriented measurement approach like *ami* [2] along with specific tools can help a medium to large critical and complex software development project improve its development process in its weakest areas and maintain ISO 9001 compliance.

Finsiel, Italy's largest IT services and consultancy group, was the prime user in this experiment and no associated partners were involved. Finsiel's customers include central and local government departments, leading banks and large industrial groups.

The baseline project was a CASE tools development project, to which a significant number of resources are assigned each year in different geographical sites, and in which several innovative technologies are used.

- The PIE is now completed and can be considered successful from several points of view:
- the approach followed in the experiment is valid, the adoption of SPICE and *ami* has been effective and the two methods appear to be complementary;
- the improvement actions defined and executed in the areas of the Project Management, Testing and Configuration Management caused a progress in the baseline project development process as shown by the specific indicators and by the process assessment performed at the end of the PIE applying the SPICE prospective standard;
- both the approach and some of the solutions within the improvement actions can be generalised and reused in a more general context within Finsiel and the IT community; indeed, a new improvement plan is being defined within a different Business Unit in Finsiel.

Finsiel S.p.A, Italy

10.19 INTOOAPP 21746

Integrated Object Oriented Approach for Application Development

The partners of this process improvement experiment want to achieve an integrated specification environment for the development and adaptation of software applications by introducing and implementing object-oriented CASE tools and methodologies. The focus has been primarily on improving the transition from user requirements to object-oriented software specification and development.

The three partners are active in the business of software development and consulting for the manufacturing industry.

The experiment consists of (a) applying the selected tool(s) and methodology to a baseline project, (b) improving existing procedures and (c) preparing the introduction at departmental or company level. The introduction of the tool and the accompanying measures are comparable at each partner's site: developers are involved in a very early stage, which increases the acceptance of the new methods, while a specific project is used to test the feasibility and to get timely feed-back on needed changes and problems.

The use of a graphical tool results in an intensified and easier interaction with the customer, who is provided with more evidence that his problem has been grasped correctly. This results in a better relation with the customer and a confident software developer. This has been possible by introducing more disciplined activities to maintain quality and traceability. Experience with and the use of state-of- the-art OO-technology plays an important role.

In the course of the experiment, iterations were needed to cope with the increased awareness of the possibilities offered by the new technology. Improvements emerged automatically as a result of the increased awareness. The tools allow narrowing the gap between user requirements, often of a functional nature, and the object-oriented analysis and design phases.

The partners have learned that iterations should be allowed in process improvement activities. To keep the discussions that arise while introducing new methods and technologies vivid, it is important to keep a steady pace to discuss and introduce new procedures. The introduction of metrics (e.g. specification time, number of iterations, post-delivery changes) along the duration of the experiment prove the importance of a continuous and measured improvement of software engineering processes. The European Commission through ESSI, the European Systems and Software Initiative is supporting the work reported.

Advanced Information Systems nv/sa
Gesellschaft für Technologie-Transfer mbH
Institut für Integrierte Produktion Hannover GmbH, Germany

10.20   ISPI 21405

Ibermatica's Software Process Improvement
Expected Impact and Experience

The experiment will have the following aims: to set up and put on work a measurement system for collecting and analysing all the failures and the change requests coming both during the development activities and after the release. to introduce within the development process activities for preventing errors and for discovering them as early as possible: process normalisation using analysis and development methodology, coding standards toward a good programming style and systematic functional testing practices introducing a testing methodology for any environment. to experiment in a controlled way with the above methodologies on a real project, and evaluating quantitatively the obtained advantages in respect to the past activities.

The baseline project, from the technical point of view is a typical one in a system with DB access and TP monitor, it will be run at branch level of the bank.

The size of developing unit is about 70 full time staff.

Business Motivation and Objectives

The objective is to set up and put on work a measurement system for collecting and analysing all the failures together with improvements to the Development Process towards better quality.

Presently, the Software Development Process is well stabilised and organised, despite the absence of a formal description of it: it is a typical waterfall model, with an initial functional analysis (producing a Functional Specification document), a technical and a detailed design (recently producing reference documents), the coding activity and the testing activity.

The Experiment

The experiment will have the following aims:

- to set up and put on work a measurement system for collecting and analysing all the failures and the change requests coming both during the development activities and after the release.
- to introduce within the development process activities for preventing errors and for discovering them as early as possible: process normalisation using analysis and development methodology, coding standards toward a good programming style and systematic functional testing practices introducing a testing methodology for any environment.
- to experiment in a controlled way with the above methodologies on a real project, and evaluating quantitatively the obtained advantages with respect to the past activities.

The baseline project, from the technical point of view is a typical one in a system with DB access and TP monitor, it will be run at branch level of the bank.

The size of developing unit is about 70 full time staff.

Ibermatica S.A, Spain

10.21   MARITA 10549

Management of a Flexible and Distributed Software Production

This paper deals with the experience ABB Robotics Products AB have gained during the transition from a traditional functional project development to a continuous component-oriented process, i.e. to build products from components, a process which an increasing number of companies may be forced to adopt to remain competitive. This implies using object-oriented technologies to promote reuse. The aim of a component-based development process is to shorten lead times to market, enabling developers to "snap together" generic components and customise them for local market requirements, or specific market segments, as these arise. Cycle time is shortened if "component development" and "product assembly" is done in parallel and if customisation can take place locally, implying the need for distributed support for component-oriented development.

The ESSI experiment, MARITA, had the goal to identify the configuration management processes needed to support component-oriented development and to automate as many of these processes as possible through the use of tools. It was found more difficult than anticipated to adopt existing tools on the market to the component-oriented process. During the experiment a number of project organisational changes had to be added. Even the development model had to be redefined. ROP does not claim the measures taken are the only possible or the best ways, there are still things to improve, but it has improved the maturity of ROP as a software supplier.

The MARITA experiment have been carried out within the framework of the ESSI Community Research Programme with a financial contribution by the Commission.

ABB Robotics Products AB, Sweden

10.22   MASLYD 24287

Metrics and Software Life Cycle Definition

ICE Computer Services identified the need for significant process improvement in various aspects of it's Software Department's activities as a result of a TRI-SPIN project in March 1996. The Software Department's primary activity is development and support of a Software Product for the Financial sector, also does an amount of bespoke software development. The findings identified a number of major shortcomings in the operations of this department which are typical of many small Software Development organisations, namely : Over dependence on specific staff for Product Knowledge in the department, unreliability of the Cost Estimation processes in place. Difficulty for new hires due to lack of clearly documented procedures and work practices. This PIE was initiated with the intention of addressing these issues.

The major lessons we have learned are (1) the potential for improvement was greater than originally envisaged and (2) the process of reviewing specific problems forced us to reconsider and confirm precisely what the business of the department is.

We have already achieved significant benefits from this process and believe that we have established a basis for further improvements as the processes developed and implemented are further refined with use. The knowledge gained from this activity should be of interest to many other small Software Development organisations many of whom have very similar problems as identified in ICE.

ICE Computer Services, Ireland

10.23 MBM 21476

Management by Metrics

Management by Metrics "MBM" experiment concerns metrics collection and exploitation in support of managers to gain an improvement in the software process. Alenia and Intecs Sistemi have already in place a defined process including the collection of many process and product metrics. However these metrics are often just thrown into a database for statistical purposes. Rarely they have a direct impact on the same process they are taken from. MBM intends to bring back those metrics into the process, for the benefit of the process.

The MBM experiment has the goal to provide a Software process and product indicators "Metrics" with a friendly user presentation. The indicators are depending on the company goals. Practised deployment of Management by Metrics is expected to move from actual level 3 (of both Intecs and Alenia) to perform a project working at maturity level 4. Inside the experiment execution, firstly technical and managerial aspects have been selected as related domain to be improved ("Company Business Goals" selection), then AMI method (Application of Metrics in Industry) rigorous approach has been applied and the detailed "metrication plan" has been derived. Automatic Support Tool(s) have been delivered and Metrics collection has started (and is currently running) to feed the "dashboard" in the two companies.

The metrics viewer "dashboard", is a highly intuitive, user-friendly presentation tool selected among commercial off-the-shelf (COTS) available solutions. The "dash-board" experimented on two quite different baseline projects, provide the managers (and quality managers), at a glance and graphically, all basic process indicators, including planned vs. actual vs. historical, flagging warning and alarm values. On a mouse click, basic process indicators show up into sub-dash-boards to provide more detailed indicators, up to the level of detail required. Management decisions (e.g. when to stop testing, increase the staff, postpone a release, improve inspections, trigger an audit on a subcontractor, etc.) are taken on a quantitative basis. Managers become familiar to read these dash-boards and to understand their dynamics. The "in action" phase for managers community has run: the benefits for involved people are therefore evident and valuable.

The Alenia and Intecs dash-board are not identical – because each company has its own business goals, Software Architecture and development Platforms. The Priorities are different and different indicators are necessary; nevertheless the "harmonisation" of the two dash-boards has been pursued with a benefit for the projects. Partnership between Alenia and Intecs Sistemi optimises the overall experiment effort and makes a first generality attempt for the great potential of technology transfer to other organisations. Differences between the two MBM-experiment "implementation details" are identified in the rest of the document.

At the conclusion of the experiment the result of SPICE assessment can be summarised as follows:

- for Alenia although the selected processes have not reached the capability level 4, their execution provides the opportunity to other process to be executed at level 4.
- for Intecs Sistemi: the capability level 4 has been reached.

This experiment is contributing at on going standardisation efforts, the Management by Metrics practice is intended to be institutionalised as part of both companies Quality Systems. The dash-board is near to become an integral appendix of all project progress reports.

Alenia, Intecs Sistemi, Italy

10.24 MEFISTO 21294

Metrics Framework for Improving SME Total Operations
Expected Impact and Experience

The impact within the SEC is expected to be: an improved metrics process leading to more accurate cost estimating identification of weaknesses in the development process the establishment of a longer term and continuing process improvement environment, through the creation of a "metrics culture". All will benefit the SEC and its customers alike. The SEC has links not only to the Ministry of Defence but also to industry, and will use these to disseminate the benefits and experiences to a wide audience.

Business Motivation and Objectives

The project addresses key areas which have a major effect on the profitability of any organisation producing software. The specific objectives are to: improve the accuracy of cost estimates use metrics to identify ways to improve the general software development process increase the effectiveness of the capture and exploitation of experience.

The Experiment

The estimating experiment consists of two parts: the first to collect data to calibrate the chosen techniques, and the second to use the new techniques and evaluate them. Evaluation will be based on a comparison of the accuracy of the estimates obtained. Estimates will be produced for a wide range of projects. The experiments for improvement and experience involve the identification of suitable metrics, the collection of associated data on a number of projects and the evaluation of the metrics. The evaluation will compare the cost of identifying and collecting the metrics with the value they give to the business.

The Software Engineering Centre (SEC) has about 130 staff.

Contact Information

Software Engineering Centre, Defence Research Agency, UK

10.25 METPRO 21323

Company Metrics Programme Introduction: A Quantitative Approach to Software Process Understanding and Improvement

The objective of the experiment has consisted in understanding the software engineering practice (and then software quality and productivity) by measurement of the product and process. The goal was to start a company metrics programme in order to drive a software process understanding and improvement. The main goals of the metrics program were:

- to provide the quantitative information essential to identify opportunities for improvement;
- to verify the advantages of the implemented changes to the development process.

The experiment has consisted on understanding and quantifying the shortcomings relevant to the following areas:

- software problem analysis and defects prevention capability;
- productivity and schedule estimation capability.

The experience gained with the execution of the experiment is fully transferable to all the companies developing software which decide to better understand and improve their development process.

The primary area/community of interest to which the experiment corresponds is:

- Industrial sector: Information Technology (any system and software supply company)
- Community of interest – System point of view: Technically oriented systems
- Community of interest – Technology point of view: any software application using high level languages, software product technology and an established process method.

The work done regards the definition of the metric program plan, described in the Annex A, the data gathering for the baseline projects, their re-engineering in electronic sheets designed by us and data validation respect to the established metrics. The results are complete for all the baseline projects and they are reported in the Annex B.

The potential for replicating the results of the experiment is due to the fact that the proposed method and metrics framework present the following advantages:

- they are life cycle independent, so their use is not affected by various development methodologies which could be utilised;
- they are simple to understand and easy to apply.

Dataspazio S.p.A., Italy

10.26   MIDAS 21244

Measurable Improvement of Development, Deployment and Operation of Interbank Automation Software

The project aims at a measurable improvement in the reliability and availability of interbank services offered by SIA, the organisation in charge of running, developing, and maintaining the National Inter-bank Network of Italy. Such improvement is achieved by establishing an effective CM process, i.e. to define CM procedures and policies, to select and customise automated tools supporting CM activities and to experiment the new CM process in a baseline project. A suitable measurement program was defined – using the Goal/Question/Metrics (GQM) technique – and executed in order to objectively assess the effectiveness of the new CM practice.

This document describes the achievements of the MIDAS project. The document is addressed to both managers and technical people. In fact both organisational and business-oriented issues, as well as technical information (mainly excerpts from the deliverables) are reported, in order to provide a picture of the project as comprehensive as possible, and to allow readers to be informed about all relevant issues concerning the establishment of CM and measurement processes.

Work done

- CM policies and tools: this is the core activity of the project, since CM is the main innovation introduced in SIA with the experiment [1]. The following steps were performed: • Definition of the CM process for the pilot project development environment. The pilot project is the NRO project. NRO will provide a full range of services for the management and operation of the SIA network. It also provides APIs and interfaces to allow SIA customers to interface their own applications with SIA services.. It is one of the most strategic product that SIA will deliver in the next five years.
- Selection and customisation of a supporting tool (CCC/Harvest).
- Deployment of the CM system for the NRO software, training of NRO project people, establishment of an on-line support service (help desk).
- Optimisation of the CM system, according to the results of measurements, monitoring, problem reports and spontaneous feed-back.
- Definition of the GQM plan and the measurement plan to assess the effectiveness of introducing CM in SIA.

- Execution of the GQM measurement program: results are reported in [3,13] and briefly outlined in section 4.1 of this document
- External dissemination: the MIDAS project, its objectives and results have been presented in several conferences and meetings.
- Internal dissemination: MIDAS objectives and technical and managerial implications were discussed in SIA, involving both people from the pilot project, people from other projects and departments, and also some suppliers.

Lessons learned in the project and reported in this document concern the establishment of CM in a controlled way (with a special reference to the integration of process modelling, improvement and measurement), optimisations of the process (specially as far as data collection, process monitoring, support and enforcing are concerned), tool selection and customisation, management and cost issues.

SIA, Italy

10.27 MIFOS 23602

Metrics Based Improvements for SMEs
Expected Impact and Experience

The main technical benefits expected out of MIFOS include: identification of process improvements, better control of projects and, improved quality in software products. Commercial benefits include reduction of software development costs, reduction of the lead-time for software products and increased product reliability during customer use. Through this PIE, INASCO will gain experience in establishing a measurements based improvements framework.

Business Motivation and Objectives

INASCO's main business concern is to provide reliable products, as well as to improve its market competitiveness. To the satisfaction of this common business concern, the objective of the MIFOS experiment is to establish at INASCO a systematic framework for software quality measurements, which will be associated to specific business and technical goals.

The Experiment

The MIFOS experiment will introduce the Goal-Question-Metric (GQM) approach to INASCO's RTD department, focusing on a typical project as a baseline. The initial step of this PIE involves the setting-up and integration of the experiment with the baseline project, as well as the necessary personnel training. Subsequently, the main steps of the GQM approach will be followed and implemented in the context of the baseline project. The four main phases of the experiment are software development process analysis and primary goals definition, primary goals analysis, measurements plan implementation and, exploitation of measurements. The baseline projects involves development of engineering software for materials applications.

Through the MIFOS experiment, a systematic measurements based improvements framework will be established at INASCO's RTD department leading to improved software products quality and consequently, to increased competitiveness for INASCO. The MIFOS experiment will take place at INASCO's Research Technology and Development department which employs 7 highly qualified software engineers.

Contact Information

INASCO, Greece

10.28   MMM 21718

Metrics Measurement and Management

KoDa GmbH, a small business software developing enterprise has conducted a process improvement experiment (PIE), that is financially supported by the EU within the ESSI programme. This PIE was targeted to introduce measurement in the software engineering of the company. The chosen approach was the Goal Question Metric method after the first preparatory steps of the PIE.

Following this methodical approach lead to the discovery of insufficient process descriptions, to the refinement of the process and the introduction of additional process steps. This forced our focus on the guideline to keep things simple and the target to allow for measurement activities in the future not more than 4% of project effort.

The conclusion of the PIE is that measurement is possible even in a small company but care must be taken with the first difficult steps in order to control effort and cost. We had no difficulties with regard to personal objections but a lot of engagement of our engineers due to the open cultural climate of our company. But in the longer run we recognised that additional measures have to be taken to keep the motivation and attitude to support this PIE and the goals behind it.

The strategy to rely on good consulting in parallel with our own studies of literature and the approach to first try to manage our task by available means and organisation and then look for tool support was right for us but we were aware of the high costs of doing so and now we desire to have simple tools for our needs available at the market.

Measurement is not only possible in a SME but also worthwhile. The investment can be controlled and the value can directly be related to the goals. There are also – in our case at least (see annex 9.7) – unintended advantages if you promote and maintain a measurement culture, keep an open mind, allow for flexibility and support responsibilities and competence of your project leaders and engineers.

Available within our company is now an environment for effort collection and the various GQM and measurement plans according to GQM as well as a history database to store the main results and support estimations.

KoDa GmbH, Germany

10.29 MOOD 21443

Metrics for Object Oriented Developments
Expected Impact and Experience

The experiment will pull our improvement plans forward by between 2-3 years, depending on how quickly we can institutionalise the results of the experiment.

When both projects have been completed, the results collected, compared and reviewed, we shall update our Delivery Management System. The change to our own operational processes is the key to retention of the learning from this experiment. The ability to reduce development times through re-use and predict end-product quality through a proven database of experience will enhance our commercial proposals significantly.

Business Motivation and Objectives

Parallax Group plc are a rapidly expanding concern with major focus in the application development arena. A commitment to quality and improved management of projects is a demonstration of the Parallax objectives and the organisation is moving swiftly through the process of gaining a full TickIt assessment as well as advancing through the Capability Maturity Model. We will also be changing our focus on process from the CMM to SPICE.

The increasing number and complexity of projects managed by Parallax has emphasised the need to accurately predict time, cost and software quality. We believe that this is a challenge faced by most organisations in our business sector. Together with our associate contractor, The University of Warwick, we will attempt to identify and prove a set of metrics which will facilitate the choice of an Object Oriented methodology and accurately predict cost, time and software quality at project commencement.

The Experiment

This experiment has three clear stages. The first stage is to develop a set of metrics which we can use to describe and quantitatively predict the performance of the development process, when using an OO methodology, and the quality of the resultant software product. The metrics should also describe how re-usable the software is.

The second phase will be the development of an application during which metrics will be collected and reviewed. The chosen project will be developed twice. One will be a normal development project at Parallax Group plc. This is the baseline project. We will choose a development taking about 18 man months over 6 months elapsed which has an OO analysis phase as well as an OO development. The second project will be a parallel development of the same functionality at the University of Warwick using Eiffel as a development methodology.

The third phase will be the review of both our predicted and collected results. Additionally the two projects will be compared with each other.

Parallax currently employs 150 people. The direct participants in this project number 8 people. Additionally a control group of 25 people has been established to assist in surveys, review of results and collation of metrics on existing projects. This provides a significant amount of empirical data with which to work.

Parallax plc, UK

10.30 PITA 21305

Process Improvement Through AMI

This report describes acquired experiences during the execution and until the conclusion of the ESSI Process Improvement Experiment PITA (Process Improvement Through AMI). PITA introduced the AMI framework (Application of Metrics in Industry), a well established Software Process Improvement method based on the Goal-Question-Metric (GQM) approach to software development practices, aiming at systematic and value-adding measurements. The experiment was carried out at Intracom's Software Development Centre (SWDC).

PITA, involved a formal assessment based on CMM as a means of identifying weak process areas that should be improved, followed by application of AMI to a typical baseline project. Objectif Technologie was chosen to act as a trainer, CMM assessor and consultant in the introduction of AMI. One of the most important activities in PITA was to use AMI as a framework for the consolidation and harmonisation of various business and process improvement goals as well as the utilisation of already existing metrics acquired from previous software process improvement (SPI) activities. Such pre-existing goals and metrics were taken into account and reused in preparing the PITA Goal Tree, the GQM Plan and the Measurement Plan. The approach followed for the baseline project is gradually taken up by other projects as well, while several dissemination events were planned and performed, targeting both the Greek and the European software development markets.

The main activities of PITA run until March 97, while several dissemination events as well as ongoing reuse/tailoring of the AMI method in other projects (besides the baseline), took place thereafter. In addition, SPI activity that AMI helped to trigger and initiate (at the organisation level and in other ongoing development projects), is progressing well supported by AMI. Finally, in-service measurement results (i.e. while the software product is in customer use) from the baseline project are not yet complete, due to the usually long life-cycle of Intracom's software projects, which in this case was even further prolonged for reasons completely independent from the PITA experiment; still tracking of measurement results is being performed as planned.

Means to address the PITA objectives are as follows:

- establishment of a systematic GQM-based framework for software metrics (see Annex for GQM overview)
- introduction of a formal assessment (SEI/CMM based) to establish software development process maturity
- implementation of the identified improvement actions in the baseline project and organisation

Intracom SA, Greece

10.31   PRIME 21670

Practical Reuse Improvement Metrics
Expected Impact and Experience

The experiment should achieve an improved reuse measurement process, an improved software development process and a good understanding of Goal Question Metrics as a tool to drive process improvement. This will result in reduced costs on future projects, a method for demonstrating the cost savings and also further benefit approved from any process improvements in the future.

Software metrication is a difficult business. The very nature of it tends to introduce extra expense and a perceived "Non value added" activity. This leads to inaccurate measurements because the engineers providing the data haven't bought into the justifications. There are two important factors in making this experiment successful, firstly to demonstrate that there is value in the process, secondly in spending time ensuring that the process for collecting data is unobtrusive (Ideally invisible) and thus encouraging consistent and correct data.

The results will be of interest to European software developers whose level of re-use is significant, and more generally, organisations looking to identify process improvements. Understanding of industrial reuse will be improved through a practical investigation of the mechanisms necessary both for evaluating the benefits of reuse and improving a process incorporating reuse. The work will aid European software developers to create a managed and systematic reuse programme.

Business Motivation and Objectives

The experiment motivation is to reduce the costs of producing Real Time Engine Control systems and to therefore be more competitive in the market place. To achieve this the procedures for systematic reuse of previously developed and tested software must be put in place. Accurate measurement of the reuse process and it's effect are vitally important for effective process improvement and demonstration of cost reduction.

The experiment should provide useful data in three main areas of software development. Firstly the use of the Goal Question Metric approach as a means of process measurement and improvement for a reuse process and a process that includes reuse. Secondly in showing how the resultant data is effective in demonstrating a cost reduction due to reuse. Lastly in the use of Goal Question Metrics as a driver for process improvements.

The Experiment

The experiment will use the Goal Question Metric approach to assess and improve the existing reuse measurement process. Using the revised reuse process the software development process incorporating reuse will be measured and the results assessed to infer process improvements.

Current expectations of reuse on the baseline project are 50%. The aim of this experiment is to attempt to increase this reuse to around 80% or at least to provide process improvement recommendations to do so.

The target project selected for PRIME is the development of an engine controller for a BR715 engine on the McDonnell Douglas MD95. This project poses greater reuse challenges than previous applications in that it features engine and airframe, as well as engine control hardware and software changes. The project will begin in May 1996 with the commencement of the first software development. This will conclude in October the same year. This phase will be followed by further software packages.

RoSEC software represents a team of around 50 software engineers with a wealth of experience in the development of embedded real time systems to flight critical standards. The earlier application from which the baseline project is to be built is a software system of around 210,000 lines of source code. This figure includes 100,000 lines of ADA or assembler source code, 46,000 lines of design annotations and 64,000 lines of comments. The size of the MD95 application will be a similar order of magnitude.

Contact Information

Rolls Smiths Engine Controls, UK

10.32 PROVE 21417

Quality Improvement through Verification Process

Cad.Lab S.p.A., a CAD/PDM systems producer based in Italy, carried out the Process Improvement Experiment (PIE) PROVE to improve the quality of its software products by implementing a measurable verification process in parallel with the software development cycle. Two approaches were experimented: dynamic verification (testing) and static verification (inspection). The goal of high software quality is obvious: to produce software that works flawlessly, but the quality has to be reached without hindering development; thus the verification process had to be compatible with other priorities like time-to-market and adding leading-edge features to the product. As product complexity increases and customers' demand for high quality software grows, the verification process is becoming a crucial one for software producers. Unfortunately, even if verification techniques have been available for a few years, little experience in their application can be found among commercial software producers. For this reason we believe that our experience, will be of significant relevance for a wider community, not least because it could demonstrate the feasibility of a structured and quantitative approach to verification in a commercial software producer whose products sell on the national and international market.

- By setting up a verification method and supporting it with an automated infrastructure we were able to demonstrate the following results on a baseline project, based on our flagship product for three-dimensional design, Eureka:
- less errors are escaping from our ordinary quality control
- more reliability is assured in the subsequent releases through which our product evolves
- verification activities are more productive because they can relay on a replicable set of procedures which now form the core of our non-regression quality control
- quantitative data on the correctness of the product are gathered and analysed continuously

Some key sentences summarise the *lessons that we consider most valuable* for whoever will repeat a similar experiment: "A cultural growth on testing is paramount" "Developers won't accept change which does not provide a clear return on their effort investment" "Provide senior managers the results which are useful to pursuing their business strategy"

PROVE received the financial contribution of the European Commission under the ESPRIT/ESSI Programme. The project lasted 21 months.

Cad.Lab S.p.A., Italy

10.33 QUALIMET 23982

Improving Software Products Quality through the Use of Metrics

Quality requirements of industrial software are very high and the correctness of the source code is of great importance for this purpose. Traditionally, the correctness of a program has been checked through an exhaustive set of test cases that usually consider the program as a black box. It is well known that it is impossible to check the whole behaviour of the program through exhaustive tests, so an static analysis of the source code at an early stage can be of great help in order to pay special attention to those parts of the source code that are specially complex or not well written.

This paper presents the work that has been carried under QUALIMET, ESSI Project 23982 which is funded by the Commission. The objective of QUALIMET was to improve the software development process, introducing a set of style norms to be used when coding in C++, and a set of metrics to be used on the source code in order to check its quality. The different aspects that have been covered in this project are:

- Definition of a set of style norms to be used when coding in C++. A "Style Guide for programming in C++" has been obtained through the work of an internal work-group. This guide has been defined taking into account the experience of the people in the work-group and existing guidelines for programming in C++.
- Selection of a set of metrics to be applied on the C++ source code. A Metrics Model has been defined following the GQM Paradigm. Thresholds and corrective actions have been defined for all metrics.
- Selection of a software metrics tool that support the metrics selected in the previous point and that can be integrated in the current environment for software development. LOGISCOPE was selected as the measurement tool.
- Usage of the selected style norms, metrics and tool in a baseline project which consists on the development of a distributed control system. In fact, the metrics model has also been applied to another project apart from the baseline one.

The Style Norms for programming in C++ have been used in the baseline project. The Metrics Model was implemented in LOGISCOPE, defining thresholds and corrective actions, reports were also defined as well as roles inside the company. The model has been validated through its application to two projects: the baseline project called RECETAS and another project called VIDOC.

The style norms for programming in C++ have been disseminated internally in order to be used in any new development in C++. Special emphasis has been placed in the idea that it is the result of a work-group and that it must be seen as dynamic, which means that it can be changed after collecting suggestions from its use. It must be noted that the programming style guide and the metrics model have been well accepted by the people.

Main key lessons that have been learned from the experiment are:

- Importance of following a methodology for selecting the metrics that best fit the objectives of the company.
- Difficulty of defining thresholds and corrective actions.
- Importance of validating thresholds before its real use.
- Importance of top management support.

It is possible to say that it has been obtained a way of quantitatively knowing what is the quality of the design and source code, which means it is possible to start to know where we are and to establish ways of improving the quality.

It has been demonstrated that the quality model is a valid solution for its extension inside the company. For this reason, this methodology is going to be introduced in the current environment for software development. In fact, the Style Guide for programming in C++ has already been introduced and is being used in all new C++ developments inside ROBOTIKER.

ROBOTIKER, Spain

10.34 RECOMPOSE 24256

Reuse in Component Based Software Engineering
Expected Impact and Experience

An increased reuse maturity level for the whole organisation is expected to be the major benefit of the experiment. Improvements in the software engineering process will lead to better quality. The flexible component based infrastructure will make it easier to adapt new technologies and make us competitive in the rapidly changing software industry. From the commercial point of view, this will form the basis for an increased competitiveness on the existing market and on the evolving international market.

Business Motivation and Objectives

Software Innovation is a software company that bases it's business on sales of it's two "off-the-shelf" products, SalesMaker and ProArc, and on development of customer specific solutions. Both products are targeted at the high-end market, SalesMaker mainly at large sales-organisations and ProArc mainly at document management in the offshore business. The company has experienced a rapid growth the last three years. Larger projects and larger project teams have been needed to meet the customers demand. This rapid growth has created a new environment, in which communication between development teams have been reduced and reuse is incorporated on an opportunistic level only.

The purpose of this PIE is to achieve measurable improvements in the company's development process, through developing mechanisms that allow us to build reusable components and modules on a company wide basis. The goal is to arrive at increased quality, flexibility and productivity through both organised reuse and object oriented, component based system development.

The Experiment

The experiment is to change the existing development process to a well-defined component-based development process with emphasis on reusable components. An object-oriented system development method for client/server systems will be selected. The project management model will be adopted to incorporate reuse activities, resources and documentation, enabling the project managers of the two products to plan and track the baseline project. Metrics will be selected and then used to evaluate both the quality and the reusability of components. The improved development process will be applied to our baseline project, the development of new Win32 based versions of our two products. Software Innovation has 82 employees of which 50 are working with system development. The baseline project is planned to allocate 12-16 persons over a 1.5 year period.

Contact Information

Software Innovation, Norway

10.35 REPRO 21513

Reuse Process and Organisation
Expected Impact and Experience

We anticipate that the REPRO experiment will lead to a defined reuse maturity level for the organisation, where the projects deliver results according to long-term product plans, and not only to satisfy one single customer. This again, will lead to a more stabile core of the ProRetail system. It is anticipated that this core will continue to grow and include functionality from future customers, making a delivery more a matter of configuring the right system. When incorporating these standards, we will create systems quicker with reduced development costs, thus making us more competitive. We anticipate this will lead to more contracts with potentially higher profit margins.

Business Motivation and Objectives

Provida is a SME currently being evaluated as a vendor in a number of international markets, including Europe, South America and Australia. In order to stay competitive, we must offer flexible and modularised systems at short notice. The key factor for Provida in meeting this challenge is to reduce time-to-market by introduction of organised reuse. Organised reuse will increase productivity in our development process, which in turn will have a major impact on the competitive situation for Provida – especially in new markets. Hence, our objectives with REPRO are to implement development procedures and roles focusing on reuse, to build libraries of reusable components and hence, improve quality, increase productivity and reduce time-to-market.

The Experiment

The Experiment will introduce organised reuse in our development process, focusing on the following key reuse areas:

- Organisation and Project management
- Development for, respectively with reuse
- Repository management
- Metrics and measurements

To do this, we have identified certain improvement steps; To introduce specific organisational roles, responsible for reuse, such as Domain expert, Repository Manager, Component co-ordinator, Component expert, and Reuse co-ordinator. To introduce a new tool for Repository. To improve and document our development procedures in Process Engineer. To use metrics and measurements, in order to show the cost-benefit of the above mentioned improvement steps. The project will be focused around a technical upgrade of the loan and card modules in ProRetail. ProRetail is a retail banking system running on an MVS mainframe with CICS and DB/2. The upgrade has two major objectives; to reuse the functionality of the existing older version, and to reuse the core functionality of the already upgraded parts of ProRetail (in particular the deposits system – ProDeposits). The project has a budget of 3-4 mill. ECU.

Contact Information

Provida ASA, Norway

10.36 ROAR 10645

Renovate Applications and Optimise Developments through Quality Assurance and Code Restructuring

The project concerns ways of cutting code maintenance costs. Three different aspects have been involved :

- automatic control to ensure that PACBASE programs meet their programming standards,
- search for standards concerning the structural complexity of the code (written in PACBASE and in COBOL),
- automatic restructuring of COBOL code.

By implementing controls to ensure that programming standards are met, we hope to decrease the cost of maintaining programs. Not only do we find the poorly written programs more easily, we also acquire knowledge about programmers who frequently program in a "doubtful" way. Normally the lack of knowledge about PACBASE and good programming is the cause, and these controls give us a way to determine who needs extra training in a particular subject. The tool we have been using is called PQC.

The idea of the second stage was to develop programming standards for the structure of the code. The expected benefits were both to restructure old, poorly written programs and to prevent new, un-maintainable programs from being put into use. In order to do that we collected many data from a sample of programs by the use of a tool called LOGISCOPE. By comparing them with the opinion of the programmer, we wanted to see which criteria determine if a program is complicated or not. Unfortunately we did not find any criteria that in a clear way expressed the complexity of the programs. Several factors (type of program, interactive or batch, language etc.) made us split the sample into different categories, but we still did not find any correlation. Finally we decided to halt this part of the project. We found that the technology transfer from the supplier of LOGISCOPE did not reach our expectations.

The third and final section concerns the automatic restructuring of old programs, with poor (or no) internal structure. By finding software that does this without, or almost without, the work of the programmer we hope to bring down the cost of maintaining old COBOL applications. We were, of course, looking for a software package that guarantees the same functioning for both the restructured program and the old one. We also need software that can treat the BULL and IBM commands and COBOL 1 and 2. The tools we have chosen are called ECrevise and REVOLVE. The tool ECrevise is the restructuring tool. This tool is very easy to use and to implement but it has some bugs and a very bad hot line. So in these conditions, it seems difficult to generalise its use. The tool REVOLVE is a tool to help to maintain programs. This tool is also easy to use and to implement and we think it is a better solution to increase the productivity, to control the costs and to improve the pereniality of our applications.

We thank the Commission without whom this project would not have been possible. So often this kind of project either has to be put on one side, or undertaken without enough time or money to provide the best conditions for its success. With the support of the Commission we have the opportunity to work on new subjects and to really implement them in the work place. Further action on these three aspects is now planned :

- PQC : its use is generalised in other Informatique CDC entities which use PACBASE case tool. In GIRET, its use is possible in integration environment and mandatory in acceptance environment and the method department of GIRET has produced a users' guide for all the staff,
- LOGISCOPE : although we halted the experimentation in GIRET department, we have installed a self service station in our method department in PARIS for the other entities of Informatique CDC and we make a lot of measurements of code quality in COBOL and in C,
- finally for the third part, we obtained inconclusive results with the restructuring tool, so we gave up this action on the COBOL code. But we are starting a vast project on the "changing millennium" and we are studying a possible solution with tools such as REVOLVE.

Informatique CDC

10.37 SQUEME 21271

Software Quality Environment and Measurement
Business Motivation and Objectives

Due to the rapid pace of technology evolution and the increasing complexity of the projects, it has been decided to establish a Quality infrastructure and a Measurement System to provide information about the current situation. This will help achieve a continuous process improvement and increasing quality, productivity and client's satisfaction.

The Experiment

The experiment will apply the following Standards and Models to define a Quality Model for the whole system area: Demings, IEEE, SEI, ISO 9001. We have constituted two work groups working in parallel to define a Quality Model and a Measurement Program. This experiment is divided into 3 Work Packages:

- WP1 deals with requirements definition and refinement of needs.
- WP2 Project Development, relates to the establishment a Quality Model and a Metrics Program based on international standards and supported with tools. Training is considered as a major requirement to reach the goal.

- WP3 is the implementation on the baseline project. We have selected "Other Companies Billing" which requires accurate timing and quality.

After the evaluation of the results there is a plan to disseminate them.

Iberia Sistemas employs 600 persons, 12 of them are involved in SQUEME project.

Expected Impact and Experience

SQUEME is expected to give improved clients satisfaction and better management capabilities taking into account projects and services rendered by IT. Once we know our productivity and Quality level, we will be able to start an improvement plan in some areas.

Contact Information

Iberia Airlines, Spain

10.38 SWAT 23855

Software Automated Testing in a Real-time Environment
Expected Impact and Experience

The current test process relies heavily on manual testing. By automating testing, an increase in the reliability of the product software will be achieved, concurrently with a decrease in the time taken to carry out the testing. The decrease in the test time will allow the product to reach the market place earlier, leading to commercial advantage. Additionally the discovery of software defects earlier in the software lifecycle leads to reduced defect repair costs and improved customer perceptions. The experience gained will be applicable to other real-time software applications within TSc and other interested companies.

Business Motivation and Objectives

Software produced by INPS is aimed at automating its social security services and therefore it is highly related to the continuous law changes and needs for new services to the community. By the definition of a comprehensive document process during the software life cycle and of well specified Verification and Validation activities we want to improve the control over the whole software development process and, consequently, the ability to timely adequate our services to customer requirements.

The Experiment

The intent of this project is to define a set of document standards together with the definition of clear rules and roles involved in the document flow management. Moreover we intend to experiment Verification and Validation activities to be executed on the outputs of each phase. Available environments as Lotus Notes for document management and a metrication tool as Metrication (by SPC) for collection and analysis of metrics (also derived by V&V activities) will be experimented in PIE project.

Major activities in the experiment will be: PIE management, PIE qualification and monitoring; Set up of the IDEA experiment, inclusive of training, definition of a methodology defining document and V&V processes, software tools selection and acquisition, preparation of technological layout; Application of defined methodology on top of the baseline project (methodology tailoring, definition of baseline project plans, production of specified documents, application of defined procedures on software development products, collection and analysis of metrics); internal and external dissemination of results.

The baseline project selected for this PIE concerns the reengineering of software used to collect requests and to order payments of unemployment indemnities to specific workers categories, a limited project but highly representative of our typical software production. It will be carried out by an IT peripheral software development structure (SIR – Bari), already owning a noticeable experience on this particular application domain, with the control and supervision of the IT central structure (DCTI- Roma).

The whole IT department of INPS employs about 800 people in Italy, while the involved peripheral structure employs about 20 people.

Contact Information

Telecom Sciences Corp. Ltd,UK

10.39 TEPRIM 21385

Test Process Improvement Library of Reusable Test Cases, Centralised Test Documentation Management, Metrics

In order to gain cost reduction, greater quality (product, service) and better customer satisfaction the TEPRIM PIE aimed to improve the testing process by implementing:

- An electronic test documentation management system, based on a centralised repository of all the test data (Product specification test plan, test cases, errors, cost, etc.);

- The automatic recording and automatic re-execution of test cases;
- The review of metrics and measurements according to product evaluation model defined in ISO/IEC 9126 and the implementation of process metrics;

In fact testing phase is, for us, the most intensive labour, time consuming phase in the software project life-cycle, in addition, testing effort is about 30% of the total project effort and the activities are based on the knowledge of few specialists.

The TEPRIM project ran from January 1996 till June 1997 and all project activities were successfully completed.

The TEPRIM project results are addressed to software companies whose core activities are software development, software maintenance and related services. Particularly the test data model and the specific testing environment managed can be easily reproduced in the companies which have the AS/400 or PC platform for software development, maintenance and PC platform for testing activities. Some figures, diagrams and graphical images have been included in the annexes to help the processing of the report.

Here is a brief summary of the work done and the results achieved:

- Initial process assessment of Engineering processes (ENG.5 Integrate and test software – ENG.7 Maintain system and Software) according to the SPICE model (see Annex A). The conformity profile (weakness and strengths) of the selected PIE processes were identified and specific improvement steps were established.
- A final formal assessment of the same processes (ENG.5 and ENG.7) according to SPICE model. The initial assessment in comparison with the final assessment has brought out, in objective way, the improvement obtained from the PIE execution.
- Identification of adequate software testing tools (available on the market) and the building up of a new testing environment on PC platform (Annex B). The new testing environment is based on interactive testing tools for testing recording/playback, tools for test data documentation and data error tracking.
- Identification of a new test data model (Annex E) and the building up of an electronic documentation management system working in C/S architecture with a repository of all the test data records (Annex F). A total of 40 data were selected to cover test plan, test case information, test execution data and test errors.
- Execution of two pilots with 450 test cases in electronic form and reusable, 170 test cases recorded and re-executable, test errors stored and all test data usable for statistic and improvement.
- Identification, experimentation and validation of a Quality profile (set of metrics) for the Business Management System (BMS) product following the AMI approach and the ISO/IEC 9126 (Annex C).
- Acquisition of advanced skills on testing tools and methodologies, on SPICE assessment model and on process/product metrics (AMI approach).
- Introduction of a workgroup organisation for testing management activities.

Specific internal and external dissemination activities were implemented to give a wide visibility of the experiment and the availability of a web page (http://max.tno.it/esssiteprim/teprim.htm). The results achieved were considered very positive and the use of new testing environment was extended to other software product development projects. Plans are in place for Company wide implementation of TEPRIM and for further dissemination of activities on both internal and external levels. The TEPRIM project has been funded by the Commission of European Communities (CEC) as a Process Improvement Experiment under the ESSI programme.

IBM Semea Sud, Italy

Index

Druck: Strauss Offsetdruck, Mörlenbach
Verarbeitung: Schäffer, Grünstadt